the mishnah

ARTSCROLL MISHNAH SERIES / A NEW
TRANSLATION WITH A COMMENTARY **YAD
AVRAHAM** ANTHOLOGIZED FROM TALMUDIC
SOURCES AND CLASSIC COMMENTATORS.

Published by

Mesorah Publications, ltd

ששה סדרי **משנה**

FIRST EDITION
First Impression ... November, 1986

Published and Distributed by
MESORAH PUBLICATIONS, Ltd.
1969 Coney Island Avenue
Brooklyn, New York 11223

Distributed in Israel by
MESORAH MAFITZIM / J. GROSSMAN
Rechov Harav Uziel 117
Jerusalem, Israel

Distributed in Europe by
J. LEHMANN HEBREW BOOKSELLERS
20 Cambridge Terrace
Gateshead
TYNE AND WEAR
England NE8 1RP

ISBN
0-89906-293-8 (hard cover)
0-89906-294-6 (paperback)

Typography by CompuScribe at ArtScroll Studios, Ltd.
1969 Coney Island Avenue / Brooklyn, N.Y. 11223 / (718) 339-1700

Printed in the United States of America by Moriah Offset
Bound by SEFERCRAFT Brooklyn, N.Y.

◄§ Seder Nezikin Vol. I(c):
מסכת בבא בתרא
Tractate Bava Basra

Translation and anthologized commentary by
Rabbi Matis Roberts

Edited by:
Rabbi Yehezkel Danziger

This volume is dedicated
to the memory of

Irving Bunim

ר' יצחק מאיר בן ר' משה ז"ל

ד' טבת תשמ"א

Irving Bunim was a pioneer of pioneers.
His list of accomplishments defies belief:
Founder and leader of Young Israel,
Hero of Hatzalah,
Leader and president of Yeshivas Rabbi Jacob Joseph,
Right hand and confidant of
  Hagaon Harav Aharon Kotler זצ"ל,
Builder, partner and pillar of Beth Medrash Govoha,
Author, teacher and lecturer,
Great leader of Torah in his generation,
  and model for future generations,
And all this, while setting a peerless standard
  of integrity in commerce.
His devotion to Klal will inspire Jews
  as long as his sterling memory endures.
America's flourishing Torah life will forever be nourished
  by the oasis called Reb Yitzchak Meir Bunim.

יהי זכרו ברוך

תנצב"ה

הסכמה

Rabbi Moshe Feinstein
455 F. D. R. Drive
New York, N. Y. 10002

משה פיינשטיין
ר"מ תפארת ירושלים

בע"ה

[חתימת יד הרב משה פיינשטיין]

בע"ה

הנני מברך בזה את ידידי הרב הנכבד מהר"ר מאיר יעקב בן ידידי הרב הגאון ר' אהרן שליט"א זלאטאוויץ ואת ידידי הרב הנכבד מהר"ר נתן שערמאן שליט"א שעמדו בראש הנהלת **חברת ארטסקרול,** אשר הוציאו כבר הרבה חבורים חשובים בשפה אנגלית לזכות את הרבים, וגם הוציאו על משניות כרך אחד ועכשיו מוציאים לאור עוד כרך שני, ויש בו לקוטים מספרי רבותינו מפרשי משניות על כל משנה ומשנה, מלוקטים בטוב טעם ע"י תלמידי חכמים חשובים ומומחים לרבים, והוא לתועלת גדול להרבה אינשי ממדינה זו שלא התרגלו מילדותם במשניות, וגם יש הרבה שבעוה"ש"ת התקרבו לתורה ויראת שמים כשכבר נתגדלו ורוצים ללמוד, שיוכלו ללמוד משניות בנקל בשפה המורגלת להם, שלכן הם ממזכי הרבים שזכותם גדול ואני מברכם שיצליחם השי"ת בחבור זה ובעוד כרכים.

וגם אני מברך בזה את ידידי הרב הנכבד מאד עסקן ותומך גדול לתורה ולתעודה מוהר"ר אלעזר גליק שליט"א אשר עזר הרבה להדפסת משניות אלו לזכר נשמת בנו המנוח החשוב מאד מר **אברהם יוסף** ז"ל ונקרא הפירוש **יד אברהם** על שמו והוא זכות גדול לעילוי נשמתו בלמוד הרבים. יהי זכרו ברוך. וע"ז באתי על החתום בער"ח אלול תש"מ.

משה פיינשטיין

יעקב קמנצקי

RABBI J. KAMENECKI

38 SADDLE RIVER ROAD

MONSEY, NEW YORK 10952

בע"ה

יום ה' ערב חג השבועות תשל"ס, פה מאנסי.

כבוד הרבני איש החסד שוע ונדיב מוקיר רבנן מר אלעזר נ"י בליק שלו' וברכת כל טוב.

מה מאד שמחתי בהודעי כי כבודו רכש לעצמו הזכות שייקרא ע"ש בנו המנוח הפירוש מבואר על כל ששת סדרי משנה ע"י "ארטסקראל" והנה חברה זו יצאה לה מוניטין בפירושה על תנ"ך, והבה נקוה שכשם שהצליחה בתורה שבכתב כן תצליח בתורה שבע"פ. ובהיות שאותיות "משנה" הן כאותיות "נשמה" לפיכך טוב עשה בכורונתו לעשות זאת לעילוי נשמת בנו המנוח אברהם יוסף ע"ה, ומאד מתאים השם "יד אברהם" לזה הפירוש, כדמצינו במקרא (ש"ב י"ח) כי אמר אין לי בן בעבור הזכיר שמי וגו'. ואין לך דבר גדול מזה להפיץ ידיעת תורה שבע"פ בקרב אחינו שאינם רגילים בלשון הקדש. וד' הטוב יהי' בעזרו ויוכל לברך על המוגמר. וירוה רוב נחת מכל אשר אתו כנפש מברכו.

יעקב קמנצקי

YESHIVAT TELSHE   ישיבת טלז
Kiryat Telshe Stone   קרית טלז-סטון
Jerusalem, Israel   ירושלים

(הנוסח בכתב יד)

אנדרייך ציונ"י,
מרדכי

בע"ה — ד' בהעלותך — לבני א"י, תשל"ט — פה קרית טלז, באה"ק

מע"כ ידידי האהובים הרב ר' מאיר והרב ר' נתן, נר"ו, שלום וברכה נצח!

אחדשה"ט באהבה ויקר,

לשמחה רבה היא לי להודע שהרחבתם גדול עבודתכם בקודש לתורה שבע"פ, בהוצאת המשנה בתרגום וביאור באנגלית, וראשית עבודתכם במס' מגילה.

אני תקוה שתשימו לב שיצאו הדברים מתוקנים מנקורת ההלכה, וחזקה עליכם שתוציאו דבר נאה ומתוקן.

בפנותכם לתורה שבע"פ יפתח אופק חדש בתורת ה' לאלה שקשה עליהם ללמוד הדברים במקורם, ואלה שכבר נתעשרו מעבודתכם במגילת אסתר יכנסו עתה לטרקלין חדש וישמשו להם הדברים דחף ללימוד המשנה, וגדול יהי' שכרכם.

יהא ה' בעזרכם בהוספת טבעת חדשה באותה שלשלת זהב של הפצת תורת ה' להמוני עם לקרב לב ישראל לאבינו שבשמים בתורה ואמונה טהורה.

אוהבכם מלונ"ח,
מרדכי

מכתב ברכה

RABBI SHNEUR KOTLER
BETH MEDRASH GOVOHA
LAKEWOOD, N. J.

בע״ה

שניאור קוטלר

בית מדרש גבוה

לייקוואוד, נ. דז. ‏

[handwritten text]

בשורת התרחבות עבודתם הגדולה של סגל חבורת ,,ארטסקרול״, המעתיקים ומפרשים, לתחומי התושבע״פ, לשים אלה המשפטים לפני הציבור כשלחן ערוך ומוכן לאכול לפני האדם [ל' רש״י], ולשימה בפיהם — לפתוח אוצרות בשנות בצורה ולהשמיעם בכל לשון שהם שומעים — מבשרת צבא רב לתורה ולימודה [ע' תהלים ס״ח י״ב בתרגום יונתן], והיא מאותות התעוררות ללימוד התורה, וזאת התעודה על התנוצצות קיום ההבטחה ,,כי לא תשכח מפי זרעו״. אשרי הזוכים להיות בין שלוחי ההשגחה לקיומה וביצועה.

יה״ר כי תצליח מלאכת שמים בידם, ויזכו ללמוד וללמד ולשמור מסורת הקבלה כי בהרקת המים החיים מכלי אל כלי תשתמר חיותם, יעמוד טעמם בם וריחם לא נמר. [וע' משאחז״ל בכ״מ ושמרתם זו משנה — וע׳ חי׳ מרן רי״ז הלוי עה״ת בפ׳ ואתחנן] ותהי׳ משנתם שלמה וברורה, ישמחו בעבודתם חברים ותלמידים, ,,ישוטטו רבים ותרבה הדעת״, עד יקויים ,,אז אהפוך אל העמים שפה ברורה וגו׳ ״ [צפני׳ ג׳ ט׳, עי׳ פי׳ אבן עזרא ומצודת דוד שם].

ונזכה כולנו לראות בהתכנסות הגליות בזכות המשניות כל׳ חז״ל עפ״י הכתוב ,,גם כי יתנו בגוים עתה אקבצם״, בגאולה השלמה בב״א.

הכו״ח לכבוד התורה, יום ו' עש״ק לס׳ ,,ויוצא פרח ויצץ ציץ ויגמול שקדים״, ד׳ תמוז התשל״ט

יוסף חיים שניאור קוטלר
בלאאמו״ר הגר״א זצוק״ל

ב״ה

ישיבה דפילאדעלפיא

בכבוד יקר׳ לידיד ידיד ישראל, ולבושלינים לכל דבר שבקדושה
הרבני הנדיב המפורסם ר׳ אליעזר הכהן גליק נ״י

ארצה״ב באהבה

בשורה טובה שמעתי שכב׳ מצא את המקום המתאים לעשות יד ושם להנציח זכרו של בנו **אברהם יוסף ע״ה שנקטף** בנעוריו. ״ונתתי להם בביתי ובחומתי יד ושם״. אין לו להקב״ה אלא ד׳ אמות של הלכה בלבד. א״כ זהו בית ד׳ לימוד תורה שבע״פ וזהו המקום לעשות יד ושם לנשמת בנו ע״ה.

נר ד׳ נשמת אדם אמר הקב״ה נרי בידך ונרך בידי. נר מצוה ותורה אור, תורה זהו הנר של הקב״ה וכשישמרים נר של הקב״ה שעל ידי הפירוש ״יד אברהם״ בשפה הלעוזית יתברבה ויתפשט לימוד ושקיעת התורה בבתי ישראל. ד׳ ישמור נשמת אדם.

בנו אברהם יוסף ע״ה נתברך בהמדה שבו נכללות כל המדות, לב טוב והיה אהוב לחבריו. בלמדו בישיבתנו היה לו הרצון לעלות במעלות התורה וכשעלה לארצנו הקדושה היתה בדעתו המבוקשו להמשיך בלמודיו. ביקוש זה ימצא מלואו על ידי הרבים המבקשים דרך ד׳, שהפירוש ״יד אברהם״ יהא מפתח להם לים התלמוד.

התורה נקראת ״אש דתי״ ונמשלה לאש ויש לה הכח לפעפע ברזל לפצוץ כוחות האדם, הניצוץ שהאיר רבי רבנו הרב שרגא פייויעל מנדלוויץ זצ״ל שמרת עליו, ועשה חיל. עכשיו אתה מסייע להאיר נצוצות בנשמות בני ישראל שיעשה חיל ויהא לאור גדול.

תקוותי עזה שכל התלמידי חכמים שנדרכה רוחם להוציא לפועל מלאכה ענקית זו לפרש המשניות כולה, יצא עבודתם ברוח פאר והדר ויכוונו לאמיתה של תורה ויתקדש ויתרבה שם שמים על ידי מלאכה זו.

יתברך כב׳ וב׳יב לראות ולרוות נחת רוח מצאצאיו.

הכו״ח לכבוד התורה ותומכיה עש״ק במדבר תשל״יט

אלי׳ שווי

מכתב ברכה

דוד קאהן · · · · · · · · · · · ביהמ"ד גבול יעבץ
ברוקלין, נוא יארק

[מכתב בכתב יד]

בס"ד כ"ה למטמונים תשל"ט

כבוד רחימא דנפשאי, עושה ומעשה
ר' אלעזר הכהן גליק נטריה רחמנא ופרקיה

שמוע שמעתי שכבר תקעת כפיך לתמוך במפעל האדיר של חברת ארטסקרול — הידוע בכל קצווי
תבל ע"י עבודתה הכבירה בהפצת תורה — לתרגם ולבאר ששה סדרי משנה באנגלית. כוונתך להנציח
זכר בנך הנחמד אברהם יוסף ז"ל שנקטף באבו בזמן שעלה לארץ הקודש בתקופת התרוממות הנפש
ושאיפה לקדושה, ולמטרה זו יכונה הפירוש בשם "יד אברהם"; וגם האיר ה' רוחך לגרום עילוי לנשמתו
הטהורה שעי"ז יתרבה לימוד התורה שניתנה בשבעים לשון, על ידי כלי מפואר זה.
מכיוון שהנני מכיר היטיב שני הצדדים, אוכל לומר לדבק טוב, והנני תקוה שיצליח המפעל הלזה לתת
יד ושם וזכות לנשמת אברהם יוסף ז"ל. חזקה על חברת ארטסקרול שתוציא דבר נאה מתוקן ומתקבל
מתחת ידה להגדיל תורה ולהאדירה.
והנני מברך אותך שתמצא נוחם לנפשך, שהאבא זוכה לברא, ותשבע נחת — אתה עם רעיתך תחיה —
מכל צאצאיכם היקרים אכי"ר

ידידך עז
דוד קאהן

Preface

אָמַר ר׳ יוֹחָנָן: לֹא כָּרַת הקב״ה בְּרִית עִם יִשְׂרָאֵל אֶלָּא עַל־תּוֹרָה שֶׁבְּעַל
פֶּה שֶׁנֶּאֱמַר: „כִּי עַל־פִּי הַדְּבָרִים הָאֵלֶּה כָּרַתִּי אִתְּךָ בְּרִית ..."
R' Yochanan said: The Holy One, Blessed is He, sealed a
covenant with Israel only because of the Oral Torah, as it is
said [Exodus 34:27]: For according to these words have I
sealed a covenant with you ... (Gittin 60b).

With gratitude to Hashem Yisborach we present the Jewish public
with Bava Basra, the third tractate of Seder Nezikin. Following the
successful completion of Moed and Nashim, work is proceeding not
only on the rest of Nezikin but on the other three other sedarim as well.
All of this is thanks to the vision and commitment of MR. AND MRS.
LOUIS GLICK. In their quiet, self-effacing way, they have been a major
force for the propagation of Torah knowledge and the enhancement of
Jewish life for a generation. The commentary to the mishnayos bears the
name YAD AVRAHAM, in memory of their son AVRAHAM YOSEF GLICK
ע״ה. An appreciation of the niftar will appear in Tractate Berachos. May
this dissemination of the Mishnah in his memory be a source of merit for
his soul. תנצב״ה.

By dedicating the ArtScroll Mishnah Series, the Glicks have added a
new dimension to their tradition of service. The many study groups in
synagogues, schools and offices throughout the English-speaking world
are the most eloquent testimony to the fact that thousands of people
thirst for Torah learning presented in a challenging, comprehensive, and
comprehensible manner.

We are proud and grateful that such venerable luminaries as MARAN
HAGAON HARAV YAAKOV KAMINETZKI זצ״ל and להבל״ח MARAN HAGAON
HARAV MORDECHAI GIFTER שליט״א have declared that this series should
be translated into Hebrew. Boruch Hashem, it has stimulated readers to
echo the words of King David: גַּל־עֵינַי וְאַבִּיטָה נִפְלָאוֹת מִתּוֹרָתֶךָ, Uncover
my eyes that I may see wonders of Your Torah (Psalms 119:18).

May we inject two words of caution:

First, although the Mishnah, by definition, is a compendium of laws,
the final halachah does not necessarily follow the Mishnah. The

development of halachah proceeds through the Gemara, commentators, codifiers, responsa, and the acknowledged poskim. Even when our commentary cites the Shulchan Aruch, the intention is to sharpen the reader's understanding of the Mishnah, but not to be a basis for actual practice. In short, this work is meant as a first step in the study of our recorded Oral Law — no more.

Second, as we have stressed in our other books, the ArtScroll commentary is not meant as a substitute for the study of the sources. While this commentary, like others in the various series, will be immensely useful even to accomplished scholars and will often bring to light ideas and sources they may have overlooked, we strongly urge those who can, to study the classic seforim in the original. It has been said that every droplet of ink coming from Rashi's pen is worthy of seven days' contemplation. Despite the exceptional caliber of our authors, none of us pretends to replace the study of the greatest minds in Jewish history.

The author of this volume, RABBI MATIS ROBERTS, currently serving as mashgiach ruchni of Yeshiva Shaar HaTorah of Kew Gardens, N.Y., is familiar to ArtScroll Mishnah readers from his fine work on tractates Gittin and Kiddushin. His manuscript was edited by RABBI YEHEZKEL DANZIGER, whose work is well known from earlier volumes of the Mishnah Series.

We are also grateful to the staff of Mesorah Publications: RABBI HERSH GOLDWURM, whose encyclopedic knowledge is always available; REB ELI KROEN whose very fine graphics production of this volume, carries on the tradition of REB SHEAH BRANDER, who remains a leader in bringing beauty of presentation to Torah literature; RABBI AVIE GOLD, SHIMON GOLDING, YOSEF TIMINSKY, MICHAEL ZIVITZ, YEHUDAH NEUGARTEN, LEA FREIER, MRS. ESTHER FEIERSTEIN, MRS. MALKA HELFGOTT, MRS. SIMIE KORN, MRS. FAIGIE WEINBAUM, MRS. JUDI DICK, and ESTIE ZLOTOWITZ.

Finally, our gratitude goes to RABBI DAVID FEINSTEIN שליט״א and RABBI DAVID COHEN שליט״א, whose concern, interest, and guidance throughout the history of the ArtScroll Series have been essential to its success.

Rabbi Nosson Scherman / Rabbi Meir Zlotowitz

כ״ד מרחשון תשמ״ז / November 26, 1986
Brooklyn, New York

מסכת בבא בתרא
Tractate Bava Basra

The Publishers are grateful to

TORAH UMESORAH

and

YAD AVRAHAM INSTITUTE

for their efforts in the publication of the

ARTSCROLL MISHNAH SERIES

General Introduction to Bava Basra

◆§ The Tractate

Bava Basra (lit. *the last gate*) is the third and concluding tractate of the set of three *Bavos*, of which *Bava Kamma* (first gate) and *Bava Metzia* (middle gate) are the earlier volumes. Together these tractates define the bulk of the Torah's civil law — damages, litigations, personal liabilities and responsibilities, and property rights and transactions. *Bava Basra* deals primarily with the last of these categories — property rights and transactions.

In connection with these topics, there are two concepts which underlie many of the mishnah's rulings. These are the concept of a קִנְיָן, *formal act of acquisition*, and the judicial principle of הַמּוֹצִיא מֵחֲבֵרוֹ עָלָיו הָרְאָיָה, *the burden of proof lies on the one seeking to exact property from the other*.

◆§ קִנְיָן [kinyan], Act of Acquisition

Torah law stipulates that a transfer of property from one owner to another can be effected only through a *kinyan*, formal act of acquisition. Mere agreement — whether written or oral — and in some instances even payment, are insufficient to effect a transfer, which can only be accomplished through one of these legally defined formal acts. In the absence of such an act, the property does not change hands, the agreement is not binding, and either party can renege. This applies whether the transfer is a sale or a gift. Similarly, property and monetary agreements of any kind (e.g., easements, waivers) are finalized only with an appropriate *kinyan*. The *kinyan* is performed by the person acquiring the property, at the behest of the one giving it up.

Different types of acts are mandated for different types of property. For example, real estate is acquired through כֶּסֶף, *payment*; שְׁטָר, (handing over) a bill of sale; and חֲזָקָה [*chazakah*], an act of possession (see *Kiddushin* 1:5 and *Yad Avraham* comm. there). [*Chazakah*, the act of possession, is discussed below in mishnah 3:3.] Movable property, on the other hand, cannot be acquired through any of these acts, even payment, but is acquired only through one of several acts which at least symbolically indicate taking physical possession of the object being acquired. These are: הַגְבָּהָה, *hagbahah*, lifting the object being acquired; מְשִׁיכָה, *meshichah*, drawing or pulling it; מְסִירָה, *mesirah*, grasping hold of it (*Kiddushin* 1:4,5; see *Yad Avraham* comm. there). *Hagbahah* may be used in any situation in which it is practical. *Meshichah* and *mesirah* are valid as methods of acquisition only where the object is too heavy or unwieldly to be lifted readily.

The operative theory for the act of *meshichah* is that the new owner draws the object into his sphere by pulling it into an area which either belongs to him or which he has the right to use *(Rashbam* 76b). For this reason, in order for an article to be acquired by *meshichah,* the act must take place in a property which is at least partially owned by the buyer or in a *simta* — a recess off the side of a public thoroughfare in which people do not generally walk but in which they may put down their objects *(Rashbam* 84b). If the article is in a public thoroughfare or the property of the seller, where the buyer's pulling the object does not indicate ownership, *meshichah* is not valid *(Gem.* 76b) unless he pulls it completely out of that area and into his property or a *simta* *(Gem.* 84b; see comm. to *Kiddushin* 1:4).

In addition to the direct acts of acquisition described above, movable property may also be formally acquired through real property in two ways. The first is simply by being in the receiver's land or utensil at the time of transaction. This is known as קִנְיַן חָצֵר, lit. *acquisition by courtyard.* The second way is by the mechanism of אַגַב, *agav* [lit. *along with*], the rule that where a transaction involves both movable and real property, formal acquisition of the land by any method appropriate to it brings with it formal acquisition of the movables as well.

הַמּוֹצִיא מֵחֲבֵרוֹ עָלָיו הָרְאָיָה — The Burden of Proof Lies ...

A basic principle of Torah law regarding monetary litigations is הַמּוֹצִיא מֵחֲבֵרוֹ עָלָיו הָרְאָיָה, *the burden of proof lies upon the one seeking to exact property from the possession of another (Bava Kamma* 46b). That is, if one person is in possession of property and another claims it as his, the court must assume it belongs to the one presently in possession of it and the burden of proof lies on the claimant to prove otherwise. Though the holder's possession of the property does not prove his ownership of it, it establishes a presumption of ownership which the claimant must refute. [The modern-day equivalent of this is the dictum, 'Possession is ninetenths of the law.']

Physical possession — holding the object in question on one's person or in one's property — establishes a presumption of ownership only in the case of movable property. The law concerning real property, however, is different. Here simple presence in a field or house is not sufficient since it is impossible to prevent people from ever entering one's property. Rather, presumption of ownership is assigned to the last person known to have owned the property (מָרָא קַמָּא). For an occupant to supercede the last known owner and achieve presumptive ownership [thereby removing the necessity for him to prove that the land is his], he must occupy the property for three consecutive years. This rule is discussed at length in ch. 3.

◄§ Chapter Summary

There are primarily six topics addressed in this tractate. The first of these is partnerships, and when and how they can be dissolved by one of the

partners. Also included in this discussion are the regulations concerning the partitions required between adjoining properties to preserve privacy (chapter 1).

The second topic is that of the limits placed on a person's use of his property because of the negative effects his activities will have on his neighbors and their property. The mishnah defines which activities are permitted despite their effect on neighbors and which are regulated by that concern (chapter 2).

The tractate next discusses the rules of חֲזָקָה [*chazakah*], the point at which continuous occupation or use of a property grants the occupant legal possession and presumed ownership of that property [see above]. Also defined is when the right to pursue those activities normally barred from a jointly owned property can be established by use of that property and *chazakah* (chapter 3).

The fourth topic is that of purchases; what is assumed to have been included in a purchase without having been specified in the contract and what is not assumed to have been included unless specified. This discussion is divided into two sections — one in regard to real estate (chapters 4, 6, 7) and one concerning movable property (chapter 5, beginning of 6).

The fifth subject is inheritance. This includes the laws delineating how inheritance is apportioned and how uncertainties concerning inheritance are resolved (chapters 8, 9). Also discussed are the special rules governing sickbed wills [מַתְּנַת שְׁכִיב מְרַע] (8:5; 9:6,7).

The final area of discussion is that of legal documents. The mishnah deals with the correct manner in which a document must be drawn, the resolution of contradictory statements within a single document, the validity of partially faded documents and the legal remedies for faded ones, and the rights which the bearer of a document enjoys (chapter 10).

[א] **הַשֻּׁתָּפִין** שֶׁרָצוּ לַעֲשׂוֹת מְחִצָּה בֶּחָצֵר
בּוֹנִין אֶת הַכֹּתֶל בָּאֶמְצַע. מְקוֹם
שֶׁנָּהֲגוּ לִבְנוֹת גָּוִיל, גָּזִית, כְּפִיסִין, לְבֵנִים, בּוֹנִים;

יד אברהם

Chapter 1

The first two chapters of this tractate delineate the rules governing relations between neighbors and their legal rights and obligations towards each other regarding the use of their adjoining properties. Chapter 1 deals primarily with the right of partners who dissolve their partnership and divide their property (thereby becoming neighbors) to demand that a partition be erected between their properties: where and when this is required, how large it must be, who must pay for it and related issues.

1.

When two people share a piece of land either one can force the other to dissolve the partnership and divide the property as long as each one's share will be large enough to be used for the same purpose for which the land had previously been used *(Meiri* from mishnah 6). If the resulting shares will be insufficient, neither can force the other to divide the property. However, one can then demand of the other that he either buy him out or sell out to him [גוּד אוֹ אָגוּד] *(Gemara* 13a; see commentary to mishnah 6).

Our mishnah deals with a courtyard adjoining two houses which is jointly owned by the owners of those houses. In such a case, one partner can force the other to dissolve the partnership and divide the courtyard only if each will be left with an area of at least four cubits by four cubits,[1] which is the minimum area deemed necessary to maintain the function of a courtyard for each house (mishnah 6). In the case of our mishnah, the courtyard did not have these dimensions, but the partners agreed to the division anyway.

The issue under discussion here is הֶיזֵק רְאִיָּה, *loss of privacy* [lit., *the damage of seeing*], i.e., the loss of privacy which results from a neighbor's ability to see into one's privately owned area. In earlier times, the courtyard in front of the house was the place where most of a person's daily activities were performed *(Rashi)*, and loss of privacy there is considered a form of damages. Therefore, after dividing up the courtyard, one can demand of the other that he share in the expenses of building a partition between them. The existence of this right is debated in the *Gemara* (2b, 3a), and the prevailing opinion is that it is enforceable for a courtyard *(Rif; Rosh; Tos.; Rambam, Shecheinim* 2:14).

הַשֻּׁתָּפִין — *Partners*

I.e., two people whose houses shared

a common courtyard which they owned jointly *(Rashi)*.[2]

1. There are various opinions as to the precise length of a cubit, ranging from 18 to 24 inches (see General Introduction to ArtScroll *Eruvin*).

2. [The law given here requiring them to share in the expense of erecting a partition between their courtyards would seem to apply equally to neighbors who were never partners (see *Choshen Mishpat* 154:8). The reason the mishnah states this law in terms of partners may be that anyone building a courtyard encloses it on all sides to give himself privacy. Thus, it would be extremely unlikely to find two separately built courtyards open to each other. The only

1
1

1. Partners who agreed to the partition of a courtyard build the wall in the middle. Wherever
they are accustomed to build [with] untrimmed
stones, [or] hewn stones, [or] half-bricks, [or] bricks,

YAD AVRAHAM

שֶׁרָצוּ לַעֲשׂוֹת מְחִצָּה בְחָצֵר — *who agreed to
the partition of a courtyard*

The partners agreed to divide[1] the
courtyard. Their agreement was necessary because the courtyard was not of
sufficient size to allow one of them to
demand a division [i.e., it was less than
4x8 cubits, so that it could not be
divided into two shares of 4x4]. This
agreement was formalized by each of
them making a חֲזָקָה, *chazakah* (an act of
acquisition of land which is performed
by doing something which shows
possession — e.g., digging up part of the
land — see *Kiddushin* 1:5), in his share
(*Rav* from *Gemara* 3a).

Although the *Gemara* says they each made
a *chazakah*, the wording is used loosely,
because once one of them performs an act of
acquisition in his half, the other half is
automatically acquired by his partner (*Rosh;
Nimmukei Yosef*).

However, some explain the *Gemara's*
wording to be literal, because they rule that
the type of *chazakah* made here need not be
the full *chazakah* normally required for
acquisition. Since they already own the land
and are now only dividing it, it is sufficient if
each of the partners walks along the borders
of his share. Since this *chazakah* is less than
the standard *chazakah*, however, they must
both perform this act in order for it to be
effective, and it is for this reason that the
Gemara speaks of both having made a
chazakah (*Beis Yosef* to *Choshen Mishpat*
157 from *Hagahos Maimonios*).

בּוֹנִין אֶת הַכֹּתֶל — *build the wall*

Each of them can force the other to
contribute half the expense of building a

partition four cubits high to insure their
privacy (*Rashi* 2a).

בָּאֶמְצַע. — *in the middle.*

I.e., each of them must also provide
half of the space for the wall from his
property (*Rav*), even the one who is not
interested in building the partition (*Tos.*
2b).

The same law would apply if one
partner compelled the other to divide a
courtyard which was of sufficient size
to allow for a forced apportionment (see
preface). The mishnah chooses a case in
which both partners' consent is
necessary to teach that neither can say
that he agreed to apportionment only on
the assumption that he would not have
to build a partition [since he did not
stipulate this at the time of division]
(*Tos.* 2b).

מְקוֹם שֶׁנָּהֲגוּ לִבְנוֹת גְּוִיל, — *Wherever they
are accustomed to build [with] untrim-
med stones,*

These are stones whose rough
surfaces have not been hewn to a
smooth finish (*Rav* from *Gem.* 3a).

גָּזִית, — *[or] hewn stones,*

Stones which have been smoothed
down (ibid.).

כְּפִיסִין, לְבֵנִים, — *[or] half-bricks, [or]
bricks,*

A standard full brick was three handbreadths long by three handbreadths
wide. Thus, a half-brick was 1½
handbreadths by 3 (*Rav* from *Gem.* 3b,
Eruvin 1:3).

likely case for this to happen is when a courtyard began its existence serving as a common yard
for several adjacent houses — i.e., a jointly held courtyard — and the residents then decided to
divide the yard and separate from each other — in short, partners who agreed to the division of
a courtyard.]

1. Although the word מְחִצָּה usually denotes a wall or fence, it is used here to mean a division
(see *Numbers* 31:43).

הַכֹּל כְּמִנְהַג הַמְּדִינָה. בְּגָוֵיל, זֶה נוֹתֵן שְׁלֹשָׁה
טְפָחִים, וְזֶה נוֹתֵן שְׁלֹשָׁה טְפָחִים; בְּגָזִית, זֶה נוֹתֵן
טְפָחַיִם וּמֶחֱצָה, וְזֶה נוֹתֵן טְפָחַיִם וּמֶחֱצָה;
בִּכְפִיסִין, זֶה נוֹתֵן טְפָחַיִם, וְזֶה נוֹתֵן טְפָחַיִם;
בִּלְבֵנִים, זֶה נוֹתֵן טֶפַח וּמֶחֱצָה, וְזֶה נוֹתֵן טֶפַח
וּמֶחֱצָה. לְפִיכָךְ אִם נָפַל הַכֹּתֶל, הַמָּקוֹם וְהָאֲבָנִים
שֶׁל שְׁנֵיהֶם.

יד אברהם

בּוֹנִים; הַכֹּל כְּמִנְהַג הַמְּדִינָה. — *they build; all in accordance with the custom of the province.*

Each of the partners can compel the other to share in the expense of building the type of wall which is normally used in that locale. This must conform only to the standard used to partition jointly owned courtyards, not the general standard for walls in that area (*Maggid Mishneh, Shecheinim* 2:15). If the local custom allows for a partition made from twigs or the foliage of palm trees, that too is sufficient as long as one cannot see through it *(Rav* from *Gemara* 4a).[1]

If one of the partners is willing to build the entire wall on his own property of some less sturdy material, there is a question whether the other can demand that he share instead in the cost of building a sturdier wall in accordance with the local custom in order to protect himself against the danger of collapse and the lack of privacy which would ensue (see *Rosh, Nimmukei Yosef*).

Where there is no established custom, the materials listed in the mishnah must be used (*Nimmukei Yosef*).

בְּגָוֵיל, זֶה נוֹתֵן שְׁלֹשָׁה טְפָחִים, וְזֶה נוֹתֵן שְׁלֹשָׁה טְפָחִים; — *For untrimmed stones, each one provides three handbreadths* [lit. this one provides ... and this one provides ...];

[A wall made of untrimmed stones must be made six handbreadths wide,

and each of the neighbors must provide three handbreadths of his property for its construction.]

Although even a thinner wall is sufficient to obstruct vision, they each have a right to demand a wall this thick because of the fear that a less sturdy wall may collapse and his privacy will be violated until the partition is rebuilt (*Nimmukei Yosef*).

Despite having previously stated that the size of the wall is regulated by local custom, the mishnah specifies these dimensions to teach that even if the local custom is to build a thicker wall from these materials neither partner can compel the other to adhere to the custom. However, if local custom allows for a thinner wall, neither can be compelled to contribute to anything more than that (*Tos.* 2a). Others contend that local custom can define only the type of material used to build the wall; the thickness necessary for each type of partition is that which is stated in the mishnah, and a local custom to make it thicker or thinner is disregarded (*Rosh*).

בְּגָזִית, זֶה נוֹתֵן טְפָחַיִם וּמֶחֱצָה, וְזֶה נוֹתֵן טְפָחַיִם וּמֶחֱצָה; — *for hewn stones, each one provides two and a half handbreadths;*

I.e., the total for these walls is one handbreadth thinner than for untrim-

---

1. However, if local custom permits a partition so flimsy that it does not entirely obstruct vision, that custom has no validity and either partner can demand a thicker partition (*Tos.* 2a as explained by *Meiri*).

they build; all in accordance with the custom of the province. For untrimmed stones, each one provides three handbreadths; for hewn stones, each one provides two and a half handbreadths; for half-bricks, each one provides two handbreadths; for bricks, each one provides one and a half handbreadths. Therefore, if the wall fell, the place and the stones belong to both of them.

YAD AVRAHAM

med stones. The latter's thickness must be greater because of its many protrusions (*Rav* from *Gem.* 3a).

בִּכְפִיסִין, זֶה נוֹתֵן טְפָחַיִם, וְזֶה נוֹתֵן טְפָחַיִם; — *for half-bricks, each one provides two handbreadths;*

Such a wall is built from a double layer of half-bricks (i.e., two half-bricks lying side by side, which adds up to a width of three handbreadths) plus a handbreadth of mortar in between to hold them together (ibid.).

בִּלְבֵנִים, זֶה נוֹתֵן טֶפַח וּמֶחֱצָה, וְזֶה נוֹתֵן טֶפַח וּמֶחֱצָה. — *for bricks, each one provides one and a half handbreadths.*

Such a wall is built from a single layer of whole bricks. Whole bricks are three handbreadths wide, and since the entire thickness of the wall is composed of a single layer of bricks, no mortar is necessary (ibid.).

לְפִיכָךְ, אִם נָפַל הַכֹּתֶל, הַמָּקוֹם וְהָאֲבָנִים שֶׁל שְׁנֵיהֶם. — *Therefore, if the wall fell, the place and the stones belong to both of them.*

Since both partners are required by law to share equally in the building of the wall, if the wall collapses, the two are presumed to be equal partners in the materials of the wall and in the ground

upon which it stood. Thus, even if the wall fell entirely into the property of one of the partners and he claims that the wall is completely his, the two partners divide the wall evenly, and we do not require the one who does not have possession to bring proof of his ownership (*Rav, Rashi* from *Gem.* 4a). Even if they remained in the one's possession over a period of time without any protest on the part of the other, they must be divided equally, because it is considered self-evident that neither put up the wall on his own when he had the right to compel the other to share in the expense (*Tos.* 2a).

The fact that they divide the space evenly is obvious, since there is no way for either to assume possession more than the other [as physical possession of land is not evidence of ownership (see 3:1)]. The mishnah mentions it only along with the stones (ibid.).

Although the mishnah is discussing a case in which one could not compel the other to divide the courtyard, the one holding the stones in his possession is not believed to say that the other agreed to divide only on condition that the former build the wall himself. Since they both need their privacy, it can be assumed that they both desired to provide for it (*Rosh*).

2.

This mishnah continues the discussion concerning one's right to compel his neighbor to build a partition between their properties, in this case in regard to a garden and a field of grain.

וְכֵן [ב] בְּגִנָּה, מָקוֹם שֶׁנָּהֲגוּ לִגְדּוֹר, מְחַיְּבִין
אוֹתוֹ. אֲבָל בְּבִקְעָה, מָקוֹם שֶׁנָּהֲגוּ שֶׁלֹּא
לִגְדּוֹר, אֵין מְחַיְּבִין אוֹתוֹ. אֶלָּא אִם רוֹצֶה, כּוֹנֵס
לְתוֹךְ שֶׁלּוֹ, וּבוֹנֶה, וְעוֹשֶׂה חָזִית מִבַּחוּץ. לְפִיכָךְ,

יד אברהם

וְכֵן בְּגִנָּה, — *Similarly, a garden*

The rule stated above requiring the owners of adjacent properties to put up partitions between their courtyards applies to adjoining gardens as well (*Rav; see below*).

מָקוֹם שֶׁנָּהֲגוּ לִגְדּוֹר, מְחַיְּבִין אוֹתוֹ. — [*is treated generally as*] *a place where they were accustomed to fence off, [and] we obligate him [to do so]*.

I.e., a garden in a place where there is no clear-cut local custom is treated as the equivalent of a garden which is in a place where there is a set custom to fence off adjoining gardens. Consequently, two partners dividing their garden (*Rashi*) or someone buying an unfenced garden adjoining other gardens (*Rav, Rambam Comm.*) is obligated to join in erecting partitions between them (*Rav from Gemara* 4a). However, if the prevailing custom is not to build, he cannot be compelled to build (*Rosh*).[1]

The issue here is not loss of privacy as in the case of courtyards, since the gardens of those days were simply plots for growing vegetables, not general use

areas requiring privacy (*Rashba*). Rather it is a matter of the fear of the damage caused by עַיִן הָרַע, *evil eye*, when one person views the other's possessions with jealousy (*Rashi*, see *Gem.* 2b; *Nimmukei Yosef* to 4a). For this reason, in stating the obligation to build a partition between courtyards, the previous mishnah did not take local custom into consideration as does the present mishnah in the case of a garden. Since the need for privacy in a courtyard is great, because that is where a person performs most of his activities, the right to demand a wall for a courtyard exists even in a place where local custom does not demand it (*Nimmukei Yosef from Rashba*).

Others contend that here too the issue is the problem caused to one's garden by a neighbor's ability to see inside. Because a person performs some private activities even in his garden [although not to the same degree as in his courtyard], he has a right to demand privacy there as well, as long as there is no custom to the contrary (*Yad Ramah* 4).[2]

1. *Rambam (Shecheinim* 2:17) states that one who buys a garden surrounded by other gardens is obligated to build a wall between his garden and the others even in a place where the custom is not to build walls between gardens. In this a buyer is treated more strictly than a neighbor, who cannot be forced to put up a partition between gardens where the custom is not to do so (*Maggid Mishneh;* see also *Shulchan Aruch, Choshen Mishpat* 158:1 and 2). This is because it is assumed that the seller's intent is that the buyer take all necessary precautions to prevent damage to the neighboring gardens. Thus, he is committed to this arrangement [if he did not specify otherwise] (*Tos. Yom Tov;* see further, *Kesef Mishneh* ad loc. and *Ketzos HaChoshen* 158:2). *Ravad* disputes this and considers a purchaser to be no different than a neighbor, neither of whom may be compelled where the custom is not to put a wall (*Maggid Mishneh*).

2. *Rambam (Shecheinim* 2:16; responsum cited by *Migdal Oz* there) is of the opinion that neither privacy nor evil eye are serious concerns in a garden or a field, and the issue here is only that of building a partition to separate the two properties so that anyone crossing over that partition will be clearly identified as an intruder. Accordingly, he considers a partition ten

1
2

2. **S**imilarly, a garden [is treated generally as] a place where they were accustomed to fence off, [and] we obligate him [to do so]. However, a valley [is treated generally as] a place where they were accustomed not to fence off, [and] we do not obligate him [to do so]. Rather, if he desires, he should withdraw into his own [field], build [a fence], and make a mark on the outside. Therefore, if the wall

YAD AVRAHAM

The literal translation of this section would read: *Similarly, in a garden, in a place where they were accustomed to fence off, we compel him [to do so]; but in a valley, in a place where they were accustomed not to fence off, we do not compel him [to do so].* The implication of this would be that in the case of a garden one can be compelled to erect a partition only in places where there is a definite custom to do so. But where there is no clear-cut custom — e.g., in a new community or where the custom varies (*Yad Ramah*) — one could not be compelled to share in putting up a partition. By contrast, a field would in general require a partition unless there was a clear-cut custom to the contrary. Thus, the obligation to put up a partition would be greater in a field than in a garden — a completely illogical situation, since the need for privacy is obviously greater in a garden than in a field! For this reason, the *Gemara* (4a) explains that the mishnah is really addressing the question of gardens and fields in places where the custom is not well defined. In such places, a garden is treated as if the custom was to require partitions, while a field is treated as if the custom was not to require partitions. The translation has followed this explanation.

אֲבָל בְּבִקְעָה, מְקוֹם שֶׁנָּהֲגוּ שֶׁלֹּא לִגְדּוֹר, אֵין מְחַיְּבִין אוֹתוֹ. — *However, a valley [is treated generally as] a place where they were accustomed not to fence off, [and] we do not obligate him [to do so].*

The open areas were divided into

separate fields for the purpose of growing grain. If these fields were located in a place where there is no set custom concerning the obligation to fence off the fields, they are treated the same as if they were in a place where the custom was not to build a partition, and a reluctant neighbor cannot be compelled to contribute (*Rav from Gemara* 4a).

אֶלָּא אִם רוֹצֶה, כּוֹנֵס לְתוֹךְ שֶׁלּוֹ, וּבוֹנֶה, וְעוֹשֶׂה חָזִית מִבַּחוּץ. — *Rather, if he desires, he should withdraw into his own [field], build [a fence], and make a mark on the outside.*

If one of the owners of the neighboring fields desires to build a fence, he must build it in his own field. To prove that the wall is entirely his, he should plaster a cubit at the top of the wall with lime. This mark should be placed on the outside of the wall (i.e., his neighbor's side of the wall), rather than on his own, because if he were to place it on the inside of the wall, a dishonest neighbor could place a layer of lime on *his* side of the wall and thereby negate the former's proof of sole ownership. This way, his neighbor's only recourse is to scrape off the lime, the effect of which is discernible (*Rav* from *Gem.* 4b).[1]

handbreadths high sufficient in these cases, and it is not necessary to build a wall of four cubits as in a courtyard. Other dispute this and require a wall of four cubits here as well (*Ramban* cited by *Maggid Mishneh, Shecheinim* 2:16).

1. Once someone relies on a mark for proof of ownership, he will guard against his neighbor's trespassing to place a mark on his side [which is, relative to the neighbor, the outside part of the wall] (*Yad Ramah*).

אָם נָפַל הַכּֽתֶל, הַמָּקוֹם וְהָאֲבָנִים שֶׁלּוֹ. אִם עָשׂוּ
מִדַּֽעַת שְׁנֵיהֶן, בּוֹנִין אֶת הַכּֽתֶל בָּאֶמְצַע וְעוֹשִׂין
חָזִית מִכָּאן וּמִכָּאן. לְפִיכָךְ, אִם נָפַל הַכּֽתֶל,
הַמָּקוֹם וְהָאֲבָנִים שֶׁל שְׁנֵיהֶם.

[ג] **הַמַּקִּיף** אֶת חֲבֵרוֹ מִשָּׁלֹשׁ רוּחוֹתָיו, וְגָדַר
אֶת הָרִאשׁוֹנָה, וְאֶת הַשְּׁנִיָּה, וְאֶת
הַשְּׁלִישִׁית, אֵין מְחַיְּבִין אוֹתוֹ. רַבִּי יוֹסֵי אוֹמֵר: אִם

יד אברהם

The word חָזִית is derived from the word מֶחֱזֶה — i.e., something which is seen in order to indicate ownership (Rambam Comm.). Others explain that it means edge, and refers to the mark on the edge of the wall (Rashi 4a).

לְפִיכָךְ, אִם נָפַל הַכּֽתֶל, הַמָּקוֹם וְהָאֲבָנִים שֶׁלּוֹ. — Therefore, if the wall fell, the space and the stones belong to him.

[I.e., we rely on the evidence of the mark to prove ownership.]

There is a dispute among the authorities whether such a mark can also be relied upon to award ownership of the wall of a courtyard in this manner (Rosh), or whether the assumption that they would definitely share in its construction outweighs it (Ri Migash; Nimmukei Yosef).

אִם עָשׂוּ מִדַּעַת שְׁנֵיהֶן, בּוֹנִין אֶת הַכֹּתֶל בָּאֶמְצַע וְעוֹשִׂין חָזִית מִכָּאן וּמִכָּאן. — If they made [it] by common consent, they build the wall in the middle and make marks on both sides.

When they put up the wall they make marks on both sides of it to indicate that they both shared equally in its construction (Rav). Although if neither were to make a mark it would also be clear that the wall belonged to both of them, the Rabbis were concerned that one of them might manage to place an

illicit mark to indicate that it is his; they therefore recommended that both place marks and thereby avoid subsequent difficulties (Gem. 4a).

We are not concerned that one of them built the wall himself and placed a mark on his neighbor's side, and that the latter managed subsequently to place one on the opposite side illicitly, because once someone relies on a mark for evidence of his ownership he will guard against the possibility of his neighbor entering his property to place another. Only in a case where no mark at all is placed are we apprehensive that one of the neighbors might manage to place one on the opposite side unnoticed (Yad Ramah).

Alternatively, in most cases, one of the neighbors pays the other to see to the building of the partition. Therefore, at the time of building it would be relatively easy for the latter to place a mark on the opposite side unnoticed. Once the wall has already been built, it becomes much more difficult to do so and we are therefore not concerned about it (Rabbeinu Yonah).

לְפִיכָךְ אִם נָפַל הַכֹּתֶל, הַמָּקוֹם וְהָאֲבָנִים שֶׁל שְׁנֵיהֶם. — Therefore, if the wall fell, the place and the stones belong to both of them.

[Since there were marks on both sides of the wall, we have proof of shared ownership.]

3.

הַמַּקִּיף אֶת חֲבֵרוֹ מִשָּׁלֹשׁ רוּחוֹתָיו, — [If] someone surrounds his neighbor on three sides [lit. from his three

directions],

I.e., the man owns the land on three sides of another person's field (Rashi).

fell, the space and the stones belong to him. If they made [it] by common consent, they build the wall in the middle and make marks on both sides. Therefore, if the wall fell, the place and the stones belong to both of them.

3. [I]f] someone surrounds his neighbor on three sides, and he fences off the first, second, and third [sides], we do not obligate him. R' Yose says: If

YAD AVRAHAM

וְגָדַר אֶת הָרִאשׁוֹנָה, וְאֶת הַשְּׁנִיָּה, וְאֶת הַשְּׁלִישִׁית, — *and he fences off the first, second, and third [sides],*

The owner of the outer fields built a partition between his land and that of his neighbor, thereby enclosing the inner field on three sides. The inner field remains open, however, on the fourth side (*Rashi; Baal Hamaor; Rambam, Shecheinim 3:3*).

Others explain that he built a partition around the outer fields, thereby protecting the inner one as well from being damaged by roving animals coming from outside both fields. The outer and inner fields remain completely open to each other, however (*Ri Migash; Yad Ramah*).

אֵין מְחַיְּבִין אוֹתוֹ. — *we do not obligate him.*

The owner of the inner field cannot be obligated to share in the expense of the partition, because the wall does not fully protect his field since it is still open on the fourth side (*Rav*). Although the partition gives him privacy by blocking his neighbors on those three sides from seeing inside his field (see mishnah 1), one is not compelled to build a wall between fields for that purpose unless there is a local custom to do so (see mishnah 2), which is not the case of our mishnah. Thus he cannot be forced to pay for this benefit (*Rashi*).

Others contend that even in a situation in which neighbors are obligated to build a

partition to ensure privacy, if one of them proceeded to build it on his own he cannot collect from the other unless the latter's field is completely enclosed and fully protected from view (*Baal Hamaor*).

As implied by the mishnah, if the owner of the outer fields built a partition to enclose his neighbor's field on the fourth side as well, the latter is obligated to share in the expense of all four walls (*Rav from Gem. 4b*). Although mishnah 2 taught that one is not compelled to build a partition of four cubits between fields to ensure privacy, a ten-handbreadth wall to keep animals from entering the field can be demanded (*Tos. Yom Tov from gloss to Rashi 4b*). Therefore, if that is provided by one of them, the other is obligated to contribute half of the expense. However, he does not have to pay for half the value of the wall which was built, only for half the price of a picket fence, since that would provide ample protection for his needs (*Rav from Gem. 4b*).

Others contend that there is no obligation to build any partition whatsoever between fields, and indeed, if the owner of the inner field made it clear from the outset that he had no intention of sharing in the expense of the wall, he would no longer be obligated to do so. However, in the case of our mishnah, he did not do so. Consequently, since a field needs a fence and the owner of the inner field benefits from it, he is obligated to pay his share (*Rambam; Nimmukei Yosef*).[1]

---

1. These authorities cite as a parallel the *Gemara's* ruling in *Bava Metzia* (101a) that one who plants trees in another person's field without his permission is reimbursed for his expenses or

עָמַד וְגָדַר אֶת הָרְבִיעִית, מְגַלְגְּלִין עָלָיו אֶת הַכֹּל.

[ד] כֹּתֶל חָצֵר שֶׁנָּפַל, מְחַיְּבִין אוֹתוֹ לִבְנוֹתוֹ עַד אַרְבַּע אַמּוֹת. בְּחֶזְקַת שֶׁנָּתַן עַד שֶׁיָּבִיא רְאָיָה שֶׁלֹּא נָתַן. מֵאַרְבַּע אַמּוֹת וּלְמַעְלָה, אֵין מְחַיְּבִין אוֹתוֹ. סָמַךְ לוֹ כֹּתֶל אַחֵר, אַף עַל פִּי שֶׁלֹּא נָתַן עָלָיו אֶת הַתִּקְרָה, מְגַלְגְּלִין עָלָיו אֶת

יד אברהם

רַבִּי יוֹסֵי אוֹמֵר: אם עָמַד וְגָדַר אֶת הָרְבִיעִית, מְגַלְגְּלִין עָלָיו אֶת הַכֹּל. — *R' Yose says: If he stood up and fenced off the fourth [side], we devolve [the obligation for] all of it upon him.*

If the owner of the outer fields fenced off the fourth side of the field, the owner of the inner field becomes obligated to pay half the actual expenses of all four walls, even if he built a wall which is more expensive than the minimally required partition. In this, R' Yose disputes the anonymous first *Tanna* who, in such a case, requires the owner of the inner field to pay only half the costs of a picket fence, as explained above (*Rav from Gem.* 4b). Since he has benefited from his neighbor's expense — and since he did not protest at the time the fourth wall was built (*Meiri*) — he must pay for the benefit he actually receives, not only that which was minimally necessary [and a wall provides better protection than a picket fence] (*Yad Ramah to Gem.* 4b; see *Bava Kamma* 21b). Certainly, if the owner of the inner fields added the

fourth wall to the three built by the other, he must share in the expenses of the other three walls as well, since he thereby indicates his desire for the protection provided by those walls (*Rav; see Gem.* 5a).

The halachah follows the opinion of R' Yose (*Rav from Gem.*).

Rambam (*Shecheinim* 3:4) states that he is obligated to share equally in the expense only if the wall was built on both their properties. If it is not on his property, he has no right to use the wall, and he is therefore required to pay only a small portion of the cost, as evaluated by the court. *Ravad* contends that he must pay a full share and he therefore shares in the ownership of the wall. Consequently, he is permitted to make use of it and only the space upon which the wall stands belongs exclusively to the one who built it.

If the owner of the outer fields fenced off the inner field on two sides, and his neighbor fenced off the third, leaving the fourth still unprotected, there is a dispute among the authorities whether the former can demand of the latter that he share in the cost of the first two walls (*Beis Yosef, Choshen Mishpat* 158; *Rama* ibid. §7).

4.

As explained in mishnah 1, owners of adjoining courtyards can compel each other to share in the expenses of building a partition between them to protect their privacy, and they are therefore assumed to be partners in any wall which separates them. The following mishnah elaborates on when one is assumed to have contributed his share of the building expenses.

כֹּתֶל חָצֵר שֶׁנָּפַל, מְחַיְּבִין אוֹתוֹ לִבְנוֹתוֹ עַד אַרְבַּע אַמּוֹת. — [If] the wall of a courtyard fell, we obligate him to rebuild it to [a height of] four cubits.

paid for the value of the improvement, whichever is less, provided the field is one which could be expected to have trees planted in it.

1
4

he stood up and fenced off the fourth [side], we
devolve [the obligation for] all of it upon him.

4. **[**I**f]** the wall of a courtyard fell, we obligate him
to rebuild it to [a height of] four cubits. [Each
is] presumed to have contributed until [the other]
brings proof that he did not contribute. From four
cubits and upward, we do not obligate him. [If] he
built another wall near it, even though he did not
[yet] place a roof upon it, we [nevertheless] devolve

YAD AVRAHAM

If the wall dividing the courtyards of
two neighbors collapsed (see mishnah
1), each can obligate the other to join in
rebuilding the wall to a height of four
cubits. This height is sufficient to
maintain privacy between the two
courtyards (Rav).

[If one refuses, the other can sue him
in court to collect half the expenses of
the wall. Thus the wording, we (the
court) obligate him.]

בְּחֶזְקַת שֶׁנָּתַן עַד שֶׁיָּבִיא רְאָיָה שֶׁלֹּא נָתַן. —
[Each is] presumed to have contributed
until [the other] brings proof that he did
not contribute.

If either neighbor claims that he paid
for the entire wall himself and now
demands that the other reimburse him
for half, while the other insists that he
contributed his share at the time of
construction, the latter is believed that
he paid. Since it is common knowledge
that neighbors are obligated to pay for a
partition between them, we assume that
the one would not have built the
partition on his own without first
exacting payment from his neighbor —
either voluntarily or in court. Thus,
unless the claimant brings witnesses
that he demanded that his neighbor
contribute his share and the latter
refused, he cannot collect (Rav; Rashi).

Others contend that even this would not
be sufficient evidence, since it is possible that
he was only delaying until he would have
money to pay. Rather, he must bring

witnesses who were with this neighbor since
the time the claimant began building the wall,
and who can testify that he did not pay.
Alternatively, if he can prove that the
neighbor had been obligated by a court to
pay and had refused, the neighbor is not
assumed to have paid afterwards unless he
can furnish proof that he did (Rosh).
Another possibility is that witnesses testify
that he had previously admitted to owing the
money and he does not claim to have fulfilled
his obligation since then [but rather that he
paid from the outset] (Meiri).

Even if the wall is unfinished, he is
assumed to have paid his share of whatever
has been built, because his obligation to
contribute for each bit of construction takes
effect as it occurs (Yad Ramah from Gem.
5b).

מֵאַרְבַּע אַמּוֹת וּלְמַעְלָה, אֵין מְחַיְּבִין אוֹתוֹ. —
From four cubits and upward, we do not
obligate him.

Despite the fact that the original wall
had been higher than four cubits and he
had contributed to the extension at that
time, once the wall has collapsed and
must be rebuilt he cannot be forced to
contribute a second time to this extension (Nimmukei Yosef; Meiri).

This may be deduced from the mishnah's
statement of this ruling in regard to a wall
which collapsed, rather than one being built
for the first time. The only purpose of this is
to teach that even if it was originally higher
than four cubits there is no obligation to
rebuild it to that height if it collapses (Meiri).

סָמַךְ לוֹ כֹתֶל אַחֵר, אַף עַל פִּי שֶׁלֹּא נָתַן עָלָיו
אֶת הַתִּקְרָה, — [If] he built another wall

הַכֹּל. בְּחֶזְקַת שֶׁלֹּא נָתַן עַד שֶׁיָּבִיא רְאָיָה שֶׁנָּתַן.

[ה] **כּוֹפִין** אוֹתוֹ לִבְנוֹת בֵּית שַׁעַר וְדֶלֶת לֶחָצֵר.
רַבָּן שִׁמְעוֹן בֶּן גַּמְלִיאֵל אוֹמֵר: לֹא
כָל הַחֲצֵרוֹת רְאוּיוֹת לְבֵית שַׁעַר.
כּוֹפִין אוֹתוֹ לִבְנוֹת לָעִיר חוֹמָה, וּדְלָתַיִם,
וּבְרִיחַ. רַבָּן שִׁמְעוֹן בֶּן גַּמְלִיאֵל אוֹמֵר: לֹא כָל

יד אברהם

near it, even though he did not [yet] place a roof upon it,

After one of them raised the wall beyond the required four cubits, the other built another wall of equal height alongside it, obviously for the sake of laying a roof from one wall to the other to cover the area in between. However, he did not yet lay the roof and has thus not yet made use of the first wall (Rav).

מְגַלְגְּלִין עָלָיו אֶת הַכֹּל. — we [nevertheless] devolve [the obligation for] all of it upon him.

Since he has shown that he desires the additional height of the wall partitioning their yards, he is required to pay his share of its added height (Rav; see Tos. 5a). [He is assumed to have already paid his share of the basic wall, as explained above.]

Although we cannot be certain that he will actually support his roof on the partitioning wall, the fact that he will be using it as a wall for the house he will be building is sufficient to obligate him to pay his share of it (Nimmukei Yosef).

To be obligated in half the expense he must gain ownership of half the wall (as explained at the end of the previous mishnah). To accomplish this requires a formal acquisition (קִנְיָן), and this occurs by virtue of the fact that half of it is standing in his courtyard. Although acquisition by the fact of something being within one's property requires that the original owner tell him to take possession in that manner, it is obvious that the neighbor who built the wall wished him to share in its ownership so that he would share in its expenses (Nimmukei

Yosef).

If the additional wall was higher than four cubits but smaller than the partitioning wall, or its length was shorter than that of the partition, he must pay only for that part of the partitioning wall which corresponds to his own. However, if he built it in a manner which indicates that he intends to add to it — e.g., he made notches on the top of his wall to allow for further building — he is obligated even now to pay his share of the entire partition (Rambam, Shecheinim 3:1 from Gem. 6a).

בְּחֶזְקַת שֶׁלֹּא נָתַן עַד שֶׁיָּבִיא רְאָיָה שֶׁנָּתַן. — [He is] presumed not to have contributed until he brings proof that he did contribute.

If the one who raised the partition above four cubits asks his neighbor for payment after that neighbor built another wall of corresponding height next to it, and the latter claims that he already paid his share of the heightened partition at the time he built his wall, he is not believed unless he can produce proof to that effect. This is because the obligation to contribute under these circumstances is not well known, and he would therefore not pay unless directed to do so by the court (Rav from Gem. 5b).

From the fact that the mishnah makes no distinction, it is clear that even if the neighbor who built the second wall is well versed in the law he is presumed not to have paid. It was necessary to enact the law in this manner, because otherwise anyone could claim he knew the law and therefore paid from the

[the obligation for] all of it upon him. [He is] presumed not to have contributed until he brings proof that he did contribute.

5. We compel him to build a gatehouse and a door for the courtyard. Rabban Shimon ben Gamliel says: Not all courtyards require a gatehouse. [We] compel him to build for the town a wall, double-doors, and a crossbar. Rabban Shimon ben

YAD AVRAHAM

outset, which would negate the effect of the law itself. This way, if one is well versed in the law, he is also aware that he must pay before witnesses, and if he does not do so, he has only himself to blame *(Yad Ramah)*.

5.

The mishnah now deals with the responsibility of the residents of homes which adjoin a common courtyard to share in the expenses towards maintaining the privacy of the courtyard. It also takes up the similar issue of the responsibilities of the citizens of a town towards the expenses for the protection of the town.

כּוֹפִין אוֹתוֹ — *We compel him*

The owners of the homes adjoining a common courtyard may legally compel any of their group who refuses to join in the expenses of the courtyard to contribute his fair share *(Rav)*.

לִבְנוֹת בֵּית שַׁעַר — *to build a gatehouse*

Courtyards commonly had a gatehouse for a watchman to sit in its shade and prevent passersby from disturbing the privacy of the courtyard *(Rav)*. Alternatively, the gatehouse itself blocked the opening of the courtyard and thereby concealed the courtyard from public view *(Nimmukei Yosef)*.

However, if the gatehouse is one which prevents poor people from being heard when they come to the courtyard entrance to beg for assistance, it is considered a travesty of a Jewish residence, and no one can be compelled to contribute to its construction *(Meiri to Gem. 7b)*.

וְדֶלֶת — *and a door*

A door was placed at the entrance of the courtyard *(Rav)* so that the courtyard could be locked *(Meiri)*.

לֶחָצֵר. — *for the courtyard.*

[Since these are necessary for the courtyard, every resident is required to contribute.]

רַבָּן שִׁמְעוֹן בֶּן גַּמְלִיאֵל אוֹמֵר: לֹא כָל הַחֲצֵרוֹת רְאוּיוֹת לְבֵית שַׁעַר. — *Rabban Shimon ben Gamliel says: Not all courtyards require* [lit. *are fit for*] *a gatehouse.*

Only a courtyard which is near a public thoroughfare requires this type of protection and therefore only in such a case can the residents be compelled to contribute to its construction. The first *Tanna*, however, contends that all courtyards require a gatehouse because sometimes there is so much traffic in the public thoroughfare that it spills over into the adjoining alleys and disturbs the privacy of courtyards not immediately adjacent to the public domain *(Rav from Gem. 7b)*. The halachah follows the first *Tanna (Rav; Rambam, Shecheinim 5:1; Choshen Mishpat 161:1)*.

כּוֹפִין אוֹתוֹ לִבְנוֹת לָעִיר חוֹמָה, וּדְלָתַיִם, וּבְרִיחַ. — *[We] compel him to build for the town a wall, double-doors, and a crossbar.*

Citizens of a town can compel each

הֶעֲיָרוֹת רְאוּיוֹת לְחוֹמָה. כַּמָּה יְהֵא בָעִיר וִיהֵא
כְּאַנְשֵׁי הָעִיר? שְׁנֵים עָשָׂר חֹדֶשׁ. קָנָה בָהּ בֵּית
דִּירָה, הֲרֵי הוּא כְּאַנְשֵׁי הָעִיר מִיָּד.

[ו] אֵין חוֹלְקִין אֶת הֶחָצֵר עַד שֶׁיְּהֵא אַרְבַּע
אַמּוֹת לָזֶה וְאַרְבַּע אַמּוֹת לָזֶה; וְלֹא אֶת
הַשָּׂדֶה עַד שֶׁיְּהֵא בָהּ תִּשְׁעָה קַבִּין לָזֶה וְתִשְׁעָה
קַבִּין לָזֶה. רַבִּי יְהוּדָה אוֹמֵר: עַד שֶׁיְּהֵא בָהּ תִּשְׁעַת

יד אברהם

other to contribute to the expense of putting up these protective devices (Meiri). [The wall surrounded the town, necessitating large doors (double-doors) to permit entry and exit from the town, and a crossbar to lock these doors.]

The obligation is based on the degree of need for this protection. If the purpose of the wall is to protect against thieves from outside the town, the contribution demanded from each resident depends upon his wealth and his proximity to the edge of the town. These factors determine his vulnerability to loss, and they therefore determine the extent of his need for these protections (Gem. 7b; Rashi). If there is also fear of bodily harm, all people are equally at risk regardless of their degree of wealth, and the tax assessment should reflect this consideration. Similarly, in a time of general upheaval or war, those in the center of the city are just as vulnerable as those at the outskirts, and proximity to the wall of the town is therefore not a factor (Rosh).

Torah scholars need not contribute to this tax, because they are guarded by their Torah and require no other protection (Gem. 7b; see Yoreh Deah 243:2 and commentators ad loc. concerning present-day application of this principle).

רַבָּן שִׁמְעוֹן בֶּן גַּמְלִיאֵל אוֹמֵר: לֹא כָל הֶעֲיָרוֹת רְאוּיוֹת לְחוֹמָה. — Rabban Shimon ben

Gamliel says: Not all towns require a wall.

According to Rabban Shimon ben Gamliel, only those towns which are near the border of a hostile people require a protective wall. The Tanna Kamma, however, maintains that all towns require protection because hostile troops sometimes penetrate beyond the borders to invade the interior (Rav from Gem. 7b). The halachah follows the Tanna Kamma (Rav; Choshen Mishpat 163:1; Sema).

כַּמָּה יְהֵא בָעִיר וִיהֵא כְּאַנְשֵׁי הָעִיר? — How long must one be in the town to be [treated] like [one of] the citizens of the town?

I.e., to be obligated to contribute to the expenses of the town's protection (Choshen Mishpat 163:2). [Other taxes have different residency requirements; see Gem. 8a, Yoreh Deah 256.]

שְׁנֵים עָשָׂר חֹדֶשׁ. — Twelve months.

[Twelve months in a city gives one resident status so that he must pay for the protection of the city.] In later times, when people tended to move more often, it became customary to require a contribution after thirty days (Rav).

קָנָה בָהּ בֵּית דִּירָה, הֲרֵי הוּא כְּאַנְשֵׁי הָעִיר מִיָּד. — [However, if] he bought a house there, he is immediately [treated] like [one of] the citizens of the town.

By buying a house in the town he indicates that he intends to stay in this

1
6

Gamliel says: Not all towns require a wall. How long must one be in the town to be [treated] like [one of] the citizens of the town? Twelve months. [However, if] he bought a house there, he is immediately [treated] like [one of] the citizens of the town.

6. **W**e do not divide a courtyard unless there are four cubits for each one; nor [do we divide] a field unless there are nine *kavs* for each one. R′

YAD AVRAHAM

town *(Yad Ramah)*. However, if he inherited a house or received one as a gift, this ruling would not apply, since there is no indication of a decision to become a permanent resident *(Yad Ramah)*.

Some say that if he rented a house for a twelve-month period, he is also considered a citizen of the town *(Beis Yosef to Choshen Mishpat 163)*.

6.

As noted in the preface to mishnah 1, each partner can compel the other to divide the object or property which they share if the share which each of them will receive can still perform the function of the whole. This mishnah is the source of that law and discusses its application.

אֵין חוֹלְקִין אֶת הֶחָצֵר — *We do not divide a courtyard*

Two people owning houses sharing a common courtyard cannot compel each other to divide that courtyard *(Rav)*.

עַד שֶׁיְּהֵא אַרְבַּע אַמּוֹת לָזֶה וְאַרְבַּע אַמּוֹת לָזֶה; — *unless there are four cubits for each one* [lit. *four cubits for this one and four cubits for that one*];

I.e., unless they will each be left with an area of at least four cubits by four cubits *(Meiri; Yad Ramah)*. This is the minimum amount of space required by a person for those activities commonly performed in the courtyard. This figure does not include another square of four cubits which must be retained in front of the door to each house for loading and unloading *(Rav from Gem. 11a)*. If either of the houses has more than one

door, four by four cubits must be allotted for each door, and only then can the remainder be divided if it is large enough to be split into two lots of four by four cubits *(Choshen Mishpat 171:2)*.[1] [Thus, the total area required before a courtyard may actually be divided is substantially more than four by eight cubits; an exact figure cannot be given, however, because it depends on the number of doors opening into the courtyard.[2]]

וְלֹא אֶת הַשָּׂדֶה עַד שֶׁיְּהֵא בָה תִּשְׁעָה קַבִּין לָזֶה וְתִשְׁעָה קַבִּין לָזֶה. — *nor [do we divide] a field unless there are nine kavs for each one.*

One partner cannot compel the other to divide a grain-field which they share unless each of them will be left with a plot of land large enough to plant nine

1. However, this applies only if they built their homes in an open space and later closed off a common courtyard; if they bought or inherited the lot together, they must divide the courtyard equally, irrespective of the number of doors each has (ibid. 172:1,2).

2. However, one may not simply add doors to his house and thereby gain space in the courtyard, as will be explained in 3:7.

חֲצָאֵי קַבִּין לָזֶה וְתִשְׁעַת חֲצָאֵי קַבִּין לָזֶה. וְלֹא אֶת
הַגִּנָּה עַד שֶׁיְּהֵא בָה חֲצִי קַב לָזֶה וַחֲצִי קַב לָזֶה.
רַבִּי עֲקִיבָא אוֹמֵר: בֵּית רֹבַע. וְלֹא אֶת הַטְּרַקְלִין,
וְלֹא אֶת הַמּוֹרָן, וְלֹא אֶת הַשּׁוֹבָךְ, וְלֹא אֶת
הַטַּלִּית, וְלֹא אֶת הַמֶּרְחָץ, וְלֹא אֶת בֵּית הַבַּד, עַד
שֶׁיְּהֵא בָהֶן כְּדֵי לָזֶה וּכְדֵי לָזֶה. זֶה הַכְּלָל: כָּל
שֶׁיֵּחָלֵק וּשְׁמוֹ עָלָיו חוֹלְקִין; וְאִם לָאו, אֵין חוֹלְקִין.
אֵימָתַי? בִּזְמַן שֶׁאֵין שְׁנֵיהֶם רוֹצִים; אֲבָל בִּזְמַן
שֶׁשְּׁנֵיהֶם רוֹצִים אֲפִלּוּ בְּפָחוֹת מִכָּאן יַחֲלֹקוּ.

יד אברהם

kavs of seed in it. Any plot smaller than that is too small to be worth the effort of plowing and sowing (Tos. 11a).

A kav is one-sixth of a seah, which is the amount of seed planted in an area fifty by fifty cubits.[1] Thus, nine kavs equal one and a half seah, and an area large enough for planting nine kavs is equal to 3750 square cubits (Yad Ramah; Tos. Yom Tov).

רַבִּי יְהוּדָה אוֹמֵר: עַד שֶׁיְּהֵא בָה תִּשְׁעַת חֲצָאֵי קַבִּין לָזֶה וְתִשְׁעַת חֲצָאֵי קַבִּין לָזֶה. — R' Yehudah says: Unless there are nine half-kavs for each one.

R' Yehudah does not dispute the statement of the first Tanna; rather he is giving the figures for his locale. The land there was extremely fertile, and an area half the size of that required by the first Tanna — i.e., 1875 square cubits — was sufficient for that amount of grain (Rav from Gem. 12a).

The mishnah's figures are for Eretz Yisrael. In Babylonia, where the land was less fertile, a field which required plowing and planting could not be divided against the will of either of the partners unless each of them was left with an area requiring a day's work,

enough to make the effort worthwhile (Gem. 12a, Tos., see Tos. Yom Tov).

וְלֹא אֶת הַגִּנָּה עַד שֶׁיְּהֵא בָה חֲצִי קַב לָזֶה וַחֲצִי קַב לָזֶה. — Nor [do we divide] a garden unless there is half a kav for each one.

[One cannot compel his partner to divide their vegetable garden unless they will each be left with an area of at least 208⅓ square cubits.]

רַבִּי עֲקִיבָא אוֹמֵר: בֵּית רֹבַע. — R' Akiva says: A quarter-kav.

In R' Akiva's view, an area in which one-fourth of a kav can be planted (Rav) — i.e., 104⅙ square cubits — is sufficient for a forced apportionment. The halachah is in accordance with the opinion of the first Tanna (Yad Ramah; Choshen Mishpat 171:2).

Others contend that R' Akiva does not dispute the first Tanna, but is discussing a locale where the land was more fertile — just as R' Yehudah did above (see Nimmukei Yosef).

וְלֹא אֶת הַטְּרַקְלִין, — Nor [do we divide] a salon,

Whose minimum area is ten by ten cubits (Meiri from mishnah 6:4; see comm. there).

---

1. Kav and seah are actually volume measures; they are transposed into area measures by calculating the size of a field in which this volume of barley seed may be planted; see Yad Avraham to ArtScroll Eruvin 2:3.

1
6

Yehudah says: Unless there are nine half-*kavs* for each one. Nor [do we divide] a garden unless there is half a *kav* for each one. R' Akiva says: A quarter-*kav*. Nor [do we divide] a salon, nor a hall, nor a dovecote, nor a cloak, nor a bathhouse, nor an olive press, unless there is enough for this one and enough for that one. This is the rule: Anything which can be divided and [still] retain its name we divide; but if not, we do not divide [it]. When? When they do not both consent; but when they both consent they may divide with even less than this. However, they may

YAD AVRAHAM

וְלֹא אֶת הַמּוֹרָן, — *nor a hall,*

This was another type of aristocratic structure. According to some, it was a small tower built overlooking a garden (*Aruch*).

וְלֹא אֶת הַשּׁוֹבָךְ, וְלֹא אֶת הַטַּלִּית, וְלֹא אֶת הַמֶּרְחָץ, וְלֹא אֶת בֵּית הַבַּד, עַד שֶׁיְּהֵא בָּהֶן כְּדֵי לָזֶה וּכְדֵי לָזֶה. — *nor a dovecote, nor a cloak, nor a bathhouse, nor an olive press, unless there is enough for this one and enough for that one.*

[None of the above may be divided against the will of either of the partners unless the division will leave a proper share for each, as the mishnah will now explain.]

זֶה הַכְּלָל: כָּל שֶׁיֵּחָלֵק וּשְׁמוֹ עָלָיו חוֹלְקִין; — *This is the rule: Anything which can be divided and [still] retain its name we divide;*

If after a shared object is divided equally, each half will still [provide the function of that object and thereby] retain its name, each of the partners can compel the other to divide it (*Rav*).

וְאִם לָאו, אֵין חוֹלְקִין. — *but if not, we do not divide [it].*

[If after being divided the resulting shares are inadequate to perform their original function, and thus do not retain their original name, neither can force the other to divide the object of their

partnership and thereby destroy its usefulness. E.g., half a small salon would result in an apartment whose usefulness and value is not the same as a salon's. Similarly, half a cloak or olive press is useless.] However, even in such a case, one may demand of the other that he either sell out his share to him or buy out his share for the appropriate price (*Rav from Gem.* 13a; *Meiri*). Others contend that he may even set an exaggerated price for the item as long as he allows the other the choice of whether to buy or sell (*Rashi; Rosh; Choshen Mishpat* 171:6).

Partners in a courtyard, however, cannot impose this type of settlement upon each other because a courtyard is considered essential to the needs of the house (*Rosh*).

אֵימָתַי? בִּזְמַן שֶׁאֵין שְׁנֵיהֶם רוֹצִים; אֲבָל בִּזְמַן שֶׁשְּׁנֵיהֶם רוֹצִים אֲפִלּוּ בְּפָחוֹת מִכָּאן יַחֲלֹקוּ. — *When? When they do not both consent; but when they both consent they may divide with even less than this.*

The above rule applies only when one partner wants to continue the joint ownership while the other does not. If they both agree to divide, they may do as they please. This is obvious, of course, and it is stated only to preface the following statement of the mishnah (*Rashi*).

[21]   THE MISHNAH/BAVA BASRA — Chapter One: *HaShutafin*

וְכִתְבֵי הַקֹּדֶשׁ אַף עַל פִּי שֶׁשְּׁנֵיהֶם רוֹצִים לֹא יַחֲלֹקוּ.

[א] לֹא יַחְפֹּר אָדָם בּוֹר סָמוּךְ לְבוֹרוֹ שֶׁל חֲבֵרוֹ, וְלֹא שִׁיחַ, וְלֹא מְעָרָה, וְלֹא אַמַּת הַמַּיִם, וְלֹא נִבְרֶכֶת כּוֹבְסִין אֶלָּא אִם כֵּן הִרְחִיק מִכֹּתֶל חֲבֵרוֹ שְׁלֹשָׁה טְפָחִים, וְסָד בְּסִיד.

יד אברהם

וְכִתְבֵי הַקֹּדֶשׁ אַף עַל פִּי שֶׁשְּׁנֵיהֶם רוֹצִים לֹא יַחֲלֹקוּ. — However, they may not divide Holy Scriptures even if they both consent.

I.e., a scroll of a Sefer Torah, Prophets and Writings (Rav) may not be cut up to be divided even if both consent, because it is considered a desecration of their sanctity to cut them up (Rashi). This rule applies only to books written on one scroll. Separate scrolls, however, may be divided among partners if they wish (Rav from Gem. 13b). Nevertheless, one cannot coerce the other to do so, since each has need of a full set of the books of the Bible (Gem. ibid.). However, if they share two volumes of the same book, one can force the other to divide them (Meleches Shlomo).

Chapter 2

This chapter deals with the limits placed on the use of one's own property because of the damage it causes to a neighbor's property. Obviously, a person may use his property for whatever he wishes if he locates the objectionable activity far enough away from any neighbor to avoid damaging anyone. Thus, the restrictions are formulated in terms of how far from a neighbor's property a person must distance the undesirable matter.

There is a fundamental dispute among the *Tannaim* whether or not one is obligated to distance objectionable activities from the boundaries of his neighbor's property if no immediate damage will result but the potential for future damage exists (see below, mishnah 10, s.v. ר' יוסי, and mishnah 11). R' Yose maintains that one is not so obligated unless there is some immediate damage, and the halachah follows his view (Gem. 17b, 22b; Rambam, Shecheinim 10:5).

1.

The first mishnah discusses the prohibition against damaging one's neighbor's water cistern by digging nearby in his own field. If the neighboring field is watered by irrigation and therefore requires cisterns, one is forbidden to dig a pit in his own field within three handbreadths of the common boundary. If his neighbor's field relies on rain water, and cisterns are not needed and thus not likely to be dug, one is permitted to dig a cistern anywhere in his own field, even along its border (Meiri from Gem. 17b).

לֹא יַחְפֹּר אָדָם בּוֹר סָמוּךְ לְבוֹרוֹ שֶׁל חֲבֵרוֹ, — A man may not dig a pit near the pit of another,

A property owner may not dig a pit near the pit of his neighbor because seepage from the water in his pit could damage his neighbor's pit (Rambam, Shecheinim 9:1; Choshen Mishpat 155:10 from Gem. 19a). Even according to R' Yose, who holds that one may place something in his property despite the damage it may cause in the course of

not divide Holy Scriptures even if they both consent.

1. **A** man may not dig a pit near the pit of another, nor a ditch, nor a vault, nor a water channel, nor a launderer's pool unless he distanced [them] three handbreadths from the other's wall and plastered [them] with lime.

YAD AVRAHAM

time to a neighbor, as long as it causes no immediate damage (mishnah 2), he may still not dig near his neighbor's pit. The very act of digging directly weakens the walls of the first pit *(Gem., Rashi* 17b), and since this damage takes place immediately, one is prohibited to dig a pit adjacent to his neighbor's pit.

Some explain that R' Yose obligates him to distance his pit because of the seepage as well as the digging, since the seepage begins as soon as the water is placed in the pit *(Meiri).*

וְלֹא שִׁיחַ, וְלֹא מְעָרָה, — *nor a ditch, nor a vault,*

These are all types of water cisterns. In contrast to a pit, which is roundish, the שִׁיחַ, *ditch,* is long and narrow, while the מְעָרָה, *vault,* or grotto, is roofed *(Rav).*

וְלֹא אַמַּת הַמַּיִם, וְלֹא נִבְרֶכֶת כּוֹבְסִין — *nor a water channel, nor a launderer's pool*

A launderer's pool is a square pit in which rain water is collected and in which clothing is washed *(Rav).*[1]

Although these are generally not as deep as a pit, ditch, or vault, they may still not be placed immediately adjacent to someone else's pit because of the damage they may cause. Additionally, the mishnah teaches that though the water within a water channel flows (and is therefore less prone to seepage), while the launderer's pool is not necessarily permanent — since a launderer may

change his trade *(Rashi)* — one must still distance them from the border of his neighbor's property *(Gem.* 19a).

אֶלָּא אִם כֵּן הִרְחִיק מִכֹּתֶל חֲבֵרוֹ שְׁלֹשָׁה טְפָחִים, — *unless he distanced [them] three handbreadths from the other's wall,*

A person may not dig any of these various cisterns within three handbreadths[2] of the wall of his neighbor's cistern. However, since these cisterns are not above-ground constructions but merely cavities in the ground, the wall of these cisterns is itself defined as being the three handbreadths of land surrounding it *(Rav* from *Gem.* 17b). Thus, the actual distance between the edge of one hole and the other is six handbreadths *(Rav).*

In a field requiring irrigation, one may not encroach within three handbreadths of his neighbor's land even if his neighbor does not yet have a cistern near the boundary, since it is entirely possible that he will install one there. Thus, the first neighbor to dig also has to distance his cistern three handbreadths from the common border, and when the second neighbor digs his cistern, therefore, it suffices for him to locate it three handbreadths away from the border as well. However, in a non-irrigated field, where there is no reason to assume that a cistern will be installed, one may locate his cistern right at the

1. This refers only to a pool in which clothes are soaked; one in which they are scrubbed must be distanced four cubits from a neighbor's cistern (ibid.) because of the splashing of the water *(Gem., Rashi* 19a).

2. There are six handbreadths to a cubit. Since there are various opinions as to the conversion of cubits to inches, ranging from eighteen to twenty-four inches, the size of a handbreadth ranges from three to four inches.

מַרְחִיקִין אֶת הַגֶּפֶת, וְאֶת הַזֶּבֶל, וְאֶת הַמֶּלַח,
וְאֶת הַסִּיד, וְאֶת הַסְּלָעִים מִכְּתָלוֹ שֶׁל חֲבֵרוֹ
שְׁלשָׁה טְפָחִים וְסָד בְּסִיד. מַרְחִיקִין אֶת הַזְּרָעִים,
וְאֶת הַמַּחֲרֵשָׁה, וְאֶת מֵי רַגְלַיִם מִן הַכֹּתֶל שְׁלשָׁה
טְפָחִים.

יד אברהם

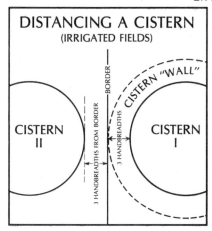

boundary as long as his neighbor does
not have one there. Thus, if the
neighbor should later decide to place
one in that area too, he must distance
himself the full six handbreadths (*Gem.*
17b; *Rambam, Shecheinim* 9:10;
Choshen Mishpat 155:18).

As explained above (s.v. לא יחפר), it is R′
Yose's view that one is obligated to distance
his cistern from that of his neighbor only
because of the effects of the digging.
Nevertheless, when digging a water cistern,
once one must take the potential effects of
the digging into consideration, he is obligated
to prevent damage from seepage as well, and
he must therefore distance his hole a total of
six handbreadths from his neighbor's hole
(*Tos.* 17a). Consequently, when digging a pit
not meant to contain water he need not
distance his hole this much, but only in
accordance with the estimate of experts as to
its capacity to cause damage (*Rashba* cited by
Beis Yosef, Choshen Mishpat 155:12; *Rama*
155:10; see *Beur HaGra*, ibid.). Others,
however, contend that even the damage
caused by digging itself could extend up to
six handbreadths and thus this distance is

required regardless of what the hole will hold
(*Ran* cited by *Shitah Mekubetzes; Nimmukei
Yosef*).

וְסָד בְּסִיד. — *and plastered [them] with
lime.*

In addition to separating his pit from
that of his neighbor by six
handbreadths, he must coat the inside of
it with lime to prevent seepage (*Rambam, Shecheinim* 9:1; *Choshen Mishpat*
155:10). Others rule that although one
should provide both safeguards, once he
has provided one of them his neighbor
cannot compel him to add the other
(*Rosh*, as explained by *Ketzos
HaChoshen* 155:5,7, *Nesivos
HaMishpat* 155:9). [The *Gemara* (19a)
actually takes up this issue, and the
dispute cited here is based on conflicting
views of the *Gemara's* conclusion
(ibid.).]

מַרְחִיקִין אֶת הַגֶּפֶת, וְאֶת הַזֶּבֶל, וְאֶת הַמֶּלַח, וְאֶת
הַסִּיד, וְאֶת הַסְּלָעִים מִכְּתָלוֹ שֶׁל חֲבֵרוֹ שְׁלשָׁה
טְפָחִים — *One must distance olive refuse,*

2
1

One must distance olive refuse, manure, salt, lime, and stones three handbreadths from the wall of another or plaster [it] with lime. One must distance seeds, a plow, and urine three handbreadths from the wall.

YAD AVRAHAM

manure, salt, lime, and stones three handbreadths from the wall of another

This refers to the wall of a building, not that of a cistern. All of these items generate heat which may damage a nearby wall *(Rav; Rashi).* Olive refuse is the olive pulp remaining after the olives have been pressed for their oil *(Rav).* This generates heat as it decays. The stones referred to here are flint stones *(Rashi)* which also generate heat which can therefore damage a neighbor's wall *(Rav),* or corrode the surrounding ground and thereby weaken the wall's foundation *(Tos. 19a).*

וְסָד בְּסִיד. — *or plaster [it] with lime.*

I.e., instead of distancing his potentially damaging substances he may coat his neighbor's wall with plaster to protect it from the effects of the heat and thus place these items next to the wall *(Tif. Yis.).* In this case, all agree that either preventive measure is sufficient by itself, because the damage is not as great as in the previous cases *(Tos. 17a).*[1] [Some versions of the mishnah say explicitly אוֹ סָד בַּסִיד, *or he must plaster with lime* (see *Tos. Yom Tov*).]

Most authorities maintain that according to R' Yose (see preface), one is permitted to place these items near the boundary of his property if his neighbor has no wall there at the time, because there is no damage being inflicted at the time he places them *(Nimmukei Yosef; Tur Choshen Mishpat* 155:47; *Sema* 155:17). However, others rule that even R' Yose would prohibit this *(Rashi, Rif* cited by *Tur* ibid; see *Sema* 155:73 for the

reason).

מַרְחִיקִין אֶת הַזְּרָעִים, — *One must distance seeds,*

One may not plant seeds within three handbreadths of his neighbor's wall (see below), because they loosen the earth and thereby undermine the foundation of the wall *(Rav from Gem.* 19b)

וְאֶת הַמַּחֲרֵשָׁה, — *a plow,*

I.e., one may not plow within three handbreadths of a neighbor's wall — even if he plows only around trees and does not plant any seeds *(Rav from Gem.* 19a) — because the plowing itself weakens the foundation *(Rashi).*

וְאֶת מֵי רַגְלַיִם — *and urine*

Urine dissolves bricks of dried clay; therefore one must urinate at least three handbreaths away from a wall of that material. If the wall is of stone, one handbreadth is sufficient; if it is of granite, no separation is necessary *(Rav from Gem.* 19a).

מִן הַכֹּתֶל שְׁלֹשָׁה טְפָחִים. — *three handbreadths from the wall.*

[The three items mentioned above must all be distanced from a neighbor's wall by three handbreadths.] Plastering is not mentioned here because these affect the ground beneath the wall rather than the wall itself, and plastering the wall would be to no avail *(Meiri).* The fact that the mishnah includes urine in this group indicates that it, too, cannot be prevented from damaging a wall by coating the wall with plaster *(Beis Yosef, Choshen Mishpat* 155).

1. [When lime (calcium oxide) is mixed with water, a chemical reaction takes place in which a great deal of heat is released. The resulting substance is calcium hydroxide, which is used as plaster. Once it dries it no longer gives off heat, and in fact protects the wall.]

וּמַרְחִיקִין אֶת הָרֵחַיִם שְׁלֹשָׁה מִן הַשֶּׁכֶב, שֶׁהֵן
אַרְבָּעָה מִן הָרֶכֶב; וְאֶת הַתַּנּוּר שְׁלֹשָׁה מִן הַכְּלְיָא,
שֶׁהֵן אַרְבָּעָה מִן הַשָּׂפָה.

[ב] **לֹא** יַעֲמִיד אָדָם תַּנּוּר בְּתוֹךְ הַבַּיִת אֶלָא אִם
כֵּן יֵשׁ עַל גַּבָּיו גֹּבַהּ אַרְבַּע אַמּוֹת. הָיָה
מַעֲמִידוֹ בָּעֲלִיָּה, צָרִיךְ שֶׁיְּהֵא תַחְתָּיו מַעֲזִיבָה
שְׁלֹשָׁה טְפָחִים, וּבְכִירָה, טֶפַח. וְאִם הִזִּיק, מְשַׁלֵּם

יד אברהם

וּמַרְחִיקִין אֶת הָרֵחַיִם — *One must distance a mill*

The action of the upper stone grinding against the lower stones sets up both vibrations and noise which can be damaging to a nearby wall, and the mill must therefore be distanced from neighboring walls (*Rav, Meiri* from *Gem.* 20b).

שְׁלֹשָׁה מִן הַשֶּׁכֶב, שֶׁהֵן אַרְבָּעָה מִן הָרֶכֶב; — *three [handbreadths as measured] from the lower millstone, which is four [as measured] from the upper millstone;*

The radius of the upper stone of a mill is one handbreadth less than that of the lower one (*Rav; Tos. Yom Tov*). [Thus, if he places the mill so that the lower stone is three handbreadths from his neighbor's wall, the upper stone will be four handbreadths distant.]

This distance is sufficient only for mills small enough to be operated by hand. Larger ones, e.g., those powered by animals, must be removed a greater

distance to avoid causing damage (*Rama, Choshen Mishpat* 155:7).

The mishnah mentions the lower stone, although it is stationary and causes no damage, because the fact that it rests on the ground allows for precise measurement. It mentions the upper stone, because that is the one which does the actual grinding and thereby causes the damage (*Tif. Yis.*).

וְאֶת הַתַּנּוּר שְׁלֹשָׁה מִן הַכְּלְיָא, שֶׁהֵן אַרְבָּעָה מִן הַשָּׂפָה. — *and an oven [by] three [handbreaths as measured] from the base, which is four [as measured] from the rim.*

I.e., from the top of the base. The heat of an oven is also damaging to a wall and it must therefore also be distanced three handbreadths away from a neighbor's wall. This distance is measured from the oven's base which was one handbreadth wider than its rim. The oven itself fits onto the rim of the base and the wall of the oven will therefore actually be four handbreadths from the wall (*Rav*).

2.

לֹא יַעֲמִיד אָדָם תַּנּוּר בְּתוֹךְ הַבַּיִת — *A man may not place an oven in a house*

I.e., a house in which the ground floor is owned by one person and the second floor by another (*Tos. Yom Tov* from *Rambam, Shecheinim* 9:11, and *Tos.* to *Bava Kamma* 61b; *Meiri*). In such a case, each has the right to compel

the other to take precautions against causing a fire (*Tur Choshen Mishpat* 155:1). The house referred to here is the ground floor.

Rashi to *Bava Kamma* goes further and explains the mishnah to be discussing the right of even the townspeople to compel the owner of a

2
2

One must distance a mill three [handbreadths as measured] from the lower millstone, which is four [as measured] from the upper millstone; and an oven [by] three [handbreadths as measured] from the base, which is four [as measured] from the rim.

2. A man may not place an oven in a house unless there is a height of four cubits above it. [If] he wished to place it in the upper story, there must be a [layer of] plaster three handbreadths [thick] beneath it, and for a stove, one handbreadth. If it caused

house to take steps to prevent a fire from breaking out in his house (see also *Tos.* there and *Tur Choshen Mishpat* 155:3).

אֶלָּא אִם כֵּן יֵשׁ עַל גַּבָּיו גֹּבַהּ אַרְבַּע אַמּוֹת. — *unless there is a height of four cubits above it.*

I.e., at least four cubits of empty space between the top of the oven and the ceiling are required to assure that the ceiling will not catch fire *(Rav)*.

This applied to the ovens of Talmudic times, which opened from the top, so that there was a risk of the oven's flame shooting straight up. Those of medieval times opened from the side and therefore, according to many authorities, required a space of only three handbreadths between the top of the oven and the ceiling to prevent heat damage *(Nimmukei Yosef)*. Others disputed this and ruled that since these latter-day ovens were larger and therefore gave off more heat than the smaller ovens of Talmudic times, they too required a space four cubits *(Tur Choshen Mishpat* 155:1 from *R' Yehudah of Barcelona)*, or even more *(Tur* from *Rosh)*, despite their being side-opening ovens (see *Choshen Mishpat* 155:1).

הָיָה מַעֲמִידוֹ בָעֲלִיָּה, צָרִיךְ שֶׁיְּהֵא תַחְתָּיו מַעֲזִיבָה שְׁלֹשָׁה טְפָחִים, — *[If] he wished to place it in the upper story, there must be a [layer of] plaster three handbreadths [thick] beneath it,*

Before the owner of the upper story

may place an oven on the floor of his apartment, there must be a layer of some sort of plaster three handbreadths thick covering the floor beneath the oven in order to insulate it. There must also be a space of four cubits above the oven to prevent the roof from going up in flames *(Rav)*.

This applies to a private oven. The oven of a baker, which is in constant use, requires a plaster base of four handbeadths *(Gem.* 28b).

וּבְכִירָה, טֶפַח. — *and for a stove, one handbreadth.*

The stoves of those days were similar to ovens *(Rashi)*, but were smaller, with smaller fires *(Rav;* see *Tos. Yom Tov;* see *Yad Avraham* to *Shabbos* 3:1,2). Thus, when placed in an upper story, a plaster base of one handbreadth is sufficient *(Tur Choshen Mishpat* 155). Nevertheless, four cubits of space are still required above the stove just as for an oven *(Sema* 155:2; see *Tur* 155:1).

Others disagree and maintain that just as a stove requires only one-third the protection of an oven beneath it, so too it requires only one-third its protection from above. Therefore, a space of one and one-third cubits — eight handbreadths — is sufficient *(Yad Ramah)*. A third view is that one handbreadth is sufficient above it as well as beneath it *(Nimmukei Yosef;* see *Tur*

בבא
בתרא
ב/ג

מַה שֶׁהִזִּיק. רַבִּי שִׁמְעוֹן אוֹמֵר: לֹא אָמְרוּ כָּל הַשִּׁעוּרִין הָאֵלּוּ אֶלָּא שֶׁאִם הִזִּיק פָּטוּר מִלְּשַׁלֵּם.

[ג] **לֹא** יִפְתַּח אָדָם חֲנוּת שֶׁל נַחְתּוֹמִין וְשֶׁל צַבָּעִין תַּחַת אוֹצָרוֹ שֶׁל חֲבֵרוֹ, וְלֹא רֶפֶת בָּקָר. בֶּאֱמֶת, בַּיַּיִן הִתִּירוּ, אֲבָל לֹא רֶפֶת בָּקָר. חֲנוּת שֶׁבֶּחָצֵר — יָכוֹל לִמְחוֹת בְּיָדוֹ וְלוֹמַר לוֹ,

יד אברהם

Choshen Mishpat 155:1).
The stove of a baker requires a base of three handbreadths (Gem. 20b).

וְאִם הִזִּיק, מְשַׁלֵּם מַה שֶׁהִזִּיק. — If it caused damage, he must pay for the damage.

Although he took the necessary precautions, he is still liable if any damage occurs (Rav), because the constant potential for hazard engendered by the regular use of an oven should lead a person to constantly check it and be perpetually on guard against its damaging his neighbor, even after having taken the required legal precautions (Rif to Bava Kamma 61b).

Some authorities maintain that this ruling applies only to an oven, because its damage is clear and visible and one is therefore responsible to prevent it. The objects cited in the previous mishnah as requiring precautionary distancing because of their potential for causing damage do not inflict such obvious damage. Therefore, if one took

the necessary precautions for them but they caused damage anyway, he is not obligated to pay for those damages (Meiri). Others contend that even if one took the required precautions he is obligated to pay except in those cases in which the damage is caused indirectly [see mishnah 5] (Rosh, cited by Tur 155:50).

רַבִּי שִׁמְעוֹן אוֹמֵר: לֹא אָמְרוּ כָּל הַשִּׁעוּרִין הָאֵלּוּ אֶלָּא שֶׁאִם הִזִּיק פָּטוּר מִלְּשַׁלֵּם. — R' Shimon says: They stated all these measurements only so that if it caused damage, he [should be] exempt from paying.

[Since the Sages formulated these precautionary distances as law, one who observes them has done all he can be expected to do. Consequently, if damage results despite his adherence to these codes, he is exempt.]

The halachah is in accordance with the opinion of the first Tanna (Rav; Rambam, Shecheinim 9:11; Choshen Mishpat 155:1).

3.

לֹא יִפְתַּח אָדָם חֲנוּת שֶׁל נַחְתּוֹמִין וְשֶׁל צַבָּעִין תַּחַת אוֹצָרוֹ שֶׁל חֲבֵרוֹ, — A man may not open a bakery or a dye shop [lit. a baker's or dyer's shop] under the storehouse of another,

One may not open these stores beneath his neighbor's storehouse of grain or oil (Rashi 20b), even if he leaves the required space above the oven (see previous mishnah), because the con-

stant smoke and heat produced by the ovens of these establishments is detrimental to the produce being stored (Rashi 18a, Yad Ramah).

[A dye shop is a workshop in which fabric is dyed. This involves boiling the dye (see Shabbos 1:6, Keilim 5:5).]

If one stored other products, such as dates or pomegranates, it is not clear whether this ruling would apply (Gem.

2
3

damage, he must pay for the damage. R' Shimon says: They stated all these measurements only so that if it caused damage, he [should be] exempt from paying.

3. **A** man may not open a bakery or a dye shop under the storehouse of another, nor a cattle shed. In truth, in [the case of a storehouse of] wine, they permitted [these], except for a cattle shed.
A store in a courtyard — one can block him by

YAD AVRAHAM

20b). Therefore, though one may not open such a shop beneath those storehouses, if he did so he cannot be compelled to remove it (*Meiri*).

וְלֹא רֶפֶת בָּקָר. — *nor a cattle shed.*
The odor (*Rashi; Rambam; Nimmukei Yosef*) and heat (*Rambam, Shecheinim* 9:12) of a cattle shed have a detrimental effect on produce.

This is prohibited even according to R' Yose (see preface to chapter), despite the fact that the damage from the odor does not begin as soon as the cattle shed is opened. This is because when he later works in the stall and shovels the manure to remove it, that increases the effect, and that damage is directly inflicted by him. Since it is inevitable that the maintenance of a cattle shed will include this activity, the owner of the storehouse can prevent him from opening it in the first place (*Yad Ramah*).

If he opened a bakery, dye shop or cattle shed before his neighbor placed a storehouse above it, he cannot be compelled to close them, even if his neighbor subsequently uses the upper story for storage (*Gem.* 20b).

בֶּאֱמֶת, — *In truth,*
This term denotes that the halachah is in accordance with the following statement beyond any doubt (*Tos. Yom Tov* to *Bava Metzia* 4:11, s.v. באמת).

בְּיֵין הִתִּירוּ, — *in [the case of a storehouse of] wine they permitted [these],*
The Sages permitted one to open a bakery or a dyer's shop beneath a wine

storehouse because the smoke is not harmful to the wine and the heat is in fact beneficial (*Rav* from *Gem.* 20b).

However, this was stated only concerning the wine of the Land of Israel [where the mishnah was compiled]; elsewhere, if it is known that the heat or smoke is harmful to the wine of that area, it is prohibited, as was the case in Babylonia (ibid.).

אֲבָל לֹא רֶפֶת בָּקָר. — *except for a cattle shed.*
The odor emanating from a cattle shed is harmful to wine as well as to the other produce (*Rashi*).

Even according to the view that the damage from a cattle shed is due to its heat, it is nevertheless of a different nature than that of an oven, and it causes the wine to spoil (*Meiri*).

חֲנוּת שֶׁבֶּחָצֵר — יָכוֹל לִמְחוֹת בְּיָדוֹ — *A store in a courtyard — one can block him* [lit., *protest in his hands*]
If one of the residents of a courtyard wants to open up a store there, the neighbors can prevent him from doing so (*Rav*).

Rashba rules that even if the store opened with the permission of the neighbors, they can later revoke their consent, because they did not realize how it would affect them. This is derived from the deviation of the wording here from that of the previous cases — i.e., *a store in a courtyard — one can protest it*, rather than *a man may not open a store in a courtyard*, indicating that a protest can be lodged against a store even after it has

„אֵינִי יָכוֹל לִישֵׁן מִקּוֹל הַנִּכְנָסִין וּמִקּוֹל הַיּוֹצְאִין."
עוֹשֶׂה כֵלִים, יוֹצֵא וּמוֹכֵר בְּתוֹךְ הַשּׁוּק. אֲבָל אֵינוֹ
יָכוֹל לִמְחוֹת בְּיָדוֹ וְלוֹמַר לוֹ „אֵינִי יָכוֹל לִישֵׁן לֹא
מִקּוֹל הַפַּטִּישׁ," וְלֹא „מִקּוֹל הָרֵחַיִם," וְלֹא „מִקּוֹל
הַתִּינוֹקוֹת."

[ד] **מִי** שֶׁהָיָה כוֹתְלוֹ סָמוּךְ לְכוֹתֶל חֲבֵרוֹ לֹא

יד אברהם

opened with permission (Rashba).

וְלוֹמַר לוֹ „אֵינִי יָכוֹל לִישֵׁן מִקּוֹל הַנִּכְנָסִין וּמִקּוֹל
הַיּוֹצְאִין." — by claiming [lit. and say to
him], 'I cannot sleep due to the noise of
those entering and leaving [lit. and the
noise of those leaving].'

The basis for their protesting the
opening of a store in their courtyard is
that the noise of the customers'
occasional arguments will disturb their
sleep (Meiri). Others contend that noise
alone is insufficient grounds for
preventing a member of the courtyard
from exercising his rights of ownership
but that this is symptomatic of the
primary concern that the customers
crowd the courtyard and thereby
inconvenience the residents (Rambam;
Rashba; Ritva).

עוֹשֶׂה כֵלִים, יוֹצֵא וּמוֹכֵר בְּתוֹךְ הַשּׁוּק. — One
may make utensils [and] go out and sell
[them] in the marketplace.

Although a person can be prevented
from opening a store in a courtyard, he
cannot be prevented from making
utensils in the courtyard to sell in the
marketplace (Tos. 21a; Tos. R' Akiva).
According to some he may even accept
contracts to make utensils for others.
Although this will bring a certain
amount of traffic into the courtyard,
such workshops do not attract the
number of customers that stores do
(Tos. 20b, 21a).

אֲבָל אֵינוֹ יָכוֹל לִמְחוֹת בְּיָדוֹ וְלוֹמַר לוֹ „אֵינִי
יָכוֹל לִישֵׁן לֹא מִקּוֹל הַפַּטִּישׁ," — But one
cannot block him by claiming, 'I cannot

sleep due to the noise of the hammer,'

Since this noise is made by the
activities of the resident of the
courtyard himself, rather than his
customers, his neighbors cannot prevent him from performing those
activities (see Rav). Moreover, it was
accepted practice (in earlier times) for a
man to pursue his trade within his own
house; therefore, he could not be
prevented from doing so. Commerce,
however, ordinarily took place in the
marketplace, and therefore one who
wants to do otherwise must obtain the
consent of his neighbors (Meiri).

Alternatively, in the case of the store,
the noise takes place in the courtyard,
which belongs to all the residents; they
thus have a claim as to how it should be
used. In the case of a craftsman,
however, it takes place in his own home
(Sema, Choshen Mishpat 156:10).

Others contend that neighbors have
no right to prevent noise in any case;
their only legitimate complaint is the
inconvenience caused by the crowding
of their courtyard, which is not
applicable in this case (Rashba; see
above s.v. ולומר לו).

Another view is that neighbors have the
right to restrict even the noise made by a
resident in his own house. The rulings of this
mishnah apply only to a case in which they
originally allowed him to perform those
actvities in his house, in which case they
cannot retract [see 3:5] (Rambam,
Shecheinim 6:12; Maggid Mishneh).
Although in the previous case (according to
this view) they could revoke their consent to

claiming, 'I cannot sleep due to the noise of those entering and leaving.' One may make utensils [and] go out and sell [them] in the marketplace. But one cannot block him by claiming, 'I cannot sleep due to the noise of the hammer,' or, 'the noise of the mill,' or, 'the noise of the children.'

4. One whose wall was near the wall of another

YAD AVRAHAM

his store, that is because the noise in that situation is generated by others who have no rights in the courtyard whatsoever *(Maggid Mishneh,* ibid.).

וְלֹא ,,מְקוֹל הָרֵחַיִם," — *or, 'the noise of the mill,'*

Nor may the members of a courtyard stop one of their number from opening a mill in his home on the grounds that the noise of the grinding is disturbing (see *Tos.* 20b).

וְלֹא ,,מְקוֹל הַתִּינוֹקוֹת." — *or, 'the noise of the children.'*

The residents of a courtyard may also not prevent one of their number from opening a class to teach Torah to children in his home. Although this will result in an increase of noise and traffic generated by outsiders, the Rabbis permitted it for the sake of spreading Torah study *(Rav from Gem.* 20b), by increasing the availability of Torah instruction *(Nimmukei Yosef).*

A teacher of secular studies, however, does not enjoy this dispensation *(Rav from Rambam Comm.).*

4.

The flow of pedestrian traffic past a wall is beneficial to it because the constant tread of footsteps hardens the ground at its base and thereby strengthens its foundation *(Gem.* 22b). Consequently, someone building a wall on an adjacent property is constrained from building it in a way which will block the traffic from passing by the first wall *(Gem.* 22b). The mishnah now takes up this law.

This law applies to a courtyard wall in a newly settled town,[1] since the ground there has not yet been hardened. However, the wall of a courtyard in an old town does not require this reinforcement, having been amply hardened by the tread of the many people passing by through the years *(Rav from Gem.* 22b). It also applies to the wall of a garden even in an old town, because gardens are not much walked in, and their ground therefore requires hardening from the footsteps of those passing by outside their walls. However, a wall less than four cubits long does not require this support and it is not necessary to leave space opposite it when building another wall *(Rav).*

מִי שֶׁהָיָה כֹתְלוֹ סָמוּךְ לְכֹתֶל חֲבֵרוֹ — *One whose wall was near the wall of another*

A man's wall stood perpendicular to

the end of his neighbor's wall, to which it was connected *(Rav; Rambam Comm.* and *Hil. Shecheinim* 9:9; see *Maggid Mishneh* there).[2]

1. Some authorities say that this refers to a town less than sixty years old *(Mordechai).* Others contend that as long as there are inhabitants who still remember its settlement, it is considered new *(Tos. Yom Tov).*

2. *Rav* and *Rambam's* understanding follows that of *Ri Migash* and is seemingly based on an alternate text of the *Gemara's* explanation of our mishnah; see *Maggid Mishneh* and *Lechem Mishneh.*

יִסְמֹךְ לוֹ כֹתֶל אַחֵר אֶלָּא אִם כֵּן הִרְחִיק מִמֶּנּוּ
אַרְבַּע אַמּוֹת. וְהַחַלּוֹנוֹת — מִלְמַעְלָן, וּמִלְמַטָּן,
וּמִכְּנֶגְדָּן, אַרְבַּע אַמּוֹת.

יד אברהם

לֹא יִסְמֹךְ לוֹ כֹתֶל אַחֵר אֶלָּא אִם כֵּן הִרְחִיק
מִמֶּנּוּ אַרְבַּע אַמּוֹת. — *may not place
another wall near it unless he distances
[it] four cubits from it.*

He may not add another wall
perpendicular to his first and parallel to
that of his neighbor unless he leaves a
space of four cubits between them —
i.e., between his new wall and that of his
neighbor — to allow for people to walk
between them and harden the ground at
its base (*Rav; Rambam* loc. cit.). This is
prohibited even according to R' Yose
because the damage is considered to
have begun as soon as people are
prevented from walking there (*Tos.
22b*).

He was allowed to build the first,
perpendicular wall (*Maggid Mishneh*)
because it does not entirely prevent
people from walking by the neighbor's
wall. By putting up a second wall,
however, he creates a cul-de-sac which,
if it is less than four cubits wide, will not
be entered at all (*Derishah, Choshen
Mishpat* 155:13; see *Tos. Yom Tov*).

Actually, the same would be true if only
two walls were involved and he put up that
second wall parallel to the first and within
four cubits of it. By creating such a long and
narrow alley (rather than a cul-de-sac), he
also shuts off all traffic past the first wall.
The *Tanna* chose a case involving three walls

to make the point that even though traffic
has already been substantially reduced by the
perpendicular wall, he may still not choke off
the area entirely (*Sema* 155:30; see *Tos. Yom
Tov*).

Others reverse this reasoning and contend
that only in the case of three walls is he
obligated to leave a space of four cubits; but
in a two-wall case, where he is only putting
up a parallel wall, as long as a path remains
between the walls people will continue to
pass through even if it is narrower than four
cubits (*Lechem Mishnah* to *Hil. Shecheinim*
9:9; see *Tos. Yom Tov*).

Others explain the mishnah to refer
to one whose wall was *parallel* to his
neighbor's wall at a distance of four
cubits [the minimum distance away
from a neighbor's wall that one may
build a wall]. The mishnah teaches that
though these two walls have been facing
each other in close proximity for a long
time, with the result that the ground
between them has been heavily tram-
pled by the traffic moving through this
narrow area, if the wall should collapse
and need to be replaced, he [still] may
not place another wall near it [i.e.,
parallel to his neighbor's wall] unless he
distances it four cubits (*Rosh; Tur
Choshen Mishpat* 155:13; see *Rashba,
Nimmukei Yosef* and *Meiri* for other
explanations of this mishnah).

Some commentators maintain that, in

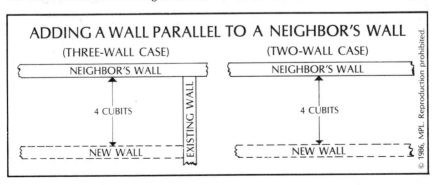

ADDING A WALL PARALLEL TO A NEIGHBOR'S WALL

(THREE-WALL CASE)　　　　　　(TWO-WALL CASE)

NEIGHBOR'S WALL　　　　　　　NEIGHBOR'S WALL

4 CUBITS　　EXISTING WALL　　　4 CUBITS

NEW WALL　　　　　　　　　　NEW WALL

may not place another wall near it unless he distances [it] four cubits from it. And [with regard to] windows — [he must leave] four cubits above them, below them, and opposite them.

YAD AVRAHAM

general, a man has no claim on his neighbor that he sacrifice the use of part of his land in order to allow for the reinforcement of the former's wall. The mishnah is discussing a case in which the owner of the wall was allotted his garden or courtyard by the government, or where he acquired it from property which had previously belonged to no one. It is therefore understood that he acquired rights (though not ownership) to the area alongside the wall as well, to ensure that it remain open to the public so as to allow for the wall's reinforcement (*Nimmukei Yosef*). However, this is not universally accepted (see *Choshen Mishpat* 155:12-14 and *Ketzos HaChoshen* 155:6).

— וְהַחַלּוֹנוֹת — And [with regard to] windows —

If one wishes to build a wall opposite the window of his neighbor's house (*Tif. Yis.*, see *Gem.* 2b).

— מִלְמַעְלָן, וּמִלְמַטָּן, וּמִכְּנֶגְדָּן, אַרְבַּע אַמּוֹת. [he must leave] four cubits above them, below them, and opposite them.

I.e., when building walls opposite windows he must either build them low enough so that the windows remain four cubits *above* the tops of the walls, or high enough so that the windows are four cubits *below* the tops of the walls, in both cases so that someone standing on top of the wall will not be able to see into the window. Similarly, regardless of their height, he must distance all these walls four cubits away from any windows [opposite them] to allow light to reach the window (*Rav, Rambam Comm.* from *Gem.* 22b).

According to this explanation, the terms *above them*, etc., refer to the proposed walls — he must leave a height of four cubits *above them*. It is not clear,

LOSS OF PRIVACY DUE TO PROXIMITY OF WALL

WINDOW

If the top of the wall is within a height of four cubits of the neighbor's window — either above or below it — someone standing on top of the wall can see into the window.

though, why the mishnah should refer to walls in the plural — *them*. Rashi, on the other hand, has *them* refer to the windows (to which the plural is more appropriate) — i.e., he must raise the wall *above them* (i.e., any windows) four cubits, or keep it that distance below them (*Tos. Yom Tov*). [As far as the actual law is concerned, there is no difference between these two explanations.]

If the wall was parallel to the window, he would in any case be obligated to leave four cubits space in order to allow for people to walk by on the ground and thereby reinforce the wall, as explained

[ה] **מַרְחִיקִין** אֶת הַסֻּלָּם מִן הַשּׁוֹבָךְ אַרְבַּע
אַמּוֹת, כְּדֵי שֶׁלֹּא תִּקְפֹּץ
הַנְּמִיָּה; וְאֶת הַכֹּתֶל מִן הַמַּזְחִילָה אַרְבַּע אַמּוֹת,
כְּדֵי שֶׁיְּהֵא זוֹקֵף אֶת הַסֻּלָּם.
מַרְחִיקִין אֶת הַשּׁוֹבָךְ מִן הָעִיר חֲמִשִּׁים אַמָּה;

יד אברהם

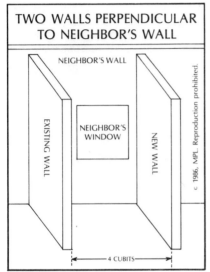

TWO WALLS PERPENDICULAR TO NEIGHBOR'S WALL

NEIGHBOR'S WALL

EXISTING WALL

NEIGHBOR'S WINDOW

NEW WALL

© 1986, MPL. Reproduction prohibited.

← 4 CUBITS →

above (*Gem.* 22b).[1] Thus, if this were the case of the mishnah, it would be a repetition of the ruling stated previously. The *Gemara* (ibid.) therefore explains the mishnah to be discussing the building of two walls perpendicular to his neighbor's house, one on each

side of his window. In such a case, the small amount of space blocked off by these walls would not prevent people from walking by most of the neighbor's wall (*Rashi*). It is therefore necessary for the mishnah to tell us that he must leave four cubits of space between the walls to allow the sunlight to reach the window. [Thus, there are four cubits of open space directly opposite the window.]

There is a dispute among the authorities whether the four cubits between the two walls includes the width of the window (*Rambam Comm.* and *Hil. Shecheinim* 7:3; see *Tos. Yom Tov*), or is in addition to it (*Rosh*).

Some authorities maintain that where the walls are perpendicular to the side of the window rather than directly opposite it is not sufficient to raise the wall four cubits higher than the window, because it is still possible to crouch on the edge of the wall and see inside the window. Therefore, he must build the wall with a slanted top so as to prevent anyone from climbing on top of it (*Rashi, Tos.* from *Gem.* 22b). Others understand the *Gemara's* conclusion to be that either raising it four cubits above the window or slanting its top is sufficient (*Rambam Comm., Hil. Shecheinim* 7:3).

5.

מַרְחִיקִין אֶת הַסֻּלָּם מִן הַשּׁוֹבָךְ אַרְבַּע אַמּוֹת, — *One must distance a ladder four cubits from a dovecote,*

If someone has a dovecote in his courtyard near the wall which stands between his property and that of his neighbor, the latter may not stand a

ladder near the wall unless he places it at least four cubits away from the dovecote (*Rav; Rashi*).

כְּדֵי שֶׁלֹּא תִּקְפֹּץ הַנְּמִיָּה; — *so that a marten should not spring [into it]*;

So that a marten[2] should not climb

1. This would be true even in an old city because a house contains furniture and utensils which prevent people within from walking across the dirt floor near the wall and thereby reinforcing the wall from within. Thus, it is like a garden (*Tos.* 22b; see *Tos. R' Akiva*).

2. The translation follows one cited by *Rashi, Chullin* 52b.

5. **O**ne must distance a ladder four cubits from a dovecote, so that a marten should not spring [into it]; and a wall four cubits from a gutter, so that he can stand a ladder [there].

One must distance a dovecote fifty cubits from a

YAD AVRAHAM

the ladder and jump into the dovecote and kill the doves (Rav; Rashi).

This ruling applies even according to R' Yose whose view (mishnah 11) is that a person is not required to distance a potential source of damage from his neighbor's property unless the hazard is immediate (see chapter preface). In the case of our mishnah the hazard is considered immediate because the animal may climb the ladder and spring from it as he places it near the wall. Although he cannot be held accountable even if this happens, since he is only an indirect cause of that damage (גְּרָמָא בְּנִזָקִין), he is nevertheless required to take measures to prevent such an occurrence (Gem. 22b).

According to Tur (Choshen Mishpat 155:15), one must not only distance the ladder four cubits from the dovecote, but he must remove it four cubits from the entire wall, since otherwise the animal can jump from the ladder to the wall and from there to the dovecote. Most authorities permit leaning the ladder against the wall as long as it is four cubits away from the dovecote (Rashi 22b; Rambam, Shecheinim 9:7; see Bach and Perishah). By removing it that distance, one has moved it far enough from the dovecote so that the marten cannot jump directly from the ladder into the dovecote, and he has thereby avoided creating any immediate hazard. Although it can still use the ladder as access to the top of the wall and from there reach the dovecote, this hazard is not immediate and one is not required to prevent it, according to R' Yose (Perishah, Choshen Mishpat 155:15).

וְאֶת הַכֹּתֶל מִן הַמַּזְחִילָה אַרְבַּע אַמּוֹת, כְּדֵי שֶׁיְּהֵא זוֹקֵף אֶת הַסֻּלָּם. — and a wall four cubits from a gutter, so that he can stand a ladder [there].

One who builds a wall parallel to the gutter of his neighbor's roof must leave

a space of four cubits between them in order to allow his neighbor enough space to lean a ladder there to climb up and clean out his gutter (Rav).

The space in question is the property of the owner of the wall, and yet the mishnah nonetheless requires him to leave it open for the servicing of his neighbor's gutter. It is clear from this that the owner of the roof has somehow acquired an easement in the yard below related to the servicing of his gutter. Some authorities maintain that the mishnah's ruling applies only in a case where the neighbor explicitly acquired this right from him. The mishnah teaches that in such a case, four cubits of space must be left to allow for that privilege (Tos.; Rosh). Others, however, rule that if someone's neighbor puts up a gutter adjacent to his property and he does not protest, the neighbor automatically acquires the right to use his yard to service it (Rambam, Shecheinim 9:8; see 7:7).

Although blocking access to the gutter by building a wall right next to it would not cause the neighbor to suffer any harm until sometime later when he must clean his gutter, even R' Yose (preface to mishnah 2) would agree that such a wall cannot be built. Since the owner of the gutter has an easement in his neighbor's property related to the needs of his gutter, the construction of the wall violates those rights immediately (Nimmukei Yosef).

The word מַזְחִילָה comes from the word זוֹחֵל, to flow, because the water from the roof runs into the gutter and flows to the ground (Tos. Yom Tov).

מַרְחִיקִין אֶת הַשּׁוֹבָךְ מִן הָעִיר חֲמִשִּׁים אַמָּה; — One must distance a dovecote fifty cubits from a town;

וְלֹא יַעֲשֶׂה אָדָם שׁוֹבָךְ בְּתוֹךְ שֶׁלּוֹ אֶלָּא אִם כֵּן יֵשׁ
לוֹ חֲמִשִּׁים אַמָּה לְכָל רוּחַ. רַבִּי יְהוּדָה אוֹמֵר: בֵּית
אַרְבַּעַת כּוֹרִין, מְלֹא שֶׁגֶר הַיּוֹנָה. וְאִם לְקָחוֹ, אֲפִלּוּ
בֵּית רֹבַע, הֲרֵי הוּא בְּחֶזְקָתוֹ.

[ו] **נִפּוֹל** הַנִּמְצָא בְּתוֹךְ חֲמִשִּׁים אַמָּה הֲרֵי הוּא
שֶׁל בַּעַל הַשּׁוֹבָךְ; חוּץ מֵחֲמִשִּׁים

יד אברהם

Doves generally feed on the food which lies within a radius of fifty cubits around them (Gem. 23a). Consequently, one who establishes a dovecote in an unused area outside of town must locate it at least fifty cubits beyond the edge of the town to prevent his doves from eating the produce laid out on roofs to dry (Rav; Tos.), or growing in people's gardens (Rashi; see Tos. Yom Tov). Having been removed that distance they no longer pose a threat, since they will find their fill before reaching the town's limits (Rashi 23a).

Although situating the dovecote closer by would not cause any immediate damage, one is obligated to distance it even according to R' Yose. This is because the doves are considered his property by Rabbinic law, and he is thus responsible for the damage they inflict the same as for the damage inflicted by any of his animals [see Bava Kamma 1:1] (Ritva; Nimmukei Yosef).

Some authorities, however, maintain that if he did not heed this law and they went and damaged, he is not liable (Meiri; see Ketzos HaChoshen 155:9).

וְלֹא יַעֲשֶׂה אָדָם שׁוֹבָךְ בְּתוֹךְ שֶׁלּוֹ אֶלָּא אִם כֵּן יֵשׁ לוֹ חֲמִשִּׁים אַמָּה לְכָל רוּחַ. — and a man may not build a dovecote within his own property unless he owns fifty cubits [of land] in every direction.

Since a person is not allowed to locate a dovecote within fifty cubits of other people's property (Rav), he cannot locate a dovecote in the middle of his own property unless he owns at least fifty cubits of land around that site in

every direction. This rule is all-inclusive and applies even if there is ample food for the doves within a smaller area (Nimmukei Yosef) and the food planted in the fields is not clearly visible (Tos.) Regardless, he may not locate his dovecote there if he does not have an additional fifty cubits in every direction.

רַבִּי יְהוּדָה אוֹמֵר: בֵּית אַרְבַּעַת כּוֹרִין, — R' Yehudah says: An area of four kor,

I.e., he must have an area of one beis kor on each side of the dovecote, not just fifty cubits. A beis kor is the area in which thirty seah can be planted (Rav) — 75,000 square cubits. This comes to a distance of 273.86 cubits in each direction (Tos. Yom Tov).

מְלֹא שֶׁגֶר הַיּוֹנָה. — the extent of a dove's flight.

I.e., the distance they fly at one time without pause (Rav; Rashi). Rambam (Comm.) renders שֶׁגֶר, a flock — i.e., the distance a flock of doves flies. R' Yehudah maintains that one must guard against damage the doves might cause for this entire distance, not only the first fifty cubits within which they usually find their fill of food (Tos.). The halachah follows the opinion of the first Tanna (Rav; Rambam, Gezeilah 6:9; Choshen Mishpat 155:24).

וְאִם לְקָחוֹ, — If he bought it,

If a man bought a field which already contained a dovecote (Rav).

אֲפִלּוּ בֵּית רֹבַע, — even [if it is within] an area of a quarter-kav,

Even if the dovecote is centered in an

2

6

town; and a man may not build a dovecote within his own property unless he owns fifty cubits [of land] in every direction. R' Yehudah says: An area of four *kor*, the extent of a dove's flight. If he bought it, even [if it is within] an area of a quarter-*kav*, it retains its standing.

6. A young dove which was found within fifty cubits [of a dovecote] belongs to the owner of the dovecote; beyond fifty cubits, it belongs to its

YAD AVRAHAM

area of only a fourth of a *kav* within his property *(Rav)*, which comes to approximately 10.2 cubits in each direction *(Rambam Comm.)*.

הֲרֵי הוּא בְחֶזְקָתוֹ. — *it retains its standing.*
The dovecote retains its current status and the buyer may keep it where it is. Since the previous owner had maintained it there without his right to do so being contested, we assume that he obtained this right from his neighbors, either by paying them for it or by their waiver of their right to bar him[1] *(Gem. 23a)*.

Although we would not make this assumption on behalf of the original owner and he would only prevail if he explicitly claimed that this was the case *(Yad Ramah)*, the buyer has no way of knowing what occurred before he acquired the property, and the court therefore makes this claim on his behalf *(Gem. ibid.)*.

6.

Having discussed how far a dovecote must be distanced from other people's property, the mishnah deviates from the theme of this chapter to discuss the ownership of a dove found in the vicinity of a dovecote *(Meiri)*.

Ordinarily, when a dove is found any place but in a dovecote, the one who finds it may keep it even if there is a dovecote nearby, and he need not worry that it flew out of that dovecote. The reason for this is that the greater number of doves in the world at large outweighs the factor of the dove's proximity to a specific dovecote as an indication of its point of origin. However, our mishnah considers the case of a young dove which cannot yet fly, whose possible starting points for reaching this spot are more limited *(Gem. 23b)*.

נִפּוֹל — *A young dove*
I.e., one which cannot yet fly, but rather hops along on its feet *(Tos. Yom Tov from Gem. 23b)*.

הַנִּמְצָא בְּתוֹךְ חֲמִשִּׁים אַמָּה — *which was found within fifty cubits* [of a dovecote]
It was found within fifty cubits of

one dovecote, while all other dovecotes were more than fifty cubits away *(Rashi)*.

הֲרֵי הוּא שֶׁל בַּעַל הַשּׁוֹבָךְ; — *belongs to the owner of the dovecote;*
The bird is assumed to have come from the nearby dovecote *(Meiri)*,

1. A waiver is obtained by their failure to protest the establishment of the dovecote so close to their property. There is a dispute whether this takes effect immediately *(Rambam, Shecheinim 11:4)*, or only after a failure to protest over a period of three years *(Yad Ramah; see further, 3:5)*.

אַמָּה, הֲרֵי הוּא שֶׁל מוֹצְאוֹ. נִמְצָא בֵּין שְׁנֵי
שׁוֹבָכוֹת, קָרוֹב לָזֶה, שֶׁלּוֹ; קָרוֹב לָזֶה, שֶׁלּוֹ. מֶחֱצָה
עַל מֶחֱצָה, שְׁנֵיהֶם יַחֲלקוּ.

[ז] **מַרְחִיקִין** אֶת הָאִילָן מִן הָעִיר עֶשְׂרִים
וְחָמֵשׁ אַמָּה; וּבֶחָרוּב וּבַשִּׁקְמָה,
חֲמִשִּׁים אַמָּה. אַבָּא שָׁאוּל אוֹמֵר: כָּל אִילַן סְרָק
חֲמִשִּׁים אַמָּה. אִם הָעִיר קָדְמָה, קוֹצֵץ וְאֵינוֹ נוֹתֵן

יד אברהם

because a bird which must hop generally ranges no more than fifty cubits from its point of origin (*Gem.* 23b). This is the distance it needs to cover to find its food (*Sema* 260:31; see mishnah 5). Since it is also unlikely to have been dropped by a passerby (because people carrying doves are generally careful not to drop them), the bird is assumed to have reached the spot under its own power from the dovecote (*Tos.* 23b). Others explain the mishnah to be discussing a case in which the dove was found in the path of a vineyard, along which people seldom pass (*Nimmukei Yosef*; see below).

חוּץ מֵחֲמִשִּׁים אַמָּה, הֲרֵי הוּא שֶׁל מוֹצְאוֹ. — *beyond fifty cubits, it belongs to its finder.*

If the dove was found more than fifty cubits from any dovecote, whoever finds it may keep it. At this distance it is not likely to have come from a dovecote on its own, and it is more reasonable to assume that it was dropped by someone passing by. Since this person has certainly given up hope of recovering it because there is no way to identify it as his, the finder may keep it (*Nimmukei Yosef*). This is the law for any lost article whose owner has despaired of recovering it (see *Bava Metzia* 2:1).

Some contend that it cannot be assumed that the owner discovered his loss and

despaired of recovering it. Rather, the mishnah must be discussing a dove found in an area where most of the passersby are gentiles (*Sema* 260:32; see *Shach* there 22), whose lost article one is not obligated to return (*Choshen Mishpat* 259:3).

נִמְצָא בֵּין שְׁנֵי שׁוֹבָכוֹת, — [*If*] *it was found between two dovecotes,*

I.e., within fifty cubits of two dovecotes (*Rav; Yad Ramah; Meiri*).

Rashi (24a) explains that this case of the mishnah may even refer to a dove more than fifty cubits from the two dovecotes, because a dove in a vineyard tends to move beyond that radius as long as its dovecote remains in sight. Nevertheless, our doubt centers on these two dovecotes only, because all other dovecotes are blocked from sight by the vineyard, and a young dove will not hop to where it can no longer see its nest (*Rashi* 24a; see *Rama, Choshen Mishpat* 260:8).

קָרוֹב לָזֶה, שֶׁלּוֹ; קָרוֹב לָזֶה, שֶׁלּוֹ. מֶחֱצָה עַל מֶחֱצָה, שְׁנֵיהֶם יַחֲלקוּ. — [*if it was*] *closer to this one, it is his; [if it was] closer to that one, it is his. [If it was] equidistant [from both], they divide [it].*

Since there is a reasonable chance of its having come from either of these dovecotes, our doubt is resolved on the basis of greater proximity and we assume that it came from the closer one.

However, the *Gemara* (23b) points out that this holds true only as long as both dovecotes house an equal number of birds. If one is larger than the other, the probability is greater that this

finder. [If] it was found between two dovecotes, [if it was] closer to this one, it is his; [if it was] closer to that one, it is his. [If it was] equidistant [from both], they divide [it].

7. One must distance a tree twenty-five cubits from a town; and in [the case of] carob or sycamore trees, fifty cubits. Abba Shaul says: Any non-fruit bearing tree [requires] fifty cubits. If the town was there first, he cuts down [the tree] and does not pay compensation; but if the tree was there first,

YAD AVRAHAM

dove came from the cote with the larger number of doves. This brings two of the Torah's principles for resolving doubtful situations — רוֹב, *majority*, and קֵרוֹב, *proximity* — into conflict. The *Gemara* establishes that wherever these two principles conflict, *majority* takes

precedence over *proximity* (רוֹב וְקֵרוֹב הוֹלְכִין אַחַר הָרוֹב). Thus, where the dove was closer to one cote but the other housed a larger number of doves, the dove would be awarded to the owner of the larger dovecote (see further *Sotah* 9:2 and *Yad Avraham* comm. there).

7.

The mishnah now returns to the discussion of objects which must be placed a certain distance away from other people's property because of the damage they may cause.

מַרְחִיקִין אֶת הָאִילָן מִן הָעִיר עֶשְׂרִים וְחָמֵשׁ אַמָּה; — *One must distance a tree twenty-five cubits from a town;*

For esthetic reasons, it was ordained that a town should be surrounded by a broad clearing, uncluttered by overhanging branches, to lend an air of grace to its design (*Rav* from *Gem.* 24b). This law applies only to towns in Eretz Yisrael (*Maggid Mishneh, Shecheinim* 10:1 from *Rashba; Tur Choshen Mishpat* 155:27), and only when the land is in the hands of the Jewish people (*Beis Yosef* ibid.).

Although there is a law prohibiting the seeding of land surrounding a town for an area of one thousand cubits (*Arachin* 9:8, see *Tos. Yom Tov* there), that does not apply to the planting of trees (*Gem.* 24b).

וּבֶחָרוֹב וּבְשִׁקְמָה, חֲמִשִּׁים אַמָּה. — *and in*

[*the case of*] *carob or sycamore trees, fifty cubits.*

Because their branches extend further (*Rav*).

אַבָּא שָׁאוּל אוֹמֵר: כָּל אִילָן סְרָק חֲמִשִּׁים אַמָּה. — *Abba Shaul says: Any non-fruit bearing tree [requires] fifty cubits.*

According to Abba Shaul, the presence of such trees in the immediate vicinity of the town is considered unbecoming (*Rav*). The halachah does not follow Abba Shaul (*Tos. Yom Tov* from *Rambam, Shecheinim* 10:1).

אִם הָעִיר קָדְמָה, קוֹצֵץ וְאֵינוֹ נוֹתֵן דָּמִים; — *If the town was there first, he cuts down [the tree] and does not pay compensation;*

If the town preceded the tree, the town may cut down the tree (*Rambam Comm.*) without compensating the owner of the tree, since the latter had no right to plant it there.

The singular [*he*] used here refers first to the town's agent [*he cuts it down*] (*Rambam Comm.*) and then to the collective ownership

דָּמִים; וְאִם הָאִילָן קָדַם, קוֹצֵץ וְנוֹתֵן דָּמִים. סָפֵק
זֶה קָדַם סָפֵק זֶה קָדַם, קוֹצֵץ וְאֵינוּ נוֹתֵן דָּמִים.

[ח] מַרְחִיקִין גֹּרֶן קָבוּעַ מִן הָעִיר חֲמִשִּׁים
אַמָּה. לֹא יַעֲשֶׂה אָדָם גֹּרֶן
קָבוּעַ בְּתוֹךְ שֶׁלּוֹ אֶלָּא אִם כֵּן יֶשׁ לוֹ חֲמִשִּׁים אַמָּה
לְכָל רוּחַ, וּמַרְחִיק מִנְּטִיעוֹתָיו שֶׁל חֲבֵרוֹ וּמִנִּירוֹ
כְּדֵי שֶׁלֹּא יַזִּיק.

יד אברהם

of the town [(he) does not pay] (Rav; Rashi; Tos. Yom Tov).

Others explain that this too refers to the person who cuts down the tree, since it is with him that the owner of the tree must deal (Rambam Comm.; Tos. 24b).

וְאִם הָאִילָן קָדַם, קוֹצֵץ וְנוֹתֵן דָּמִים. — but if the tree was there first, he cuts [it] down and pays compensation.

[If the tree was there before the town was, the town may still cut down the tree but the owner of the tree must be compensated since, when he planted the tree, it was permissible for him to do so.] Nevertheless, the tree is cut down before payment is rendered, because otherwise, no one will take it upon himself to advance the money for

payment and the tree will not be removed (Gem. 24b). This way, once the tree is cut down, its owner will demand payment (Meiri), and those responsible will then be able to collect the money to pay him (Rambam Comm.).

סָפֵק זֶה קָדַם סָפֵק זֶה קָדַם, קוֹצֵץ וְאֵינוּ נוֹתֵן דָּמִים. — [If there is] doubt [whether] this one was first or that one, he cuts [it] down and does not pay compensation.

Since the tree is removed regardless of which came first, there is no basis for its owner to prevent them from cutting it down. However, he cannot exact compensation, because it is not certain whether it is due him (Rav from Gem. 24b).

8.

מַרְחִיקִין גֹּרֶן קָבוּעַ מִן הָעִיר חֲמִשִּׁים אַמָּה. — One must distance a fixed threshing floor fifty cubits from a town.

This refers to a threshing floor for large piles of grain. The grain in this place is winnowed by being shoveled and tossed in the air for the wind to separate the grain from its chaff. Consequently, it must be located at least fifty cubits away from the town so that the wind-swept chaff should not injure

any townspeople (Rav from Gem. 24b)[1] or damage their property (Rashi).

Such damage is an immediate consequence of his actions, since the chaff is blown towards the town as soon as he throws it into the wind. Thus, even though he is not legally liable if damage occurs, since he is only considered to have indirectly caused the damage (גְּרָמָא) which was actually the result of the wind's force, he is

1. If the piles in the threshing place are small enough for the grain to be separated from the chaff by the wind without being tossed in the air, some authorities rule that the Rabbis did not require him to distance it from the town at all, because it is not a permanent fixture, and because the damage which may be done is negligible (Ritva; Nimmukei Yosef). Others

he cuts [it] down and pays compensation. [If there is] doubt [whether] this one was first or that one, he cuts [it] down and does not pay compensation.

8. One must distance a fixed threshing floor fifty cubits from a town. One may not establish a fixed threshing floor within his own property unless he owns fifty cubits [of land] in every direction, and he must distance [it] from the plantings of his neighbor and from his plowed-over areas so that it should not damage [them].

YAD AVRAHAM

nevertheless prohibited to cause it even according to R' Yose [see chapter preface] *(Ritva; Nimmukei Yosef;* see commentary to mishnah 5, s.v. כדי שלא תקפץ).

If the threshing place preceded the town, he must nevertheless remove it when the town is built, but the townspeople must compensate him for his loss. If it is unknown which was first, he must remove it without compensation *(Rama, Choshen Mishpat* 155:22; see previous mishnah).

לֹא יַעֲשֶׂה אָדָם גֹּרֶן קָבוּעַ בְּתוֹךְ שֶׁלּוֹ אֶלָּא אִם כֵּן יֶשׁ לוֹ חֲמִשִּׁים אַמָּה לְכָל רוּחַ, — *One may not establish a fixed threshing floor within his own property unless he owns fifty cubits [of land] in every direction,*

I.e., even if it is surrounded by fields and there is no danger of injuring people, he must still leave fifty cubits in every direction to avoid damaging his neighbor's plants and fields, as will now be explained *(Nimmukei Yosef; Rambam, Shecheinim* 10:2).

וּמַרְחִיק מִנְּטִיעוֹתָיו שֶׁל חֲבֵרוֹ וּמִנִּירוֹ — *and he must distance [it] from the plantings of his neighbor and from his plowed-over areas*

This is the reason for the previous statement: He must leave fifty cubits around the threshing floor in order to distance it from the young shoots of his neighbor's field and from his plowed areas *(Nimmukei Yosef; Rambam, Shecheinim* 10:2; *Tos. Yom Tov).*

נִיר refers to the areas plowed over in the summer for the sake of destroying any weeds and grass which the land may contain *(Rav).*

Tur (Choshen Mishpat 155) cites this as a separate case from the previous one. Thus, the earlier statement of the mishnah teaches that one must distance his threshing floor from fields because it may harm the seeds, and this one tells us that even the shoots of the plants, as well as the plowed areas, can be harmed by chaff *(Perisha,* ibid. §28).

בְּדֵי שֶׁלֹּא יַזִּיק. — *so that it should not damage [them].*

The decaying chaff will dry out the shoots of the plants and damage the plowed areas *(Rav).*

This mishnah mentions the concern over damage explicitly, unlike any of the others in this chapter, because the previous mishnah dealt with an ordinance enacted not to protect against damage but to enhance the scenic charm of the town. As explained above, that enactment is only applicable to towns in

contend that even so he is required to distance it from the town's edge but that he need not move it fifty cubits away. Rather, a smaller separation is sufficient, the distance being determined by its capacity to cause damage *(Yad Ramah; Meiri).*

[ט] **מַרְחִיקִין** אֶת הַנְּבֵלוֹת, וְאֶת הַקְּבָרוֹת,
וְאֶת הַבֻּרְסְקִי מִן הָעִיר חֲמִשִּׁים
אַמָּה. אֵין עוֹשִׂין בֻּרְסְקִי אֶלָּא לְמִזְרַח הָעִיר. רַבִּי
עֲקִיבָא אוֹמֵר: לְכָל רוּחַ הוּא עוֹשֶׂה חוּץ
מִמַּעֲרָבָה, וּמַרְחִיק חֲמִשִּׁים אַמָּה.

[י] **מַרְחִיקִין** אֶת הַמִּשְׁרָה מִן הַיָּרָק, וְאֶת
הַכְּרֵישִׁין מִן הַבְּצָלִים, וְאֶת

יד אברהם

Eretz Yisrael, and it is therefore necessary to clarify that this law is due to concern for actual damage and thus applies everywhere. In addition, since potential damage is the basis of this restriction, the townspeople may, if they wish, waive their rights and allow him to place his threshing floor there. They may not, however, do so where the scenic beauty of Eretz Yisrael is at stake (*Rashba; Ritva*).

9.

מַרְחִיקִין אֶת הַנְּבֵלוֹת, וְאֶת הַקְּבָרוֹת, וְאֶת הַבֻּרְסְקִי מִן הָעִיר חֲמִשִּׁים אַמָּה. — *One must distance carcasses, graves, and a tannery fifty cubits from a town.*

Rotting animal carcasses, [shallow] graves, and tanneries (where hides are made into leather) all emit foul odors, and they must therefore be moved away from a town (*Rav; Meiri*).

אֵין עוֹשִׂין בֻּרְסְקִי אֶלָּא לְמִזְרַח הָעִיר. — *One may establish a tannery only to the east of a town.*

[Even after distancing the tannery fifty cubits from the town, he may still only locate it to the east of the town.] This is because an east wind is ordinarily a gentle wind which is not strong enough to carry the odor to the town from that distance. Only when divine retribution has been decreed upon an area does the east wind blow strongly (*Rav; Rashi*; see *Tos. Yom Tov*). Others explain that it is rare for there to be an east wind at all in the Mideast, where this law was stated. Thus, this is the least likely direction for any odor to be carried from (*Rambam*

Comm., cf. Tos. 25a; Yad Ramah).

רַבִּי עֲקִיבָא אוֹמֵר: לְכָל רוּחַ הוּא עוֹשֶׂה חוּץ מִמַּעֲרָבָה, — *R' Akiva says: He may establish it in any direction except to the west,*

Prayers are said facing westward, since that is the direction in which the Divine Presence manifests itself most directly (*Rav* from *Gem.* 25a). [Therefore, it would be a profanity to place a tannery, with its foul odor, on that side of the town.] Although today we actually pray facing eastward, that is because the Temple site in Jerusalem is to our east. In Jerusalem, though, the Temple was located on the west side of the city (*Meiri*).

The first *Tanna* maintains, however, that the Divine Presence manifests itself in all directions equally (*Tos. Yom Tov*; cf. *Yad Ramah*).

וּמַרְחִיק חֲמִשִּׁים אַמָּה. — *and he must distance [it] fifty cubits.*

I.e., in all other directions, he must distance the tannery fifty cubits from

9. One must distance carcasses, graves, and a tannery fifty cubits from a town. One may establish a tannery only to the east of a town. R' Akiva says: He may establish it in any direction except to the west, and he must distance [it] fifty cubits.

10. One must distance a flax pool from vegetables, and leeks from onions, and mustard plants

YAD AVRAHAM

the town; but he may not place it at any distance to the west (Gem. 25a).

The halachah follows the opinion of the first Tanna (Rav; Rambam, Shecheinim 10:4, Choshen Mishpat 155:23).

10.

מַרְחִיקִין אֶת הַמִּשְׁרָה מִן הַיָּרָק, — One must distance a flax pool from vegetables,

[Before the fiber of flax stems may be processed into linen, their stems must be retted (soaked) for several days to break down their woody tissues and dissolve the substances binding together the fiber cells. The stems were tied in bunches and then immersed in pools or ponds. After several days of soaking, the water in the pool becomes polluted from the substances it absorbs and toxic to growing plants.] Thus a person must place his soaking pool at a safe distance so as not to damage the vegetables of his neighbor (Rav).

וְאֶת הַכְּרֵישִׁין מִן הַבְּצָלִים, — and leeks from onions,

Leeks diminish the sharpness of onions which grow too close to them (Rambam Comm.).

וְאֶת הַחַרְדָּל מִן הַדְּבוֹרִים. — and mustard plants from bees.

He must distance his mustard plants from the beehives of his neighbor (Tif. Yis.) because the mustard, when eaten by the bees, ruins the honey by rendering it pungent (Rav; Rambam Comm., Shecheinim 10:5). Alternatively, the bees are bothered by the sharp taste of the mustard and therefore

consume their honey (Meiri; Rashi to 18a).

The mishnah does not specify the distance required between these objects. Some commentators maintain that no set distance is given; one must place them where he is certain they will not cause damage (Yad Ramah; Meiri). Others say that the mishnah relies on the distance stated in the previous mishnah — fifty cubits — to apply here as well (Ritva; Nimmukei Yosef).

Some state that, according to this Tanna, it is prohibited to place any of these potentially damaging items near the property of a neighbor, even if the latter presently has no object which is susceptible to damage, because he may subsequently decide to place it there. Thus, for example, one would not be allowed to place mustard near the boundary even if his neighbor has no bees at present. Moreover, even if one planted mustard in the middle of his own field and later sold half the field, leaving the mustard plants on the border, if the buyer should then place beehives in his property, the seller would have to remove his mustard plants so that they should not cause damage to the beehives (Rashi to 18b; see Tos. there; Ketzos HaChoshen 155:11). Others contend that it is permitted to plant mustard near one's neighbor's field as long as the latter has no bees there at the time, and having done so, he need not remove it if his neighbor sub-

הַחַרְדָּל מִן הַדְּבוֹרִים. רַבִּי יוֹסֵי מַתִּיר בַּחַרְדָּל.

[יא] **מַרְחִיקִין** אֶת הָאִילָן מִן הַבּוֹר עֶשְׂרִים
וְחָמֵשׁ אַמָּה, וּבֶחָרוּב וּבַשִּׁקְמָה,
חֲמִשִּׁים אַמָּה, בֵּין מִלְמַעְלָה בֵּין מִן הַצַּד. אִם
הַבּוֹר קָדְמָה, קוֹצֵץ וְנוֹתֵן דָּמִים; וְאִם אִילָן קָדַם,

יד אברהם

sequently places beehives there *(Rabbeinu Tam,* cited by *Tos.* 18b).[1]

A third view concurs with this last opinion with one exception. If someone had mustard plants and beehives near each other in his field and then sold the land containing the mustard to one and the parcel containing the bees to another, the new owner of the mustard plants must remove them from the proximity of the bees. Although ordinarily (according to this view) once he planted the mustard there permissibly his neighbor would have no right to place beehives nearby and thereby force him to move his mustard, in this case the latter's bees were also placed there permissibly; consequently, it is the one causing the damage who must take the necessary steps to prevent it *(Ramban).*

רַבִּי יוֹסֵי מַתִּיר בַּחַרְדָּל. — *R' Yose permits [it in the case of] the mustard plants.*

I.e., the owner of the mustard plants need not distance them from the bee-hives because he can turn the claim around and demand that the owner of the bees distance his bees from the mustard so that the bees not eat the leaves of his plants *(Rav* from *Gem.* 25b). The first *Tanna* maintains that the bees do not cause real damage to the mustard, since the seeds are inside the pod and thus inaccessible *(Rashi),* and any leaves consumed grow back *(Gem.* 18b).

This implies that R' Yose disputes the ruling of the *Tanna Kamma* only in regard to mustard, but not in the other cases. However, the *Gemara* (18b) concludes that R' Yose disagrees in all of these cases, because he maintains that a person using his field for his own purposes has no obligation to prevent that usage from damaging his neighbor's field unless the damage begins immediately upon the placement of the harmful object (see next mishnah). Rather, the burden rests on the one threatened with the loss to distance himself and avoid damage. Thus, in these cases, at the time the leek is planted it does not yet damage the onions; when the mustard seed is planted in the ground the bees cannot eat it until it grows;[2] and when he digs a pool and soaks flax in it, the water does not damage his neighbor's vegetables until it sits for a while and becomes polluted. R' Yose's focus on the mustard plants is only because he feels that even the *Tanna Kamma* should agree that the obligation should not fall on the mustard farmer to distance his plants from the beehives since he is being equally damaged by the bees *(Rambam Comm., Rosh).*

1. Actually, this question is dealt with by the *Gemara.* The *Gemara* (18a) in fact states that one may not place mustard plants near the boundary of his neighbor's property even if he has no bees. However, *Rabbeinu Tam's* reading of the *Gemara's* conclusion (18b) has it that the *Gemara* retracts this position.

2. It is difficult to understand why this reason is necessary; even without this factor, the damage caused by the mustard is not immediate because the bees must first come and eat it before any damage will occur to the honey *(Hasogos Chavos Yair* to *Rif.* 25a).

from bees. R' Yose permits [it in the case of] the mustard plants.

11. One must distance his tree twenty-five cubits from a pit, and in [the case of] carob or sycamore trees, fifty cubits, whether from above or from the side. If the pit was there first, he cuts [it] down and pays compensation; if the tree was there first, he may not cut [it] down. [If it is] uncertain

YAD AVRAHAM

This implies that according to R' Yose, he need not distance his leeks or mustard plants from his neighbor's property at all[1] (*Tur Choshen Mishpat* 155; see *Derisha* 45 there).

Others contend that a distance of three handbreadths is required in all these cases, even according to R' Yose (*Rambam, Shecheinim* 10:5).

11.

מַרְחִיקִין אֶת הָאִילָן מִן הַבּוֹר עֶשְׂרִים וְחָמֵשׁ אַמָּה, — *One must distance his tree twenty-five cubits from a pit,*

A man may not plant a tree within twenty-five cubits of his neighbor's water cistern because the Rabbis assessed that the roots of a tree may spread up to that distance and thereby damage the cistern (*Yad Ramah; Meiri*).

וּבֶחָרוּב וּבַשִּׁקְמָה, חֲמִשִּׁים אַמָּה, — *and in [the case of] carob or sycamore trees, fifty cubits,*

Their roots spread to a greater distance than those of other trees (*Rav; Rashi; Yad Ramah*).

בֵּין מִלְמַעְלָה — *whether from above*

I.e., whether the tree and cistern are situated on a slope, one above the other (*Rav*). If the tree is higher, the roots will damage the cistern itself; if the cistern is higher, the roots will weaken the ground beneath it (*Gem.* 25b).

בֵּין מִן הַצַּד. — *or from the side.*

I.e., where the tree and cistern are near each other on level ground (*Rav*).

אִם הַבּוֹר קָדְמָה, קוֹצֵץ וְנוֹתֵן דָּמִים; — *If the*

pit was there first, he cuts [it] down and pays compensation;

[If the cistern was dug before the tree was planted, the owner of the cistern may have the tree removed, but he must compensate his neighbor for it.] Although generally speaking the offending party is required to remove his threatening items without compensation, a tree is different, either because it is not capable of causing damage when it is first planted (*Rav*), or because its removal involves substantial long-term loss (*Tos.* 18b, s.v. ואי). Accordingly, the Rabbis did not obligate him to remove it for the sake of a single individual without compensation (*Rav*). [This is in contrast to a tree planted near a town, where the public benefit is at stake, in which case the Rabbis did not mandate compensation if the town was there first, as taught in mishnah 7.]

וְאִם אִילָן קָדַם, — *if the tree was there first,*

[If the tree was planted before the cistern was dug.]

According to those who maintain that one may not place an object which can cause

1. The flax pool is an exception because he must still observe the rules governing the placement of a cistern; see mishnah 1 (*Rosh*).

לֹא יָקֵץ. סָפֵק זֶה קָדַם וְסָפֵק זֶה קָדַם, לֹא יָקֵץ. רַבִּי
יוֹסֵי אוֹמֵר: אַף עַל פִּי שֶׁהַבּוֹר קוֹדֶמֶת לָאִילָן לֹא
יָקֵץ, שֶׁזֶּה חוֹפֵר בְּתוֹךְ שֶׁלּוֹ וְזֶה נוֹטֵעַ בְּתוֹךְ שֶׁלּוֹ.

[יב] **לֹא** יִטַּע אָדָם אִילָן סָמוּךְ לִשְׂדֵה חֲבֵרוֹ
אֶלָּא אִם כֵּן הִרְחִיק מִמֶּנּוּ אַרְבַּע
אַמּוֹת, אֶחָד גְּפָנִים וְאֶחָד כָּל אִילָן. הָיָה גָדֵר

יד אברהם

סָפֵק זֶה קָדַם וְסָפֵק זֶה קָדַם, לֹא יָקֵץ. — [If it is] uncertain which was first, he may not cut [it] down.

Since the right to cut is unclear, the owner of the tree cannot be made to suffer the loss of his tree out of doubt. This is consistent with the rule for any case of uncertainty regarding monetary issues, in which the ruling is made in favor of the defendant (Rambam Comm.).

רַבִּי יוֹסֵי אוֹמֵר: אַף עַל פִּי שֶׁהַבּוֹר קוֹדֶמֶת לָאִילָן לֹא יָקֵץ, שֶׁזֶּה חוֹפֵר בְּתוֹךְ שֶׁלּוֹ וְזֶה נוֹטֵעַ בְּתוֹךְ שֶׁלּוֹ. — R' Yose says: Even if the pit preceded the tree he may not cut [it] down, because this one digs within his property and that one plants within his property.

R' Yose maintains that in any case where the placement of the harmful object does not immediately damage his neighbor, it is up to the one who is being damaged to protect himself (עַל הַנִּזָּק לְהַרְחִיק עַצְמוֹ) — by removing his vulnerable item from the proximity of the threatening object (Yad Ramah from Gem. 25b, Rambam, Shecheinim 6:7; Choshen Mishpat 155:32).

damage near his neighbor's field even if the field does not presently contain anything vulnerable (see comm. to previous mishnah, s.v. ואת החרדל), this mishnah is discussing a case in which a man who had a tree in the middle of his field sold part of the field to another, thus leaving the tree near his border (Tos. R' Akiva from Gem. 18a). Alternatively, the field in question is one which is watered by the rain and does not require irrigation; thus, his neighbor's digging of a cistern is an unlikely event which he is not obligated to anticipate (Yad Ramah; see mishnah 1).

לֹא יָקֵץ. — he may not cut [it] down.

[Since the tree was planted there legitimately, the owner of the cistern may not cut it down. This is again in contrast to a tree growing at the outskirts of a town, where, because of the public interest, they may cut down even a tree which antedates the town (mishnah 7), as Rav explained above.]

According to the opinion that a potential hazard which was placed permissibly must nevertheless be removed once it actually threatens, a tree is an exception to this rule because of the large financial loss involved (Tos. 18b, s.v. ואי).

12.

לֹא יִטַּע אָדָם אִילָן סָמוּךְ לִשְׂדֵה חֲבֵרוֹ — A man may not plant a tree near the field of another

Whether that field is a field of trees or of grain (Rav).

אֶלָּא אִם כֵּן הִרְחִיק מִמֶּנּוּ אַרְבַּע אַמּוֹת, — unless he distances [the tree] four cubits from it,

A person needs a space of four cubits around his tree in order to maneuver his

which was first, he may not cut [it] down. R' Yose says: Even if the pit preceded the tree he may not cut [it] down, because this one digs within his property and that one plants within his property.

12. **A** man may not plant a tree near the field of another unless he distances [the tree] four cubits from it, whether vines or any other tree. [If]

YAD AVRAHAM

plow around it. If his tree is within four cubits of his neighbor's field he will have to tread in his neighbor's field in order to plow around his tree. To avoid this, he must distance his tree four cubits away from the boundary (*Rav* from *Gem.* 26a).

This is required even according to R' Yose, because the owner of the tree causes the damage himself by entering into his neighbor's field; therefore, the latter may prevent him from creating a situation which will eventually lead to that damage (*Yad Ramah*).

According to *Rashi*, who maintains that the *Gemara's* conclusion is that it is prohibited to place a potentially damaging object near a neighbor's field even if there is nothing vulnerable in that field at present (see comm. to mishnah 10, s.v. ואת החרדל), he would be required to distance his tree twenty-five cubits from his neighbor's field, since the neighbor might some day decide to dig a cistern there (see previous mishnah). Accordingly, the mishnah is discussing a case in which there is a section of rock between the two fields and there is thus no danger of the tree's roots spreading into the neighboring field (*Tos. R' Akiva* from *Gem.* 18a). Nevertheless, he must leave four cubits of space to allow for maneuvering the plow around the tree (*Tos.* 18a, s.v. המפסיק).

אֶחָד גְּפָנִים וְאֶחָד כָּל אִילָן. — *whether vines or any other tree.*

The rule about distancing a tree at least four cubits from a neighbor's field applies to all trees, not only vines. This

is stated to preclude equating this law with the laws of *kilayim* — the prohibition of planting vines together with other species — in which the requirement to distance four cubits pertains only to a vineyard (*Tos.* 26a).

The four-cubit restriction applies only in Eretz Yisrael, where they used long plows. In Babylonia — as well as in all other lands (*Rav; Rambam Comm.*) — they used a shorter plow, and a space of two cubits was sufficient (*Rav* from *Gem.* 26a). Nevertheless, even in these places, if he is planting a tree near his neighbor's vine, he must distance it four cubits (*Rav* from *Gem.* 26a), so that when he chases away the birds sitting on top of his tree his action should not directly cause them to alight on the nearby vineyard and cause damage (*Nimmukei Yosef*).[1]

Rosh contends that the required distance cannot be set at just four cubits; rather, it must be at a sufficient distance from the vineyard that the birds cannot reach it in one swoop from the tree, even if this turns out to be more than four cubits. Within this distance it is prohibited even according to R' Yose, because their alighting on the vines would be a direct result of his chasing them.

However, some commentators explain the reason for the distancing to be because the tree offers the birds a perch from which to see and be tempted by the vineyard (*Rabbeinu Yonah*). According to this explanation, the obligation to prevent this is only if one is transplanting a grown tree [so that the possibility of its causing damage begins as soon as he places it in the ground (see mishnah 5)]. However, if he plants seeds

1. The same applies to a tree which is near a grain field (*Tos.* 26a; *Rama, Choshen Mishpat* 155:25).

בִּנְתַיִם, זֶה סוֹמֵךְ לַגָּדֵר מִכָּאן, וְזֶה סוֹמֵךְ לַגָּדֵר מִכָּאן.

הָיוּ שָׁרָשִׁים יוֹצְאִין לְתוֹךְ שֶׁל חֲבֵרוֹ, מַעֲמִיק שְׁלֹשָׁה טְפָחִים, כְּדֵי שֶׁלֹּא יְעַכֵּב אֶת הַמַּחֲרֵשָׁה. הָיָה חוֹפֵר בּוֹר, שִׁיחַ, וּמְעָרָה, קוֹצֵץ וְיוֹרֵד, וְהָעֵצִים שֶׁלּוֹ.

[יג] אִילָן שֶׁהוּא נוֹטֶה לִשְׂדֵה חֲבֵרוֹ, קוֹצֵץ מְלֹא הַמַּרְדֵּעַ עַל גַּבֵּי הַמַּחֲרֵשָׁה; וּבֶחָרוּב וּבַשִּׁקְמָה, כְּנֶגֶד הַמִּשְׁקֹלֶת. בֵּית הַשְּׁלָחִין, כָּל הָאִילָן כְּנֶגֶד הַמִּשְׁקֹלֶת. אַבָּא שָׁאוּל אוֹמֵר: כָּל

יד אברהם

for a new tree, he need not distance them at all, because there is no possibility of immediate damage (*Tos.* loc. cit., s.v. אבל; *Rama* loc. cit.; see *Sema* ibid. §59).

הָיָה גָּדֵר בִּנְתַיִם, זֶה סוֹמֵךְ לַגָּדֵר מִכָּאן, וְזֶה סוֹמֵךְ לַגָּדֵר מִכָּאן. — [*If*] *there was a fence in between, this one may approach the fence on this side and that one may approach the fence on that side.*

[Since there is no possibility of trespassing in the neighbor's field when a fence divides them, there is no reason to distance the tree from the boundary.] Although this is obvious, the mishnah mentions it in order to teach us that the reason for the required distance is to avoid the possibility of trespassing (*Nimmukei Yosef*).

הָיוּ שָׁרָשִׁים יוֹצְאִים לְתוֹךְ שֶׁל חֲבֵרוֹ, מַעֲמִיק שְׁלֹשָׁה טְפָחִים, כְּדֵי שֶׁלֹּא יְעַכֵּב אֶת הַמַּחֲרֵשָׁה. — [*If*] *the roots extended into his neighbor's [property], he may [cut them off] to a depth of three handbreadths, so that they should not impede the plow.*

The owner of the field may cut away the roots of the tree to a depth of three handbreadths to allow him to plow his land (*Rav*). Since the roots are in his property, he has the right to do so even though this will harm the tree

(*Rambam, Shecheinim* 10:7).

As explained above (s.v. אלא אם כן הרחיק), according to *Rashi's* understanding of the *Gemara's* conclusion, our mishnah, which permits planting a tree up to four cubits from a neighbor's property, must refer to a case in which an area of rock separates them to prevent the roots from penetrating his property. That being the case, how could the mishnah now discuss a case in which the roots did penetrate?

The *Gemara* (18a) answers that this part of the mishnah deals with a case in which there was no such rocky area, and the tree was planted improperly. Although in such a case the affected neighbor may force him to cut down his tree, he would have to compensate him for it (see mishnah 11). The mishnah teaches us that he is permitted to cut away the roots to a depth of three handbreadths even without offering remuneration (*Ritzba* cited by *Tos.* 18a). Alternatively, the mishnah is discussing a case in which the tree was placed there permissibly — e.g., he owned the entire field and then sold half to another, leaving the tree on the border (*Tos.* ibid; cf. *Meiri* to 18a; *Tos. R' Akiva*).

הָיָה חוֹפֵר בּוֹר, שִׁיחַ, וּמְעָרָה, קוֹצֵץ וְיוֹרֵד, — [*If*] *he was digging a pit, a ditch, or a vault, he may cut downward,*

[If the one into whose property the roots grew decided to dig a cistern of

there was a fence in between, this one may approach the fence on this side and that one may approach the fence on that side.

[If] the roots extended into his neighbor's [property], he may [cut them off] to a depth of three handbreadths, so that they should not impede the plow. [If] he was digging a pit, a ditch, or a vault, he may cut downward, and the wood belongs to him.

13. **[I**f] a tree's [branches] extend over the field of another, he may cut [them] off to the height of an ox-goad raised over the plow; with a carob or sycamore tree, [he may cut them] along the plumb line. [In the case of] an irrigated field, [he may cut the branches of] any tree along the plumb line. Abba

any kind, he may cut — and thereby destroy the roots of his neighbor's tree — to any depth he requires.]

וְהָעֵצִים שֶׁלוֹ. — *and the wood belongs to him.*

In both of the above cases (*Tos. Yom Tov*) the wood which is cut from the roots belongs to the owner of the

property into which they extended. However, this is true only for the roots which extend beyond sixteen cubits from the trunk of the tree; any roots cut within sixteen cubits belong to the owner of the tree. Since they provide the tree's nourishment (*Rav from Gem.* 26b), they are considered an integral part of it (*Meiri;* cf. *Tos. Yom Tov*).

13.

אִילָן שֶׁהוּא נוֹטֶה לִשְׂדֵה חֲבֵרוֹ, — [*If*] *a tree's* [*branches*] *extend over the field of another,*

[I.e., they hang over a neighboring field.]

קוֹצֵץ מְלֹא הַמַּרְדֵּעַ עַל גַּבֵּי הַמַּחֲרֵשָׁה; — *he may cut* [*them*] *off to the height of an ox-goad raised over the plow;*

The owner of the field into which the branches protrude may cut them off to the height necessary to allow room for a man who is driving a plow to pass under the branches and raise his ox-goad over the plow in order to prod the oxen (*Meiri*).

וּבְחָרוּב וּבְשִׁקְמָה, — *with a carob or*

sycamore tree,

The branches of these two species of trees are very long and thick (see mishnah 7) and thus block out a great deal of sunlight, which is detrimental to the field (*Rav; Rashi*).

כְּנֶגֶד הַמִּשְׁקֹלֶת. — [*he may cut them*] *along the plumb line.*

The owner of the affected field may cut away any branches overhanging his property until they are in line with a plumb line hanging from the tree directly over the borderline between the two properties — i.e., anything within the airspace of his property (*Meiri*).

בֵּית הַשְּׁלָחִין, כָּל הָאִילָן כְּנֶגֶד הַמִּשְׁקֹלֶת. — [*In*

אִילָן סְרָק כְּנֶגֶד הַמִּשְׁקֹלֶת.

[יד] אִילָן שֶׁהוּא נוֹטֶה לִרְשׁוּת הָרַבִּים, קוֹצֵץ
כְּדֵי שֶׁיְּהֵא גָמָל עוֹבֵר וְרוֹכְבוֹ. רַבִּי
יְהוּדָה אוֹמֵר: גָמָל טָעוּן פִּשְׁתָּן אוֹ חֲבִילֵי זְמוֹרוֹת.
רַבִּי שִׁמְעוֹן אוֹמֵר: כָּל הָאִילָן כְּנֶגֶד הַמִּשְׁקֹלֶת
מִפְּנֵי הַטֻּמְאָה.

יד אברהם

the case of] an irrigated field, [he may cut the branches of] any tree along the plumb line.

If the field over which the branches extend requires irrigation, the owner of that field may cut off the branches of any tree which extends over his property. Such a field is very dry and needs the moisture provided by the dew, which the branches catch and prevent from reaching the field below (Rav, Rambam Comm.). Furthermore, additional sunlight is needed for the proper absorption of even the moisture which comes from irrigation (Nimmukei Yosef).

אַבָּא שָׁאוּל אוֹמֵר: כָּל אִילָן סְרָק כְּנֶגֶד הַמִּשְׁקֹלֶת.

— Abba Shaul says: [He may cut] any non-fruit bearing tree along the plumb line.

Abba Shaul disputes the first statement of the mishnah and rules that any non-fruit bearing tree whose branches extend over a field, even a field which does not require irrigation, can be cut back completely to the borderline (Rav and Gem. 27b). In his view the Sages allowed the overhang to be maintained only for the sake of protecting trees which bear fruit (Yad Ramah).

The halachah does not follow the opinion of Abba Shaul (Rav; Rambam, Shecheinim 10:8; Choshen Mishpat 155:26).

14.

אִילָן שֶׁהוּא נוֹטֶה לִרְשׁוּת הָרַבִּים, קוֹצֵץ כְּדֵי שֶׁיְּהֵא גָמָל עוֹבֵר וְרוֹכְבוֹ. — [If] a tree extends over the public domain, one may cut [it] so that a camel can pass [beneath it] with its rider.

If the branches of someone's tree extend into public property and impede passersby, the overhanging branches may be cut off to a height sufficient to allow a camel to pass beneath with his rider sitting upright (Meiri).

רַבִּי יְהוּדָה אוֹמֵר: גָמָל טָעוּן פִּשְׁתָּן אוֹ חֲבִילֵי זְמוֹרוֹת. — R' Yehudah says: A camel bearing flax or bundles of branches.

He may cut only to the height necessary to allow a camel bearing a

load of flax or branches to pass through. It is not necessary to allow for the height of the rider, because the rider can bend over when passing under the branches (Rav from Gem. 27b). The Tanna Kamma, however, is concerned that the rider may not notice the branches and be injured as he goes by (Yad Ramah).

We do not allow them to cut off the branches completely, to ensure that they do not grow back again. Rather, each branch is cut when it grows beyond the area permitted (Gem.).

רַבִּי שִׁמְעוֹן אוֹמֵר: כָּל הָאִילָן כְּנֶגֶד הַמִּשְׁקֹלֶת מִפְּנֵי הַטֻּמְאָה. — R' Shimon says: The

Shaul says: [He may cut] any non-fruit bearing tree along the plumb line.

14. [I]f] a tree extends over the public domain, one may cut [it] so that a camel can pass [beneath it] with its rider. R' Yehudah says: A camel bearing flax or bundles of branches. R' Shimon says: The entire tree [is cut] along the plumb line because of *tumah.*

YAD AVRAHAM

entire tree [is cut] along the plumb line because of tumah.

R' Shimon allows the entire overhang to be cut away until the tree extends only to the border of the public property. Otherwise, if a piece of flesh from a corpse finds its way under the branches, anyone passing by would be rendered *tamei* (ritually contaminated) by virtue of having passed under a covering which also covers part of a dead body *(Rav* from *Gem.;* see *Ohalos* 8:2 and *Yad Avraham* comm. to ArtScroll *Nazir* 7:3). The first *Tanna,* however, considers this unlikely *(Tif. Yis.).*

The halachah is in accordance with the first opinion cited in the mishnah *(Rav; Rambam, Nizkei Mamon* 13:26; *Choshen Mishpat* 417:4).

Chapter 3

A basic principle of Torah law regarding monetary litigations is הַמּוֹצִיא מֵחֲבֵרוֹ עָלָיו הָרְאָיָה, *the burden of proof lies upon the one seeking to exact property from the possession of another (Bava Kamma* 46b). That is, if one person is in possession of property and another claims it as his, the court must assume it belongs to the one presently in possession of it and the burden of proof lies on the claimant to prove his claim. [The modern-day equivalent of this is the dictum, 'Possession is nine-tenths of the law.']

Physical possession — holding the object in question on one's person or in one's property — suffices to establish a presumption of ownership only for movable property. The law concerning real property is different. Here simple presence in a field or house is not enough since it is impossible to prevent people from ever entering one's property. Rather, presumptive ownership is assigned to the last person known to have held to the property (מָרָא קַמָּא). Thus when a person known to have owned a property claims that the one presently occupying it is an illegal squatter, the burden of proof is on the occupant to prove that he acquired the property from the previous owner.

It follows from this that whenever one purchases real property he must safeguard the bill of sale to protect his property from being illegally reclaimed by the seller. The Sages, however, recognized that people generally could not be expected to hold onto this document forever. Consequently, they ruled that after three years of continuous occupancy, during which the occupant used the property in the manner appropriate to that property, the burden of proof in any litigation shifts from the occupant to the previous owner. Thus, if the previous owner should contest ownership of the field or house after three years of occupancy by someone else, the occupant is believed in his claim that he bought the property even if he cannot

[א] **חֶזְקַת הַבָּתִּים,** וְהַבּוֹרוֹת, וְהַשִּׁיחִין,
וְהַמְּעָרוֹת, וְהַשּׁוֹבָכוֹת,
וְהַמֶּרְחֲצָאוֹת, וּבֵית הַבַּדִּין, וּבֵית הַשְּׁלָחִין,
וְהָעֲבָדִים, וְכָל שֶׁהוּא עוֹשֶׂה פֵרוֹת תָּדִיר —
חֶזְקָתָן שָׁלֹשׁ שָׁנִים מִיּוֹם לְיוֹם. שְׂדֵה הַבַּעַל

יד אברהם

produce the document of sale, and it is up to the former owner to prove otherwise.[1]

This three-year possession is voided if the previous owner protests before two witnesses sometime during the three years that the person in possession of his field is holding it illicitly *(Gem. 59b)*.[2] It is assumed that word of this protest will reach the occupant of the field and that he will be alerted to hold onto his deed for three additional years following the protest *(Gem. 2a)*.

The legal term for this three-year possession and the presumption of ownership that follows from it is חֲזָקָה, *chazakah*,[3] and this is the term which will be used in the commentary. This chapter will discuss the various regulations governing the establishment of such a *chazakah* and its limits.

1.

The first mishnah discusses the extent which a property must be utilized to establish the three-year *chazakah*. There are two categories of property in regard to this matter: those which provide benefit throughout the year and those whose benefits are seasonal. Properties belonging to the first category require a full three years of utilization to establish a *chazakah*; those of the latter category have their ownership established in less time, as explained below.

---

1. There is a dispute among the *Rishonim* whether the three-year rule derives from the lack of protest by the previous owner for such an extended period or whether it is simply a Rabbinic ordinance instituted to protect buyers. According to one view, the utilization of a property for even one year without eliciting any protest from its previous owner would be sufficient proof of ownership. However, since a new owner can generally be expected to keep his bill of sale for three years, during that time his inability to produce a deed negates the proof of his occupancy. Therefore, it is only after three years that the lack of protest on the part of the previous owner over the holder's continuous use of the property is sufficient to establish the credibility of the holder's claim that he bought the property *(Ramban; Ritva)*.

Others contend that this rule is not because the lack of protest is seen as a form of evidence but that it is simply a Rabbinic ordinance to protect buyers. The Rabbis observed that, as a general rule, people tended to lose track of their deeds after three years. They therefore enacted a rule that after three years of possession one is assumed to have acquired the land and he no longer requires a document to that effect. Nevertheless, if during the three-year occupation the previous owner lodges a protest against the possession of the occupant, the possession is nullified and the occupant must take measures to retain his bill of sale for another three years *(Rosh; Ketzos HaChoshen* 140:2; cf. *Rabbeinu Yonah; Rashba)*.

2. *Rambam* rules that the previous owner must include in his protest the fact that he intends to claim it from the occupant in court *(Hil. Toein VeNitan* 11:7 from *Gem.* 39a; see *Rashbam* ad loc.).

3. The term *chazakah* has other meanings as well. It refers to a type of formal transaction by which real property can be acquired *(Kiddushin* 1:3,5), and, in its most common usage, to the

3
1

1. Possession of houses, pits, ditches, vaults, dovecotes, bathhouses, olive presses, irrigated fields, slaves, and anything which provides benefit continually — [must be] three years from day to day. A field watered by rain must be possessed three

YAD AVRAHAM

חֶזְקַת הַבָּתִּים, — *Possession of houses,*

One derives benefit from houses year-round by living in them.

וְהַבּוֹרוֹת, וְהַשִּׁיחִין, וְהַמְּעָרוֹת, — *pits, ditches, vaults,*

All of these are used throughout the year to hold water *(Yad Ramah).*

וְהַשּׁוֹבָכוֹת, וְהַמֶּרְחֲצָאוֹת, — *dovecotes, bathhouses,*

These are also used throughout the year (ibid.).

וּבֵית הַבַּדִּין, — *olive presses,*

These too are used all year. Although most people press all their olives immediately after they are picked, there are those who store them and press them little by little throughout the year *(Tos.).* Alternatively, olive presses are used for other oils (e.g., sesame oil) as well, and their use is thus not confined to the olive season *(Nimmukei Yosef; Meiri).*

וּבֵית הַשְּׁלָחִין, — *irrigated fields,*

Since irrigation ditches must be dug in these fields, they can be watered at all times and produce different fruits throughout the year — each in its appropriate season *(Rav; Yad Ramah).*

The term is derived from the word מַשְׁלְהֵי (with an interchange of the ה and ח), the Aramaic translation of עָיֵף, *tired* — i.e., a tired or thirsty field *(Rashi, Moed Katan 2a).*

וְהָעֲבָדִים, — *slaves,*

[Since slaves provide year-round service they must be utilized during the entire three years to establish a *chazakah*.]

The *Gemara* (36a) states that one cannot prove ownership of sheep or other living creatures by virtue of

simple possession in the manner of other movable property. Since living beings are capable of independent movement, they may simply have wandered onto his property on their own. This, however, does not disqualify them from the three-year *chazakah* rule. Thus, slaves who remain in one's possession for three years without any objection being raised by the previous owner can be assumed to have been acquired legitimately *(Rav from Gem.* 36a).

Some authorities are of the opinion that this applies to other living creatures as well *(Rashbam 36a; Tur Choshen Mishpat 135).* Others, however, differentiate between slaves and other living creatures, maintaining that ownership over animals cannot be established even by three years of possession *(Rambam, Toein VeNitan 10:4, see Maggid Mishneh* there; *Choshen Mishpat 135:2).* This is because their acquisition is not generally recorded in a document and the reasoning behind the three-year *chazakah* is therefore not applicable *(Sema 135:3 from Tur;* cf. *Shach 135:3,* and *Beur HaGra,* ibid.).

וְכָל שֶׁהוּא עוֹשֶׂה פֵּרוֹת תָּדִיר — *and anything which provides benefit* [lit. *produces fruit] continually —*

[I.e., anything else which provides benefit throughout the year, similar to the items listed above.]

חֶזְקָתָן שָׁלשׁ שָׁנִים מִיּוֹם לְיוֹם. — *[must be]* [lit. *their possession is] three years from day to day.*

One can establish ownership by virtue of possession only if he retains and uses these properties for three full years. These three years must be consecutive. If they are not, though he uses the property for a total of three

---

legal presumption of the status quo for objects or people whose halachic status has come into question.

חֶזְקָתָהּ שָׁלשׁ שָׁנִים, וְאֵינָהּ מִיּוֹם לְיוֹם. רַבִּי יִשְׁמָעֵאל אוֹמֵר: שְׁלשָׁה חֳדָשִׁים בָּרִאשׁוֹנָה, וּשְׁלשָׁה בָּאַחֲרוֹנָה, וּשְׁנֵים עָשָׂר חֹדֶשׁ בָּאֶמְצַע, הֲרֵי שְׁמֹנָה עָשָׂר חֹדֶשׁ. רַבִּי עֲקִיבָא אוֹמֵר: חֹדֶשׁ בָּרִאשׁוֹנָה, וְחֹדֶשׁ בָּאַחֲרוֹנָה, וּשְׁנֵים עָשָׂר חֹדֶשׁ בָּאֶמְצַע, הֲרֵי אַרְבָּעָה עָשָׂר חֹדֶשׁ. אָמַר רַבִּי יִשְׁמָעֵאל: בַּמֶּה דְבָרִים אֲמוּרִים? בִּשְׂדֵה לָבָן. אֲבָל

יד אברהם

years, no *chazakah* is established (*Gem.* 29a). In such a case, the previous owner can claim that he did not bother to protest the occupant's use of his property because the occupant's relinquishing his use at some point during the three-year period indicated that he had no intention of establishing proprietorship (*Rashbam* 29a).

שְׂדֵה הַבַּעַל — *A field watered by rain*

I.e., a non-irrigated field which relies solely on rain-water. Such a field can produce fruit only once a year (*Rav*).

חֶזְקָתָהּ שָׁלשׁ שָׁנִים, וְאֵינָהּ מִיּוֹם לְיוֹם. — *must be possessed three years, but not from day to day.*

I.e., it need not be used three full years from day to day (*Rav*). Since the normal benefit from three years of possession of these fields includes only one regular crop each year, one who exploits the produce of the field for three consecutive years in the manner in which the owner of such a field ordinarily benefits thereby indicates ownership (*Yad Ramah*).

[This ruling represents the anonymous opinion of the Sages, which will be disputed by R' Yishmael and R'

Akiva below (see *Gem.* 36b).]

Others see this statement not as an independent view but as the introductory phrase to the opinions of R' Yishmael and R' Akiva. Thus, the mishnah states that the use of such a field need not be from day to day, but that its precise duration is the subject of a controversy between R' Yishmael and R' Akiva, as the mishnah proceeds to explain (*Rashi*).[1]

רַבִּי יִשְׁמָעֵאל אוֹמֵר: שְׁלשָׁה חֳדָשִׁים בָּרִאשׁוֹנָה, — *R' Yishmael says: Three months in the first,*

According to R' Yishmael, to qualify for a *chazakah* in a field watered by rain the occupant need not use it three full years, since it only produces one crop a year in any case. Rather, in the first year, it is sufficient if he condenses a full growing season into just the last three months of the year — i.e., the months of Tammuz, Av and Elul (*Yad Ramah*) — by planting and harvesting a crop during that time (*Rashi*). This can be achieved with such crops as barley, oats, and lentils (*Rav*).[2]

וּשְׁלשָׁה בָּאַחֲרוֹנָה, — *three in the last,*

Similarly, in the last of the three years, rather than making use of the field for the entire year, it is sufficient if

---

1. Accordingly, the view of the Sages quoted by the *Gemara* comes from an outside source but is not mentioned in the mishnah.

2. *Rashi* states that he must plant and harvest the entire crop during these three months in order for them to count as a year towards his *chazakah*. *Tosafos* (28a), however, understand R' Yishmael's view to be that it is not necessary for him to harvest the crop within the three months. As long as he plants the field and retains possession of it throughout these three months, and in the meanwhile picks some of the unripe plants to use as animal fodder, the three-month period counts as a year.

3
1

years, but not from day to day. R' Yishmael says: Three months in the first, three in the last, and twelve months in between, [for] a total of eighteen months. R' Akiva says: One month in the first, one month in the last, and twelve months in between, [for] a total of fourteen months. R' Yishmael said: In regard to what is this said? In [regard to] a field of grain.

YAD AVRAHAM

he condenses its growing season into the first three months of that year — Tishrei, Cheshvan and Kislev (Yad Ramah) — by planting and harvesting a crop during that time (Rashi).

וּשְׁנֵים עָשָׂר חֹדֶשׁ בָּאֶמְצַע, — and twelve months in between,

[Since this field produces only one crop a year, the field must be held the entire middle year in order for it to be possessed and used for three consecutive growing seasons.]

Technically, it would be possible to plant and harvest three crops within fifteen months — by planting one crop three months before Nissan and harvesting it in Nissan, planting a second crop and harvesting again that summer, and then planting the following year three months before Nissan so that the third harvest is ready in Nissan. Nevertheless, R' Yishmael requires a minimum of eighteen months with one full year of possession in the middle of the three-crop cycle. Without at least one full year in the middle, his possession is not sufficiently significant to serve as a basis for a chazakah (Tos. 28a).

Furthermore, the three-month periods at the end of the first year and the beginning of the third count as a full year only if the previous owner did not work the field during the other months of those years. If he did, the fractions do not count as full years and the eighteen-month chazakah is not valid (Meiri).

הֲרֵי שְׁמֹנָה עָשָׂר חֹדֶשׁ. — [for] a total of eighteen months.

According to some commentators, this seemingly redundant phrase teaches that the years of possession must be consecutive (see Ritva; Tos.

Yom Tov; cf. Tos.; Tos. R' Akiva Eiger; Mahariach).

רַבִּי עֲקִיבָא אוֹמֵר: חֹדֶשׁ בָּרִאשׁוֹנָה, וְחֹדֶשׁ בָּאַחֲרוֹנָה, וּשְׁנֵים עָשָׂר חֹדֶשׁ בָּאֶמְצַע, הֲרֵי אַרְבָּעָה עָשָׂר חֹדֶשׁ. — R' Akiva says: One month in the first, one month in the last, and twelve months in between, [for] a total of fourteen months.

According to R' Akiva, even if the occupant of the field benefits only from vegetables or unripe grain (which he cuts for animal fodder), it suffices to establish a chazakah. Since these can be grown and harvested in as little as one month, even one-month fractions of the first and last years count as full years toward the establishment of the chazakah (Rav).

Others contend that he need not plant and harvest a crop in these one-month periods, but that simply planting a crop and holding the field for a month while that crop is growing suffices to establish possession for the first and last years according to R' Akiva (Tos. 28a).

אָמַר רַבִּי יִשְׁמָעֵאל: בַּמֶּה דְבָרִים אֲמוּרִים? — R' Yishmael said: In [regard to] what is this said?

In regard to what type of field have we ruled that a rain-watered field requires a minimum of eighteen months to establish a chazakah (Rav).

בִּשְׂדֵה לָבָן. — In regard to a field of grain [lit. a white field].

A grain field requires three different growing seasons to establish a chazakah because its entire crop is harvested at one time (Rav).

[55]   THE MISHNAH/BAVA BASRA – Chapter Three: *Chezkas HaBattim*

בְּשָׂדֶה אִילָן, כָּנַס אֶת תְּבוּאָתוֹ, מָסַק אֶת זֵיתָיו,
כָּנַס אֶת קֵיצוֹ, הֲרֵי אֵלוּ שָׁלשׁ שָׁנִים.

[כ] שָׁלשׁ אֲרָצוֹת לַחֲזָקָה: יְהוּדָה, וְעֵבֶר
הַיַּרְדֵּן, וְהַגָּלִיל. הָיָה בִיהוּדָה

יד אברהם

A grain field is called a white field either because the absence of any trees to provide shade leaves the field totally sunlit (*Rash, Sheviis* 2:1), or because grain has a tendency to whiten as it ripens (*Rash, Peah* 3:1).

אֲבָל בְּשָׂדֶה אִילָן, — *However, in [the case of] a field of trees,*

A field of trees may contain different species each of which ripens at a different time of year (*Rav*). [Thus, it is possible to have three identifiably separate harvests in one year.]

כָּנַס אֶת תְּבוּאָתוֹ, — *[if] he gathered his crop,*

The crop referred to here is specifically the produce of the grapevine (*Rav; Rashi*). This is based on a Scriptural usage of the word תְּבוּאָה; see *Deut.* 22:9 (*Tos.* 28a). *Rambam Commentary*, however, explains this to refer to grain; i.e., a field of trees in which grain is also grown.

מָסַק אֶת זֵיתָיו, — *picked his olives,*

Hebrew has different verbs to describe the harvest of different types of fruit (see *Shabbos* 73b). מוֹסֵק is the term used for olives (*Tif. Yis.*).

כָּנַס אֶת קֵיצוֹ — *and gathered in his dried figs —*

I.e., he harvested his figs, dried them out and then brought them into his house (*Rav*).

The order in which the mishnah lists these crops is puzzling, since the first of these to ripen is figs, followed by grapes and olives.

However, it is possible that the figs were customarily left to dry on the trees before being picked, or were spread out in the fields to dry out for a long time, so that they were not finally gathered in for use until after the grapes and the olives. Alternatively, the mishnah follows the order of the calendar year, beginning with Tishrei, rather than the order of the harvest seasons, which begin in Nissan (*Tos.* 28a).

הֲרֵי אֵלוּ שָׁלשׁ שָׁנִים. — *these [count as] three years.*

These three harvests are tantamount to three years of possession and suffice to establish *chazakah* (*Rav*).

R' Yishmael understands the principle of the three-year *chazakah* differently from the Sages. He sees it as akin to, and derived from, the law of the goring bull. If a bull gores another animal, it is considered by the Torah an unexpected occurrence and the owner is therefore only liable for half the damage. If it happens three times, however, the owner is on notice that his bull is a habitual gorer, and he is from then on liable for the entire amount of any damage the bull may inflict (*Bava Kamma* 1:4, 2:4). Similarly, each time the occupant of a field raises and harvests a crop he serves notice to the previous owner that he is claiming the field as his own. Consequently, once he has taken the produce of the field three times without eliciting any protest from the previous owner, the latter's repeated silence establishes that he is no longer the owner of the property (*Gem.* 28a,b, as explained by *Tos.* 28a).[1]

1. Others explain the correlation between the two laws to be less closely matched. Nevertheless, the law of the habitually goring bull serves as a precedent for the principle that when the legal status of something changes as a result of a series of incidents, three such

However, in [the case of] a field of trees, [if] he gathered his crop, picked his olives, and gathered in his dried figs — these [count as] three years.

2. [T]here are] three lands [in Eretz Yisrael] in regard to *chazakah:* Judea, Transjordan, and the Galilee. [If] he was in Judea and [another] took

YAD AVRAHAM

The *Gemara* (36b) states that the view of the Sages is that three years are necessary to establish a *chazakah* regardless of the type of field involved. The halachah follows their opinion *(Rav from Gem.* 36b; *Choshen Mishpat* 141:1).

Even so, *Rambam (Toein VeNitan* 12:1) maintains that according to the Sages, possession for three *full* years is not necessary for a rain-watered field, which does not produce more than one regular crop a year. It is necessary only to hold it long enough to harvest the regular crop of each of the three years [rather than the eighteen- or fifteen-month growing cycle of R' Yishmael and R' Akiva]. Although the *Gemara* (29a)

explains the basis for the *chazakah* as being that a person is likely to lose his deed after three years (see preface to chapter), it actually means that he loses it after he has reaped the produce of three years. Having done so without eliciting any objection from the previous owner, he feels secure that the latter has no intention of disputing his ownership *(Nimmukei Yosef).* Most authorities, however, explain that the Sages require three *full* years of possession to establish *chazakah* for all fields, even for those which do not produce more than one crop a year *(R' Chananel,* cited by *Rashbam* to 36b; *Rosh; Rav,* see *Tos. Yom Tov). Shulchan Aruch (Choshen Mishpat* 141:1) rules in favor of *Rambam,* while *Rama* adopts the latter opinion.

2.

As noted in the chapter preface, if at any time during the three years of occupation the former owner of the land protests the fact that another is occupying his land, the *chazakah* is voided and the occupant must produce his deed in order to be awarded the field. This protest is valid even if it is issued in a different country than the one in which the land in question lies, because it is assumed that a report of the protest will spread by word of mouth to reach the person holding the field, and he will know that he must continue to hold onto his deed.

This situation pertains only where the borders between the two countries are open and there is therefore traffic from one to the other. Where the border is closed as a result of hostilities, however, it can no longer be assumed that a report of a protest issued in one land will reach the other. Hence, the absence of any objection by the owner is also meaningless since he has no way of issuing an effective protest in any case. This being the case, the *chazakah* cannot be valid *(Gem.* 38a). This situation, in turn, is by its very essence a clear warning to the present occupant of the field to safeguard his deed, and his failure to do so costs him the field *(Rav).*

שָׁלשׁ אֲרָצוֹת לַחֲזָקָה: יְהוּדָה, וְעֵבֶר הַיַּרְדֵּן, וְהַגָּלִיל. — [There are] three lands [in Eretz Yisrael] in regard to chazakah:

Judea, Transjordan, and the Galilee.
    In Mishnaic times the land of Israel was divided into three regions, each of

incidents establish the change of status. Consequently, the ownership status of a field changes from the proprietorship of its last known owner to that of the one presently in possession of it by virtue of three indications to that effect *(Ramban; Ritva).*

וְהֶחֱזִיק בַּגָּלִיל, בַּגָּלִיל וְהֶחֱזִיק בִּיהוּדָה, אֵינָה
חֲזָקָה, עַד שֶׁיְּהֵא עִמּוֹ בַּמְּדִינָה. אָמַר רַבִּי יְהוּדָה:
לֹא אָמְרוּ שָׁלֹשׁ שָׁנִים אֶלָּא כְּדֵי שֶׁיְּהֵא בְּאִסְפַּמְיָא,
וְיַחֲזִיק שָׁנָה, וְיֵלְכוּ וְיוֹדִיעוּהוּ שָׁנָה, וְיָבֹא לְשָׁנָה
אַחֶרֶת.

יד אברהם

which was considered a separate land in regard to the issue of *chazakah*, as the mishnah will explain (*Rav*).

הָיָה בִּיהוּדָה וְהֶחֱזִיק בַּגָּלִיל, בַּגָּלִיל וְהֶחֱזִיק בִּיהוּדָה, אֵינָה חֲזָקָה, — [If] he was in Judea and [another] took possession in the Galilee, [or he was] in the Galilee and [another] took possession in Judea, it is no chazakah,

If the owner of a field located in the Galilee was living in Judea, and someone occupied that field for three years, the *chazakah* is not valid. Travel between these regions was generally so sparse that it could not be assumed that word of a protest lodged in one province would reach the other province, and the situation was analogous to a border which lies between two hostile nations (*Rav; Rashbam*).[1] Accordingly, there was no point for the owner of the field to protest its occupation even if he knew of the situation, since word of his protest would not reach the occupant in any case (*Rav from Gem. 38a*). The latter, knowing that this is the situation, is clearly expected to preserve his deed. Therefore, if he cannot produce it when the case comes to court, he loses the property (*Rav; Yad Ramah, Nimmukei Yosef*).

The Gemara seems to focus on the issue of whether or not word of the protest will reach across the border, rather than word of the occupation of the land itself. This is because the absentee owner of a property constantly inquires about his property and is therefore more likely to be aware of its status than the occupant who is not expected to inquire

whether a protest has been lodged (*Tos.* 38a). *Rambam* (*Toein VeNitan* 11:2), however, understands the Gemara's primary concern to be the inability of the owner to find out that his land has been occupied. *Yad Ramah* states that both these considerations are valid, depending on the situation.

עַד שֶׁיְּהֵא עִמּוֹ בַּמְּדִינָה. — until he is with him in the [same] province.

I.e., unless the owner of the field is in the same province as the field so that his protest is certain to reach the person occupying the field. In such a case, the absence of a protest establishes a *chazakah* even if they are in different towns, because word of a protest can certainly travel from one town to another. Consequently, there is no plausible rationale for the owner of the field's failure to protest (*Rav*; see preface).

Even when the previous owner of the field lives in a foreign country which is at war with the country in which his field is, if it can be shown that he traveled to that country despite the hostilities and yet did not protest, the *chazakah* is valid (*Gem.* 30a, as explained by commentators; see *Rif*, *Rashbam*; see further *Rambam*, *Toein VeNitan* 11:3 and *Choshen Mishpat* 143:1).

אָמַר רַבִּי יְהוּדָה: לֹא אָמְרוּ שָׁלֹשׁ שָׁנִים — R' Yehudah said: They said three years only [lit. they did not say three years, only]

R' Yehudah has a different approach to the three-year *chazakah*. He maintains that if a person is silent about the occupation of his land for even one day that is ample proof that he sold it to the

---

1. *Rambam Commentary* explains that in Mishnaic times the borders between these areas were actually closed. This was the result of the many tensions and outright hostilities which plagued those times (*Meiri; Yad Ramah*).

3
2

possession in the Galilee, [or he was] in the Galilee and [another] took possession in Judea, it is no *chazakah*, until he is with him in the [same] province. R' Yehudah said: They said three years only so that [in case] one is in Spain and [another] takes possession [of the field] for one year, they have one year to travel and notify him, and he can return the following year.

YAD AVRAHAM

person occupying it, even if the latter cannot produce a deed. In R' Yehudah's opinion the three-year time span for *chazakah* was not based on the assumption that a buyer holds his deed that long but was a design to cover all possible situations, even one such as described below (*Rav*).

אֶלָּא כְּדֵי שֶׁיְּהֵא בְּאַסְפָּמְיָא — *so that [in case] one is in Spain*

Spain was one year's travel from Eretz Yisrael in the times of the Mishnah (*Rashbam*). The Rabbis based the *chazakah* on this limit because it was extremely rare for a person to travel further away from home than that (*Tos.* 38a).

וְיַחֲזִיק שָׁנָה, — *and [another] takes possession [of the field] for one year,*

In which time it can be assumed that the occupation of the field has become public knowledge (*Rashbam* 38a).

וְיֵלְכוּ וְיוֹדִיעוּהוּ שָׁנָה, — *they have one year to travel and notify him,*

[I.e., there should be a year's time for word of the occupation to travel and reach the owner of the field in Spain.]

וְיָבֹא לְשָׁנָה אַחֶרֶת. — *and he can return the*

following year.

The third year of the three-year *chazakah* period allows the owner of the field time after hearing about its illicit occupation to return to Eretz Yisrael and issue a protest (*Rashbam* 38a). Although he could issue it from afar, the mishnah advises him to return to his field in order to prevent the occupant from consuming its produce, for which it will be difficult to exact payment afterwards (*Gem.* 39a).

According to R' Yehudah, if the previous owner remains in the same district as his field — and is thus immediately aware of anyone occupying his field — *chazakah* takes effect immediately, unless he issues a protest at that point (*Rashbam* 38a from *Gem.* 41a).

Similarly, according to R' Yehudah, the *chazakah* of three years is valid even between Judea and Galilee (*Rav; Rashbam* 38a; *Yad Ramah*), because he maintains that this time span was designated for those situations in which spreading word of the occupation is difficult (*Yad Ramah*). The halachah does not follow the view of R' Yehudah (*Rav, Choshen Mishpat* 143:1).

3.

The following mishnah discusses the limits of *chazakah* — what type of claim it can support and who is excluded from establishing a *chazakah* by virtue of his legitimate access to someone else's property.

[59]   THE MISHNAH/BAVA BASRA – Chapter Three: *Chezkas HaBattim*

[ג] **כָּל** חֲזָקָה שֶׁאֵין עִמָּהּ טַעֲנָה אֵינָהּ חֲזָקָה.
כֵּיצַד? אָמַר לוֹ ,,מָה אַתָּה עוֹשֶׂה בְּתוֹךְ
שֶׁלִּי!" וְהוּא אָמַר לוֹ ,,שֶׁלֹּא אָמַר לִי אָדָם דָּבָר
מֵעוֹלָם," אֵינָהּ חֲזָקָה. ,,שֶׁמְּכַרְתָּ לִי," ,,שֶׁנָּתַתָּ לִי
בְּמַתָּנָה," ,,אָבִיךְ מְכָרָהּ לִי," ,,אָבִיךְ נְתָנָהּ לִי
בְּמַתָּנָה," הֲרֵי זוֹ חֲזָקָה. וְהַבָּא מִשּׁוּם יְרֻשָּׁה אֵינוֹ
צָרִיךְ טַעֲנָה.

יד אברהם

כָּל חֲזָקָה שֶׁאֵין עִמָּהּ טַעֲנָה — *Any possession not accompanied by a claim.*

I.e., any three-year possession of real estate which is not accompanied by a claim on the part of the occupant that he is holding the property because he legally acquired it (*Rav*).

אֵינָהּ חֲזָקָה. — *is not a chazakah.*

Despite being held for three consecutive years, such possession cannot serve to establish ownership. Three years of holding a property in the absence of any protest by the previous owner does not transfer ownership from the owner to the holder — it merely serves as evidence that such a transaction has previously taken place. Therefore, it is only useful if the present occupant claims that he either bought the property or received it as a gift from the previous owner. If he does not make such a claim, then it is clear that the property still belongs to the previous owner despite his three years of possession (*Nimmukei Yosef*).

The mishnah's ruling applies as well to those instances in which *chazakah* is established in less than three years. For example, the *Gemara* 6a states that one can have a *chazakah* to maintain his right to use someone else's wall as a support for his own beam. In this case a *chazakah* is established as soon as the owner of the wall sees his neighbor bracing his beam against the wall and fails to protest (*Rashbam* 6a). Such a *chazakah* is also valid only if it is backed by a claim that the owner of the wall sold or gave him this right.

Similarly, simple possession of a movable object does not impart ownership but serves only as evidence that a transfer of ownership took place. Consequently, if the holder does not claim any transaction, his possession of the object proves nothing (*Nimmukei Yosef*). It is to these and similar cases that the mishnah alludes with the words *any possession* (*Rashbam* 41a).

כֵּיצַד? אָמַר לוֹ ,,מָה אַתָּה עוֹשֶׂה בְּתוֹךְ שֶׁלִּי?" — *How so? [If] he said to him, 'What are you doing in my [property]?'*

[The previous owner of the field demanded this explanation of its present occupant.]

וְהוּא אָמַר לוֹ ,,שֶׁלֹּא אָמְרוּ-לִי אָדָם דָּבָר מֵעוֹלָם," — *and he replied, 'Because no one ever said anything to me,'*

[I.e., the occupant does not claim to have acquired the field, but justifies his occupancy only on the basis that he held the land all this time without ever being challenged.]

אֵינָהּ חֲזָקָה. — *it is not a chazakah.*

[Since he admits to being a squatter, the property is returned to its owner, as explained above.]

Although this ruling appears obvious, the mishnah teaches by it that the court does not suggest to the occupant that what he really means to claim is that he bought the land but, having lost his deed and not knowing the laws of *chazakah*, refrained from saying so (*Gem.* 41a) to avoid making what seemed to him an even more fraudulent-sounding claim (*Tos.*). Suggesting such a claim exceeds the court's responsibility to *speak up for the mute* (*Proverbs*

3. **A**ny possession not accompanied by a claim is not a *chazakah*. How so? [If] he said to him, 'What are you doing in my [property]?' and he replied, 'Because no one ever said anything to me,' it is not a *chazakah*. [But if he replied,] 'You sold [it] to me,' [or] 'You gave [it] to me as a gift,' [or] 'Your father sold it to me,' [or] 'Your father gave it to me as a gift,' it is a *chazakah*. One who comes [to a property] by virtue of inheritance does not require a claim.

YAD AVRAHAM

31:8) [the principle which requires the court to plead on behalf of a defendant any plausible legal claims which he lacks the knowledge to claim for himself טַעֲנִינָן); see below, s.v. [אֵינוּ צָרִיךְ טַעֲנָה (*Gem.* 41a). However, if he offers this explanation on his own, it is accepted despite his initial failure to make this claim.

Although the occupant's *chazakah* is not valid, the claimant must bring evidence that the land was previously his or his father's in order to take possession away from the occupant (*Rambam, Toein VeNitan* 14:12; *Choshen Mishpat* 146:9).

שֶׁמָּכַרְתָּ לִי,״ ,,שֶׁנָּתַתָּ לִי בְּמַתָּנָה,״ ,,אָבִיךְ מְכָרָהּ לִי,״ ,,אָבִיךְ נְתָנָהּ לִי בְּמַתָּנָה,״ הֲרֵי זוֹ חֲזָקָה. — [But if he replied,] 'You sold [it] to me,' [or] 'You gave [it] to me as a gift,' [or] 'Your father sold it to me,' [or] 'Your father gave it to me as a gift,' it is a chazakah.

[If the occupant offers any of these claims as the basis for his possession, his three years of occupation serve as a *chazakah* to establish his ownership.]

וְהַבָּא מִשּׁוּם יְרֻשָּׁה — One who comes [to a property] by virtue of inheritance

Someone who inherited a property from his father and then occupied the land for three years (*Rav*).

אֵינוֹ צָרִיךְ טַעֲנָה. — does not require a claim.

He is not required to know how his father came into possession of the land

(*Rav*). Since a person is not necessarily privy to such information (*Rashbam* 41a), and since his undisputed possession these three years lends credence to a claim of ownership, the court is obliged to consider on his behalf the claim that his father purchased the land from the previous owner before he died and passed it on to his son (*Rashbam* 41b). This is an instance of the principle of טַעֲנִינָן, *judicial pleading* [lit. *we (the court) claim*]; i.e., the judicial responsibility to plead on behalf of a defendant any plausible legal claim which he lacks the knowledge to claim with certitude for himself.

Nevertheless, since this claim is based on the assumption that his father purchased the property, the occupant must at least bring proof that his father occupied the field for at least one day. Without such proof the court cannot plead on his behalf (*Rav* from *Gem.* 41b).

The same ruling applies to one who claims to have acquired the land from a third party who had previously acquired it from the original owner. Although the current occupant has no way of proving that the person from whom he bought the field had actually purchased it from the original owner, based on his three-year *chazakah* the court would plead on his behalf that such was indeed the case. Here, too, the holder of the property would have to prove that the man who sold it to him had in fact occupied the property at least one day before selling it (*Gem.* 41b).

If he claimed to know that his father occupied the land for one day, but he has no independent proof of this, some authorities maintain that he is believed by virtue of a *miggo*. This is a judicial principle which means that wherever a litigant could have invented a claim more advantageous to his case had he wished to lie, which the court would have been compelled to accept, his choice of a less advantageous claim indicates that he is telling the truth. In this case, too, if he wished to lie, the occupant of the field had a better claim to make than that he had inherited it from his father — namely, that he himself purchased the land from the claimant. Such a claim would immediately give him ownership of the field since it is backed by his three-year *chazakah*. The fact that he does not claim this, but claims instead to have inherited the land from his father whom he saw occupying it for one day, indicates that he is telling the truth about this, since a liar would have chosen the simpler and better lie (see *Gem.* 41b). Thus, the property is awarded to the occupant the same as it would be awarded to him if he brought witnesses to establish his father's occupancy (*Tos.* 30a).

Others contend that this is not sufficient (*Ramban*) because *miggo* suffices only when, given the conclusion of the *miggo*, all doubts are resolved. In this case, however, even if we believe him that his father lived there one day, we must still make the further assumption that the father had acquired the land, and *miggo* is not strong enough evidence to be carried to that extent (*Nimmukei Yosef*).

If the occupant claims that he saw his father (or the person from whom he bought the field) acquire it from the claimant, he is believed on the strength of his *chazakah* even without producing witnesses to that effect, the same as if he had claimed that he had bought it himself (*Gem.* 41b; *Choshen Mishpat* 146:14).[1]

The mishnah now lists those who are excluded from establishing a *chazakah* in a property due to their position of trust or privilege in that property, which allows them constant access to it.

הָאֻמָּנִין, — *Craftsmen,*

The legal basis for *chazakah*, whether in the case of movable property or real property, is that the possession serves as evidence of ownership. Thus, it is only effective when there is no other likely explanation to account for the object in question being in this person's possession legally (and we don't assume without evidence that he stole it). Consequently, when a craftsman holds an object which is known to have belonged to another, his possession cannot serve as evidence that he acquired it from the latter, since it is equally possible that he was given the object to repair.

If there are no witnesses to the fact that the object is in the possession of the craftsman, he is believed to say that he bought it by virtue of a *miggo* that he could have denied having it at all (*Rav* from *Gem.* 45a-46a). However, in such a case, he is required to take an oath to support his claim of having purchased it, since had he denied having it at all he would also have had to swear the Rabbinically ordained oath (שְׁבוּעַת הֶסֵּת) imposed on one who makes such a total denial of a claim (see *Shevuos* 40b). Thus, unless he swears an oath to buttress his

---

1. The *Gemara* states that he is believed with this claim because he could just as easily have claimed to have bought it from the previous owner himself — a claim which would certainly have been accepted on the basis of his *chazakah*. Thus, his claim is supported by the principle of *miggo* (see comm.). However, *Ketzos HaChoshen* (146:12) points out that the *Gemara* has no need to resort to *miggo* since even without that proof he is believed, because his *chazakah* is now accompanied by a legitimate claim of ownership. In *Ketzos'* view, the *Gemara* in fact may mean nothing more than this; see there.

present claim of having bought the object, he lacks a *miggo*, because the option of denying that he has the object at all, which requires an oath to be effective, is then less attractive to him — since swearing falsely is something even a liar wishes to avoid *(Rav)*.

Rif, however, disputes this and rules that such a *miggo* is not sufficient to exact property from its previous owner. Therefore, even if the craftsman could have denied possessing the object, but admits to holding it, he is not believed to say he acquired it.

Others explain the mishnah to be discussing the three-year *chazakah* for real property, similar to the other cases listed below. According to this explanation, the mishnah refers to a case where a craftsman was hired to build or do other work on someone's property, and he lived on that property for three years while performing the work. The mishnah teaches that since his presence there is accounted for by his employment, it cannot serve as evidence of acquisition *(Rambam Comm.; Yad Ramah; Meiri)*.

Similarly, if a slave [whose possession indicates ownership only if maintained for three years (see mishnah 1)] was sent to a craftsman for training and remained with him for three years, this possession is not considered proof of ownership *(Yad Ramah)*.

וְהַשֻּׁתָּפִים, — *partners,*

Partners in a property that is not large enough to be divided between them (see 1:6) often implement their partnership by dividing its usage by time. Therefore, if one of them used the land for three years, it does not prove that he bought out his partner, since the terms of their partnership may call for each of them to occupy the land for that length of time. Accordingly, the mishnah here refers only to a partnership in a small property. However, if the property is large enough for each of them to use half of it, and one held the entire area for three years, it is a valid *chazakah* *(Rav from Gem. 42b; Rashbam)*.

וְהָאֲרִיסִין, — *sharecroppers,*

A sharecropper is paid for his labor out of the crop he raises and thus his consumption of that crop over three years does not indicate ownership. Although a sharecropper customarily receives only a percentage of the crop for his labor, even his taking all the produce of the field for three consecutive years does not establish his ownership of the field. This is because the mishnah refers to a sharecropper who served the father of the present owner, and who is thus treated by him as the administrator of the estate rather than as a tenant *(Rav from Gem. 46b, Rambam Comm.)*. The current landlord, having grown up under the sharecropper's management of the estate, does not question the sharecropper's distribution of the produce *(Rambam, Toein VeNitan 13:5)*. However, a new sharecropper brought in by the present landlord would be able to establish a *chazakah* if he kept all the produce of the field instead of only a percentage of it *(Rav from Gem.)*.

In *Rashbam's* understanding of the *Gemara*, the mishnah refers to a sharecropper whose family has served in that position to this family for generations. In such a situation, it is not unusual for them to devise an arrangement whereby the sharecropper gets the produce for several years consecutively and then the owner receives it for the next few. With a new sharecropper, though, the owner would not agree to such a long-term arrangement, and the sharecropper's retention of all the produce for three consecutive years would therefore confer a *chazakah*.

וְהָאַפּוֹטְרוֹפִּין — *and administrators*

Someone who was appointed to administer the estate of another cannot prove from his possession and use of the land for three years that he has acquired it, because his official access to the estate negates his *chazakah* *(Nimmukei Yosef)*.

אֵין לָהֶם חֲזָקָה. אֵין לְאִישׁ חֲזָקָה בְּנִכְסֵי אִשְׁתּוֹ,
וְלֹא לְאִשָּׁה חֲזָקָה בְּנִכְסֵי בַעֲלָהּ, וְלֹא לְאָב בְּנִכְסֵי
הַבֵּן, וְלֹא לְבֵן בְּנִכְסֵי הָאָב. בַּמֶּה דְּבָרִים אֲמוּרִים? בְּמַחֲזִיק. אֲבָל בְּנוֹתֵן

יד אברהם

The *Gemara* (*Bava Metzia* 39a,b) rules that a *chazakah* cannot be established on the property of a minor because he is not sophisticated enough to protest an illegal occupation of his land (*Rashi*). There is a dispute among the authorities whether someone who occupied the field of a minor and then retained it for three more years after the latter came of age has established a *chazakah* over the property (*Rambam, Toein VeNitan* 14:7; *Ravad* ibid.). According to the view that a valid *chazakah* is established, our mishnah teaches that an administrator is an exception to this rule, in that he cannot establish *chazakah* even after the minor whose property he administers comes of age (*Rambam*, ibid. 13:7). Those who maintain that such a *chazakah* is not valid for anyone explain the mishnah, which singles out an administrator, to be discussing someone who was appointed administrator to the estate of a person already of age (*Yad Ramah; Meiri, Sema* 149:46; but see *Lechem Mishneh* loc. cit. 13:7).

אֵין לָהֶם חֲזָקָה. — *have no chazakah.*

[Their possession does not constitute proof of ownership, as explained.]

If there is no evidence that the person in possession was a partner, sharecropper, or administrator, he is believed in his claim that he acquired the property, even if he admits to this status. This is by virtue of a *miggo* [see above s.v. אֵינוֹ צָרִיךְ טַעֲנָה] that he could have denied the existence of that status (*Meiri; Rambam* loc. cit. 13:3).

אֵין לְאִישׁ חֲזָקָה בְּנִכְסֵי אִשְׁתּוֹ, — *A man has no chazakah in the property of his wife,*

A man who took all the produce of his wife's field for himself for three years cannot prove from this that he acquired the field from her because the husband has the legal right to use that produce for as long as they are married (see *Kesubos* 4:4). Moreover, even in a case in which he waived that right in advance of their marriage, his possession of her field does not constitute a *chazakah*, because a wife is likely to allow her husband to consume produce which belongs to her even when he is not legally entitled to it. Thus, his consumption of it does not demonstrate ownership (*Rav* from *Gem.* 49a).[1]

The mishnah clearly implies that if he could produce a document that she had sold him the land, it would be accepted. However, this is true only of נִכְסֵי מְלוֹג, *melog* (usufructuary) *properties*. This is the property which a wife brings into the marriage and gives over to the husband for his use, but to which she retains title.[2] Since the husband has no rights whatsoever to the actual property but only to its output, she would not agree to sell it to him simply to please him if she did not mean it wholeheartedly. However, if she sold him נִכְסֵי צֹאן בַּרְזֶל, *fixed-value property*, the sale is not valid. This is property which she brings into the marriage and gives to him with the stipulation that, in the event of divorce or the husband's death, she receives the property at

1. However, if he dug ditches in the land or otherwise impaired it she is likely to protest, and if she doesn't his *chazakah* is valid (*Yad Ramah* §195 from *Gem.* 50b; *Tur, Choshen Mishpat* 149:10; *Rama* 149:9; see *Sema* 12). Others, based on a different assessment of the *Gemara's* conclusion, rule that under *no* circumstances can a husband establish a *chazakah* over his wife's property (*Rif, Rosh* as explained by *Beis Yosef* 149:6; *Rambam, Toein VeNitan* 13:8 as explained by *Maggid Mishneh; Shulchan Aruch, Choshen Mishpat* 149:9 as explained by *Sema* 11; cf. *Shach* 8).

2. See below, preface to 9:9, and General Introductions to ArtScroll *Yevamos* p. 12 and *Kesubos* p. 5, for a fuller explanation of these terms.

3
3

nistrators have no *chazakah*. A man has no *chazakah* in the property of his wife, nor does a woman have a *chazakah* in the property of her husband, nor a father in the property of his son, nor a son in the property of his father.

In regard to what is this stated? In [regard to] one who holds possession. But in [the case of] one who

YAD AVRAHAM

its value as it stood at the time of the marriage, with any rise or fall in the value of the property going to the husband. Thus, to a large extent the property is already in the hands of the husband and it would not be easy for her to refuse to sell it to him completely (see *Yad Avraham* comm. to *Gittin* 5:6, s.v. מקחו בטל). Consequently, if she did sell it to him, she can believably claim that she did so only to please him, but did not really consent to the sale (*Rav* from *Gem.* 49b-50a).

וְלֹא לְאִשָּׁה חֲזָקָה בְּנִכְסֵי בַעֲלָהּ, — *nor does a woman have a chazakah in the property of her husband,*

I.e., even if he designated a specific field for her support and she took the yield of a different field for three years, it is no *chazakah*. A man will allow his wife to take his produce even when she is not legally entitled to it; consequently, her consumption of it does not demonstrate her ownership of the property (*Rav* from *Gem.* 51a).

Here, too, the implication is clear that if she can document her acquisition of the field it is valid. However, this is true only if he gave her the land as a gift. If he sold it to her, he can claim that she had hidden away money which belonged to him and the sale was a ruse to retrieve it (*Rav* from *Gem.* 51a).

וְלֹא לְאָב בְּנִכְסֵי הַבֵּן, וְלֹא לְבֵן בְּנִכְסֵי הָאָב. — *nor a father in the property of his son, nor a son in the property of his father.*

In a case where a son is still being supported by his father, neither will prevent the other from taking from his personal property and consequently such taking is not proof of ownership. Once they have separated, however, this no longer holds true, and the *chazakah*

is valid (*Gem.* 47a, 52a; *Choshen Mishpat* 149:4).

The term *chazakah* has several meanings. It has been used up to this point to mean the three-year possession of property which serves as evidence of ownership. The mishnah now contrasts the *chazakah* of proof with the *chazakah* of acquisition — the formal act of possession by which a person obtains title to real property.

בַּמֶּה דְּבָרִים אֲמוּרִים? — *In regard to what is this stated?*

In regard to what type of *chazakah* were the limits mentioned above applied (*Rav; Rambam Comm.*)? Alternatively, in regard to what type of *chazakah* is a three-year possession required (*Rashbam; Yad Ramah; Nimmukei Yosef*)?

בְּמַחֲזִיק. — *In [regard to] one who holds possession.*

I.e., one who occupies land which another claims is his (*Rav* from *Gem.* 52b).

It is difficult to understand how this thought is indicated by the word בְּמַחֲזִיק, which is the form of the word which would be used regardless of the type of *chazakah* intended. The Gemara (52b) states, therefore, that the text of the mishnah is missing a phrase which reads as follows: *In regard to what is this stated? In [regard to] a possession against which there is a claim* (see *Rashbam*) — e.g., if the [putative] seller says, 'I did not sell,' and the [putative] buyer says, 'I bought.' *But [in the case of] a possession against which there is no claim* — e.g., one who gives a gift ... if he ... it is a chazakah.

בבא
בתרא
ג/ד
מַתָּנָה, וְהָאַחִין שֶׁחָלְקוּ, וְהַמַּחֲזִיק בְּנִכְסֵי הַגֵּר,
נָעַל, וְגָדַר, וּפָרַץ כָּל שֶׁהוּא, הֲרֵי זוֹ חֲזָקָה.

[ד] **הָיוּ** שְׁנַיִם מְעִידִין אוֹתוֹ שֶׁאֲכָלָהּ שָׁלֹשׁ

יד אברהם

,אֲבָל בְּנוֹתֵן מַתָּנָה — *But in [the case of] one
who gives a gift,*

If someone gives another a gift of
land and tells him to perform an act of
chazakah acquisition and thereby
acquire it, the recipient assumes
immediate ownership with that act of
chazakah (as described below), and the
giver can no longer retract (*Rav* from
Gem. 53a). If the giver is present when
the recipient performs the act of
chazakah, it is valid even if he did not
explicitly tell him to make a chazakah
and acquire it (*Gem.* 52b). Furthermore,
even those individuals listed above,
whose possession of a property does not
prove their ownership of it, can still
acquire that property by such an *act of
chazakah* (*Rav*). The same rules apply
to one who sells a property to another
(*Tos. Yom Tov* from *Gem.* 52b).

,וְהָאַחִין שֶׁחָלְקוּ — *brothers who divide,*

Similarly, brothers who inherit
property and agree on its division can
each acquire their share by an act of
chazakah, after which none of them can
renege on the division (*Rav*). If there are
only two brothers, it is not even
necessary for both to perform acts of
chazakah; if just one of them makes a
chazakah in his half he acquires it and
the other half therefore automatically
goes to the other (*Tos. Yom Tov*).

,וְהַמַּחֲזִיק בְּנִכְסֵי הַגֵּר — *and one who takes
possession of the property of a convert,*

If a convert dies and leaves no
children or grandchildren, his property
is ownerless and available to anyone
who takes possession of it (*Rav*). [This
is in contrast to a natural-born Jew who,
because he is at least distantly related to
all other natural-born Jews, can never
die without an heir. Only a convert,
whose familial connection with his

gentile relations is legally severed when
he becomes a Jew (*Yevamos* 62a), can
die without any heirs whatsoever.]

,נָעַל — *[if] he closed off,*

I.e., he put up a door (*Rav*).

There are several opinions as to the precise
nature of this act of chazakah. *Rashbam*
(53a) says that he must either put up a door
or place a lock on an already existing door.
Merely closing and locking a door, however,
is not sufficient. *Tosafos* (52b) maintain that
closing the door and thereby preventing
anyone from entering is a valid chazakah,
while *Rosh* requires that he lock it with a key
as well. Some authorities contend that just as
closing the door is a chazakah, so too is
opening one which was locked (*Yad Ramah*).
Others dispute this analogy (*Rosh; Ritva*).
There is another opinion that one must close
the door and then open it (*Rambam,
Mechirah* 1:10; see *Maggid Mishneh*) in
order to show that he closed it for the sake of
acquisition and not at the behest of the owner
(*Kesef Mishneh*). See *Choshen Mishpat*
192:3.

,וְגָדַר — *fenced off,*

I.e., he enclosed the property (*Rav*).

וּפָרַץ — *or breached*

I.e., he made an opening in the
enclosure to allow entrance into it
(*Rashbam* 42a).

,כָּל שֶׁהוּא — *somewhat,*

The word *somewhat* refers back to all
three of these actions. I.e., he need not
completely open the passageway or
enclose the property. It is sufficient if he
narrows an opening through which
people pass easily and makes it more
difficult for them to get through, or he
widens an opening which was difficult
to go through, and makes it easier to
enter (*Gem.* 53a).

In reference to the first case, *closed off,* the
meaning of the term *somewhat* is ambiguous,

3
4

gives a gift, brothers who divide, and one who takes possession of the property of a convert, [if] he closed off, fenced off, or breached somewhat, it is a *chazakah*.

4. **[I**f] two [witnesses] testified on his behalf that

YAD AVRAHAM

and its interpretation varies in accordance with the different explanations of the nature of that act of *chazakah* noted above. According to those who maintain that he must build a door, the term *somewhat* is used in the same manner as in the other cases — i.e., he makes it more difficult to pass through *(Rashbam)*. According to the other opinions, *somewhat* refers to the fact that these smaller measures are sufficient, and it is not necessary to actually build a new door *(Nimmukei Yosef)*.

הֲרֵי זוּ חֲזָקָה. — *it is a chazakah.*

[By demonstrating possession with one of these acts of *chazakah*, he acquires the property.]

4.

The testimony of two (or more) witnesses can be challenged and discredited in one of two ways.[1] The first is by הַכְחָשָׁה, the *contradictory testimony* of two other witnesses. When faced with such conflicting testimony, the court is forced to disregard the testimony of both sets of witnesses, because there is no way to determine which ones are telling the truth *(Rambam, Eidus* 18:2). However, neither set of witnesses is permanently discredited and both may testify in a future case *(Gem.* 31b).

The Torah also decrees a second way of challenging testimony. This is where the later witnesses do not contradict the testimony of the earlier witnesses, but impugn their ability to have seen what they claim to have seen. This they do by testifying that they were with the first witnesses in one place at the very moment those witnesses claim to having seen an event happen in another place. In this instance, the Torah decrees that the latter witnesses are to be believed and the earlier ones discredited. The Torah further decrees that the false witnesses are to be punished by inflicting upon them whatever penalty they sought to impose upon the victim of their scheme. Thus, if their testimony would have caused the victim to lose money, they must pay him that amount as a penalty. If their testimony would have caused him to be executed, they are executed instead. [However, the penalty is not imposed unless the court had already issued a ruling based on their false testimony. It is also not imposed once the court has carried out that improper ruling. The witnesses are liable for the *zomemim* penalty only in the period between the handing down of the ruling and its implementation *(Makkos* 5b).]

Repudiation of the testimony in this manner is called הַזָּמָה, *hazamah*, and the discredited witnesses are referred to as זוֹמְמִים, *zomemim (Deut.* 19:16-21; *Makkos,* chapter 1).

הָיוּ שְׁנַיִם מְעִידִין אוֹתוֹ שֶׁאֲכָלָה שָׁלֹשׁ שָׁנִים, — *years,*
[*If*] *two* [*witnesses*] *testified on his behalf that he ate its* [*produce*] *three*

[Two witnesses testified on behalf of a certain person that he had for three

1. The witnesses themselves can be impeached on a variety of other grounds, for instance, by showing that they are known to be untrustworthy or unqualified to serve as witnesses *(Sanhedrin* 3:3). The testimony itself, however, once it has passed the judge's examination and been accepted by the court, can only be challenged directly in these two ways.

בבא שָׁנִים, וְנִמְצְאוּ זוֹמְמִים, מְשַׁלְּמִין לוֹ אֶת הַכֹּל.
בתרא שְׁנַיִם בָּרִאשׁוֹנָה, וּשְׁנַיִם בַּשְּׁנִיָּה, וּשְׁנַיִם בַּשְּׁלִישִׁית,
ג/ד מְשַׁלְּשִׁין בֵּינֵיהֶם. שְׁלֹשָׁה אַחִים, וְאֶחָד מִצְטָרֵף

יד אברהם

years consumed the produce of a field which had previously belonged to another but which this occupant claimed to have bought. Based on this testimony, his *chazakah* was established and the court awarded him the field.]

וְנִמְצְאוּ זוֹמְמִים, — *and they were found to be zomemim*,

[I.e., it was established through the testimony of others that these witnesses were not in the vicinity of the land in question during the time of the alleged *chazakah*. Thus, the occupant's claim of *chazakah* collapses, and in the absence of any other proof that he bought the field, the field is returned to the original owner. In addition, the witnesses are now subject to a penalty for having testified falsely.]

מְשַׁלְּמִין לוֹ אֶת הַכֹּל. — *they pay him everything*.

As a penalty for their false testimony, the witnesses must pay the original owner the value of the land they tried to take from him by their testimony

(Rashbam).

They must also pay him the value of any produce which the occupant had consumed during those three years, since their false testimony establishing the occupant's *chazakah* deprived the original owner of the right to recover the value of this produce from the occupant. This is indicated by the mishnah's use of the word *everything* (Rosh).[1] However, others suggest that *everything* may simply be used to contrast this case with the next one, in which each pair of witnesses pays only one-third (Ritva, Nimmukei Yosef).

Seemingly, the supposed buyer occupied the field at the time the previous owner brought him to court, and thus the original declaration by the court awarding the occupant the field took effect immediately. This raises the question of how the witnesses can be subject to the *zomemim* penalty, when the law is that the penalty can only be imposed when the improper ruling resulting from the false testimony was not yet carried out (Makkos 5b).

Some answer that this exception to the

1. Although these witnesses have been discredited, the occupant's claim itself has not been shown to be a lie. His loss of the field to the previous owner occurs only because he has neither a bill of sale to show that he bought the field, nor credible witnesses to support his claim of a three-year *chazakah*. Accordingly, the occupant does not have to repay the original owner for the produce he claims to have consumed during these three years — even though he admits to having taken it — since if we accept that he took that produce, we must also accept that he has a valid *chazakah* and award him the field.

By the same token, the *zomemim* witnesses cannot, in such a case, be compelled to pay for the produce either, since, having been proven false, there is no valid evidence that the occupant took anything whatsoever. Consequently, *Rosh*, who interprets this mishnah as teaching that the witnesses are subject to a penalty payment for the produce, explains that there are other witnesses here who testify that the occupant took the yield of two years but they know nothing about the third year. Thus, once the field is awarded to the original owner, the occupant must pay for the two years worth of produce which he is now seen to have illegally taken. This being the case, the false witnesses (who claimed to have seen three years of *chazakah*) must pay a penalty for having sought to deprive the original owner of this repayment. The mishnah's ruling that they must pay *everything* does not refer to *all* the produce but only to that part of it verified by other sources. It is for this reason that *Ritva* avoids interpreting *everything* as referring to the produce and sees it instead as merely a contrast to the next case.

he ate its [produce] three years, and they were found
to be *zomemim*, they pay him everything. [If] two
[testified] concerning the first [year], two concerning
the second [year], and two concerning the third
[year], they divide it in three among them. [If they
were] three brothers, and one joined with them, these

YAD AVRAHAM

zomemim penalty does not apply to monetary judgments, because money can always be returned and its transfer is therefore analogous to a sentence which has not yet been executed (*Nimmukei Yosef* from *Tos.*; cf. *Tos.* to *Bava Kamma* 4b). Alternatively, the mishnah is discussing a case in which the one claiming a *chazakah* on the field was not occupying it at the time the court ruled on it, and the ruling has therefore not yet been implemented (*Nimmukei Yosef* from *Ritva*).

שְׁנַיִם בָּרִאשׁוֹנָה, וּשְׁנַיִם בַּשְּׁנִיָּה, וּשְׁנַיִם בַּשְּׁלִישִׁית, — [If] two [testified] concerning the first [year], two concerning the second [year], and two concerning the third [year],

[I.e., the *chazakah* was established by three pairs of witnesses, each of them attesting to one year's occupation of the field.]

One of the rules of testimony is that in order to be received by the court it must be a complete testimony, i.e., it must by itself directly affect some legal matter. Any testimony which by itself has no legal consequences and is relevant only in conjunction with that of other witnesses regarding the same aspect of the case is not valid at all. For example, a child who has reached the age of majority does not become an adult under Torah law until two pubic hairs have grown (*Niddah* 6:11). Thus, when a youth of bar- or bas-mitzvah age must engage in some legal act for which majority is Biblically required, and it is not yet clear that he has developed such signs of physical maturity, witnesses are required to testify to having examined the youth and found at least two hairs (*Niddah* 52b; *Even Haezer* 155:17). Should two witnesses testify to having found one hair in the upper part of the pubic area, while two others attest to having discovered another hair in the lower

pubic area, neither testimony is accepted because neither set is testifying to anything which, taken on its own, has any legal consequence. This is derived from the verse (*Deut.* 19:15), *By the testimony of two witnesses ... shall a matter be established* — i.e., testimony to be valid must establish a *[full] matter, not half a matter* [דָּבָר וְלֹא חֲצִי דָבָר] (*Gem.* 56b).

This being the rule, the question arises why the testimony of any of these three sets of witnesses should be accepted at all, since not one of them is relating that a full *chazakah* has been established.

Rif and *Tos.* (56b) answer that each of these testimonies would be effective on its own even if no *chazakah* is established, because it would obligate the occupant to pay the owner for the produce he consumed during that year. Alternatively, testimony is only invalidated for being incomplete if it was possible for the witnesses to have observed the entire matter at one time. In this case, however, the three testimonies could not have been observed simultaneously (*Rashbam* 56b).

מְשַׁלְּשִׁין בֵּינֵיהֶם. — *they divide it in three among them.*

Each pair must pay one-third of the loss they sought to cause the owner of the field (*Rav*).

Some maintain that this applies only if it is apparent that the three pairs acted in collusion. Otherwise, each pair can claim that they testified with the sole intent of making the occupant of the field pay for the produce he consumed and never intended the owner any harm (*Yad Ramah; Meiri*). Others contend that such a claim is not credible since it was the occupant of the field who brought them all to court to testify (*Tos.* 56b).

שְׁלֹשָׁה אַחִים, וְאֶחָד מִצְטָרֵף עִמָּהֶם, — *[If they were] three brothers, and one joined*

עִמָּהֶם, הֲרֵי אֵלּוּ שָׁלֹשׁ עֵדֻיּוֹת; וְהֵן עֵדוּת אַחַת
לַהֲזָמָה.

[ה] אֵלּוּ דְּבָרִים שֶׁיֵּשׁ לָהֶם חֲזָקָה וְאֵלּוּ דְבָרִים
שֶׁאֵין לָהֶם חֲזָקָה: הָיָה מַעֲמִיד בְּהֵמָה
בֶּחָצֵר, תַּנּוּר, וְכִירַיִם, וְרֵחַיִם, וּמְגַדֵּל תַּרְנְגוֹלִין

יד אברהם

with them,

If three brothers testified to the *chazakah*, each of them attesting to a separate year of possession, and they were joined by a fourth individual unrelated to them who testified to all three years of possession *(Rav)*.

הֲרֵי אֵלּוּ שָׁלֹשׁ עֵדֻיּוֹת; — *these are three testimonies;*

This fourth witness combines in turn with each of the three brothers to form a separate pair testifying in regard to each of the three years of *chazakah*. Therefore, even though two brothers cannot testify together on one matter (see *Makkos* 6a), their testimony in this case is valid, because none of the brothers is attesting to the same fact *(Rav)*.

וְהֵן עֵדוּת אַחַת לַהֲזָמָה. — *but they are one testimony in regard to hazamah.*

Another of the rules of *zomemim* witnesses is that all of those who testify together must be shown to be *zomemim*

before the penalty for *hazamah* can be applied to any of them *(Makkos* 1:7). In our case, therefore, since none of their testimonies could have established a *chazakah* except in conjunction with the others, they are considered as one testimony in regard to the laws of *hazamah*, and none of them can be punished unless they are all shown to be *zomemim* *(Rav; Meiri)*.

If they are all discredited, each of the brothers pays one-sixth of the fine — half of what he falsely testified about — while the fourth witness, who testified about all three years, pays one-half *(Meiri; Rambam, Eidus* 21:7).

When they are all discredited through *hazamah*, each of the three brothers is in effect being fined partially due to the testimony of his brothers, since without his brothers' testimony no *chazakah* would have been established. Nevertheless, since this is only an indirect result of their testimony, it does not violate the principle that one cannot be punished through the testimony of a relative *(Nimmukei Yosef)*.

5.

The mishnah now discusses another aspect of *chazakah*, viz., that a person's use of someone else's property for his own needs can establish his right to continue doing so. There is a dispute among the authorities whether the *chazakah* discussed in this mishnah and the next requires three years of use and a claim of acquisition in order to be valid or not. *Rav* follows the view of *Rashbam* (57a), *Ramban*, and *Tur* *(Choshen Mishpat* 140:19) that these *chazakos* are no different than the standard one — they all require three years to be established and are valid only when it is claimed that the rights were formally acquired. The view of the *Geonim* (cited by *Meiri*), *Ri Migash* and *Rambam* *(Shecheinim* 5:5), however, is that in the situations with which the following mishnah deals, where one partner in a property uses it in the presence of the other for a purpose not customary to such a property and the

are three testimonies; but they are one testimony in
regard to *hazamah*.

5. **T**hese are circumstances for which there is
chazakah, and these are circumstances for
which there is no *chazakah*: [If] he kept an animal in
the courtyard, [or] an oven, a stove, or a mill, or he
raised chickens or placed his manure in the

YAD AVRAHAM

latter does not object, his lack of objection is seen as a waiver and the other may
continue to utilize the property in this manner.[1] For this, no formal transaction or
claim of acquisition is required in order to establish such a *chazakah*, nor are three
years of use necessary; rather the *chazakah* takes effect immediately.[2]

אֵלּוּ דְבָרִים שֶׁיֵּשׁ לָהֶם חֲזָקָה, — *These are*
circumstances for which there is
chazakah [lit. *things which have*
chazakah],

These are ways in which a person's
utilization of another's property establishes his right to continue doing so
(*Rav*). As explained in the prefatory
note, according to many authorities this
chazakah can only be established over
the course of three years (*Rav*), and is
effective only as evidence to support a
claim that he formally acquired the right
to continue this use (*Rashbam; Nim-*
mukei Yosef). According to others, it
takes effect immediately (if no protest
has been registered), because the other
partner's silence in the face of this
restricted use demonstrates his waiver
of the restriction (*Rambam, Shecheinim*
5:5).

וְאֵלּוּ דְבָרִים שֶׁאֵין לָהֶם חֲזָקָה: — *and these*
are circumstances for which there is no
chazakah:

[Certain types of use are not likely to
bother the owner, and his lack of protest

is therefore no basis for *chazakah*.
Thus, he can, at some later date, block
the further usage of the property in this
manner.]

הָיָה מַעֲמִיד בְּהֵמָה בְּחָצֵר, — *[If] he kept an*
animal in the courtyard,

One of the partners kept his animal in
a jointly owned courtyard (*Rav* from
Gem. 57b), though a courtyard is not
ordinarily used for such purposes
(*Rashbam; Meiri*).

תַּנּוּר, וְכִירַיִם, — *[or] an oven, a stove,*

In Talmudic times both of these
cooking units were hollow earthenware
containers which were filled with coals
to heat them (see ArtScroll *Shabbos*,
3:1,2). Both were movable objects
(*Rashbam* 57a).

וְרֵחַיִם, — *or a mill,*

I.e., a hand-powered mill [for
grinding small amounts of grain]
(*Rashbam* 57a).

וּמְגַדֵּל תַּרְנְגוֹלִין — *or he raised chickens*

I.e., he raised them in the jointly
owned courtyard (*Yad Ramah*).

---

1. *Rambam*, however, agrees that if one establishes such use in a property in which he is not a
part owner, he cannot claim that the owner waived his rights in favor of the user, since one
does not readily give up his property rights to another.

2. Even among those who follow this opinion, some maintain that if no act was done to
indicate that the usage was meant to be permanent, the *chazakah* takes effect only after thirty
days (*Ravad, Shecheinim* 7:7; see *Yad Ramah* §10).

וְנוֹתֵן זִבְלוֹ בֶּחָצֵר, אֵינָהּ חֲזָקָה. אֲבָל עָשָׂה מְחִצָּה
לִבְהֶמְתּוֹ גְּבוֹהָהּ עֲשָׂרָה טְפָחִים, וְכֵן לַתַּנּוּר, וְכֵן
לַכִּירַיִם, וְכֵן לָרֵחַיִם, הִכְנִיס תַּרְנְגוֹלִין לְתוֹךְ הַבַּיִת,
וְעָשָׂה מָקוֹם לְזִבְלוֹ עָמוֹק שְׁלֹשָׁה אוֹ גָּבוֹהַּ שְׁלֹשָׁה,
הֲרֵי זוֹ חֲזָקָה.

[ו] **הַמַּרְזֵב** אֵין לוֹ חֲזָקָה, וְיֵשׁ לִמְקוֹמוֹ חֲזָקָה.

יד אברהם

וְנוֹתֵן זִבְלוֹ בֶּחָצֵר, — *or placed his manure in the courtyard,*

[Animal manure was collected and stored for use as fertilizer (see *Sheviis* ch. 3).]

אֵינָהּ חֲזָקָה. — *it is not a chazakah.*

In all of these cases, the use of the courtyard even over a period of three years does not establish a *chazakah*. A person is not likely to object to his partner's use of their common courtyard in this manner, since he makes no structural changes in the property (*Rashbam; Maggid Mishneh* to *Rambam, Shecheinim* 5:5).

Another opinion mentioned in the *Gemara* (57b) is that if he kept these objects in the courtyard in front of the houses the *chazakah* would be valid, because a person would ordinarily not allow even his partner to do so. The mishnah is discussing a case in which they were placed in a jointly owned backyard, where clutter is less bothersome to people (*Rashbam*). This opinion is the one cited by *Rif* and *Rosh* (see *Tur, Choshen Mishpat* 161; *Beis Yosef, Perisha* ad loc; *Shach* ibid., 146:20).

If a person performed these activities over a period of three years in a courtyard in which he was not a partner, it would constitute a valid *chazakah*, because the owner would not allow him to do so if he had not sold him this right (*Gem.* 57b; see *Rav*).[1]

אֲבָל עָשָׂה מְחִצָּה לִבְהֶמְתּוֹ גְּבוֹהָהּ עֲשָׂרָה טְפָחִים, וְכֵן לַתַּנּוּר, וְכֵן לַכִּירַיִם, וְכֵן לָרֵחַיִם, — *However, [if] he made a partition ten handbreadths high for his animal, or [he did] so for the oven, stove, or mill,*

[If one of the partners built a partition in the jointly owned courtyard to facilitate any of the above-mentioned usages, this structural alteration would be expected to elicit a protest even from a partner.]

הִכְנִיס תַּרְנְגוֹלִין לְתוֹךְ הַבַּיִת, — *[or] he placed chickens in the house,*

[Similarly, if one placed his chickens in a jointly owned house (rather than a courtyard), this would be intolerable even to his partner.] Although no structural change was made, the other partner would be expected to object to the chickens dirtying his house (*Nimmukei Yosef*).

וְעָשָׂה מָקוֹם לְזִבְלוֹ עָמוֹק שְׁלֹשָׁה אוֹ גָּבוֹהַּ שְׁלֹשָׁה, — *or he made a [storage] place for manure three [handbreadths] high or three [handbreadths] deep,*

He built a border three handbreadths high in which to place the manure so that it would not spread across the courtyard, or he dug a hole three handbreadths deep for this purpose (*Rashbam* 57a).

הֲרֵי זוֹ חֲזָקָה. — *this is a chazakah.*

1. As explained in the footnote above, even *Rambam*, who considers the *chazakah* of the cases listed in this mishnah to take effect immediately, agrees that the usages presently under discussion cannot establish a *chazakah* in another's courtyard in less than three years. If this were not the case, one would not be able to permit someone to use his property temporarily as a favor for fear of having him establish an irrevocable *chazakah* there.

3
6
courtyard, it is not a *chazakah*. However, [if] he made a partition ten handbreadths high for his animal, or [he did] so for the oven, stove, or mill, [or] he placed chickens in the house, or he made a [storage] place for manure three [handbreadths] high or three [handbreadths] deep, this is a *chazakah*.

6. **A** drainspout has no *chazakah*, but its place has

YAD AVRAHAM

If he maintains any of these for three years without objection from his partner the *chazakah* is valid. His utilization of their joint property in any of these ways would be expected to elicit a protest, and if it did not, it is evident that the rights were sold or given away *(Rav)*.

As explained above, according to *Rambam*, such a *chazakah* takes effect immediately and does not require any transaction. The failure to protest immediately the violations of their partnership constitutes a legal waiver of rights. However, if he did any of these things in a property in which he was not a partner, *Rambam* agrees that it is a *chazakah* only if he did so for three years *(Shecheinim 5:5; Toein VeNitan 12:14)*. Furthermore, a claim of waiver would not be acceptable in this case and the *chazakah* would therefore only be valid if he claims to have bought the right to build the wall or place his chickens or manure *(Maggid Mishneh)*.

6.

This mishnah continues the previous mishnah's delineation of the circumstances for which there is *chazakah* and those for which there is not. Accordingly, the dispute mentioned above, whether the *chazakah* is one of three years in support of a claim of having acquired the rights in question or whether it is an immediate *chazakah* based on the silence of the owner constituting a consent and waiver of his rights, applies here as well *(Meiri; Beis Yosef 153:2; see Rashbam 58b)*.[1]

הַמַּרְזֵב — *A drainspout*
I.e., a small pipe which juts out from the gutter running along the edge of a roof. This drains the water from the gutter and directs it away from the wall of the house. The water, in this case, is being directed into a neighbor's courtyard *(Rav; Rashbam)*.

אֵין לוֹ חֲזָקָה, — *has no chazakah,*
The right to locate the drainspout at a specific point along the gutter cannot be established by *chazakah* *(Rav* from

Gem. 58a).

וְיֵשׁ לִמְקוֹמוֹ חֲזָקָה. — *but its place has a chazakah.*
The right to have the water drain into that courtyard at some point, however, is established by *chazakah* and the affected neighbor cannot demand that the drainspout be removed entirely. The owner of the courtyard retains only the right to have the drainspout moved to the other end of the gutter *(Gem.* 58b), because it makes no difference to the

1. *Rav* (s.v. ולצורית), however, seemingly follows the view of *Yad Ramah*, that the two mishnayos are not identical. Rather, while the previous mishnah discussed a *chazakah* of three years, the *chazakah* in this mishnah takes effect immediately. [The difference between the two is apparently that in the previous mishnah the structural alteration was made in property jointly owned by another and the right to use it can therefore not be obtained (in this view)

הַמַּזְחִילָה יֵשׁ לָהּ חֲזָקָה. סֻלָּם הַמִּצְרִי אֵין לוֹ
חֲזָקָה, וְלַצּוֹרִי יֵשׁ לוֹ חֲזָקָה.
חַלּוֹן הַמִּצְרִית אֵין לָהּ חֲזָקָה, וְלַצּוֹרִית יֵשׁ לָהּ

יד אברהם

owner of the gutter where in his neighbor's courtyard the drainspout runs out (Rav). Furthermore, the drainspouts of those times were not fixed to a particular spot on the gutter and could easily be shifted. Thus, there was never any reason for the owner of the neighboring courtyard to protest its precise location (Rashbam).

By the same token, the owner of the courtyard has a right to prevent the owner of the drainspout from removing it, since the former has a chazakah to receive the spout's water (Gem. 59a). Thus, while the latter can shift the spout along the gutter, he cannot entirely remove it from over his neighbor's courtyard (Rambam, Shecheinim 8:5).

הַמַּזְחִילָה — A gutter

I.e., the gutter which extends along the edge of the roof (Rav).

יֵשׁ לָהּ חֲזָקָה. — has a chazakah.

In contrast to a drainspout's position, a gutter's placement along the edge of the roof is permanent in nature. Consequently, the silence of the owner of the courtyard indicates his consent to its placement and he cannot subsequently demand that it be removed (Rav, Rashbam 58b).[1]

סֻלָּם הַמִּצְרִי — An Egyptian ladder

A small, portable ladder (Rav) with fewer than four rungs (Gem. 59a).

אֵין לוֹ חֲזָקָה, — has no chazakah,

If one placed it in his neighbor's property in order to climb up to a low roof or dovecote, it does not establish a chazakah to allow him to continue to keep it there. A person does not

ordinarily object to the placement in his property of a small, portable object which can be easily removed at any time, and his silence consequently proves nothing (Rav; Rashbam). Therefore, if the owner of the property should decide to build on it, his neighbor cannot prevent him from doing so on the grounds that he will have to remove his ladder (Rambam, Shecheinim 8:4).

Some contend that the mishnah cannot be referring to placing a ladder in someone else's property because that would mean that the person would constantly have to enter the property in order to use his ladder — something to which anyone would object. Rather, they explain the mishnah to be discussing a case in which one placed a ladder in his own property but leaned it against the wall of his neighbor (Yad Ramah, Tur Choshen Mishpat 153:20).

Rambam (Shecheinim 8:4) maintains that since one cannot establish a chazakah for his small ladder in another's property merely by placing it there, and since placing it there does not damage the property in any way, one may not prevent his neighbor from doing so unless he needs the space. This is because of the rule that the court compels one not to act in the manner of Sodom (כּוֹפִין עַל מִדַּת סְדוֹם) — i.e., with unreasonable selfishness (Maggid Mishneh). Others rule that one cannot be compelled to allow someone else to use his property and that such usage is not included in that rule (Tur, Choshen Mishpat 153:21).

The mishnah's ruling to this point refers to a portable ladder. However, if he fixed it into that spot with nails, its presence does constitute a chazakah (Nimmukei Yosef).

without a formal transaction. In the case of the following mishnah, however, his alteration is made within his own property, though it affects his neighbor's. Thus, only the affected person's consent and waiver is required, and this can be established by his silence alone (see Yad Ramah §11).]

1. As explained in the prefatory note, according to some it is his prolonged silence over three years which serves as proof of his sale of these rights, while according to others his immediate silence constitutes a waiver.

3
6

6. A drainspout has no *chazakah*, but its place has a *chazakah*. A gutter has a *chazakah*. An Egyptian ladder has no *chazakah*, but a Tyrian [ladder] has a *chazakah*.

An Egyptian window has no *chazakah*, but a

וְלַצּוּרִי יֵשׁ לוֹ חֲזָקָה. — *but a Tyrian [ladder] has a chazakah.*

This is a larger ladder, with four or more rungs *(Tif. Yis.)*. The weight of such a ladder makes it difficult to move and renders it equivalent to one fixed to that spot *(Eruvin 78a)*. Consequently, the lack of protest leads to a *chazakah* *(Nimmukei Yosef)*.

Above (2:4) the mishnah taught that when building a wall one must distance it at least four cubits from a neighbor's window to avoid blocking out its light. Because of this, the owner of a property can enjoin the owner of an adjacent house from opening a permanent window facing his property because allowing that window to remain would prevent him from someday building a wall directly opposite it. Additionally, if the window overlooks his courtyard, he may protest its opening on the grounds that its presence deprives him of his privacy by allowing him to be observed in the courtyard from the window (see mishnah 7).

The following ruling of the mishnah delineates when a failure by the owner of a property to protest the opening of a window in an adjacent building results in a *chazakah* being established for the window's continued presence.

חַלּוֹן הַמִּצְרִית — *An Egyptian window*

As the mishnah will explain below, this is a window which is too small for a person to fit his head through it.

אֵין לָהּ חֲזָקָה, — *has no chazakah,*

If someone made such a window in the wall of his house opening out onto his neighbor's courtyard, the neighbor's

failure to object to it does not establish a *chazakah* for that window. As the *Gemara* (59a) explains, this is because the mishnah refers here to a window made more than four cubits above floor-level. Consequently, the owner of the courtyard can claim that he did not protest the installation of the window because such a small opening lacks permanence *(Rabbeinu Tam, Tos. 59a)* [and he is therefore not concerned that the other will establish a *chazakah* for its presence]. At the same time, since it is above eye-level, it does not intrude on his privacy *(Rav)*. Therefore, if the latter decides to build a wall opposite that window, the owner of the window cannot prevent him, since he has not established his right to have a window there.

However, if such a window was opened in the wall *within* four cubits of the floor, and thus within eye-range of the occupants, the owner of the courtyard's failure to protest this threat to his privacy does establish a *chazakah* and the window may no longer be blocked off *(Rav; Rabbeinu Tam; Rosh)*.

Furthermore, even though the owner of a courtyard does not necessarily feel threatened by a small window above four cubits, he can, if he wishes, prevent the owner of the house from opening even such a window because of the possibility that an occupant of the house will invade his privacy by standing on a stool to watch him through the window *(Rav from Gem. 59a)*.

If the window was made specifically for light, it has a *chazakah*[1] *(Rav from*

---

1. Some maintain that this ruling refers only to a window which is the sole source of sunlight for that room, because it is then clearly a permanent fixture *(Rashbam)*. Others rule that it

חֲזָקָה. אֵיזוֹ הִיא חַלּוֹן הַמִּצְרִית? כָּל שֶׁאֵין רֹאשׁוֹ
שֶׁל אָדָם יָכוֹל לִכָּנֵס לְתוֹכָהּ. רַבִּי יְהוּדָה אוֹמֵר:
אִם יֵשׁ לָהּ מַלְבֵּן, אַף עַל פִּי שֶׁאֵין רֹאשׁוֹ שֶׁל אָדָם
יָכוֹל לִכָּנֵס לְתוֹכָהּ, הֲרֵי זוֹ חֲזָקָה.
הַזִּיז — עַד טֶפַח יֵשׁ לוֹ חֲזָקָה, וְיָכוֹל לִמְחוֹת.

יד אברהם

Gem. 59b), because such a window is obviously intended as a permanent fixture, and the owner of the courtyard should have protested. The mishnah is discussing a window which was built for the sake of watching one's property through it (Rashbam).

וְלַצּוֹרִית יֵשׁ לָהּ חֲזָקָה. — but a Tyrian [window] has a chazakah.

If he made a Tyrian window, which is a window large enough for a man to place his head through it (see below), and the owner of the neighboring courtyard did not protest this intrusion in his privacy, a chazakah is established. Therefore, the neighbor may no longer build a wall opposite it and block it (Rav). The chazakah of this larger type window is established even if it is more than four cubits above the floor (Rav; Rabbeinu Tam). Although at this height it is above eye-level and does not pose a significant threat to the courtyard's privacy, the large size of the window shows that it is a permanent alteration, and the failure to protest its installation therefore establishes its chazakah (Rabbeinu Tam as explained by Rosh).[1]

The view presented to this point reflects the explanation of Rav, who follows Rabbeinu Tam, Rambam (Shecheinim 7:6) and others in understanding the Gemara's (59a) distinction between a window above four cubits and one within four cubits to refer to the small, Egyptian windows. In this view the presence of large, Tyrian windows generates a chazakah regardless of their height.

Others, most notably Rashbam and Ravad (Shecheinim 7:6), interpret the Gemara's distinction regarding the height of the window to refer to the Tyrian windows rather than the Egyptian ones. In this view small windows never establish a chazakah for their presence, even if they are within four cubits of the floor and thus at eye-level, because their smallness and impermanence account for the owner of the courtyard's failure to protest their presence. It is only in the case of large windows that one would expect to elicit a protest, and therefore it is only in the case of large windows that the absence of a protest generates a chazakah. According to this view, it is in the case of the larger, Tyrian windows that the Gemara states that no chazakah can be established for windows set above four cubits from the floor. The owner of the courtyard can say that he did not protest the installation of such a high window — despite its size and permanence — because he considered the height of the window sufficient protection for his privacy.[2]

applies even where there are other windows as well, because once a window has been added to give extra light it is unlikely to be removed (Ritva).

1. Maggid Mishneh (Shecheinim 7:6) offers a different reason for this. As explained by Lechem Mishneh there, it is that with a large window there is greater concern for loss of privacy in the courtyard because of the greater temptation for the inmates of the house to stand on a stool and look out. With a tiny window, the temptation is much less due to the limited field of vision offered by a small hole. [Thus, even if the larger size window is also impermanent, its installation should still elicit a protest from the owner of the courtyard about his loss of privacy.]

2. As taught in mishnah 1:1, the right to privacy in one's property is paramount and extends even to forcing a neighbor to share in the expense of putting up a partition between their properties. As will be seen in the next mishnah, this right is what allows one to block his

3
6

Tyrian [window] has a *chazakah*. What is an Egyptian window? Any [window] through which a man's head cannot enter. R' Yehudah says: If it has a frame, even though a man's head cannot enter it, it establishes a *chazakah*.

A protrusion — down to a handbreadth it has a *chazakah*, and one can protest [its placement]. [But if

YAD AVRAHAM

אֵיזוֹ הִיא חַלּוֹן הַמִּצְרִית? כָּל שֶׁאֵין רֹאשׁוֹ שֶׁל אָדָם יָכוֹל לִכָּנֵס לְתוֹכָהּ. — *What is an Egyptian window? Any [window] through which a man's head cannot enter.*

[As explained above.]

רַבִּי יְהוּדָה אוֹמֵר: אִם יֶשׁ לָהּ מַלְבֵּן, אַף עַל פִּי שֶׁאֵין רֹאשׁוֹ שֶׁל אָדָם יָכוֹל לִכָּנֵס לְתוֹכָהּ, הֲרֵי זוֹ חֲזָקָה. — *R' Yehudah says: If it has a frame, even though a man's head cannot enter it, it establishes a chazakah.*

Framing out a window indicates that it is intended to be a permanent fixture. Therefore, whatever its size, the one whose courtyard it overlooks would be expected to issue a protest, and if he did not do so it is evidence of his acquiesence (*Meiri*).

— הַזִּיז — *A protrusion* —

I.e., a piece of stone or wood which protrudes from a wall and extends into a neighboring courtyard. The extension is a handbreadth or more long (*Rav*) and at least a handbreadth wide (*Yad Ramah; Meiri*).

עַד טֶפַח יֶשׁ לוֹ חֲזָקָה, — *down to* [lit. *until*] *a handbreadth it has a chazakah,*

I.e., if the protrusion is any length down to a handbreadth (but not smaller) it can establish a *chazakah* for its presence. Since it is of significant size, the lack of protest by the owner of the courtyard indicates acquiescence to its presence (*Rashbam*). Therefore, the owner of the courtyard can no longer build in a manner which will block off that protrusion and negate its use (*Rav*).

Yad Ramah maintains that only the use of the protrusion as a ledge upon which to place

neighbor from opening a window overlooking his courtyard. According to most authorities this right can be waived through a failure to protest, and a *chazakah* may be established for the window's continued presence despite the resulting loss of privacy in the courtyard. Although mishnah 1:1 taught that there could be no *chazakah* to negate the right to a partition, that was because nothing overt was done to challenge the right of privacy. The installation of a window, however, actively challenges the courtyard's previous privacy, and the failure to protest this therefore indicates acquiescence (*Maggid Mishneh, Shecheinim* 2:14 from *Ri Migash; Choshen Mishpat* 154:8). Additionally, the loss of privacy due to a window is not as great as in a totally open courtyard; consequently, its waiver can be binding (*Rosh*).

In explaining the mishnah as referring to a window overlooking a courtyard and dealing with the issue of lost privacy, the commentary has followed this view, which is shared by *Rav, Rashbam, Rabbeinu Tam, Rambam* and others.

However, some authorities maintain that this right cannot be compromised even by a failure to protest, and no *chazakah* can negate it (*Rif* cited by *Ritva; Ramban; Nimmukei Yosef*). Even one who remained silent over an extended period of time may later retract on the grounds that he originally thought he could bear the loss of privacy but now sees that he was mistaken (*Ramban, Ritva* to 58b; see *Choshen Mishpat* 155:36).

According to this view, the mishnah here is discussing only windows which pose no threat to privacy — such as those which do not overlook a courtyard — and which threaten only the property owner's right to build directly in front of the window. The difference between small and large windows is that the former are not generally permanent and therefore do not necessarily arouse the ire of the property owner, whereas the latter are permanent in nature

פָּחוֹת מִטֶּפַח, אֵין לוֹ חֲזָקָה, וְאֵינוֹ יָכוֹל לִמְחוֹת.

[ז] לֹא יִפְתַּח אָדָם חַלּוֹנוֹתָיו לַחֲצַר הַשֻּׁתָּפִין. לָקַח בַּיִת בְּחָצֵר אַחֶרֶת לֹא יִפְתָּחֶנָּה לַחֲצַר הַשֻּׁתָּפִין. בָּנָה עֲלִיָּה עַל גַּבֵּי בֵיתוֹ, לֹא יִפְתָּחֶנָּה לַחֲצַר הַשֻּׁתָּפִין. אֶלָּא, אִם רָצָה, בּוֹנֶה אֶת הַחֶדֶר לִפְנִים מִבֵּיתוֹ, וּבוֹנֶה עֲלִיָּה עַל גַּבֵּי

יד אברהם

things is protected by the *chazakah*, not the right to hang things from it. *Rambam* (*Shecheinim* 8:2), however, considers even this latter right established by the *chazakah*. Thus, the owner of the courtyard would have to leave him ten handbreadths of airspace beneath his protrusion (*Meiri*).

וְיָכוֹל לִמְחוֹת. — *and one can protest* [*its placement*].

The owner of the courtyard can block the original construction of the protrusion (*Rav*), because its presence causes its owner to see into the courtyard while using it (*Rashbam* 59b).

פָּחוֹת מִטֶּפַח, אֵין לוֹ חֲזָקָה, — [*But if it is*] *less than a handbreadth, it has no chazakah,*

A protrusion this small is not fit for regular use and therefore no *chazakah* can be established on the basis of the owner of the courtyard's failure to protest its existence. Consequently, he may subsequently build in a manner which will impede the use of the protrusion (*Rav*).

וְאֵין יָכוֹל לִמְחוֹת. — *and one cannot protest* [*its placement*].

The owner of the courtyard cannot prevent his neighbor from extending a protrusion this size into his airspace because it causes him no harm (*Rav*).

Since it is not large enough to keep things on it, but only to hang objects from it, he can be careful to avoid looking into his neighbor's courtyard when hanging things from it (*Gem.* 59b).[1] This is not true of one extending a handbreadth or more. Such a protrusion is used for placing things on top of it, and he must inevitably see into his neighbor's courtyard when he goes out onto it to arrange his objects (*Rosh*).

In addition, the owner of the house cannot prevent the owner of the courtyard from using the protrusion to hang things from it, because the owner of the courtyard has the right to remove it entirely if he wishes to build in that spot, since it has no *chazakah* (*Rashbam* 59b).

The above explanation of *Rav* follows the view of Rav Yehudah in the *Gemara* (59b). The *Gemara* also cites the dissenting view of Rav Huna that the owner of the courtyard *can* protest the extension of even a tiny protrusion into his airspace because of the possible loss of privacy when the owner of the house hangs things from it. In this view, the mishnah's ruling that no *chazakah* can be established for such a small protrusion refers only to the inability of the owner of the protrusion to gain the right to block the owner of the courtyard from building right

and thus should have elicited a protest to preserve the right to build (*Rashba, Nimmukei Yosef*).

1. Thus, although it is possible for him to look into the courtyard while hanging things from the protrusion, he is unlikely to do so because he does not want to be caught peeping. Only when in the normal course of usage it is impossible to avoid occasional glances into the courtyard — e.g., in the case of an overlooking window or a protrusion more than a handbreadth which allows for putting things on top of it — is their concern for loss of privacy, since no shame can be attached to these glimpses (*Rashbam* 59b).

it is] less than a handbreadth, it has no *chazakah*, and one. cannot protest [its placement].

7. A man may not open his windows onto a jointly owned courtyard. [If] he buys a house in another courtyard he may not open it onto a jointly owned courtyard. [If] he builds an attic above his house, he may not open it onto a jointly owned courtyard. However, if he wishes, he may build a room within his house, or build an attic above his

YAD AVRAHAM

next to his protrusion *(Lechem Mishneh)*. Rambam *(Shecheinim* 8:1) follows this view and rules accordingly that if the owner of the courtyard failed to protest the extension, a *chazakah* is established for its continued presence.

7.

This mishnah continues the delineation of the limits placed on the renovations a person may make on his own property due to the detrimental effect they will have on his neighbors. Some commentators maintain that all such restrictions depend upon the custom of the time and place, and that which is generally not considered objectionable cannot be blocked by neighbors *(Meiri;* see *Tos. Yom Tov; Rama, Choshen Mishpat* 154:11).

לֹא יִפְתַּח אָדָם חַלּוֹנוֹתָיו לַחֲצַר הַשֻׁתָּפִין. — **A man may not open his windows onto a jointly owned courtyard.**

I.e., he may not install a window in his house facing the courtyard. Although when people share a courtyard they must necessarily limit their private activities in that area in any case, the addition of a window facing the courtyard limits their activities even further by allowing them to be observed even by people in the house *(Gem.* 59b; Rashbam; *Tos.).* It goes without saying that one may certainly not open a window onto a courtyard in which he is not a partner *(Gem.).*

לָקַח בַּיִת בְּחָצֵר אַחֶרֶת לֹא יִפְתָּחֶנָּה לַחֲצַר הַשֻׁתָּפִין. — **[If] he buys a house in another courtyard he may not open it onto a jointly owned courtyard.**

If a partner in one courtyard buys a house in an adjoining courtyard he may not add a back door to that house to open into the first courtyard because it

would increase the flow of traffic through there *(Rav* from *Gem.* 60a). Even if he closes off the new house from its original courtyard, thereby insuring that it will not be used as a shortcut between the two courtyards, it is still prohibited because the inhabitants of the second house itself will now be using this first courtyard as their access to it *(Nimmukei Yosef, Rav).*

בָּנָה עֲלִיָּה עַל גַּבֵּי בֵיתוֹ, לֹא יִפְתָּחֶנָּה לַחֲצַר הַשֻׁתָּפִין. — **[If] he builds an attic above his house, he may not open it onto a jointly owned courtyard.**

[An attic with a separate entrance is likely to be rented or lent to others and thereby increase traffic through the courtyard.]

אֶלָּא, אִם רָצָה, בּוֹנֶה אֶת הַחֶדֶר לִפְנִים מִבֵּיתוֹ, — **However, if he wishes, he may build a room within his house,**

I.e., he may sub-divide the existing space in his house. Although this enables him to add to the number of its

בֵּיתוֹ, וּפוֹתְחָהּ לְתוֹךְ בֵּיתוֹ.
לֹא יִפְתַּח אָדָם לַחֲצַר הַשֻּׁתָּפִין פֶּתַח כְּנֶגֶד פֶּתַח
וְחַלּוֹן כְּנֶגֶד חַלּוֹן. הָיָה קָטָן, לֹא יַעֲשֶׂנּוּ גָדוֹל; אֶחָד,
לֹא יַעֲשֶׂנּוּ שְׁנַיִם. אֲבָל פּוֹתֵחַ הוּא לִרְשׁוּת הָרַבִּים
פֶּתַח כְּנֶגֶד פֶּתַח וְחַלּוֹן כְּנֶגֶד חַלּוֹן. הָיָה קָטָן,
עוֹשֶׂה אוֹתוֹ גָדוֹל; אֶחָד, עוֹשֶׂה אוֹתוֹ שְׁנַיִם.

יד אברהם

occupants, there are no limits set on the number of people one may allow to live in his house within its present dimensions (Rav from Gem. 60a). He may not, however, enlarge the current dimensions of his house [without the consent of his neighbors] (Tur, Choshen Mishpat 154:3 from Rashbam 60a).

וּבוֹנֶה עֲלִיָּה עַל גַּבֵּי בֵיתוֹ, — or build an attic above his house,

I.e., he may divide his house vertically, thereby creating a second story, since he is not actually adding to the overall size of the house (Rashbam from Gem. 60a).

וּפוֹתְחָהּ לְתוֹךְ בֵּיתוֹ. — and open it into his house.

[He may sub-divide the house in these ways only if he does not make separate entrances out to the courtyard for the newly created rooms. The doors to these rooms may only open internally, into the house.]

The above explanation is that of Rav, who follows Rashbam. Many other authorities, however, rule that the mishnah permits adding even to the overall dimensions of the house as long as he does not open separate entrances into the courtyard for the newly built rooms or floors. Since they open only into his house, they are not likely to be rented out to others (Rambam, Shecheinim 5:8; Ramban; Ritva; Nimmukei Yosef). Even if it should transpire that the new section is rented, it is no worse than taking boarders into his house, which he is certainly permitted to do. As long as

the renovation of the house does not readily lend itself to that type of use alterations are permitted (Nimmukei Yosef).

לֹא יִפְתַּח אָדָם לַחֲצַר הַשֻּׁתָּפִין פֶּתַח כְּנֶגֶד פֶּתַח — A man may not open onto a jointly owned courtyard a doorway opposite another doorway

He may not make a doorway directly opposite that of his neighbor, because he will be able to see inside the latter's home. In addition to depriving him of his privacy, this would violate the standard of modesty expected of Jews (Rashbam). This is derived from the verse (Numbers 24:2), And Balaam lifted his eyes and he saw Israel dwelling according to its tribes. 'What did he see? He saw that the entrances to their tents did not stand directly opposite each other, and he said, "These are fitting for the Divine Presence to dwell among them" ' (Gem. 60a).

וְחַלּוֹן כְּנֶגֶד חַלּוֹן. — or a window opposite another window.

[The same applies to opening a window opposite that of his neighbor.]

Although the mishnah ruled above that it is forbidden to open up any window overlooking a courtyard, the case here involves a window which had long overlooked the courtyard and had thus become sanctioned by chazakah. Now, however, the owner of the house wants to close that window and replace it with one in a different spot (Rashbam). While in regard to seeing into the courtyard there is no difference where the window is placed, he must

3
7
house, and open it into his house.

A man may not open onto a jointly owned courtyard a doorway opposite another doorway or a window opposite another window. [If] it was small, he may not enlarge it; [if there was] one, he may not make it two. However, he may open onto the public domain a doorway opposite another doorway and a window opposite another window. [If] it was small, he may enlarge it; [if] there was one, he may make it two.

nonetheless make sure not to open it directly opposite his neighbor's window so that it does not allow him to see into his neighbor's house *(Yad Ramah)*. Rather, he must locate his window slightly off line from the other window *(Rashbam)* so that he cannot see directly into it. Although he can still see in from an angle if he desires, this is something which he can do in any case by going out into the courtyard and looking from there. Thus, the placement of the window does not aggravate the problem *(Nimmukei Yosef)*.

It follows from this that if the neighbor's window is more than four cubits above the ground, in which case someone standing in the courtyard cannot see into it because of its height, the new window must be located far enough to the side so that it is impossible to see into the neighbor's window at all (ibid., as interpreted by *Tos. Yom Tov*).

Others rule that in all cases he must build his window far enough off line from his neighbor's so that he is unable to see into it *(Ritva; see Choshen Mishpat 154:3, Sema 11)*.

הָיָה קָטָן, לֹא יַעֲשֶׂנּוּ גָדוֹל; — *[If] it was small, he may not enlarge it;*
If he had a small door opening into the courtyard, he may not enlarge it, because it makes it more difficult for his neighbors to maintain their privacy *(Rav from Gem. 60a)*. The same is true for a window *(Tur 154:4)*.

אֶחָד, לֹא יַעֲשֶׂנּוּ שְׁנַיִם. — *[if there was] one,*

he may not make it two.
He may not divide a large door into two smaller doors, even if the total size of the entrance remains the same. It is easier for one using the courtyard to check whether one door is open than two; thus, to increase the number of doors constitutes a loss of the neighbors' privacy *(Rav from Gem. 60a)*.

אֲבָל פּוֹתֵחַ הוּא לִרְשׁוּת הָרַבִּים פֶּתַח כְּנֶגֶד פֶּתַח וְחַלּוֹן כְּנֶגֶד חַלּוֹן. — *However, he may open onto the public domain a doorway opposite another doorway and a window opposite another window.*

If the door or window he wishes to install faces the public domain, he need not take account of any doors or windows in the house across the road. Since the windows and doors of the house are open to public view from the street, steps must in any case be taken to protect the privacy of the house, in which case a window in the house across the street does not intrude *(Rav from Gem. 60b)*. However, if the neighbor's window is higher than the range of public view — above four cubits *(Meiri)* — this does not apply (ibid.; Rambam; Rashba; et al.). *Rashbam* (60a), however, rules that as long as a rider on a camel can see through the window, this ruling applies.

הָיָה קָטָן, עוֹשֶׂה אוֹתוֹ גָדוֹל; אֶחָד, עוֹשֶׂה אוֹתוֹ שְׁנַיִם. — *[If] it was small, he may enlarge it; [if] there was one, he may make it two.*

[ח] **אֵין** עוֹשִׂין חָלָל תַּחַת רְשׁוּת הָרַבִּים —
בּוֹרוֹת, שִׁיחִין, וּמְעָרוֹת. רַבִּי אֱלִיעֶזֶר
מַתִּיר כְּדֵי שֶׁתְּהֵא עֲגָלָה מְהַלֶּכֶת וּטְעוּנָה אֲבָנִים.
אֵין מוֹצִיאִין זִיזִין וּגְזֻזְטְרָאוֹת לִרְשׁוּת הָרַבִּים.
אֶלָּא אִם רָצָה, כּוֹנֵס תּוֹךְ שֶׁלּוֹ וּמוֹצִיא. לָקַח חָצֵר
וּבָהּ זִיזִין וּגְזֻזְטְרָאוֹת, הֲרֵי זוֹ בְחֶזְקָתָהּ.

יד אברהם

[Since the occupant of that house must in any case protect himself against public view, these measures do not affect him.]

Although the prohibition against opening a doorway directly opposite someone else's doorway is derived from Balaam's vision of the desert encampment, where the tents presumably faced each other across the camp's paths, there was, in fact, no public domain in the desert except in the encampment of the Levites *(Shabbos 96b)*. The encampment of the other tribes was similar to a jointly owned courtyard *(Rashbam)*.

The mishnah does not discuss the rules of privacy concerning neighboring homes in a common alley. Some authorities maintain that unless the alley is open at both ends, and thus serves as a thoroughfare, it is similar to a courtyard *(Ramah; Ritva; R' Yehudah Barceloni,* cited by *Tur 154:10)*. Others rule that if there are three or more houses in the alley, it is judged like a public domain *(Rashba)*.

8.

אֵין עוֹשִׂין חָלָל תַּחַת רְשׁוּת הָרַבִּים — *One may not dig [lit. make] a hole under the public domain —*

[Such an excavation might cause the street to cave in.] This is prohibited even if he accepts responsibility for any damage which may occur *(Rav, Rashbam 60a)*.

This prohibition applies only to the middle of the road, where the wagons travel. Along the sides, where people walk, there is no serious concern for damage if the hole is well covered *(Nimmukei Yosef)*.

בּוֹרוֹת, שִׁיחִין, וּמְעָרוֹת. — *pits, ditches, or vaults.*

[See commentary to mishnah 1.] These are examples of the hole mentioned above *(Rashbam)*.

רַבִּי אֱלִיעֶזֶר מַתִּיר כְּדֵי שֶׁתְּהֵא עֲגָלָה מְהַלֶּכֶת וּטְעוּנָה אֲבָנִים. — *R' Eliezer permits [it] if it is [strong] enough for a wagon loaded with stones to ride [over it].*

As long as the roadway remains fit to support heavy wagons, R' Eliezer permits digging beneath it *(Rav)*. The first *Tanna,* however, prohibits even this out of concern that the cover may in time rot without anyone being aware of it and collapse *(Gem. 60a)*.

This degree of precaution for future safety is required only when protecting the public. For private individuals, such extensive measures would not be necessary *(Nimmukei Yosef)*.

אֵין מוֹצִיאִין זִיזִין וּגְזֻזְטְרָאוֹת — *One may not extend protrusions or ledges*

זִיזִין, *protrusions,* are small extensions; גְזֻזְטְרָאוֹת, *ledges,* are larger extensions *(Rav)*.

לִרְשׁוּת הָרַבִּים. — *into the public domain.*

Because passersby might stumble over them *(Rav)*. If the ledge is above the height of a rider on a camel this concern is not pertinent and the ruling does not apply *(Rif; Yad Ramah; Rambam, Nizkei Mamon 13:24)*.

אֶלָּא, אִם רָצָה, כּוֹנֵס תּוֹךְ שֶׁלּוֹ וּמוֹצִיא —

8. One may not dig a hole under the public domain — pits, ditches, or vaults. R' Eliezer permits [it] if it is [strong] enough for a wagon loaded with stones to ride [over it].

One may not extend protrusions or ledges into the public domain. However, if he wishes, he may recess [his wall] inside his own property and extend [them]. [If] he bought a courtyard in which there are protrusions or ledges, they retain their status.

YAD AVRAHAM

However, if he wishes, he may recess [his wall] inside his own property and extend [them].

He may recess his wall back from the edge of his property and build a ledge which protrudes until the boundary *(Rav)*. Although traffic may spill over into that recess, he need no longer concern himself with the possibility of injury to passersby *(Tos. Yom Tov)*. However, after recessing the wall into his property, he may not move it back, because once land has been taken over by the public, it cannot be reclaimed for private use [see below, 6:7] *(Gem. 61b)*.

לָקַח חָצֵר וּבָה זִיזִין וּגְזֻזְטְרָאוֹת, הֲרֵי זוֹ בְחֶזְקָתָה. — *[If] he bought a courtyard in which there are protrusions or ledges, they retain their status.*

I.e., they are assumed to have been properly installed by the seller, who recessed his wall to allow for them. Since he has no way of knowing whether the ledges were legitimately extended or not, the court claims on his behalf (see above, mishnah 3, s.v. אינה חזקה) that the original owner had placed them there legally *(Rav)*. Even if the wall collapses, he may rebuild it with the ledges *(Gem. 60b)*.

Chapter 4

This chapter and the next deal with the topic of property sales — specifically, what secondary items or areas are assumed to be included in the sale and which are not included unless specified.

In determining whether some area or object which has not been specified in the contract is included in the sale of a property, the major consideration is not location but the functional relationship between the item in question and the primary property being sold. Objects which function as integral parts of the primary property and which are attached to it are assumed to be part of it and thus included in the sale. Those which are commonly used separately from the primary property are generally not included in the sale (unless specified), even if they are physically attached to it. Since it is not uncommon for people to share ownership of a single structure or even to own property within the boundaries of another person's property, mere physical connection cannot serve to establish the inclusion of a secondary object or area in the sale of the primary one. In general, the more inherently the function of the secondary property is related to that of the primary property, the less clearly its inclusion in the sale must be specified. The more something functions as an independent unit, the less likely it is to be automatically included in the sale.

The laws cited in the mishnah pertain to the generally accepted customs and

[א] **הַמּוֹכֵר** אֶת הַבַּיִת לֹא מָכַר הַיָּצִיעַ, וְאַף
עַל פִּי שֶׁהִיא פְתוּחָה לְתוֹכוֹ; וְלֹא
אֶת הַחֶדֶר שֶׁלִּפְנִים מִמֶּנּוּ; וְלֹא אֶת הַגַּג בִּזְמַן שֶׁיֵּשׁ
לוֹ מַעֲקֶה גָבוֹהַּ עֲשָׂרָה טְפָחִים. רַבִּי יְהוּדָה אוֹמֵר:
אִם יֵשׁ לוֹ צוּרַת פֶּתַח, אַף עַל פִּי שֶׁאֵינוֹ גָבוֹהַּ
עֲשָׂרָה טְפָחִים, אֵינוֹ מָכוּר.

יד אברהם

practices of that time as they related to the architectural styles and usages of those
days. However, all such regulations are dependent upon the prevailing custom in
any given time or place *(Rambam, Mechirah* 26:8). The *Tosefta* states this rule
explicitly in regard to the case discussed in mishnah 5:5; see comm. there.

1.

The first three mishnayos of this chapter consider the sale of a house. In the
custom of those days, it was common for different parts of the house to be owned
by different people. Consequently, the only parts of the structure automatically
included in the sale are those which serve as areas of residence — the primary
function of a house.

הַמּוֹכֵר אֶת הַבַּיִת לֹא מָכַר הַיָּצִיעַ, — *One who*
sells a house has not sold the annex,

This refers to a structure which was
built over the outside walls of a house or
set into the thickness of the wall itself.
Although it is attached to the house, it is
considered a separate structure and is
therefore not automatically sold along
with the house *(Yad Ramah)*. However,
if it is smaller than four cubits by four
cubits, it is not of sufficient significance
to be considered an independent
structure, and it is then dealt with as
part of the house *(Rav from Gem.* 61a).

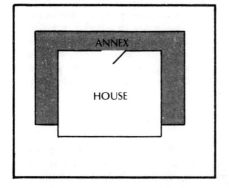

ANNEX

HOUSE

Rashbam (61a) understands this to be a
kind of colonnade attached to the outside of a
house which is enclosed by windows rather
than regular walls. Such a structure is built
for its esthetic quality and as a kind of
summerhouse in which to cool oneself on hot
days; it is therefore not considered an
integral part of the house. However, a
functional room attached to the outer walls of
a house would, in this view, go along with
the house.

The amount of money paid cannot be
used to determine what was included in
the sale, because the worth of a given
property is often dependent upon
factors other than its utilitarian value
[e.g., sentimental attachments or family
considerations] (see *Tos.* 61b; and
comm. to mishnah 4, s.v. רבי אלעזר).

וְאַף עַל פִּי שֶׁהִיא פְתוּחָה לְתוֹכוֹ; — *even*
though it opens into it;

Even if the only door to the annex
opens from the house it is still viewed as
a separate unit *(Sema* 214:2).

וְלֹא אֶת הַחֶדֶר שֶׁלִּפְנִים מִמֶּנּוּ; — *nor the*
room which is to the rear of [the house];

This type of room served as a storage
area and did not function as part of the

4
1

1. One who sells a house has not sold the annex, even though it opens into it; nor the room which is to the rear of [the house]; nor the roof when it has a parapet ten handbreadths high. R' Yehudah says: If it has a doorway, even if it is not ten handbreadths high, it is not included in the sale.

YAD AVRAHAM

house (Rashbam). Therefore, even if it can only be reached through the house, it is not automatically included in the sale (Rav).

This statement of the mishnah appears superfluous, since such a room is even less a part of the house than the annex, which the mishnah has already stated is not sold with the house. The novelty of this ruling is that even if the seller specified the dimensions of the house being sold, and the room is within those boundaries, it is still not included in the sale unless the seller specifically mentions it. Since such an area is not normally considered part of the house, the assumption must be that, in describing the dimensions, precision was sacrificed in favor of easily recognizable landmarks (Gem. 61b; Tos. Yom Tov).

Some authorities maintain that, in contrast to the annex, a room such as this is considered separate from the house even if it is less than four cubits by four cubits (Rambam, Mechirah 25:2). Others do not differentiate (Yad Ramah §2).

וְלֹא אֶת הַגָּג — **nor the roof**

In Mishnaic times, roofs were built flat and were used not only to cover a house but as functional areas as well (Aruch Hashulchan, Choshen Mishpat 214:4). [Therefore, their ownership was often independent of that of the house itself and they were thus identified separately in a bill of sale.] However, the roof must be at least four cubits square (Rambam, Mechirah 25:2; Choshen Mishpat 214:2) to be considered an entity unto itself (Meiri).

Others contend that a roof is sufficiently distinct in its function from the house to be considered a separate unit even if it is smaller than four cubits square (Yad Ramah §2).

בִּזְמַן שֶׁיֵּשׁ לוֹ מַעֲקֶה גָּבוֹהַּ עֲשָׂרָה טְפָחִים. — **when it has a parapet ten handbreadths high.**

For purposes of safety, a roof designated for use requires a fence ten handbreadths high around it (Deut. 22:8; Choshen Mishpat 427). Thus, if the fence around the roof is lower than ten handbreadths, it is obvious that the roof is not being used for any purpose other than shelter. Therefore, the roof is considered part of the house and is automatically sold along with it (Rashbam 64a; Rama; Choshen Mishpat 214:3).

רַבִּי יְהוּדָה אוֹמֵר: אִם יֵשׁ לוֹ צוּרַת פֶּתַח, אַף עַל פִּי שֶׁאֵינוֹ גָבוֹהַּ עֲשָׂרָה טְפָחִים, אֵינוֹ מָכוּר. — **R' Yehudah says: If it has a doorway, even if it is not ten handbreadths high, it is not included in the sale.**

[If the roof has a doorway, it indicates that it has been designated for use. Therefore, it is considered a separate entity even without a parapet ten handbreadths high, and it is not automatically included in the sale of the house.]

2.

This mishnah continues its discussion of which parts of a structure are automatically included in the sale of a house. The case considered here is that of a water cistern or pit. The houses of those days did not customarily contain a built-in

[85]   THE MISHNAH/BAVA BASRA – Chapter Four: HaMocher Es HaBayis

[ב] **לֹא** אֶת הַבּוֹר וְלֹא אֶת הַדּוּת, אַף עַל פִּי שֶׁכָּתַב לוֹ ,,עָמְקָא וְרוּמָא.'' וְצָרִיךְ לִקַּח לוֹ דֶרֶךְ; דִּבְרֵי רַבִּי עֲקִיבָא. וַחֲכָמִים אוֹמְרִים: אֵינוֹ צָרִיךְ לִקַּח לוֹ דֶרֶךְ. וּמוֹדֶה רַבִּי עֲקִיבָא בִּזְמַן שֶׁאָמַר לוֹ ,,חוּץ מֵאֵלּוּ,'' שֶׁאֵינוֹ צָרִיךְ לִקַּח לוֹ דֶרֶךְ. מְכָרָן לְאַחֵר, רַבִּי עֲקִיבָא אוֹמֵר: אֵינוֹ צָרִיךְ לִקַּח לוֹ דֶרֶךְ. וַחֲכָמִים אוֹמְרִים: צָרִיךְ לִקַּח לוֹ דֶרֶךְ.

יד אברהם

water reservoir. Rather, these were centrally located and the residents of the area would come to draw water from them and carry it home to store in a water barrel for later use. The mishnah, however, considers the case of a house which does contain its own private water reservoir.

לֹא אֶת הַבּוֹר — [He has] not [sold] the pit
One who sells a house is not understood to have included in the sale a pit dug in the floor of the house for use as a water reservoir. [Since houses did not usually come equipped with a private reservoir,] a reservoir could not be considered to function as part of a house (Rav). Therefore, even if a house contained one, it would not be considered an integral part of the house, and would thus not be included in its sale (Tif. Yis.).

וְלֹא אֶת הַדּוּת, — nor the cistern,
I.e., an above-ground stone structure used to store large quantities of water (Rav). Others explain that this refers to a stone-lined water cistern dug into the ground (Rashbam to 64a; see Yad Avraham comm. to ArtScroll Rosh Hashanah 3:7, s.v. או לתוך הדות).

אַף עַל פִּי שֶׁכָּתַב לוֹ ,,עָמְקָא וְרוּמָא.'' — even if he wrote [in the contract], 'the depth and the height.'
Even if the seller specified in the contract that he was selling the depth and height of the house, the various types of cisterns are not included. The contractual sense of these words denotes only the airspace above the house —

which allows him to add to the height of the building — and the ground upon which it stands, neither of which would have otherwise been included in the sale (Gem. 63b; Rashbam; cf. Rambam Comm.).

If the contract does not specify the depth and the height, the seller retains the ground beneath the house, and thus the right to dig in it as long as it does not damage the house.[1] Similarly, the seller retains the right to the airspace above the house, enabling him to extend a balcony or the like from his own house over the sold house, provided it does not rest on the roof of that house (Rashbam 63a).

According to some commentators, this ruling of the mishnah refers only to the pit and the cistern; a roof with a parapet ten handbreadths high, however, is included in the sale if the contract specifies the depth and the height (Rashbam 63b). Similarly, an annex and rear room (see mishnah 1) are also included (Nimmukei Yosef). Tosafos (63b), however, rule that the roof is not included in the stipulation of height and depth.

However, if the contract stated that he is selling from the depths of the ground to the height of the heavens, it includes even a pit and cistern [as well as a roof], because the extra wording signifies that he is selling more

---

1. Others contend that this is forbidden, since he may unwittingly cause damage. However, if the buyer digs there, the pit he digs belongs to the seller (Mahari Halevi, cited by Tur 214).

משניות / בבא בתרא — פרק ד: המוכר את.הבית   [86]

4
2

2. [H]e has] not [sold] the pit nor the cistern, even if he wrote [in the contract], 'the depth and the height.' And he must buy [back] for himself a [right-of-]way; [these are] the words of R' Akiva. The Sages, however, say: He need not buy [back] a [right-of-]way. R' Akiva, however, agrees that when he said to him, 'except for these,' he need not buy [back] for himself a [right-of-]way. [If] he sold them to another, R' Akiva says: He need not buy a [right-of-]way. The Sages, however, say: He must buy a [right-of-]way.

YAD AVRAHAM

than would be indicated with only the words 'the depth and the height' *(Rav from Gem. 63b; see Tos. R' Akiva Eiger).*

וְצָרִיךְ לִקַּח לוֹ דֶרֶךְ; דִּבְרֵי רַבִּי עֲקִיבָא. — *And he must buy [back] for himself a [right-of-]way; [these are] the words of R' Akiva.*

Although he did not sell the pit, he did sell the entire house, and this sale is assumed to be all-inclusive. This is based on the legal assumption that when a person sells something, he does so generously (בְּעַיִן יָפָה), without retaining any rights to it for himself *(Rav from Gem. 64b).* [The pit is excluded because it is not considered part of the house and therefore not the subject of the sale.] Thus, he now has no access to his pit unless he buys back a right-of-way through the house.

וַחֲכָמִים אוֹמְרִים: אֵינוֹ צָרִיךְ לִקַּח לוֹ דֶרֶךְ. — *The Sages, however, say: He need not buy [back] a [right-of-]way.*

The Sages dispute R' Akiva's legal assumption and contend that a seller is not customarily generous in his sale (מוֹכֵר בְּעַיִן רָעָה). Thus it may be assumed that he retained his right to pass through the house in order to reach his pit within (ibid.).

וּמוֹדֶה רַבִּי עֲקִיבָא בִּזְמַן שֶׁאָמַר לוֹ „חוּץ מֵאֵלּוּ," — *R' Akiva, however, agrees that when he said to him, 'except for these,'*

I.e., when he specified that he is selling him the house without the pit or cistern which is in it *(Rav).*

שֶׁאֵינוֹ צָרִיךְ לִקַּח לוֹ דֶרֶךְ. — *he need not buy [back] for himself a [right-of-]way.*

Since his exclusion of the pit or vault was unnecessary, as they would in any case not have been included in the sale, the addition of this stipulation is understood to indicate that the right-of-way which facilitates their use is also being excluded from the sale *(Rav).*

According to the Sages who maintain that even without writing 'except for these,' the right-of-way would be retained, his inclusion of that phrase does not add anything, but is understood as an effort by the seller to avoid subsequent conflict with the buyer over this somewhat ambiguous point *(Tos. Yom Tov from Rashbam 64a).*

מְכָרָן לְאַחֵר, — *[If] he sold them to another,*

The mishnah now considers the reverse case, where the owner of the house sold just the pit or cistern to another, and retained the house for himself *(Rav; Rashbam; cf. Rambam Comm., Tos. R' Akiva Eiger).*

רַבִּי עֲקִיבָא אוֹמֵר: אֵינוֹ צָרִיךְ לִקַּח לוֹ דֶרֶךְ. — *R' Akiva says: He need not buy a [right-of-]way.*

The buyer need not purchase the right-of-way to his pit, because, according to R' Akiva, the seller is

נג] הַמּוֹכֵר אֶת הַבַּיִת מָכַר אֶת הַדֶּלֶת, אֲבָל
לֹא אֶת הַמַּפְתֵּחַ; מָכַר אֶת
הַמַּכְתֶּשֶׁת הַקְּבוּעָה, אֲבָל לֹא אֶת הַמִּטַּלְטֶלֶת;
מָכַר אֶת הָאִצְטְרוֹבָל, אֲבָל לֹא אֶת הַקֶּלֶת; וְלֹא
אֶת הַתַּנּוּר וְלֹא אֶת הַכִּירַיִם. בִּזְמַן שֶׁאָמַר לוֹ
„הוּא וְכָל מַה שֶּׁבְּתוֹכוֹ," הֲרֵי כֻלָּן מְכוּרִין.

נד] הַמּוֹכֵר אֶת הֶחָצֵר מָכַר בָּתִּים, בּוֹרוֹת,

יד אברהם

generous in his sale, and the right-of-way is therefore assumed to have been included (Rav).

[R' Akiva is consistent with his previous ruling, which also assumed that the seller acts generously while retaining less for himself. Thus, when he sells the house and retains the pit, he does not retain the access; conversely, when he sells the pit and retains the house, he deals generously and includes the access.]

וַחֲכָמִים אוֹמְרִים: צָרִיךְ לָקַח לוֹ דֶרֶךְ. — *The Sages, however, say: He must buy a [right-of-]way.*

[Since they maintain that a seller retains for himself as much as possible, they do not assume that right-of-way is automatically included in the sale of the pit.]

The halachah follows the opinion of R' Akiva (Rav from Gem. 65a; Rambam, Mechirah 25:3; Choshen Mishpat 214:2).

3.

Having dealt with which parts of the overall structure of the house are considered part of the house and thus included in its sale, the mishnah now moves on to consider the status of household items within the dwelling.

הַמּוֹכֵר אֶת הַבַּיִת — *One who sells a house*
I.e., without specifying which household items are included in the sale (Rav).

מָכַר אֶת הַדֶּלֶת, — *has sold the door,*
Doors are included because anything which is attached to a house and serves its needs is considered part of the house (Rav). Similarly, a bolt which is attached to the door is also sold with the house (Meiri).

אֲבָל לֹא אֶת הַמַּפְתֵּחַ; — *but not the key;*
A key is not attached to a house and thus cannot be considered part of it (Rav). Even if it is usually left in the lock it is not considered part of the

house because it can be easily removed and, indeed, sometimes is (Rashbam 65b).

מָכַר אֶת הַמַּכְתֶּשֶׁת הַקְּבוּעָה, — *he has sold the fixed mortar,*
I.e., a mortar (for pounding spices and the like) which is set in place in the ground (Rav). Even one which was built as a utensil and then cemented into the ground [rather than being hollowed out from rocks already in place] is also considered a *fixed mortar* (Meleches Shlomo from Gem. 65b).

אֲבָל לֹא אֶת הַמִּטַּלְטֶלֶת; — *but not the portable one;*
Since it is not physically attached to the house, it is not considered part of it

3. **O**ne who sells a house has sold the door, but not the key; he has sold the fixed mortar, but not the portable one; he has sold the pedestal of the mill, but not the flour-catch; nor the oven nor the stove. When he said to him, 'It, and all that is in it,' they are all sold.

4. **O**ne who sells a courtyard has sold the houses,

YAD AVRAHAM

even though it rests permanently in one place in the house (Meiri).

מָכַר אֶת הָאִצְטְרוּבָּל, — he has sold the pedestal of the mill,

This is a round wooden pedestal on which the millstone is placed (Rav).

אֲבָל לֹא אֶת הַקֶּלֶת; — but not the flour-catch;

This is a removable utensil which is placed around the mill to collect the ground flour (Rav). According to Rashbam this is the hopper in which the wheat is placed prior to being milled (see Meleches Shlomo, Tif. Yis.).

Meiri translates אִצְטְרוּבָּל as the lower millstone of a regular mill, and קֶלֶת as the upper, removable stone. The lower stone is cemented to the ground.

וְלֹא אֶת הַתַּנּוּר וְלֹא אֶת הַכִּירַיִם. — nor the oven nor the stove.

[See comm. to 3:5, 2:2.] This mishnah is discussing a portable oven and stove, neither of which are considered part of the house (Rav).

There is an alternate version of the mishnah which reads, he has sold the oven and the stove. According to this version, the mishnah refers to ovens and stoves built into the ground which are therefore considered part of the house (Rav).

בִּזְמַן שֶׁאָמַר לוֹ ,,הוּא וְכָל מַה שֶׁבְּתוֹכוֹ,'' הֲרֵי

כֻּלָּן מְכוּרִין. — When he said to him, 'It, and all that is in it,' they are all sold.

If this clause was added to the contract, all of the utensils mentioned above are included in the sale of the house because they do, to a certain extent, relate to this house specifically. Although these items are removable, they are seldom ever taken out of the house because of their weight. Thus, their use is keyed in some measure to this particular house. However, other portable household utensils, whose use does not bind them to a specific house, are not considered to be part of the house and are not automatically sold along with it (Rav; Rashbam 65b). Others dispute this last ruling and maintain that any objects which are designated for household use — e.g., beds, mattresses, dishes and silverware — are included in this clause as long as they are in the house when it is purchased (Yad Ramah).

Even in this case, the sale does not include the annex, pit, or cistern mentioned in the first two mishnayos (Gem. 65b), because those are considered independent entities and are therefore unaffected by this clause (Yad Ramah). However, if he specified that he was selling him all that is to be found within certain specified boundaries, those are also included (Nimmukei Yosef to mishnah 5).

4.

הַמּוֹכֵר אֶת הֶחָצֵר מָכַר בָּתִּים, — One who sells a courtyard has sold the houses,

The sale includes the houses which open into the courtyard (Rav).[1]

1. In Mishnaic times, and in some parts of the world even today, houses were built in clusters around a central courtyard. Thus, the term courtyard came to mean not only the open area in

שִׁיחִין, וּמְעָרוֹת; אֲבָל לֹא אֶת הַמִּטַּלְטְלִין. בִּזְמַן
שֶׁאָמַר לוֹ ,,הִיא, וְכָל מַה שֶׁבְּתוֹכָהּ,'' הֲרֵי כֻלָּן
מְכוּרִין. בֵּין כָּךְ וּבֵין כָּךְ, לֹא מָכַר לֹא אֶת הַמֶּרְחָץ
וְלֹא אֶת בֵּית הַבַּד שֶׁבְּתוֹכָהּ. רַבִּי אֱלִיעֶזֶר אוֹמֵר:
הַמּוֹכֵר אֶת הֶחָצֵר לֹא מָכַר אֶלָּא אֲוִירָהּ שֶׁל חָצֵר.

[ה] **הַמּוֹכֵר** אֶת בֵּית הַבַּד מָכַר אֶת הַיָּם, וְאֶת
הַמַּמָּל, וְאֶת הַבְּתוּלוֹת; אֲבָל לֹא

יד אברהם

בּוֹרוֹת, שִׁיחִין, וּמְעָרוֹת; — *pits, ditches, and vaults;*

Also included in the sale of a courtyard are any pits, ditches and vaults which are inside the houses of the courtyard (*Rav*). Although they are not included in the sale of the houses, they are included in that of the courtyard. Courtyards generally contained a reservoir within them [to facilitate laundering and watering animals (*Rashba*)], while houses did not (*Ri Migash*).

Similarly, an annex, roof and rear room (mishnah 1) are also included in the sale of the courtyard (*Yad Ramah*).

אֲבָל לֹא אֶת הַמִּטַּלְטְלִין. — *but not the movables.*

Although the sale of a courtyard includes in it items not included in the sale of a house, it still does not include movable household utensils. Thus, all items listed in the previous mishnah as being excluded from the sale of a house because they are not fixed to the ground are also excluded from the sale of a courtyard, as are all other utensils designated for household use (*Rashbam* 67a).

בִּזְמַן שֶׁאָמַר לוֹ ,,הִיא, וְכָל מַה שֶׁבְּתוֹכָהּ,'' הֲרֵי כֻלָּן מְכוּרִין. — *When he said to him, 'It, and all that is in it,' they are all sold.*

If the seller specified that he is selling the courtyard and all that is in it, all

household utensils are included in the sale, and only food items are excluded (*Rashbam; Yad Ramah; Meiri*).

In contrast to one who sells his house (who does not include household utensils; see mishnah 3), one who sells an entire courtyard is assumed to be moving completely away from the area, and it would therefore involve a great deal of bother for him to haul away even these smaller items. Thus, when he expressly stipulated 'all that is in it,' it may reasonably be assumed that his intention was to rid himself of all his household goods. Furthermore, a courtyard, being a more complete habitat, includes even general household utensils. As a general rule, the larger the property one sells, the more inclusive the terms of the sale are assumed to be (*Rashbam* 65b).

Nimmukei Yosef, however, disputes this and is of the opinion that general household utensils are not included even in the sale of a courtyard. In his view the mishnah includes in the sale of a courtyard only those items listed in the previous mishnah.

בֵּין כָּךְ וּבֵין כָּךְ, לֹא מָכַר לֹא אֶת הַמֶּרְחָץ וְלֹא אֶת בֵּית הַבַּד שֶׁבְּתוֹכָהּ. — *In any case, he has not sold the bathhouse or the olive press which are in it.*

Bathhouses and olive presses are not

the middle but the whole cluster of houses opening into it, much as the word 'mall' has today come to refer to the shops lining it as well as the mall itself.

4
5
pits, ditches, and vaults; but not the movables. When
he said to him, 'It, and all that is in it,' they are all
sold. In any case, he has not sold the bathhouse or the
olive press which are in it. R' Eliezer says: One who
sells a courtyard has sold only the airspace of the
courtyard.

5. One who sells an olive press has sold the
grinding block, the millstone, and the posts;

YAD AVRAHAM

considered an integral part of a courtyard, even if they happen to be located in one (Rav). They are not generally found in courtyards and in fact their design equips them to handle the needs of several courtyards (Nimmukei Yosef). Therefore, even one who specifies that he is selling the courtyard and all that is in it is not understood to have these in mind.

רַבִּי אֱלִיעֶזֶר אוֹמֵר: הַמּוֹכֵר אֶת הֶחָצֵר לֹא מָכַר אֶלָּא אֲוִירָהּ שֶׁל חָצֵר. — *R' Eliezer says: One who sells a courtyard has sold only the airspace of the courtyard.*

R' Eliezer disputes the basic premise of the first *Tanna* and maintains that

mention of a courtyard refers only to the open space of the courtyard, not to its structures (*Tif. Yis.*). The Rabbis, however, contend that it refers to everything located in the courtyard as well, just as the Scriptural reference to the courtyard of the Tabernacle includes the Tabernacle itself as well as its yard (*Gem.* 67a).

We cannot ascertain what the sale includes from the price paid, because there are many intangible factors which may effect the value of a property to a certain individual, and the discrepancy in price may have been a result of such factors rather than incorrect payment (*Tos.* 61b, s.v. שמע מינה; see *Tos. R' Akiva Eiger*).

5.

This mishnah discusses the sale of the building containing an olive press, used to extract oil from olives. There were two basic structures in such a building, the press itself, and a mill to grind the olives into small pieces prior to pressing in order to facilitate the process. Although there were many variations of the press, the basic structure of the type discussed in our mishnah was as follows: Two upright posts supported a screw which was connected to a stone or beam. Beneath this was a container into which sacks of olives were placed, after they had been ground in the mill. Boards were placed atop these sacks across the container. The screw was then turned to lower the stone (or beam) onto the boards, thereby pressing them down on the sacks of olives and squeezing out their oil.

הַמּוֹכֵר אֶת בֵּית הַבַּד — *One who sells an olive press*
I.e., the building which houses an olive press and is designated solely for that purpose (*Rashbam* 67b).

מָכַר אֶת הַיָּם, — *has sold the grinding block,*
This was a stone with a hollow in it in which the olives were placed for

grinding (*Rav; Rambam Comm.*). Rashbam (67a) explains this to refer to the vat of the press, into which the olives were placed to be squeezed.

וְאֶת הַמֶּמָּל, — *the millstone,*
This was the top part of the mill, which ground the olives into small pieces to prepare them for the press (*Rav; Rambam Comm.*).

מָכַר אֶת הָעֲכִירִין, וְאֶת הַגַּלְגַּל, וְאֶת הַקּוֹרָה.
וּבִזְמַן שֶׁאָמַר לוֹ ,,הוּא, וְכָל מַה שֶּׁבְּתוֹכוֹ," הֲרֵי
כֻּלָּן מְכוּרִין. רַבִּי אֱלִיעֶזֶר אוֹמֵר: הַמּוֹכֵר בֵּית הַבַּד
מָכַר אֶת הַקּוֹרָה.

[ו] **הַמּוֹכֵר** אֶת הַמֶּרְחָץ לֹא מָכַר אֶת
הַנְּסָרִים, וְאֶת הַסַּפְסָלִים, וְאֶת
הַוִּילָאוֹת. בִּזְמַן שֶׁאָמַר לוֹ ,,הוּא, וְכָל מַה
שֶּׁבְּתוֹכוֹ," הֲרֵי כֻּלָּן מְכוּרִין. בֵּין כָּךְ וּבֵין כָּךְ, לֹא
מָכַר לֹא אֶת הַמְּגוּרוֹת שֶׁל מַיִם וְלֹא אֶת אוֹצָרוֹת
שֶׁל עֵצִים.

יד אברהם

According to *Rashbam*, this refers to the hollow stone at the bottom, in which the olives were placed to be ground up. *Rambam* (*Mechirah* 25:7), however, interprets this as the vat in which the ground olives were pressed.

וְאֶת הַבְּתוּלוֹת; — *and the posts;*

The posts which supported the beam of the press (*Rav*). These were attached to the ends of the press vat from two sides, and pierced opposite each other. A crossbar was placed through these slots, to which the beam [i.e., the screw which controlled the beam (R' Yisrael Belsky)] was connected (*Rashbam* 67b).

These were all automatically included in the sale of the press, because every press had its own set of these accessories, and such items were not usually rented or borrowed (*Yad Ramah*).

According to *Rashbam*, all these items were attached to the ground and thus were permanent fixtures. [This approach is valid only according to *Rashbam's* own interpretation of the items listed. According to *Rav* and *Rambam*, not all of these were permanent fixtures.]

אֲבָל לֹא מָכַר אֶת הָעֲכִירִין, — *but he has not sold the boards,*

The boards which were placed upon the sacks of olives to squeeze out their oil (*Rav*).

וְאֶת הַגַּלְגַּל, — *the screw,*

The screw turned the beam and lowered it to press down on the boards (*Rav*).

וְאֶת הַקּוֹרָה. — *or the beam.*

The beam which pressed down on the boards and supplied the pressure which squeezed the oil from the olives (*Rashbam* 67b).

These are not included in the sale, because in many cases the owner of an olive press simply borrowed or rented these items when he needed them. They were therefore not considered an integral part of the press (*Yad Ramah*).

Alternatively, since these were removable components and not permanent fixtures in the press, they were not automatically included in the purchase (*Rashbam*).

וּבִזְמַן שֶׁאָמַר לוֹ ,,הוּא, וְכָל מַה שֶּׁבְּתוֹכוֹ," הֲרֵי כֻּלָּן מְכוּרִין. — *When he said to him, 'It, and all that is in it,' they are all sold.*

[This additional clause is understood to include anything which is a necessary component of a working olive press.] However, utensils which are not necessary for the olive press but are merely kept there for safekeeping are not included in the sale (*Rashbam* 67b).

Rambam (*Mechirah* 25:7) rules that only the top stone of the mill is affected by this statement, being included in the sale only if

but he has not sold the boards, the screw, or the beam. When he said to him, 'It, and all that is in it,' they are all sold. R' Eliezer says: One who sells an olive press has sold the beam.

6. **O**ne who sells a bathhouse has not sold the boards, the benches, or the curtains. When he said to him, 'It, and all that is in it,' they are all sold. In any case, he did not sell the water reservoirs nor the stores of wood.

YAD AVRAHAM

the seller specified that he was selling all that was in it. Apparently, *Rambam* had a different version to the mishnah, which stated this ruling (*Maggid Mishneh, Kesef Mishneh*).[1]

רַבִּי אֱלִיעֶזֶר אוֹמֵר: הַמּוֹכֵר בֵּית הַבַּד מָכַר

אֶת הַקּוֹרָה. — *R' Eliezer says: One who sells an olive press has sold the beam.*

R' Eliezer includes the beam in the sale because the beam is the primary instrument for pressing the olives (*Gem.* 67b; *Rashbam*).[2]

6.

הַמּוֹכֵר אֶת הַמֶּרְחָץ — *One who sells a bathhouse*

The standard bathhouses of those times had three rooms: the innermost room for bathing, the middle room for undressing, and the outer room for waiting. The sale of a bathhouse included all three of these rooms (*Rashbam* 67b).

לֹא מָכַר אֶת הַנְּסָרִים, — *has not sold the boards,*

The boards upon which people placed their clothing (*Rav; Rambam Comm.*) were movable, and thus not part of the bathhouse (*Rashbam*). Others explain this as referring to the boards which were placed upon the floor to protect the bathers' feet from the mud and heat of the ground near the bath (*Rashbam*), or to the boards used to cover the hot water to hold in its heat (*Tos.* 67b).

וְאֶת הַסַּפְסָלִים, — *the benches,*

The benches upon which they sat. Other versions have הַסְּפָלִים, *containers,* referring to the containers in which the water for bathing was stored (*Rav*).

וְאֶת הַוִּילָאוֹת. — *or the curtains.*

I.e., the curtains which covered the entrance to the bathhouse. Alternatively, these were the towels which were kept in the bathhouse, or aprons which were worn in the bathhouse for purposes of modesty (*Rav*).

בִּזְמַן שֶׁאָמַר לוֹ ,,הוּא, וְכָל מַה שֶׁבְּתוֹכוֹ,, הֲרֵי כֻלָּן מְכוּרִין. — *When he said to him, 'It, and all that is in it,' they are all sold.*

[If the owner of the bathhouse stipulated that he was selling all contents of the bathhouse, the above items are sold along with it.]

בֵּין כָּךְ וּבֵין כָּךְ, — *In any case,*

[I.e., even if he specified the

1. This version is plausible only according to *Rambam's* opinion in his code that מַעֲל refers to the utensil into which the ground olives were placed, but not according to that which he writes in his commentary, that it refers to the top stone of the mill.

2. Although the boards seem to be as fundamental to the process as the beam, this is not actually the case. There were some olive presses which did not use these boards at all, but rather relied upon the beam itself to press the olives directly.

[ז] הַמּוֹכֵר אֶת הָעִיר מָכַר בָּתִּים, בּוֹרוֹת, שִׁיחִין, וּמְעָרוֹת, מֶרְחֲצָאוֹת, וְשׁוֹבָכוֹת, בֵּית הַבַּדִּין, וּבֵית הַשְּׁלָחִין; אֲבָל לֹא אֶת הַמִּטַּלְטְלִין. וּבִזְמַן שֶׁאָמַר לוֹ ,,הִיא, וְכָל מַה שֶּׁבְּתוֹכָהּ,'' אֲפִלּוּ הָיוּ בָהּ בְּהֵמָה וַעֲבָדִים, הֲרֵי כֻלָּן מְכוּרִין. רַבָּן שִׁמְעוֹן בֶּן גַּמְלִיאֵל אוֹמֵר: הַמּוֹכֵר אֶת הָעִיר מָכַר אֶת הַסַּנְטֵר.

[ח] הַמּוֹכֵר אֶת הַשָּׂדֶה מָכַר אֶת הָאֲבָנִים שֶׁהֵם לְצָרְכָּהּ, וְאֶת הַקָּנִים

יד אברהם

bathhouse and all its contents.]

לֹא מָכַר לֹא אֶת הַמְּגוּרוֹת שֶׁל מַיִם וְלֹא אֶת אוֹצָרוֹת שֶׁל עֵצִים — *he did not sell the water reservoirs nor the stores of wood.*

These provided the water for the bathhouse and the fuel to heat it (*Rav*). They are not included in the sale because their usefulness is not limited to the bathhouse, but may be used by the owner to supply his home as well (*Rashbam* 67b). At the same time, their storage function is not vital to the operation of the bathhouse since the owner can obtain water and wood daily (*Nimmukei Yosef*).

7.

The following mishnah discusses the sale of a privately owned town.

הַמּוֹכֵר אֶת הָעִיר מָכַר בָּתִּים, — *One who sells a town has sold the houses,*

I.e., all the houses in the town, and certainly the courtyards, which are the essence of the town (*Rav*).

בּוֹרוֹת, שִׁיחִין, וּמְעָרוֹת, מֶרְחֲצָאוֹת, וְשׁוֹבָכוֹת, בֵּית הַבַּדִּין, — *pits, ditches, vaults, bathhouses, dovecotes, olive presses,*

[Although the sale of a courtyard does not include a bathhouse and olive press which happen to be located in it (see mishnah 4), these are included in the sale of the town as a whole because they are considered an integral part of a town.]

וּבֵית הַשְּׁלָחִין; — *and irrigated fields;*

This refers specifically to gardens and orchards which belong to the town (*Rav* from *Gem.* 68a). These are called בֵּית הַשְּׁלָחִין based on the verse (*Song of Songs* 4:13): שְׁלָחַיִךְ פַּרְדֵּס רִמּוֹנִים, *Your irrigated fields are orchards of pomegranates* (*Gem.*). However, grain fields are not included in this sale, because they are less a part of the town itself than the gardens, in which the inhabitants of the town go for strolls (*Rashbam*).

There is another view in the *Gemara* (68a) which interprets irrigated fields to include grain fields as well as gardens. *Rambam* (*Mechirah* 26:1) rules in accordance with this opinion (see also *Tur* and *Choshen Mishpat* 215:4).

אֲבָל לֹא אֶת הַמִּטַּלְטְלִין. — *but not the movables.*

He has not sold the movable utensils which serve the needs of the town, such as the key to the town gates or the grain receiver for the mill, and certainly not the town's food supplies (*Rav*). Nor are the cattle and the slaves of the town included in the sale (*Meiri*).

7. One who sells a town has sold the houses, pits, ditches, vaults, bathhouses, dovecotes, olive presses, and irrigated fields; but not the movables. When he said to him, 'It, and all that is in it,' even if there were cattle and slaves in it, they are all sold. Rabban Shimon ben Gamliel says: One who sells a town has sold the sentry.

8. One who sells a field has sold the stones which are needed for it, the reeds in the vineyard

YAD AVRAHAM

וּבִזְמַן שֶׁאָמַר לוֹ "הִיא, וְכָל מַה שֶּׁבְּתוֹכָה," — אֲפִלּוּ הָיוּ בָהּ בְּהֵמָה וַעֲבָדִים, הֲרֵי כֻלָּן מְכוּרִין. *When he said to him, 'It, and all that is in it,' even if there were cattle and slaves in it, they are all sold.*

Even the cattle and slaves, which move of their own accord [and are thus more completely separated from the land], are included in the sale of the town and all its contents, and certainly the food supplies as well *(Rav)*. Although these are not included in the sale of a courtyard (see comm. to mishnah 4), the sale of an entire town is more inclusive. In addition, one who sells a town and moves away intends to take along fewer belongings than one

who is moving only from one courtyard to another *(Rashbam 65b)*.

רַבָּן שִׁמְעוֹן בֶּן גַּמְלִיאֵל אוֹמֵר: הַמּוֹכֵר אֶת הָעִיר מָכַר אֶת הַסַּנְטֵר. — *Rabban Shimon ben Gamliel says: One who sells a town has sold the sentry.*

I.e., the slave appointed to stand watch over the town *(Rav from Gem. 68a following R' Chananel)*.[1] According to this opinion, grain fields around the town, which are immobile, are certainly included in the sale *(Gem., Rashbam 68a)*. Others translate this to mean a slave appointed to keep track of the boundaries of the properties *(Rashbam)*.

8

הַמּוֹכֵר אֶת הַשָּׂדֶה מָכַר אֶת הָאֲבָנִים שֶׁהֵם לְצָרְכָּהּ, — *One who sells a field has sold the stones which are needed for it,*

I.e., the stones which had been set aside for building a wall around the field *(Rav, Tif. Yis. from Gem. 69a)*. Although these are movable, they are considered part of the field because their placement there was with the intention of fixing them in that place *(Rashbam 68b)*.

The *Gemara* (69a) cites the opinion of R' Meir (78b) that one who sells a vineyard has also sold all items which serve the needs of the vineyard. The *Gemara* here states that the extent to which service items are included is disputed by the Rabbis, who include less in the sale than does R' Meir. Accordingly, our mishnah, which discusses which objects are included in the sale of a field, must be explained according to the opinions of both R' Meir and the Rabbis.

The *Gemara* explains that, according to R'

1. The *Gemara* (68a) explains that according to the second opinion mentioned above, that בֵּית הַשְּׁלָחִין refers to *gardens* (and not grain fields), then סַנְטֵר refers to grain fields. These are included in the sale, but a watchman, who is mobile, is not. Accordingly, *Rav's* commentary does not seem consistent with the *Gemara*, since if סַנְטֵר means *watchman*, as he states here, בֵּית הַשְּׁלָחִין must refer also to grain fields and not only to gardens and orchards, as *Rav* explained above *(Tos. Yom Tov)*.

שֶׁבַּכֶּרֶם שֶׁהֵם לְצָרְכּוֹ, וְאֶת הַתְּבוּאָה שֶׁהִיא
מְחֻבֶּרֶת לַקַּרְקַע, וְאֶת מְחֻצַּת הַקָּנִים שֶׁהִיא
פְּחוּתָה מִבֵּית רֹבַע, וְאֶת הַשּׁוֹמֵרָה שֶׁאֵינָהּ עֲשׂוּיָה
בְטִיט, וְאֶת הֶחָרוּב שֶׁאֵינוֹ מֻרְכָּב, וְאֶת בְּתוּלַת
הַשִּׁקְמָה.

[ט] **אֲבָל,** לֹא מָכַר לֹא אֶת הָאֲבָנִים שֶׁאֵינָן
לְצָרְכָּהּ, וְלֹא אֶת הַקָּנִים שֶׁבַּכֶּרֶם
שֶׁאֵינָן לְצָרְכּוֹ, וְלֹא אֶת הַתְּבוּאָה שֶׁהִיא תְלוּשָׁה
מִן הַקַּרְקַע. בִּזְמַן שֶׁאָמַר לוֹ ,,הִיא, וְכָל מַה

יד אברהם

Meir, the sale of a field includes any stones which have been selected for use in a fence, even if they have merely been heaped in the field; the Rabbis, on the other hand, maintain that they must be stacked one on top of the other (in preparation for building the fence) in order to be considered part of the field.

וְאֶת הַקָּנִים שֶׁבַּכֶּרֶם שֶׁהֵם לְצָרְכּוֹ, — *the reeds in the vineyard that are needed for it,*

Reeds were split at the top and used to support clusters of grapes so that they should not be spoiled by touching the ground (*Gem.; Rashbam* 69a; cf. *Tos.*).

According to R' Meir, these are included in the sale if they have merely been split at the top; according to the Rabbis, they must actually be in use (*Gem.* ibid.).

From this statement of the mishnah, it is clear that one who sells his field to another includes any vineyards which are within that field, and they are not considered as separate entities (*Rashbam*).

וְאֶת הַתְּבוּאָה שֶׁהִיא מְחֻבֶּרֶת לַקַּרְקַע, — *the produce which is attached to the ground,*

Grain still growing from the ground is included in the sale of any field even if it is fully ripened and ready to be harvested (*Gem.* 69a).

וְאֶת מְחֻצַּת הַקָּנִים שֶׁהִיא פְּחוּתָה מִבֵּית רֹבַע, — *the clump of reeds which covers less*

than the area of a quarter-kav,

[I.e., an area in which one-fourth of a *kav* of seeds can be planted, which is 104^1/$_6$ square cubits (see comm. to 1:6, s.v. רבי עקיבא).]

Reeds which grow in a single clump less than this size are considered to be part of the field rather than an entity to themselves (*Rav*), even if the reeds themselves are thick (*Gem.* 69a, *Nimmukei Yosef*).

Some commentators translate מְחֻצַּת to mean boundary — i.e., a clump of reeds on the boundary of the field. The mishnah teaches us that even in such a case it is considered part of the rest of the field (*Yad Ramah*).

וְאֶת הַשּׁוֹמֵרָה שֶׁאֵינָהּ עֲשׂוּיָה בְטִיט, — *the watchman's hut which is not plastered* [lit. *which is not made with plaster*],

Since it is not plastered it is not considered a true house, and it is therefore viewed as part of the field (see *Rashbam* to 69a, s.v. אע"ג דקביעא) even if it is not cemented to the ground and still movable (*Gem.* 69a).

There is an alternate version of the text of the mishnah which reads וְאֶת הַשּׁוֹמֵרָה הָעֲשׂוּיָה בְטִיט — *a watchman's hut which is plastered.* [This is the version followed by R' Chananel, Rif, Rambam, Rosh, Rav (*Tos. Yom Tov*).] According to this rendition, the inclusion of the hut in the sale depends

that are needed for it, the produce which is attached to the ground, the clump of reeds which covers less than the area of a quarter-*kav*, the watchman's hut which is not plastered, the ungrafted carob tree, and a virgin sycamore.

9. However, he has not sold the stones which are not needed for it, nor the reeds in the vineyard that are not needed for it, nor the produce which is detached from the ground. When he said to him, 'It,

YAD AVRAHAM

entirely upon its permanence. Even if it is not cemented to the ground — which allows for the possibility of it being moved from the field — it is still considered part of the field, because the fact that it has been plastered indicates that it is meant to be a permanent fixture (*Yad Ramah*).[1]

וְאֶת הֶחָרוב שֶׁאֵינו מֻרְכָּב, — *the ungrafted carob tree,*
I.e., a young carob tree, not yet fully grown. When it reaches maturity, branches from other trees are grafted onto it. At that point it achieves a

special prominence of its own and is therefore considered an entity separate from the rest of the field (*Rav;* see comm. to mishnah 9, s.v. ולא את החרוב).

וְאֶת בְּתוּלַת הַשִּׁקְמָה. — *and a virgin sycamore.*
I.e., a young sycamore. As it matures, its branches are cut off, causing new and thicker branches to grow in their place (*Rav*). At that point, the tree achieves a special value and prominence causing it to be considered an entity of its own apart from the rest of the field (*Rashbam* 68b).[2] As a rule this took place after seven years (*Yad Ramah*).

9.

אֲבָל לא מָכַר לא אֶת הָאֲבָנִים שֶׁאֵינָן לְצָרְכָּה, — *However, he has not sold the stones which are not needed for it,*
I.e., those which have not yet been stacked in preparation for constructing the wall (*Gem.* 69a, *Rashbam*).
According to R' Meir, this applies only to those stones which have not even been designated for that function (see comm. to previous mishnah, s.v. המוכר).

וְלא אֶת הַקָּנִים שֶׁבַּכֶּרֶם שֶׁאֵינָן לְצָרְכּו, — *nor the reeds in the vineyard that are not*

needed for it,
I.e., reeds which are not in use to support clusters of grapes.
According to R' Meir, this refers to those reeds which have not yet been split at the top to prepare them for this function (ibid., s.v. ואת הקנים).

וְלא אֶת הַתְּבוּאָה שֶׁהִיא תְלוּשָׁה מִן הַקַּרְקַע. — *nor the produce which is detached from the ground.*
Once the produce has been harvested it is no longer considered part of the

1. *Rav* explains the mishnah to mean that the hut was cemented to the ground (rather than plastered). This would follow this alternate text but seems to contradict the *Gemara's* statement that this case of the mishnah refers even to a hut not cemented to the ground (*Tos. Yom Tov*). [However, there is yet another version of the *Gemara* cited by *Meiri* which reads, *even though it is attached to the ground,* and this may have been *Rav's* reading as well.]

2. See *Yad Avraham* comm. to ArtScroll *Sheviis* 4:5.

שֶׁבְּתוֹכָהּ,״ הֲרֵי כֻלָּן מְכוּרִין. בֵּין כָּךְ וּבֵין כָּךְ, לֹא
מָכַר לֹא אֶת מְחֶצַת הַקָּנִים שֶׁהִיא בֵּית רֹבַע, וְלֹא
אֶת הַשּׁוֹמֵרָה שֶׁהִיא עֲשׂוּיָה בְטִיט, וְלֹא אֶת
הֶחָרוּב הַמֻּרְכָּב, וְלֹא אֶת סַדַּן הַשִּׁקְמָה, וְלֹא אֶת
הַבּוֹר, וְלֹא אֶת הַגַּת, וְלֹא אֶת הַשּׁוֹבָךְ — בֵּין
חֲרֵבִין בֵּין יְשׁוּבִין.

וְצָרִיךְ לִקַּח לוֹ דֶרֶךְ; דִּבְרֵי רַבִּי עֲקִיבָא. וַחֲכָמִים
אוֹמְרִים: אֵינוֹ צָרִיךְ. וּמוֹדֶה רַבִּי עֲקִיבָא בִּזְמַן

יד אברהם

field even if it has been laid out across the field to air out and dry (Gem., Rashbam 69a).

בִּזְמַן שֶׁאָמַר לוֹ ,,הִיא ,וְכָל מַה שֶׁבְּתוֹכָהּ,״ הֲרֵי כֻלָּן מְכוּרִין. — When he said to him, 'It, and all that is in it,' they are all sold.

[If the seller specified that he is selling the field and all that is in it, all of the above items are included in the sale.]

בֵּין כָּךְ וּבֵין כָּךְ, — In any case,

[I.e., even if he said, 'It, and all that is in it.']

לֹא מָכַר לֹא אֶת מְחֶצַת הַקָּנִים שֶׁהִיא בֵּית רֹבַע, — he has not sold a clump of reeds which covers the area of a quarter-kav,

[I.e., 104$\frac{1}{6}$ square cubits; see comm. to previous mishnah.]

Even if the individual reeds are thin (Gem.), the clump is considered a field to itself and is not included in the sale (Rav). This is similar to a case in which a man sells two fields to another and specifies that he is also selling all that is in them. If there is a third field between these two, it is not included in the purchase (Rashbam 68a).

וְלֹא אֶת הַשּׁוֹמֵרָה שֶׁהִיא עֲשׂוּיָה בְטִיט, — nor the watchman's hut which is plastered,

Even if it is cemented to the ground [and is thus more likely to be considered a part of the field] (Gem. 69a), the fact that it is plastered gives it the stature of a house and it is thus considered a separate entity and not part of the field (Rashbam 69a).

According to the alternate version of

the mishnah cited in the previous mishnah, the text here reads וְלֹא אֶת הַשּׁוֹמֵרָה שֶׁאֵינָה עֲשׂוּיָה בְטִיט — nor the watchman's hut which is not plastered. Since it is not plastered, it is not considered a permanent structure in the field and it is therefore not included in its sale. Even if it is cemented to the ground, the fact that it is not plastered indicates that it is not meant to be permanent, and the cementing was only in order to facilitate its temporary presence (Yad Ramah).

Actually, this hut is certainly no less permanent than produce which has been harvested. Nevertheless, the latter is included in the purchase of the field if the seller said, 'It, and all that is in it,' while the hut is not. This is because the produce in the field belongs to the owner of the field itself and he is therefore understood to have intended to include it in those words. A watchman's hut, however, is usually the property of the watchman; therefore, even in a case in which it belongs to the owner of the field, his reference to all that is in the field is not understood to include automatically such an item, which ordinarily would not be his to sell (Yad Ramah).

וְלֹא אֶת הֶחָרוּב הַמֻּרְכָּב, — nor the grafted carob tree,

Since the mature carob tree has a value and prominence of its own, which causes people to refer to it in its own right and not merely as one of the trees of the field, it is not considered part of the field (Rashbam 68b).

וְלֹא אֶת סַדַּן הַשִּׁקְמָה, — nor the cropped

4
9

and all that is in it,' they are all sold. In any case, he has not sold a clump of reeds which covers the area of a quarter-*kav*, nor the watchman's hut which is plastered, nor the grafted carob tree, nor the cropped sycamore, nor the pit, nor the wine press, nor the dovecote — whether they are in disuse or in use.

He must buy [back] a [right-of-]way; [these are] the words of R' Akiva. The Sages, however, say: He need not. R' Akiva admits [that] when he said to him,

sycamore,

Having been trimmed of its branches, it grows to a large size and is therefore referred to independently and not as a part of the field. Thus, it is considered a separate entity. All other trees, however, are considered part of the field (*Rashbam* 68b).

וְלֹא אֶת הַבּוֹר, — *nor the pit,*

I.e., a pit dug in the middle of the field to provide water (*Rashbam* to 64b). This is not included in the sale of the field because it is of sufficient importance to be considered an entity of its own (*Nimmukei Yosef*).

וְלֹא אֶת הַגַּת, — *nor the wine press,*

A wine press located in the middle of the field (*Rashbam* 64b) is considered a separate entity and is thus not included in the sale of the field (*Nimmukei Yosef*).

The mishnah mentions a wine press when discussing a field because the term field includes a vineyard as well (see previous mishnah), and the wine presses were generally located near the vineyards. In discussing a town, however, the mishnah considers the status of an olive press, since that was more commonplace there (*Tos. Yom Tov*).

וְלֹא אֶת הַשּׁוֹבָךְ — — *nor the dovecote —*

This, too, is considered an entity to itself and it is therefore not included in the sale of the field (*Nimmukei Yosef*).

בֵּין חֲרֵבִין בֵּין יְשׁוּבִין. — *whether they are in*

disuse or in use.

This refers to the last three items cited. Whether they are still in use or have fallen into disuse — i.e., the pit has no water, there is no longer a vineyard near the wine press, and there are no doves in the dovecote — they are not included in the sale of the field (*Rashbam* 64b).

וְצָרִיךְ לִקַּח לוֹ דֶרֶךְ; דִּבְרֵי רַבִּי עֲקִיבָא. — *He must buy* [back] *a* [right-of-]*way;* [these are] *the words of R' Akiva.*

Although the pit, wine press and dovecote remain in the hands of the seller, he must repurchase from the buyer the right to pass through the field to reach them. The reason for this, as explained in mishnah 2, is because in the opinion of R' Akiva one who sells an item does so generously, i.e., without retaining any rights to that item for himself (*Rav*). The same applies to one who retained a clump of reeds which is in the field (*Yad Ramah*) or one who retained a carob or sycamore tree (*Rashbam* 70a; *Rama, Choshen Mishpat* 216:5; cf. *Maggid Mishneh, Mechirah* 26:4 from *Rashba*).

וַחֲכָמִים אוֹמְרִים: אֵינוּ צָרִיךְ. — *The Sages, however, say: He need not.*

In the Sages' opinion the seller need not repurchase the right of access to the properties he has retained, because in their view one who sells a field is not so generous as to give up his right-of-way (*Gem.* 64a).

שֶׁאָמַר לוֹ „חוּץ מֵאֵלּוּ,‟ שֶׁאֵינוֹ צָרִיךְ לִקַּח לוֹ
דֶּרֶךְ. מְכָרָן לְאַחֵר, רַבִּי עֲקִיבָא אוֹמֵר: אֵינוֹ צָרִיךְ
לִקַּח לוֹ דֶּרֶךְ. וַחֲכָמִים אוֹמְרִים: צָרִיךְ לִקַּח לוֹ
דֶּרֶךְ. בַּמֶּה דְבָרִים אֲמוּרִים? בְּמוֹכֵר, אֲבָל בְּנוֹתֵן
מַתָּנָה נוֹתֵן אֶת כֻּלָּם.

הָאַחִין שֶׁחָלְקוּ, זָכוּ בְשָׂדֶה זָכוּ בְכֻלָּם. הַמַּחֲזִיק
בְּנִכְסֵי הַגֵּר, הֶחֱזִיק בְּשָׂדֶה, הֶחֱזִיק בְּכֻלָּם.

יד אברהם

וּמוֹדֶה רַבִּי עֲקִיבָא בִּזְמַן שֶׁאָמַר לוֹ „חוּץ מֵאֵלּוּ,‟
— R' Akiva admits [that] when he said to him, 'Except for these,'

[I.e., when selling the field the seller specified that he was retaining the pit, wine press or dovecote for himself.]

שֶׁאֵינוֹ צָרִיךְ לִקַּח לוֹ דֶּרֶךְ. — he need not buy [back] a [right-of-]way.

[Since in R' Akiva's view these items would automatically be excluded from the sale of the field in any case, his explicit stipulation to that effect is superfluous, and is understood therefore to indicate that he is retaining something extra, viz., the right-of-way to reach them.]

מְכָרָן לְאַחֵר, — [If] he sold them to another,

If the owner sold any of these items to another and retained the field for himself (Rashbam 91a).

רַבִּי עֲקִיבָא אוֹמֵר: אֵינוֹ צָרִיךְ לִקַּח לוֹ דֶּרֶךְ. — R' Akiva says: He need not buy a [right-of-]way.

[The buyer need not purchase the right-of-way to his pit or wine press because the seller is assumed to have been generous in the transfer of this property and to have granted the buyer the right-of-way.]

R' Akiva would agree, however, that if the seller specified that he is selling him the pit 'but not the land,' this superfluous phrase indicates that he is not granting the buyer the right-of-way through the field (Yad Ramah).

וַחֲכָמִים אוֹמְרִים: צָרִיךְ לִקַּח לוֹ דֶּרֶךְ. — The Sages, however, say: He must buy a

[right-of-]way.

[Since in their view a seller is understood to retain for himself all that he can, we do not assume that he granted the buyer the right-of-way.]

בַּמֶּה דְבָרִים אֲמוּרִים? בְּמוֹכֵר, — In regard to what is this stated? In regard to a sale [lit. seller],

All the exclusions to property sales delineated in this chapter refer only to one who sells property (Rashbam; see glosses of Bach), because if the buyer's intention was to obtain additional items in his purchase, he should have stated so explicitly (Rav from Gem. 70a).

אֲבָל בְּנוֹתֵן מַתָּנָה נוֹתֵן אֶת כֻּלָּם. — but one who gives a gift gives all of them.

Even the Sages who maintain that a seller does not transfer his property generously agree that one who gives a gift does so magnanimously, and all related items are included in that gift [unless otherwise stipulated]. This includes not only the right-of-way to the property, but also all the items listed above as not being included in a sale unless so specified. It even includes those which are excluded despite the seller's statement that he is selling 'it, and all that is in it.' These items are excluded from a sale because their tenuous connection to the house or field being sold warrants the buyer's asking for clarification on their inclusion if he really meant to obtain them. Since he did not ask for such clarification, it is clear that he too did not expect to receive them. The recipient of a gift, however, cannot be expected to have

'Except for these,' he need not buy [back] a [right-of-]way. [If] he sold them to another, R' Akiva says: He need not buy a [right-of-]way. The Sages, however, say: He must buy a [right-of-]way. In regard to what is this stated? In regard to a sale, but one who gives a gift gives all of them.

[When] brothers divide [an inheritance], those who acquire a field acquire all of them. One who takes possession of the estate of a convert, [if] he takes possession of a field, he takes possession of all

YAD AVRAHAM

specified the inclusion of these items, because he would be embarrassed to do so *(Rav* from *Gem.* 70a). Furthermore, it may be assumed that since a gift is given in a spirit of generosity, if the giver meant to exclude them he would have indicated as much. Since he did not, it is assumed that he gave them. A sale, however, is made for the sake of receiving money, not in the spirit of generosity. Therefore, there is no reason to assume that it includes more than the objects specified *(Rashbam* 70a).

However, objects not mentioned in these mishnayos, e.g., money which is found in a field or harvested produce which no longer needs the field, are not assumed to be included in a gift, because the fact that they have no connection to the property being transferred makes it obvious that they are not included in the sale *(Rashbam).* Similarly, objects listed in this chapter as being excluded from a sale which are outside the boundaries of the property being transferred are excluded from a gift as well *(Ri Migash; Rashba).*

הָאַחִין שֶׁחָלְקוּ, זָכוּ בְשָׂדֶה זָכוּ בְכֻלָּם. — [When] brothers divide [an inheritance], those who acquire a field acquire all of them.

Brothers who inherit fields and divide them acquire all of the items contained

in those fields, even a pit, wine press, or dovecote. When dividing an estate it is understood that each one's intention is to separate completely from all the others *(Rav).*

הַמַּחֲזִיק בְּנִכְסֵי הַגֵּר, — One who takes possession of the estate of a convert,

[When a gentile converts to Judaism, all his earlier familial relationships are severed in the eyes of the law and he is considered in regard to all legal matters a newborn person *(Yevamos* 62a). Therefore, he has no heirs unless he has children after his conversion. If he dies without leaving any descendants, his estate becomes ownerless and anyone who wishes may take possession of the properties which he left.[1]]

הֶחֱזִיק בְּשָׂדֶה, הֶחֱזִיק בְּכֻלָּם. — [if] he takes possession of a field, he takes possession of all of them.

Since the only participant in this acquisition is the taker, it is understood that he means to include in this act of acquisition anything which can possibly be acquired *(Yad Ramah).* Even a carob or sycamore tree, which is considered to be separate from the field, is included, because it is similar to acquiring two adjoining fields with an act of possession in one of them, which is valid as long as there is no boundary

1. This is in contrast to a natural-born Jew who, because he is at least distantly related to all other natural-born Jews, can never die without any heir, albeit a distant one.

הַמַּקְדִּישׁ אֶת הַשָּׂדֶה הִקְדִּישׁ אֶת כֻּלָּם. רַבִּי שִׁמְעוֹן
אוֹמֵר: הַמַּקְדִּישׁ שָׂדֶה לֹא הִקְדִּישׁ אֶלָּא אֶת
הֶחָרוּב הַמֻּרְכָּב וְאֶת סַדַּן הַשִּׁקְמָה.

[א] **הַמּוֹכֵר** אֶת הַסְּפִינָה מָכַר אֶת הַתֹּרֶן,
וְאֶת הַנֵּס, וְאֶת הָעוֹגִין, וְאֶת כָּל
הַמַּנְהִיגִין אוֹתָהּ; אֲבָל לֹא מָכַר לֹא אֶת הָעֲבָדִים,
וְלֹא אֶת הַמַּרְצוּפִין, וְלֹא אֶת הָאַנְתִּיקִי. וּבִזְמַן
שֶׁאָמַר לוֹ „הִיא וְכָל מַה שֶּׁבְּתוֹכָהּ," הֲרֵי כֻלָּן
מְכוּרִין.

יד אברהם

separating them (Rav).

הַמַּקְדִּישׁ אֶת הַשָּׂדֶה הִקְדִּישׁ אֶת כֻּלָּם. — One
who consecrates a field consecrates all of
them.

If someone donates property to the
Temple, he is understood to include all
that is in that property, because one
who donates to the Temple does so
generously (Rav).

רַבִּי שִׁמְעוֹן אוֹמֵר: הַמַּקְדִּישׁ הַשָּׂדֶה לֹא הִקְדִּישׁ
אֶלָּא אֶת הֶחָרוּב הַמֻּרְכָּב וְאֶת סַדַּן הַשִּׁקְמָה. —
R' Shimon says: One who consecrates a
field has consecrated only the grafted
carob tree and the cropped sycamore.

I.e., of all the items whose inclusion
in the sale of a field is questionable, only
the grafted carob and cropped sycamore
are automatically included in the
consecration of that field. He maintains
that the intent of one who donates to the
Temple is analogous to that of one who
sells his property, and includes only the
same items as the latter. However, the
trees, which derive nourishment from
land which now belongs to the Temple,
automatically become consecrated (Rav
from Gem. 71b), since that which grows

from consecrated ground is also
consecrated (Rashbam 71b).

The Gemara (72b) concludes that R'
Shimon actually maintains that these
trees are not consecrated. Since in his
view the donor does not intend to give
them to the Temple, he retains for
himself the land from which the trees
derive nourishment in order to be able
to keep them. His statement in the
mishnah is directed to the Rabbis (i.e.,
the anonymous first Tanna); that even
they who maintain that one who
donates to the Temple does so with a
degree of generosity beyond that of a
seller, should agree that this assumption
suffices only to say that he did not
retain the land under the trees, and that
the trees are therefore consecrated.
However, all the items which this
chapter has defined as not inherently
part of the field should not be included
in the consecration at all. The Rabbis,
however, insist that one who donates to
the Temple does so with the same degree
of generosity with which he gives a gift,
and all of these items are therefore
included in the donation.

Chapter Five

This chapter continues the discussion of the subsidiary items which are included
in a sale whose details were not specified. Whereas the previous chapter focused on
the sale of real estate, the Tanna now deals with sales of movables.

of them. One who consecrates a field consecrates all of them. R' Shimon says: One who consecrates a field has consecrated only the grafted carob tree and the cropped sycamore.

1. One who sells a ship has sold the mast, the sail, the anchor, and all the oars; but he has not sold the slaves, the cargo sacks, or the cargo. [When] he said to him, 'It, and all that is in it,' they are all sold.

YAD AVRAHAM

1.

הַמּוֹכֵר אֶת הַסְּפִינָה — *One who sells a ship*
Without specifying what the purchase includes (Rav).

מָכַר אֶת הַתֹּרֶן, וְאֶת הַנֵּס, וְאֶת הָעוֹגִין, וְאֶת כָּל הַמַּנְהִיגִין אוֹתָהּ; — *has sold the mast, the sail, the anchor, and all the oars* [lit. *and all that lead it*];

All these are included in the sale even if they are not specifically listed in the contract (Rav), because they are all necessary for the proper operation of the ship and have no other function (Meiri).

אֲבָל לֹא מָכַר לֹא אֶת הָעֲבָדִים, — *but he has not sold the slaves,*
I.e., the slaves who crew the ship. Since the owner and passengers of the vessel can perform these tasks on their own if necessary, the slaves are not considered indispensable components of the ship. The sale, therefore, does not automatically include them (Meiri).

וְלֹא אֶת הַמַּרְצוּפִין, וְלֹא אֶת הָאַנְתִּיקִי. — *the cargo sacks, or the cargo.*
Neither of these is designated solely for ship use (Meiri).

Once it has been stated that the cargo sacks are not included in the sale of the ship, it goes without saying that the cargo is not sold. The mishnah only mentions this by way of introducing the next ruling, that if he specified that he is selling all that is on the vessel even the

cargo is included (Tos. 73a).

In this case, and those that follow, those items which are not included in a sale would also be excluded from a gift or consecration (see 4:9). Although it was stated in the previous chapter that all items connected to a property are included with it if that property is given as a gift or consecrated for the Temple, that applies only to the sale of real property (Rav; Rashbam 73a). There the items can be considered subsidiary to the property itself by virtue of their being physically connected to it. In the case of movables, however, the secondary articles are not part of objects of the transaction and they are therefore less subsidiary to it. Consequently, they are not automatically included even in a gift or consecration (Rav; Rashbam).

וּבִזְמַן שֶׁאָמַר לוֹ ,,הִיא וְכָל מַה שֶּׁבְּתוֹכָהּ,'' הֲרֵי כֻלָּן מְכוּרִין. — *[When] he said to him, 'It, and all that is in it,' they are all sold.*
[If the seller specified that he was selling the ship and all that was in it, all of the above items, even the cargo, are included.]

Although in regard to the properties discussed in the previous chapter the inclusionary clause does not include everything physically there unless they have some inherent relationship with it (see, e.g., mishnayos 4:4,6), the slaves [as well as the cargo sacks and cargo] are, to a large degree, related to the function and purpose of a ship, and indeed are generally to be found on one (Yad Ramah).

מָכַר אֶת הַקָּרוֹן, לֹא מָכַר אֶת הַפְּרָדוֹת; מָכַר
אֶת הַפְּרָדוֹת, לֹא מָכַר אֶת הַקָּרוֹן. מָכַר אֶת
הַצֶּמֶד, לֹא מָכַר אֶת הַבָּקָר; מָכַר אֶת הַבָּקָר, לֹא
מָכַר אֶת הַצֶּמֶד. רַבִּי יְהוּדָה אוֹמֵר: הַדָּמִים
מוֹדִיעִין. כֵּיצַד? אָמַר לוֹ „מְכֹר לִי צִמְדְּךָ בְּמָאתַיִם
זוּז,״ הַדָּבָר יָדוּעַ שֶׁאֵין הַצֶּמֶד בְּמָאתַיִם זוּז.
וַחֲכָמִים אוֹמְרִים: אֵין הַדָּמִים רְאָיָה.

[ב] **הַמּוֹכֵר** אֶת הַחֲמוֹר לֹא מָכַר אֶת כֵּלָיו.

יד אברהם

[*If*] — מָכַר אֶת הַקָּרוֹן, לֹא מָכַר אֶת הַפְּרָדוֹת;
*he sold a wagon, he did not sell the
mules;*

I.e., the team which pulls the wagon
(*Rav*). These are not included in the sale
because when speaking of a wagon
people do not ordinarily mean the team.
Therefore, even if the price paid was too
much for just a wagon, the mules are
still not included (*Nimmukei Yosef;*
citing *Ri Migash, Rambam;* see below,
s.v. הדמים מודיעין).

This is true, however, only in a case in
which the mules were not hitched to the
wagon at the time of the sale.
Otherwise, they are included in the sale
(*Rav from Gem.* 77b) if this is indicated
by the price (*Nimmukei Yosef*) [because
people will use the word 'wagon' to
refer to a completely outfitted rig].

Others interpret פְּרָדוֹת to mean the
wooden shafts (thills) by means of which the
team pulls the wagon. These are coupled to
the front of the wagon and extend out along
the sides of the team. [The harness is attached
to these shafts.] These too are excluded from
the sale only if they are not attached to the
wagon at the time of the sale (*Rav*).

If someone rents a wagon, the mules are
understood to be included even if they are
not attached, because the former is not
generally hired without the latter (*Nimmukei
Yosef*).

[*if*] — מָכַר אֶת הַפְּרָדוֹת, לֹא מָכַר אֶת הַקָּרוֹן.
he sold the mules, he did not sell the

wagon.

Even if the mules are hitched to the
wagon at the time of their sale, the
wagon is not included. Since the mules
are also used independently of the
wagon, there is no basis for including
the wagon in the term 'mules' (*Meiri;
Tur* 220:3; *Perishah* ibid.).

מָכַר אֶת הַצֶּמֶד, לֹא מָכַר אֶת הַבָּקָר; מָכַר אֶת
הַבָּקָר, לֹא מָכַר אֶת הַצֶּמֶד. — [*If*] *he sold a
yoke, he did not sell the oxen;* [*if*] *he
sold the oxen, he did not sell the yoke.*

Since people do not ordinarily refer to
the oxen when speaking of a yoke, nor
to the yoke when speaking of oxen, one
is not included in the sale of the other
(*Gem.* 77b).

According to some, the cattle are not
included in the sale of the yoke even if they
are hitched to it, because the word 'yoke'
simply does not connote cattle (*Rashbam*
77b). This is disputed, however (*Ri Migash;
Meiri*).

R' — רַבִּי יְהוּדָה אוֹמֵר: הַדָּמִים מוֹדִיעִין.
Yehudah says: The price informs [*us*].

The price charged for the yoke
indicates whether the cattle were
included in the sale. R' Yehudah is
discussing a place where people
generally refer to a yoke and cattle
separately, but there are some who use
the term 'yoke' to refer to the cattle as
well. R' Yehudah maintains that in these
circumstances, the price paid for the

[If] he sold a wagon, he did not sell the mules; [if] he sold the mules, he did not sell the wagon. [If] he sold a yoke, he did not sell the oxen; [if] he sold the oxen, he did not sell the yoke. R' Yehudah says: The price informs [us]. How so? [If] he said to him, 'Sell me your yoke for two hundred *zuz*,' it is well known that a yoke does not cost two hundred *zuz*. The Sages, however, say: The price is not proof.

2. **O**ne who sells a donkey has not sold its equip-

YAD AVRAHAM

yoke is acceptable evidence of whether the purchase included the cattle as well as the yoke *(Gem. 77b)*.

However, in a locale where the terms are never used interchangeably, R' Yehudah agrees that even if he overpaid for the yoke it cannot be assumed that the sale included the cattle. On the other hand, in a place where the term 'yoke' is commonly used to refer to the cattle as well as the yoke itself, the Rabbis would admit that the price is admissible evidence (ibid.).

In the previous case, however, even R' Yehudah agrees that the price cannot be used as an indication that the mules were included in the sale of the wagon, since people never mean the [unhitched] mules when they speak of a wagon *(Nimmukei Yosef)*.

בֵּיצַד? אָמַר לוֹ ,,מְכֹר לִי צִמְדְּךָ בְּמָאתַיִם זוּז,'' הַדָּבָר יָדוּעַ שֶׁאֵין הַצֶּמֶד בְּמָאתַיִם זוּז. — *How so? [If] he said to him, 'Sell me your yoke for two hundred zuz,' it is well known that a yoke does not cost two hundred zuz.*

Since the price is totally unreasonable for just a yoke, it indicates that the sale was meant to include the cattle as well. However, if the price paid for the yoke

was not excessive, R' Yehudah agrees that the cattle are not included *(Rashbam 77b)*.

וַחֲכָמִים אוֹמְרִים: אֵין הַדָּמִים רְאָיָה. — *The Sages, however, say: The price is not proof.*

Since most people in that place would not use the word 'yoke' to include the cattle, it cannot be deduced from the price that these individuals are from among those who do, and it is up to the buyer to prove that he purchased the cattle *(Rashbam 77b; Choshen Mishpat 220:4, Rama ibid:8; see commentators there)*.

In a case such as this, in which the price paid far exceeds the value of the yoke itself and it is impossible to attribute the buyer's overpayment to a misassessment of its value, he is understood to have given the remainder of the money as a gift. If the discrepancy is not so obvious, it would be assumed that he mistakenly overpaid, and the halachah would follow the general rules of overpayment — i.e., if he overpaid a sixth of the value, that money is refunded; if he overpaid more than that, the sale is null *(Rav from Gem. 78a)*.

2.

הַמּוֹכֵר אֶת הַחֲמוֹר לֹא מָכַר אֶת כֵּלָיו. — *One who sells a donkey has not sold its equipment.*

·· The mishnah is discussing equipment for carrying loads, such as a sack or saddlebag. This *Tanna* considers

נַחוּם הַמָּדִי אוֹמֵר: מָכַר כֵּלָיו. רַבִּי יְהוּדָה אוֹמֵר:
פְּעָמִים מְכוּרִין וּפְעָמִים אֵינָן מְכוּרִין. כֵּיצַד? הָיָה
חֲמוֹר לְפָנָיו וְכֵלָיו עָלָיו, וְאָמַר לוֹ „מְכֹר לִי
חֲמוֹרְךָ זֶה,‟ הֲרֵי כֵלָיו מְכוּרִין. „חֲמוֹרְךָ הוּא,‟ אֵין
כֵּלָיו מְכוּרִין.

[ג] **הַמּוֹכֵר** אֶת הַחֲמוֹר מָכַר אֶת הַסְּיָח. מָכַר
אֶת הַפָּרָה, לֹא מָכַר אֶת בְּנָהּ.
מָכַר אַשְׁפָּה, מָכַר זִבְלָהּ. מָכַר בּוֹר, מָכַר מֵימָיו.

יד אברהם

donkeys to be used primarily for riding, not carrying loads. Therefore, these bags cannot be presumed to have been included in the sale of the animal unless specified (*Rashbam*), even if they are on the donkey at the time of the purchase (*Rav; Rambam, Mechirah* 27:4).[1]

Riding equipment, however, such as a saddle, is included in the sale (*Rav from Gem.* 78a) if it is on the donkey at the time of sale (*Rashbam* 78a; *Yad Ramah*). In the opinion of many, it is included even if it is not on the animal at the time of the purchase (*Rav; Tos.* 78a; *Rambam,* loc. cit.).

נַחוּם הַמָּדִי אוֹמֵר: מָכַר כֵּלָיו. — *Nachum the Mede says: He has sold its equipment.*

He maintains that donkeys are primarily used for carrying loads and the sale is therefore presumed to have included the carrying bags if they are on the animal (*Gem.* 78a). Nevertheless, a saddle is also included in the sale, because the saddle is used for carrying as well as for riding (*Rashbam*).

רַבִּי יְהוּדָה אוֹמֵר: פְּעָמִים מְכוּרִין וּפְעָמִים אֵינָן מְכוּרִין. — *R' Yehudah says: Sometimes they are sold and sometimes*

they are not sold.

[R' Yehudah maintains a compromise position between the first two views.]

כֵּיצַד? הָיָה חֲמוֹר לְפָנָיו וְכֵלָיו עָלָיו, וְאָמַר לוֹ „מְכֹר לִי חֲמוֹרְךָ זֶה,‟ הֲרֵי כֵלָיו מְכוּרִין. — *How so? [If] the donkey was in front of him and its equipment was on it, and he said to him, 'Sell me this donkey of yours,' its equipment is sold.*

In this phrasing, his words 'this donkey' are construed to mean as it is now, together with its equipment.

„חֲמוֹרְךָ הוּא,‟ אֵין כֵּלָיו מְכוּרִין. — *[But if he said,] 'This is your donkey,' its equipment is not sold.*

In this phrasing, he is understood to be asking whether it is indeed the animal of the seller ['Is this your donkey?'], rather than making a statement. Therefore, there is no indication that he means to include the equipment in his purchase, and of its own it is not presumed to be included, according to R' Yehudah (*Rav from Gem.* 78b).

The halachah follows the opinion of the first *Tanna* (*Rambam, Mechirah* 27:4; *Choshen Mishpat* 220:7).

1. There is actually a discussion in the *Gemara* (78a) whether equipment on the animal is included in the sale according to this first *Tanna*. However, since the discussion is not resolved, the buyer cannot take the equipment unless it was specified at the time of the sale (*Rif; Yad Ramah; Rosh*). The commentary to this mishnah will therefore follow the view that according to this *Tanna* the carrying equipment is never included; for the other view, see *Gemara*.

ment. Nachum the Mede says: He has sold its equipment. R' Yehudah says: Sometimes they are sold and sometimes they are not sold. How so? [If] the donkey was in front of him and its equipment was on it, and he said to him, 'Sell me this donkey of yours,' its equipment is sold. [But if he said,] 'This is your donkey,' its equipment is not sold.

3. One who sells a donkey has sold the foal. [If] he sold a cow, he has not sold its calf. [If] he sold a dungheap, he has sold its manure. [If] he sold a pit,

YAD AVRAHAM

3.

הַמּוֹכֵר אֶת הַחֲמוֹר מָכַר אֶת הַסְּיָח. — *One who sells a donkey has sold the foal.*

The mishnah refers to one who specified that he was selling a nursing donkey. Since the buyer has no use for a donkey's milk, it is understood that the seller meant to include the foal along with the mother (*Rav* from *Gem.* 78b).

מָכַר אֶת הַפָּרָה, לֹא מָכַר אֶת בְּנָהּ. — *[If] he sold a cow, he has not sold its calf* [lit. *child*].

Here, too, the seller stated that he was selling a nursing cow, but it cannot be assumed in the case of a cow that the calf is being included since he may simply have intended to inform the buyer that he is getting a milk cow (*Rav* from *Gem.* 78b).

מָכַר אַשְׁפָּה, מָכַר זִבְלָהּ. — *[If] he sold a dungheap, he has sold its manure.*

Animal manure was stored in large heaps placed on top of a mound at least three handbreadths high, or in a pit of the same depth (see above, 3:5). If he sold this dung pit he has also sold its manure (*Rav*). [The manure was eventually used as fertilizer.]

מָכַר בּוֹר, מָכַר מֵימָיו. — *[If] he sold a pit, he has sold its water.*

If he sold a pit which was used for storing water, he has sold the water

which is in it even if it is not a well but a storage pit (*Meiri*).

The *Gemara* (79b) cites the opinion of the Rabbis who dispute this statement; indeed, the halachah is that one who sells a pit has not sold the water which is in it (*Rav; Rif; Rambam, Mechirah* 27:10). The reason for this is that water is not seen as having its place in the pit; rather, the pit is merely a temporary repository for the water until it is used up (*Rashba* citing *Ravad*). This is evidenced by the fact that the pit is not kept full constantly, but is refilled only when empty (*Meiri*). By contrast, in the case of a dungheap everyone agrees that the contents are sold along with the facility (*Meiri; Rambam, Mechirah* 27:10; *Choshen Mishpat* 220:16,17), because a dungheap is constantly filled with more manure and dirt to increase its content. Similarly, a dovecote and beehive (see below) are the places where the doves and bees grow and multiply (*Meiri*). [Thus, the contents of these places are intrinsically linked to them.]

Others contend that the Rabbis dispute the mishnah in all of these cases, and none of them are included in the sale of their facility (*Yad Ramah; Nimmukei Yosef* to *Gem.* 79b). Nevertheless, if he sold a *well*, the water within it is included in the sale, because the word 'well' denotes a hole with water in it

מָכַר כַּוֶּרֶת, מָכַר דְּבוֹרִים. מָכַר שׁוֹבָךְ, מָכַר יוֹנִים.
הַלּוֹקֵחַ פֵּרוֹת שׁוֹבָךְ מֵחֲבֵרוֹ, מַפְרִיחַ בְּרֵכָה
רִאשׁוֹנָה. פֵּרוֹת כַּוֶּרֶת, נוֹטֵל שְׁלֹשָׁה נְחִילִין
וּמְסָרֵס. חַלּוֹת דְּבַשׁ, מַנִּיחַ שְׁתֵּי חַלּוֹת. זֵיתִים

יד אברהם

(Nimmukei Yosef). If he consecrated any of these items to be used for the Temple, their contents are included in the donation, since one who consecrates does so generously (Nimmukei Yosef; see comm. to 4:9).

מָכַר כַּוֶּרֶת, מָכַר דְּבוֹרִים. מָכַר שׁוֹבָךְ, מָכַר יוֹנִים. — [If] he sold a beehive, he has sold the bees. [If] he sold a dovecote, he has sold the doves.

These items are all considered part of the facility in which they are found and are therefore included in their sale. However, the reverse is not true, and if he sold the manure, water, bees, or doves, their purchase does not include the dungheap, pit, beehive, or dovecote (Rashbam 78b).

An exception to this would be if he sold all of the bees or doves, in which case the hive or dovecote would be included (Tosefta 4:4). This is because a person would not empty them out if he wished to keep them, but would rather retain some bees or doves for himself (Rosh; see below).

הַלּוֹקֵחַ פֵּרוֹת שׁוֹבָךְ מֵחֲבֵרוֹ, — One who buys the production [lit. fruit] of a dovecote from another

I.e., the future production of the dovecote, the doves which will be born after the sale (Rav). Those which were already born are not included (Yad Ramah).

The mishnah refers to a case in which he sold the output for a limited period, for example a year, after which the rights revert back to the seller. Thus, the buyer's rights must be exercised with a certain degree of restraint to avoid ruining the future output of the dovecote (Rav; Rashbam).

Although according to most Tannaim one cannot sell an item which has not yet come into existence (see Gem. 79b), this sale is

construed to apply to the dovecote for its production — i.e., the buyer acquires a share in the dovecote allowing him to keep its output. Since the dovecote is in existence, the sale is valid (Rambam, Mechirah 23:9; Choshen Mishpat 212:1). Even when not explicitly stated, this interpretation can be assumed (ibid.), because a dovecote and beehive (see below) have little intrinsic value and stand primarily for the sake of their output. Therefore, they are likely to have been included in the sale of the produce if that is necessary for the validity of the purchase (Kesef Mishneh, ad loc.).

Others maintain that this cannot be assumed automatically, and the mishnah is discussing a case in which it was explicitly stated (Ravad, ad loc.; Meiri). Alternatively, the case is one in which the seller and buyer agreed to abide by the terms of the agreement even after the doves were born (Nimmukei Yosef; Meiri).

מַפְרִיחַ בְּרֵכָה רִאשׁוֹנָה. — must allow the first brace to fly.

It is the tendency of doves to bear two offspring each month, one male and one female (Rashbam 80a). Although the buyer bought the rights to the young of this dovecote, he must allow the first pair to fly with their mother (Rashbam 80a) — i.e., to remain and be raised by her (Meiri). Were he to take the entire output of that year and leave none of the young, the mother bird would also fly away, leaving the dovecote completely depopulated (Rav). Since the owner only sold him a year's production but not the dovecote itself, it is understood that the buyer cannot decimate the dovecote but must leave whatever is necessary to maintain an active dovecote (Rashbam).

The Gemara concludes that this is sufficient only if there is already one

5
3
he has sold its water. [If] he sold a beehive, he has sold the bees. [If] he sold a dovecote, he has sold the doves.

One who buys the production of a dovecote from another must allow the first brace to fly. [If he bought] the production of a beehive, he takes three swarms and [then] alternates. [If he bought] honeycombs, he must leave two combs. [If he

brace which was born before the sale, in which case the mother will be left with two sets, the previous one and the first one born after the sale. Otherwise, the buyer must leave two braces behind, because one alone will not suffice to keep the mother from flying away (*Gem.* 80a, as explained by *Rabbeinu Gershom; Yad Ramah; Rambam, Mechirah* 23:12; *Choshen Mishpat* 220:10).

Others interpret the *Gemara* differently. The buyer must leave behind not only the first brace of the mother, but also the first brace which that brace will have, because otherwise the first brace will fly away, and then the mother as well (*Rashbam* 80a). Some commentators contend that by the same token, the first brace of every subsequent generation must also be left to remain in the dovecote (*Tos.*).

פֵּרוֹת כַּוֶּרֶת, — [If he bought] the production [lit. fruit] of a beehive,

I.e., someone bought the rights to the bees which will come for the entire year from a certain beehive (*Rav*).

As in the previous case, this sale involves the problem of selling something which has not yet come into existence, and the solution offered there applies here as well.

נוֹטֵל שְׁלשָׁה נְחִילִין — he takes three swarms

Each summer a beehive produces swarms of bees at intervals of nine days. These settle on the branch of a tree where they may then be enclosed by a beekeeper in a container to form another

hive (*Rashbam* 80a). Of these swarms, the first three that come out of the hive, comprising the best bees, belong to the buyer (*Rav*).

וּמְסָרֵס. — and [then] alternates.

After taking the first three swarms, the buyer may keep only alternate swarms from the hive, because some of the offspring must remain with the queen bee in order to maintain the population of the hive (*Rav*). Since the hive itself was not included in the sale, the buyer may not completely strip it but must allow for its continued use (*Tos. Yom Tov*). It is not sufficient merely to leave the seller the final swarms comprising the most inferior bees (*Nimmukei Yosef*).

חַלּוֹת דְּבַשׁ, — [If he bought] honeycombs,

The production of a beehive is defined (by common usage) as its bees, not its honey. Thus when someone contracts to buy the production of a beehive, the honeycombs are not generally included (*Nimmukei Yosef*). However, in this case the buyer specifically contracted to buy the honey production of the beehive.

מַנִּיחַ שְׁתֵּי חַלּוֹת. — he must leave two combs.

These are necessary to provide for the bees during the winter months (*Rav*). Since he sold him the honey and not the hive, that which is necessary for the upkeep of the hive is not included in the sale (*Rashbam* 80a).

לָקַץ, מַנִּיחַ שְׁתֵּי גְרוֹפִיּוֹת.

[ד] **הַקּוֹנֶה** שְׁנֵי אִילָנוֹת בְּתוֹךְ שְׂדֵה חֲבֵרוֹ
הֲרֵי זֶה לֹא קָנָה קַרְקַע. רַבִּי מֵאִיר
אוֹמֵר: קָנָה קַרְקַע. הִגְדִּילוּ, לֹא יְשַׁפֵּה. וְהָעוֹלֶה מִן
הַגֶּזַע שֶׁלּוֹ; וּמִן הַשָּׁרָשִׁים, שֶׁל בַּעַל הַקַּרְקַע; וְאִם
מֵתוּ אֵין לוֹ קַרְקַע.

יד אברהם

זֵיתִים לָקַץ, — [If he bought] olive trees to cut,

I.e., to cut and use the wood (Tur 216:11). This is specified, because if he bought to transplant he may uproot the entire tree (Yad Ramah). When he buys the right to cut wood from a tree, however, it is understood that he is not getting the whole tree and he must thus take care not to destroy it (Meiri).

מַנִּיחַ שְׁתֵּי גְרוֹפִיּוֹת. — he must leave two branches.

He may cut the tree only down to the lowest two branches, so that the tree will be able to continue to grow (Rav; Rashbam; Meiri; Tur). Others explain this to mean that he must leave two handbreadths of the trunk, from which the tree will be able to regenerate (Rambam Comm.).

4.

הַקּוֹנֶה שְׁנֵי אִילָנוֹת בְּתוֹךְ שְׂדֵה חֲבֵרוֹ — One who buys two trees in the field of another

It was not specified, however, whether the land under the trees was included in the purchase (Rav).

הֲרֵי זֶה לֹא קָנָה קַרְקַע. — has not acquired any land.

He has not acquired the land beneath the trees or around them. His acquisition amounts only to a right to use the tree for its fruit. Should the tree die, he has only the right to take the dead wood but no right to plant a new tree on that site, since the land is not his (Rashbam 81a).

However, he does acquire a right to

use the amount of land, immediately around the trees, necessary to stand with a basket and pick the fruit. Therefore, the owner of the land may not plant anything in that area (Tur 216:8; Rama, Choshen Mishpat 216:9). In addition, he acquires the right-of-way through the field to get to the trees (Gem. 82b; Rama ibid.).[1]

The Gemara (81b) concludes that the Rabbis were actually uncertain whether the acquisition of two trees gives the buyer the land beneath them and around them — as in the case of three trees below — or not. Nevertheless, the halachah is as stated in the mishnah, because wherever the sale of a property is uncertain it remains in the possession of the seller (Tos. Yom Tov).

1. Rashbam (71a, s.v. הרי זה לא קנה) states that according to R' Akiva, who maintains that a seller transfers ownership generously (see 4:2,9), the sale of two trees would also be construed generously to include the sale of the land beneath it and around it, as in the case of three trees (see below). Thus, this mishnah reflects the view of the Sages who dispute R' Akiva. Most authorities, however, disagree with this and consider the ruling of the mishnah to be true even according to R' Akiva. In their view, R' Akiva considers accessories to the item being sold included in the sale only when they are subsidiary to it; in this case, the land is of greater value than the trees (Yad Ramah; see Rosh to 83b). Therefore, although the halachah follows the opinion of R' Akiva, it also follows the view of the first Tanna in our mishnah (Tur and Choshen Mishpat 216:8).

5
4

bought] olive trees to cut, he must leave two branches.

4. One who buys two trees in the field of another has not acquired any land. R' Meir says: He has acquired land. [If] they grew, he may not trim [them]. Whatever grows from the trunk belongs to him; from the roots, to the owner of the land; and if they died the land is not his.

YAD AVRAHAM

רַבִּי מֵאִיר אוֹמֵר: קָנָה קַרְקַע. — *R' Meir says: He has acquired land.*

In R' Meir's view when two trees are sold it is understood that a 'field of trees' is being sold and it therefore includes the land beneath them and around them in the purchase (*Rashbam* 81a).

The *Gemara* (81b) states that R' Meir considers the possibility that the purchase of even one tree would include land but that since the matter is uncertain, in effect no land is acquired unless two trees were bought.

הִגְדִּילוּ, — *[If] they grew,*

If the branches grew to extend beyond their original length (*Rav*).

לֹא יְשַׁפֶּה. — *he may not trim [them].*

The seller, who owns the land over which the branches extend, may not trim them even if their shade harms his field. Since according to the Rabbis (the anonymous *Tanna*) the buyer did not receive any land to support his trees as part of the purchase, it is understood that the seller's land is bound to the needs of the trees as long as they stand (*Rav*).

וְהָעוֹלֶה מִן הַגֶּזַע שֶׁלּוֹ; — *Whatever grows from the trunk belongs to him;*

Whatever shoots grow out from the tree above ground level belong to the owner of the tree. However, he may not leave them there to grow, because additional dirt might accumulate there and cover the base of the shoot, leaving what would appear to be a third tree.

This would enable the owner of the trees to claim that he acquired three trees and thus their land (see below). To avoid this, he is required to cut the shoot (*Rav* from *Gem.* 82a).

Actually, if a dispute should subsequently arise whether only two trees had been sold (and thus no land), with the third tree being merely a shoot of one of them, the burden of proof would fall on the buyer to prove otherwise. Nevertheless, the Rabbis decreed that the new shoot must be cut off so that the seller should not have to go through the trouble of litigation (*Nimmukei Yosef* from *Ramban*).

Sma (216:32; see also *Rashba, Ritva* cited by *Nimmukei Yosef*) contends that the buyer would be believed in such a case, because the chances of such an occurrence taking place are unlikely, and the presence of three separate trunks above ground would be acceptable as evidence that he owned three separate trees.[1]

וּמִן הַשָּׁרָשִׁים, שֶׁל בַּעַל הַקַּרְקַע; — *from the roots, to the owner of the land;*

Whatever grows out of the tree from beneath the ground is deemed as growing from the roots and belongs to the owner of the land (*Rav* from *Gem.* 82a).

וְאִם מֵתוּ אֵין לוֹ קַרְקַע. — *and if they died the land is not his.*

If the trees died, he has no right to plant others in their place because the land is not his (*Rav*). However, he does have the right to cut down the dead tree for its wood (*Gem.* 81a).

1. [Perhaps *Nimmukei Yosef* assumes that the fact that the Rabbis prohibited the owner of the trees to allow these shoots to grow, for fear that they might later be mistaken for three separate

קָנָה שְׁלֹשָׁה, קָנָה קַרְקַע. הִגְדִּילוּ, יְשַׁפֶּה;
וְהָעוֹלֶה מִן הַגֶּזַע וּמִן הַשָּׁרָשִׁין שֶׁלּוֹ, וְאִם מֵתוּ יֵשׁ
לוֹ קַרְקַע.

[ה] **הַמּוֹכֵר** רֹאשׁ בְּהֵמָה גַסָּה לֹא מָכַר אֶת
הָרַגְלַיִם; מָכַר אֶת הָרַגְלַיִם, לֹא
מָכַר אֶת הָרֹאשׁ. מָכַר אֶת הַקָּנֶה, לֹא מָכַר אֶת
הַכָּבֵד; מָכַר אֶת הַכָּבֵד, לֹא מָכַר אֶת הַקָּנֶה. אֲבָל
בַּדַּקָּה, מָכַר אֶת הָרֹאשׁ, מָכַר אֶת הָרַגְלַיִם; מָכַר
אֶת הָרַגְלַיִם, לֹא מָכַר אֶת הָרֹאשׁ. מָכַר אֶת

יד אברהם

קָנָה שְׁלֹשָׁה, — [If] *he bought three,*
I.e., he bought three separate trees in
a field, even if they were not yet fully
grown (Rambam, Mechirah 24:1).

קָנָה קַרְקַע. — *he has acquired land.*
It is considered a purchase not of
individual trees but of a field of trees.
Thus included in the purchase is the
land beneath the trees, between them,
and enough area around them to allow
him to stand with a basket to pick the
fruit (Rav from Gem. 82a,b).

This holds true only if the trees form
a triangle with each other, since it is
then uncommon to plant the area
surrounded by the trees and we view
that area as a field of trees (rather than a
field with trees in it). If they are in a
straight line, however, the land between
the trees is fit for planting and is
therefore not viewed as a field of trees
and is not included in the sale (Gem.
83b; Nimmukei Yosef; Choshen Mishpat 216:7). In addition, they must be
within sixteen cubits of each other, and
at least four cubits apart (Rav from
Gem. 83a), to allow for an ox-drawn
plow to pass between them (Rashbam).

The buyer also acquires the right-of-
way to his trees through the field, since
the halachah follows the opinion of R'

Akiva (4:2,9) that a seller transfers
ownership generously and includes the
right-of-way in the sale (Sema 216:31).

הִגְדִּילוּ, יְשַׁפֶּה; — [If] *they grew, he may
trim* [them];
If the branches protruded beyond the
land sold with the trees the seller may
trim them. Since the sale provided the
buyer with land beneath and around the
trees, the seller has not bound any of his
other land to their needs and he is,
therefore, not obligated to allow them to
extend into his property and block out
the sunlight (Rashbam). He may trim
them in accordance with the rules
delineated above (2:13) for cutting off
the branches of a neighbor's tree which
extend into one's field (Yad Ramah).

וְהָעוֹלֶה מִן הַגֶּזַע וּמִן הַשָּׁרָשִׁין שֶׁלּוֹ, —
*whatever grows from the trunk and the
roots belongs to him,*
[Since in buying three trees he bought
the land beneath them as well, whatever
grows out from the tree — whether from
the trunk or from below ground level —
belongs to the buyer.]

וְאִם מֵתוּ יֵשׁ לוֹ קַרְקַע. — *and if they died
the land is his.*
Consequently, he may plant others in
their place (Tif. Yis.).

trees, shows that they considered the possibility a reasonable one. Therefore, it stands to
reason that if the seller claimed this had indeed occurred, his position would be deemed valid
unless it was proven otherwise.]

[If] he bought three, he has acquired land. [If] they grew, he may trim [them]; whatever grows from the trunk and the roots belongs to him, and if they died the land is his.

5. One who sells the head of a large animal has not sold the legs; [if] he sold the legs, he has not sold the head. [If] he sold the trachea, he has not sold the liver; [if] he sold the liver, he has not sold the trachea. However, in [the case of] a small animal, [if] he sold the head, he has sold the legs; [if] he sold the legs, he has not sold the head. [If] he sold the trachea,

YAD AVRAHAM

5.

הַמּוֹכֵר רֹאשׁ בְּהֵמָה גַּסָּה — *One who sells the head of a large animal*

I.e., of cattle (*Rambam Comm.*). It was customary for cattle to be sold in parts (*Nimmukei Yosef*) both before and after slaughter (*Sema* 220:22).

לֹא מָכַר אֶת הָרַגְלַיִם; מָכַר אֶת הָרַגְלַיִם, לֹא מָכַר אֶת הָרֹאשׁ. — *has not sold the legs; [if] he sold the legs, he has not sold the head.*

Each of these limbs is considered significant in its own right, and not subsidiary to the other. Thus, neither is automatically included in the sale of the other (*Rabbeinu Gershom*).

This ruling applies only where there is no custom to the contrary; if there is a local custom designating that one of these be included in the sale of the other, the halachah follows the custom [because it is assumed that the intent of the principals was in accordance with the custom] (*Rav from Tosefta* 4:6). In fact, all the rulings listed throughout these chapters defining the extent and limits of a sale apply only where there is no clear local custom governing these matters. Where there is, local custom determines the halachah (*Rambam, Mechirah* 26:7,8). Although the *Tosefta* states this principle explicitly only in this case, it may be because at that time this was the only instance in which the

custom of certain locales was known to differ with the general custom defined by the mishnah (*Tos. Yom Tov*).

מָכַר אֶת הַקָּנֶה, — *[If] he sold the trachea,*

This actually refers to the lungs (*Rav; Rabbeinu Gershom; Rashbam* 83b) and even the heart (*Tos.* 83b) as well. The word *trachea* is used to describe the entire pulmonary system (or cardio-pulmonary, according to *Tos.*).

לֹא מָכַר אֶת הַכָּבֵד; מָכַר אֶת הַכָּבֵד, לֹא מָכַר אֶת הַקָּנֶה. — *he has not sold the liver; [if] he sold the liver, he has not sold the trachea.*

In a large animal each of these is significant in its own right and is thus not included in the sale of the other (*Tif. Yis.*).

אֲבָל בַּדַּקָּה, מָכַר אֶת הָרֹאשׁ, מָכַר אֶת הָרַגְלַיִם; — *However, in [the case of] a small animal, [if] he sold the head, he has sold the legs;*

The legs of small animals such as sheep and goats are inconsequential in their own right, and it was therefore customary to sell them together with the head (*Rabbeinu Gershom*).

מָכַר אֶת הָרַגְלַיִם, לֹא מָכַר אֶת הָרֹאשׁ. — *[if] he sold the legs, he has not sold the head.*

The head of even a small animal is

הַקָּנֶה, מָכַר אֶת הַכָּבֵד; מָכַר אֶת הַכָּבֵד, לֹא מָכַר אֶת הַקָּנֶה.

[ו] אַרְבַּע מִדּוֹת בְּמוֹכְרִין: מָכַר לוֹ חִטִּים יָפוֹת וְנִמְצְאוּ רָעוֹת, הַלּוֹקֵחַ יָכוֹל לַחֲזוֹר בּוֹ. רָעוֹת וְנִמְצְאוּ יָפוֹת, מוֹכֵר יָכוֹל לַחֲזוֹר בּוֹ. רָעוֹת וְנִמְצְאוּ רָעוֹת, יָפוֹת וְנִמְצְאוּ יָפוֹת, אֵין אֶחָד מֵהֶם יָכוֹל לַחֲזוֹר בּוֹ. שְׁחַמְתִּית וְנִמְצֵאת לְבָנָה,

יד אברהם

.לֹא מָכַר אֶת הַקָּנֶה — [If] he sold the trachea, he has sold the liver; [if] he sold the liver, he has not sold the trachea.

The trachea and lungs of even a small animal were considered significant, whereas the liver was not (see above).

מָכַר אֶת הַקָּנֶה, מָכַר אֶת הַכָּבֵד; מָכַר אֶת הַכָּבֵד,

considered important in its own right and is thus not included in the sale of the less important legs (*Rabbeinu Gershom*).

6.

This mishnah discusses purchases in which the quality of the item is found to be different than what had been assumed at the time of the sale. The question at hand is which party, if any, can retract after the transaction has been completed.

אַרְבַּע מִדּוֹת בְּמוֹכְרִין: — *There are four rules for dealing with sales* [lit. *sellers*]:

I.e., there are four different laws (*Rav*) dealing with sales of goods whose quality turns out to be different than originally assumed (*Nimmukei Yosef*).

מָכַר לוֹ חִטִּים יָפוֹת וְנִמְצְאוּ רָעוֹת, — [If] he *sold him superior wheat and it was found to be inferior,*

I.e., if the seller specified that the wheat he was selling was of superior quality, and it turned out to be of inferior quality (*Rav*). Nevertheless, the buyer was not overcharged because the seller included enough extra inferior wheat to equal the value of the agreed price (*Nimmukei Yosef; Yad Ramah; Tos.* 84a; see *Tos. Yom Tov*).

הַלּוֹקֵחַ יָכוֹל לַחֲזוֹר בּוֹ. — *the buyer can retract.*

Such a misrepresentation is treated similar to an overcharge, in which the rule is that the buyer has the option of retracting and getting back his money (*Rav*).

Although in cases of price-gouging, if he was overcharged by only a sixth the law is that he is entitled only to reimbursement for the overcharge but cannot void the sale,[1] that is because he received the object he desired and was cheated only in regard to the price. In this case, however, in which the item he received was not of the quality agreed upon, the sale is not binding no matter how small the discrepancy (*Rashbam* 83b).

The seller, however, cannot retract [which he might want to do if the price of the wheat rose sharply in the interim] (*Rav* from *Gem.* 84a), since it would be

1. This is the view accepted by most authorities as to the *Gemara's* (83b) conclusion on this matter (see *Choshen Mishpat* 227:2). However, *Rabbeinu Tam (Tos.* 83b) in fact understands the *Gemara's* conclusion to be that the buyer does have the option of retracting (see *Bach, Choshen Mishpat* 227:3).

he has sold the liver; [if] he sold the liver, he has not
sold the trachea.

6. There are four rules for dealing with sales: [If]
he sold him superior wheat and it was found to
be inferior, the buyer can retract. [If he sold him]
inferior [wheat] and it was found to be superior, the
seller can retract. [If he sold him] inferior [wheat] and
it was found to be inferior, [or] superior [wheat] and
it was found to be superior, neither can retract. [If he
sold him] red [wheat] and it was found to be white,

YAD AVRAHAM

unreasonable to allow him to benefit
from his having cheated *(Gem.;
Rashbam)*.

Although in a case of a mistaken purchase,
in which the buyer did not receive the article
which had been agreed upon, both the buyer
and seller can retract, that is only when the
item received is totally different from the one
agreed upon, because the sale is then
inherently void. In that case both the buyer
and seller can claim that they never intended
to be involved in the transfer of such an
article. In this case, however, the item is the
same; it is only the quality that is less than
had been promised. Therefore, only the
buyer can validly claim that it is not the
purchase to which he agreed *(Rashbam 83b,
s.v. מכר לוחטים יפות).*

רָעוֹת וְנִמְצְאוּ יָפוֹת, — *[If he sold him]
inferior [wheat], and it was found to be
superior,*

I.e., the buyer convinced the seller
that his product was of inferior quality,
and the truth turned out to be otherwise
(Nimmukei Yosef).

מוֹכֵר יָכוֹל לַחֲזוֹר בּוֹ.—*the seller can retract.*

Since the seller was deceived, he has
the option of retracting. The buyer,
however, cannot retract (if the price fell
in the interim), because his cheating
cannot work to his benefit *(Gem. 84a).*

רָעוֹת וְנִמְצְאוּ רָעוֹת, יָפוֹת וְנִמְצְאוּ יָפוֹת, אֵין
אֶחָד מֵהֶם יָכוֹל לַחֲזוֹר בּוֹ. — *[If he sold him]
inferior [wheat] and it was found to be
inferior, [or] superior [wheat] and it was*

found to be superior, neither can retract.

The buyer cannot claim in the first
case that he actually understood the
purchase to be for superior wheat, but
had called it inferior as a bargaining
ploy; nor can the seller claim in the
latter case that he had actually meant to
sell a lower grade of wheat but had
described it as higher quality in order to
strengthen his position, though these
tactics are prevalent among dealers.
Thus, regardless of which way the price
moved in the interim, neither party can
retract *(Rav),* since the produce
exchanged was consistent with that
which was specified *(Rashbam 83b).*

Others explain the mishnah to be
discussing a case in which the buyer and
seller agreed upon inferior quality
wheat, but the produce turned out to be
exceptionally inferior; or they agreed
upon a superior product, but it was
found to be of truly exceptional quality.
Neither can claim that this is not the
product to which he agreed, because the
term 'inferior' includes all degrees of
inferiority, and the term 'superior'
incorporates all levels of superiority.
Therefore, unless they specified
otherwise, the entire range of inferior or
superior produce is included in their
agreement *(Yad Ramah; Nimmukei
Yosef; Meiri).*

שְׁחַמְתִּית וְנִמְצֵאת לְבָנָה, לְבָנָה וְנִמְצֵאת
שְׁחַמְתִּית — *[If he sold him] red [wheat]*

לְבָנָה וְנִמְצֵאת שַׁחַמְתִּית; עֵצִים שֶׁל זַיִת וְנִמְצְאוּ
שֶׁל שִׁקְמָה, שֶׁל שִׁקְמָה וְנִמְצְאוּ שֶׁל זַיִת; יַיִן
וְנִמְצָא חֹמֶץ, חֹמֶץ וְנִמְצָא יַיִן — שְׁנֵיהֶם יְכוֹלִין
לַחֲזוֹר בָּהֶן.

[ז] **הַמּוֹכֵר** פֵּרוֹת לַחֲבֵרוֹ, מָשַׁךְ וְלֹא מָדַד, קָנָה;

יד אברהם

and it was found to be white, [or] white [wheat] and it was found to be red;

Each of these types of wheat has an advantage. Red wheat produces a larger quantity of flour, but white wheat bakes into a finer bread (Nimmukei Yosef).

עֵצִים שֶׁל זַיִת וְנִמְצְאוּ שֶׁל שִׁקְמָה, שֶׁל שִׁקְמָה וְנִמְצְאוּ שֶׁל זַיִת; — [or he sold him] olive wood and it was found to be sycamore, [or] sycamore and it was found to be olive;

[Here, too, there are uses for which each is superior.]

יַיִן וְנִמְצָא חֹמֶץ, חֹמֶץ וְנִמְצָא יַיִן — [or he sold him] wine and it was found to be vinegar, [or] vinegar and it was found to be wine —

Although wine is clearly more valuable than vinegar, there are instances where one is needed rather than the other (Rav from Gem. 84b; Tos. Yom Tov).

שְׁנֵיהֶם יְכוֹלִין לַחֲזוֹר בָּהֶן. — both of them can retract.

Since the item sold in each of these cases was of a different species from the one agreed upon, each can back out, because it is not at all what he contracted for. Thus, this differs from the earlier cases in which the species sold was the one contracted for and only the quality differed. There, the one who gets the better of the deal cannot retract because no one can claim that he prefers the lesser quality of an item over the better one. Consequently, in those cases only the one who loses out as a result of the misrepresentation can retract (Rashbam 83b).

Although wine and vinegar are technically regarded as the same species in regard to other laws, the legitimacy of a purchase depends upon whether the article delivered is considered an acceptable substitute for the one promised, and in this case it is not (Gem. 84b).

The mishnah chose the cases listed here to teach us that although they are somewhat similar to each other, the sale is nevertheless void. Obviously, in instances in which the article promised is totally dissimilar to the one actually delivered, the ruling would be the same (Tif. Yis.).

7.

Whenever ownership of property is transferred, the person acquiring the property must perform an appropriate קִנְיָן, formal act of acquisition, in order to receive title to the property. The halachah defines different acts of acquisition for different types of property. Real property, for example, may be acquired simply by paying for it (among other ways). This does not, however, suffice for the acquisition of movable property, which can be acquired only by the buyer's performing one of the formal acts of acquisition designated for movable property (Bava Metzia 47b).

There are essentially three formal acts of acquisition by which one can acquire ownership of movable property: הַגְבָּהָה, hagbahah, lifting the object being acquired; מְשִׁיכָה, meshichah, drawing or pulling it; מְסִירָה, mesirah, grasping hold of it (Kiddushin 1:4,5; see Yad Avraham comm. there). Hagbahah may be used in any

[or] white [wheat] and it was found to be red; [or he
sold him] olive wood and it was found to be
sycamore, [or] sycamore and it was found to be olive;
[or he sold him] wine and it was found to be vinegar,
[or] vinegar and it was found to be wine — both of
them can retract.

7. **[I**f] one sold produce to another, [if] he drew [it]
but did not measure [it], he has acquired [it];

YAD AVRAHAM

situation in which it is practical. *Meshichah* and *mesirah* are valid as methods of
acquisition only where the object is too heavy or unwieldly to be lifted readily. The
essence of all these acts is to do something to the object which symbolically indicates
its entry into the possession of the new owner.

The operative theory for the act of *meshichah* is that the new owner draws the
object into his sphere by pulling it into an area which either belongs to him or which
he has the right to use (*Rashbam* 76b). For this reason, in order for an article to be
acquired by *meshichah*, the act must take place in a property which is at least
partially owned by the buyer or in a *simta* — a recess off the side of a public
thoroughfare in which people do not generally walk but in which they may put
down their objects (*Rashbam* 84b). If the article is in a public thoroughfare or the
property of the seller, where the buyer's pulling the object does not indicate
ownership, *meshichah* is not valid (*Gem.* 76b) unless he pulls it completely out of
that area and into his property or a *simta* (*Gem.* 84b; see comm. to *Kiddushin* 1:4).

In addition to the direct acts of acquisition described above, movable property
may also be formally acquired through real property in two ways. The first is
simply by being in the receiver's land or utensil at the time of transaction. This is
known as קִנְיַן חָצֵר, lit. *acquisition by courtyard*. The second way is by the
mechanism of אַגַּב, *agav* [lit. *along with*], the rule that where a transaction involves
both movable and real property, formal acquisition of the land by any method
appropriate to it brings with it formal acquisition of the movables as well.

הַמּוֹכֵר פֵּרוֹת לַחֲבֵרוֹ, — [*If*] *one sold
produce to another,*
[As explained above, even if payment
has been received the transfer of
ownership does not take effect until a
formal act of acquisition has been
performed.]

מָשַׁךְ — [*if*] *he drew* [*it*]
The produce was in public property
and the buyer drew it into a *simta*, or
into property which was jointly owned
by himself and the seller (*Rav; Rambam
Comm.*).

וְלֹא מָדַד, — *but did not measure* [*it*],
[He did not measure the quantity of
the produce, either by weight or by

volume, and thus does not really know
exactly how much he is receiving.]

קָנָה; — *he has acquired* [*it*];
[The *meshichah* act of drawing the
produce effects a transfer of the
property to the buyer even though no
money has yet changed hands.] However, they must at least have agreed
upon a set price for each specified unit
of measure; otherwise, neither is really
committing himself to the sale since the
seller will still be trying to obtain as high
a price as possible and the buyer will be
endeavoring to bring it down (*Rav*).

Since *meshichah* is valid only for
articles too heavy to lift, the mishnah
must be referring to produce packed in

מָדַד וְלֹא מָשַׁךְ, לֹא קָנָה. אִם הָיָה פִּקֵּחַ, שׂוֹכֵר אֶת
מְקוֹמָן.
הַלּוֹקֵחַ פִּשְׁתָּן מֵחֲבֵרוֹ, הֲרֵי זֶה לֹא קָנָה עַד
שֶׁיְּטַלְטְלֶנּוּ מִמָּקוֹם לְמָקוֹם. וְאִם הָיָה בִּמְחֻבָּר
לַקַּרְקַע וְתָלַשׁ כָּל שֶׁהוּא, קָנָה.

יד אברהם

crates or sacks which are not easily lifted (Gem. 86b).

מָדַד וְלֹא מָשַׁךְ, לֹא קָנָה. — [if] he measured but did not draw [it], he has not acquired [it].

If the seller measured out the produce but the buyer did not draw it into a simta, he has not acquired the produce, even if the seller placed them in the buyer's utensils. Although a person's utensils can serve as an instrument for acquiring property for him, so that placing in them an item which he wishes to acquire effects its acquisition, they can do so only if the utensils are lying in a place where the buyer was permitted to leave them. Since the mishnah is discussing a transaction taking place in the public domain, the utensils cannot effect acquisition (Rav from Gem. 84b, 85a).

However, if the buyer himself measures out the produce, so that he lifts the fruits in the process of measuring them, his lifting is a legitimate act of hagbahah acquisition [see introduction] (Rav). Others maintain that even if the buyer measures it he does not assume ownership, because the act of measuring is done on behalf of the seller as well as the buyer and as such, it cannot be rendered an act of acquisition for the buyer (Ravad cited by Shitah Mekubetzes).

Others explain the mishnah to be discussing produce lying in a simta or in property owned jointly by the buyer and seller. Accordingly, in the earlier case, the meshichah is valid where it is. However, this would mean that if the seller measured it into the utensils of the buyer, it would be an effective transaction since the utensils would

then be in a place where the buyer was permitted to leave them. Accordingly, the mishnah refers only to a case in which they were placed in the utensils of the seller (Rashbam 84b) or directly on the ground (Tos. R' Akiva).

אִם הָיָה פִּקֵּחַ, — If he is prudent,

If the transaction is to take place in the seller's property (Rav), and if the buyer is apprehensive that the seller will renege on their agreement before the produce enters his possession, he can, if he has foresight, adopt the following precaution to prevent that (Tif. Yis.).

שׂוֹכֵר אֶת מְקוֹמָן. — he rents its space.

The buyer should rent from the seller the space in which the produce is placed, thereby making it temporarily his property. Consequently, as soon as the produce is placed there, the buyer acquires immediate ownership by dint of his (rented) courtyard (Rav).

הַלּוֹקֵחַ פִּשְׁתָּן מֵחֲבֵרוֹ הֲרֵי זֶה לֹא קָנָה עַד שֶׁיְּטַלְטְלֶנּוּ מִמָּקוֹם לְמָקוֹם. — One who buys flax from another does not acquire [it] until he moves it from place to place.

I.e., he can acquire it only by lifting it, an act of hagbahah. The mishnah refers to this as moving it from place to place because a person generally first lifts his purchase when he sets out to move it to another place (Rav).

Flax stalks have a tendency to slide out of their bundles, and it is therefore impractical to tie them into large bundles. Since it is always possible to lift the smaller flax bundles one must acquire it in that manner (Gem. 86b, as explained by Rashbam; see preface to this mishnah). Alternatively, flax bundles tend to come apart if they are pulled

[if] he measured but did not draw [it], he has not acquired [it]. If he is prudent, he rents its space.

One who buys flax from another does not acquire [it] until he moves it from place to place. If it was attached to the ground and he detached any amount, he has acquired [it].

and pulling is therefore not considered a normal way of moving flax. Accordingly, it is not an effective method of acquisition (Rabbeinu Chananel, cited by Rashbam 86b).

Rambam's view is that flax can indeed be bound in large bundles but since one can open the bundles and transport the flax in smaller lots without undue difficulty, it cannot be acquired by meshichah, even when packaged in large bundles. Only produce such as almonds or peppers which, if removed from their sack, scatter and are then difficult to transfer, can be acquired in large packages by meshichah (Rambam, Mechirah 3:2).

וְאִם הָיָה בִמְחֻבָּר לַקַּרְקַע — If it was attached to the ground

I.e., the flax being sold had not yet been cut down though it was fully ripe and waiting to be cut. Since it no longer requires the sustenance of the ground, it is considered, in regard to the laws of sales, as if it had already been cut — i.e., as movable property. Thus, it must be acquired according to the rules of movable property (Rambam Comm.; Rav as explained by Tos. Yom Tov). However, since it is still attached to the ground, it is unsuited to being acquired in the manner prescribed above — hagbahah, lifting — since that would require him to cut and lift each stalk (Rambam, Mechirah 3:18).

וְתָלַשׁ כָּל שֶׁהוּא, קָנָה. — and he detached any amount, he has acquired [it].

I.e., it is possible for him to acquire possession of all the flax by detaching just a bit of it. The Gemara (87a) explains that this refers to a case in which the seller tells the buyer to clear

for him (the seller) a bit of flax from the field. In payment for this service, the buyer is to acquire a temporary right to the land (similar to a rental) and through it all the flax on that field (Rav from Gem. 87a). Thus, by performing this minor service the buyer earns his 'wage' and acquires (temporary) possession of the field. In so doing he can also acquire possession of the flax through the mechanism of agav, the law that in a transaction involving both movable and real property, formal acquisition of the land brings along with it acquisition of the movables as well. Since flax waiting to be cut is deemed movable property, in gaining possession of the land by dint of his service, albeit temporarily, he acquires the flax along with it without any need to perform a formal act of acquisition for the flax. [The entire arrangement is, in fact, merely a legal ploy to transfer ownership of the flax to the buyer.] (Rav as explained by Tos. Yom Tov; Rambam, Maggid Mishneh, Mechirah 3:18).

Other authorities dispute Rambam's assessment that produce which is still attached to the field but no longer needs its sustenance is considered to be detached and therefore governed by the rules of movable property. In their view, as long as it is still attached it is considered to be part of the land (Rashbam 138b, s.v. האב תולש) — and it must thus be acquired in the same manner as real property (Tos. Yom Tov). Accordingly, they explain the Gemara's remarks to mean that when the buyer detaches some of the flax he is performing an act of chazakah acquisition. This is one of the methods of acquiring real property whereby one

[ח] הַמּוֹכֵר יַיִן וָשֶׁמֶן לַחֲבֵרוֹ, וְהוֹקְרוּ אוֹ שֶׁהוּזְלוּ, אִם עַד שֶׁלֹא נִתְמַלְּאַת הַמִּדָּה, לַמּוֹכֵר; מִשֶּׁנִּתְמַלְּאַת הַמִּדָּה, לַלּוֹקֵחַ. וְאִם הָיָה סַרְסוּר בֵּינֵיהֶן, נִשְׁבְּרָה הֶחָבִית, נִשְׁבְּרָה לַסַּרְסוּר.
וְחַיָּב לְהַטִּיף לוֹ שָׁלֹשׁ טִפִּין. הִרְכִּינָה וּמִצָּה, הֲרֵי

יד אברהם

performs an act in the land demonstrating his possession of it (see *Kiddushin* 1:5). Thus, by performing an

act of *chazakah* in the land he formally acquires the flax which is on it (*Rashbam* 87a; cf. *Tos.*).

8.

The delineation in the previous mishnah of how and when a buyer assumes ownership over produce which he purchases is also relevant to determining who benefits from a change in price at the time of the transaction and who is responsible if something should happen to it during that period, as the coming mishnah will explain.

הַמּוֹכֵר יַיִן וָשֶׁמֶן לַחֲבֵרוֹ, — [*If*] *one sold wine or oil to another,*

The same applies to the sale of any produce. The mishnah specifies these because of the discussion at the end of the mishnah concerning the remaining droplets (*Rashbam* 87a).

וְהוֹקְרוּ אוֹ שֶׁהוּזְלוּ, — *and it appreciated or depreciated,*

[Before the transaction was completed, the market price changed, either rising or falling. As a result, the seller wants to back out of the contract to raise his price or the buyer wants to do so to reduce it.]

The ruling of the mishnah pertains to any case in which one of the principals decides to cancel the purchase for any reason at all. The *Tanna* specified these cases because price fluctuation is the most likely reason for one of them to back out (*Tos.* 87a).

אִם עַד שֶׁלֹא נִתְמַלְּאַת הַמִּדָּה, לַמּוֹכֵר; — *if* [*it happened*] *before the measure* [i.e, the utensil used for measuring] *was filled,* [*it belongs*] *to the seller;*

When buying wine or oil, the seller would pour from his barrel into a

measuring utensil the amount being purchased and give it to the buyer. The mishnah is discussing a case in which the measuring utensil belongs neither to the buyer or seller but to a third person, who lent it to them for this purpose (*Gem.* 87a). The mishnah rules that it is understood that his intent was to lend it to the seller for measuring out the wine and oil until that job is finished, and then to lend it to the buyer to use it to hold the produce until he can transfer it to his own utensil (*Rashbam* 86b). Therefore, as long as the measure is not filled the sale is not yet finalized, because the utensil is still in the possession of the seller and thus the produce along with it (*Rav*).

מִשֶּׁנִּתְמַלְּאַת הַמִּדָּה, לַלּוֹקֵחַ. — *once the measure was filled,* [*it belongs*] *to the buyer.*

Since it was the lender's intent to lend the measure to the buyer once the measuring has been completed, as soon as that happens the buyer takes over the right to the utensil and thereby acquires the oil or wine in it [as explained in the introduction to mishnah 7] (*Rav*). Although the measuring utensil is not

8. [If] one sold wine or oil to another, and it appreciated or depreciated, if [it happened] before the measure was filled, [it belongs] to the seller; once the measure was filled, [it belongs] to the buyer. If there was a middleman between them, [and] the barrel broke, it broke for the middleman. He is obligated to let three drops drip out for him.

YAD AVRAHAM

actually the buyer's, its loan to him gives him a temporary legal right to it and this is sufficient for him to acquire other goods through it (see *Gem.* 85a).

Since the produce is acquired by dint of its being in his utensil, the ruling of the mishnah obviously applies only to a case in which the measuring utensil is sitting in a *simta* or in the property of the buyer, as explained in the introduction to mishnah 7 (*Rav* from *Gem.* 85b).

The mishnah must be discussing the measure of a third party, because if it belonged to either the buyer or the seller the ruling here would not always be viable: If it was the buyer's, the wine or oil becomes his as it is being poured into his utensil, even before the measure is full (*Gem.* 87a). This is because where the price of the full sale is pegged to the sum of its constituent units (e.g., one *hin* for twelve *sela*, one *log* per *sela*), as each line on the measuring cup marking one of those smaller units is reached, that fraction of the total sale is immediately completed and is acquired by the buyer via his utensil (*Gem.* 86b). Since the mishnah makes a general statement concerning sales, it must be presumed that it includes this not uncommon case as well (*Rashbam* 87a).

On the other hand, if the measure belonged to the seller, the produce cannot become the buyer's even after the measure was filled, since it is still in the physical possession of the seller.[1]

וְאִם הָיָה סַרְסוּר בֵּינֵיהֶן, — *If there was a middleman between them,*
I.e., the sale went through a middleman (*Rashbam*), and the measuring utensil belonged to him (*Rav* from *Gem.* 87a).

נִשְׁבְּרָה הֶחָבִית, נִשְׁבְּרָה לַסַּרְסוּר. — [and] the *barrel broke, it broke for the middleman.*
Since the barrel used for measuring was the middleman's, he acquires the produce as it enters the barrel and he must therefore bear the loss. Although the middleman is in a sense serving as an agent of acquisition for the buyer he cannot shift the loss to him (*Rav*), because the reality of the situation is that the middleman is buying from the seller and then reselling to the buyer (*Rashbam* 87a).

Others maintain that the mishnah is discussing a case in which the middleman is only a broker who does not take possession of the goods. The reason he is liable is because he was the one who poured the oil or wine into the measure and it broke through his negligence. Since he stands to profit from the transaction, he is considered a *shomer,* guardian, for the produce as long as it is in his hands and he is therefore responsible if a mishap occurs, unless it was due to an accident totally beyond his control (*Tos.* 87a; *Nimmukei Yosef; Yad Ramah*).[2]

וְחַיָּב לְהַטִּיף לוֹ שָׁלֹשׁ טִפִּין. — He is obligated

1. Even if the utensil was sitting in the property of the buyer, the oil or wine does not become his as long as it remains in the utensil of the seller (see *Gem.* 84b-86b; *Rambam, Mechirah* 4:2; *Choshen Mishpat* 200:4).

2. The advantage of this interpretation is that it explains the mishnah's switching from the topic of the appreciation or depreciation of the produce to that of the barrel breaking. According to *Rashbam,* the same point could have been made concerning a change of value in the wine or oil (*Tos.* 87a).

הוּא שֶׁל מוֹכֵר. וְהַחֶנְוָנִי אֵינוֹ חַיָּב לְהַטִּיף שָׁלֹשׁ
טִפִּין. רַבִּי יְהוּדָה אוֹמֵר: עֶרֶב שַׁבָּת עִם חֲשֵׁכָה,
פָּטוּר.

[ט] **הַשּׁוֹלֵחַ** אֶת בְּנוֹ אֵצֶל חֶנְוָנִי וּפֻנְדְּיוֹן בְּיָדוֹ,
וּמָדַד לוֹ בְּאִסָּר שֶׁמֶן וְנָתַן לוֹ אֶת
הָאִסָּר, שָׁבַר אֶת הַצְּלוֹחִית וְאִבֵּד אֶת הָאִסָּר,
חֶנְוָנִי חַיָּב. רַבִּי יְהוּדָה פּוֹטֵר שֶׁעַל מְנָת כֵּן שְׁלָחוֹ.

יד אברהם

to let three drops drip out for him.

When the liquid has been measured in the seller's measuring utensil and then poured over into the buyer's container, after the flow has ended, the seller is obligated to leave the utensil inclined until three drops from that which clings to the walls of the measure drip into the buyer's utensil (*Rav; Choshen Mishpat* 231:6).

הָרְכִּינָהּ וּמָצָה, הֲרֵי הוּא שֶׁל מוֹכֵר. — [*If*] *he turned it over and drained* [*it*], *it belongs to the seller.*

If, after waiting for those last three drops to drip out, the seller turned the barrel over onto its side until the remaining drops gathered at the bottom of the utensil, they belong to him. At this point the buyer has no expectations of receiving those drops (*Rav from Gem.* 87b), and once the owner of an object despairs of obtaining it, it becomes permissible for others to take it

(see *Bava Metzia* 2:1).

וְהַחֶנְוָנִי אֵינוֹ חַיָּב לְהַטִּיף שָׁלֹשׁ טִפִּין. — *A storekeeper, however, is not obligated to let three drops drip out.*

A storekeeper is too busy with his customers to take the time to bother with such minute amounts (*Rav*), and the Rabbis did not require him to do so (*Rashbam* 87a).

There is another version which reads, *The storekeeper is* [*also*] *obligated,* etc. (*Ri Migash; Yad Ramah*).

רַבִּי יְהוּדָה אוֹמֵר: עֶרֶב שַׁבָּת עִם חֲשֵׁכָה, פָּטוּר. — *R' Yehudah says: Only on the eve of the Sabbath, at dusk, is he exempt.*

Only just before the onset of Shabbos is the storekeeper so busy as to warrant being exempt from the obligation to wait for three more drops to drip out for the buyer (*Rav*).

The halachah follows the opinion of the first *Tanna* (*Choshen Mishpat* 231:6).

9.

The mishnah now returns to the topic mentioned in the previous mishnah — responsibility for goods involved in a transaction.

הַשּׁוֹלֵחַ אֶת בְּנוֹ אֵצֶל חֶנְוָנִי — [*If*] *someone sent his son to a storekeeper*

This refers to a child who is still a minor (*Rav*).

וּפֻנְדְּיוֹן בְּיָדוֹ, — *with a pundion in his hand,*

A *pundion* equals the value of two issars (*Rav*).

וּמָדַד לוֹ בְּאִסָּר שֶׁמֶן וְנָתַן לוֹ אֶת הָאִסָּר, — *and he measured* [*out*] *for him an issar's worth of oil and gave him an issar,*

The storekeeper gave the child an

[If] he turned it over and drained [it], it belongs to the seller. A storekeeper, however, is not obligated to let three drops drip out. R' Yehudah says: Only on the eve of the Sabbath, at dusk, is he exempt.

9. [If] someone sent his son to a storekeeper with a *pundion* in his hand, and he measured [out] for him an *issar's* worth of oil and gave him an *issar*, [if] he broke the jar or lost the *issar*, the storekeeper is liable. R' Yehudah exempts him because he sent him for that purpose. The Sages agree with R' Yehudah

YAD AVRAHAM

issar's worth of oil and an *issar* in change, in accordance with the father's instructions *(Rav)*.

שָׁבַר אֶת הַצְּלוֹחִית וְאָבֵּד אֶת הָאִסָּר, חֶנְוָנִי חַיָּב. — *[if] he broke the jar or lost the issar, the storekeeper is liable.*

[I.e., if the child broke the jar or lost the *issar*, the storekeeper is responsible for the oil and the *issar*, because the storekeeper is expected to understand that] the father did not send the child to bring him the oil but only to inform the storekeeper of his request that he prepare it for him *(Rav from Gem. 87b)*. [Therefore, his sending the oil and money back with the child is considered an act of negligence for which he is liable.]

This reasoning does not explain his liability for the jar, since the father himself sent it with the child and thereby indicated that its loss is of no concern to him. The *Gemara* (88a) therefore explains the mishnah to be discussing a case in which the storekeeper borrowed the jar to use for measuring the produce of another customer. Since someone who borrows the object of another without his knowledge is considered a thief, he retains responsibility for the object until he returns it to the owner himself, which the storekeeper did not do. He is therefore liable for whatever happens to it *(Rav; see Bava Kama 118a)*.

Although the father showed the same lack of concern for the *pundion* which he sent with the child, the storekeeper is nevertheless liable. Once the *pundion* arrived safely in the hands of the storekeeper and he accepted it, he is not free of liability for the *pundion* until the oil and *issar* reach the father. But since it was not the father's intention that the storekeeper send these back with the child, he has not discharged his obligation by doing so *(Nimmukei Yosef, Tos. 87b)*.

Others contend that the mishnah is not discussing responsibility for the money at all, only for the jar and oil *(Ri Migash; Yad Ramah; Meiri)*. Their version of the mishnah does not include the words *with a pundion in his hand*, and they explain the phrase *and gave him an issar* to be referring to the *issar's* worth of oil which he poured into the jar *(Meiri)*. The child was either not sent with the money [but was instructed to order the oil on credit] *(Meiri)*, or was sent to receive a prepaid order *(Yad Ramah)*.

רַבִּי יְהוּדָה פּוֹטֵר שֶׁעַל מְנָת כֵּן שְׁלָחוֹ. — *R' Yehudah exempts him because he sent him for that purpose.*

He maintains that the storekeeper has the right to assume that the child was sent for the purpose of purchasing the oil and taking it home to his father. Therefore, he is not liable for any damage caused by the child *(Rav)*. In regard to the jar, R' Yehudah is of the opinion that something which is borrowed without permission has the laws of a borrowed article, not a stolen one, and a borrowed article need only be returned to the place from where it was taken in order for the borrower to become free from liability *(Gem. 88a)*.

וּמוֹדִים חֲכָמִים לְרַבִּי יְהוּדָה בִּזְמַן שֶׁהַצְּלוֹחִית בְּיַד הַתִּינוֹק וּמָדַד חֶנְוָנִי לְתוֹכָהּ, חֶנְוָנִי פָּטוּר.

[י] הַסִּיטוֹן מְקַנֵּחַ מִדּוֹתָיו אַחַת לִשְׁלֹשִׁים יוֹם; וּבַעַל הַבַּיִת, אַחַת לִשְׁנֵים עָשָׂר חֹדֶשׁ. רַבָּן שִׁמְעוֹן בֶּן גַּמְלִיאֵל אוֹמֵר: חִלּוּף הַדְּבָרִים. חֶנְוָנִי מְקַנֵּחַ מִדּוֹתָיו פַּעֲמַיִם בְּשַׁבָּת, וּמְמַחֶה מִשְׁקְלוֹתָיו פַּעַם אַחַת בְּשַׁבָּת, וּמְקַנֵּחַ מֹאזְנַיִם עַל כָּל מִשְׁקָל וּמִשְׁקָל.

יד אברהם

וּמוֹדִים חֲכָמִים לְרַבִּי יְהוּדָה בִּזְמַן שֶׁהַצְּלוֹחִית בְּיַד הַתִּינוֹק וּמָדַד חֶנְוָנִי לְתוֹכָהּ, חֶנְוָנִי פָּטוּר. — The Sages agree with R' Yehudah that when the jar is in the hand of the child and the storekeeper measured into it, [that] the storekeeper is exempt.

I.e., from paying for the jar (Rav). This refers to a case in which the storekeeper took the jar only to measure for the child, not for other customers. Since it was never misappropriated, it never left the possession of the owner and the storekeeper did not become liable for its damage (Rashbam 88a).

The statement that it was *in the hands of the child* is meant in a figurative sense, that it never left the child's custody, since the storekeeper was holding it for him while he was measuring into it (Tif. Yis.). Alternatively, the mishnah uses this expression because it was customary for storekeepers to pour into the customer's jar without ever taking it from their hands. In point of fact, however, the same law applies even if the storekeeper took the jar from the child, as long as he did not use it for someone else (Meiri).

10.

A Jew is required by Torah law to make certain that his weights and measures are accurate, so that he not cheat his customers (Lev. 19:36). The next two mishnayos discuss the steps which must be taken by various dealers to maintain that accuracy.

הַסִּיטוֹן — *A wholesaler*

Since he sells only to retailers, not to private customers, he does not use his measures as often as does a retailer (Meiri).

Some commentators maintain that the term סיטון refers specifically to one who sells oil or wine (Rabbeinu Gershom; Tos. to Bava Metzia 48a, s.v. נתנה לסיטון; cf. Nimmukei Yosef here).

מְקַנֵּחַ מִדּוֹתָיו אַחַת לִשְׁלֹשִׁים יוֹם; — must clean his measures once in thirty days;

In the course of a month a layer of congealed oil and wine builds up inside these measures, diminishing their

holding capacity (Rav). [Therefore, to preserve the integrity of the measure, this film must be removed.]

וּבַעַל הַבַּיִת, אַחַת לִשְׁנֵים עָשָׂר חֹדֶשׁ. — and a householder, once in twelve months.

I.e., the farmer who sells the products of his fields to the wholesaler. Such a person uses his measures even less frequently than a wholesaler (Rav), often selling all his produce at one time (Meiri). Therefore, he need only clean his measures once a year.

רַבָּן שִׁמְעוֹן בֶּן גַּמְלִיאֵל אוֹמֵר: חִלּוּף הַדְּבָרִים. — Rabban Shimon ben Gamliel says: The

that when the jar is in the hand of the child and the storekeeper measured into it, [that] the storekeeper is exempt.

10. A wholesaler must clean his measures once in thirty days; and a householder, once in twelve months. Rabban Shimon ben Gamliel says: The reverse is true. A storekeeper must clean his measures twice a week, wipe his weights once a week, and clean the scales for every weighing.

YAD AVRAHAM

reverse is true.

In his view, it is the wholesaler who need only clean his measures once a year, because their constant use prevents the liquid from congealing. A householder, however, who does not use his measures constantly, must clean them every thirty days (Rashbam 88a). Alternatively, because a householder sells all of his produce at one time, if his measures are inaccurate, the entire loss falls on one buyer. This is not true in the case of a wholesaler in which the relatively minor loss is distributed among several buyers. Since they too are earning a profit on these products, the Rabbis were less concerned over this slight loss and did not burden the wholesaler with cleaning his measures so frequently (Meiri).

חֶנְוָנִי מְקַנֵּחַ מִדּוֹתָיו פַּעֲמַיִם בְּשַׁבָּת, — A storekeeper must clean his measures twice a week,

A storekeeper must clean his measures more frequently because, as explained above (mishnah 8), he is not required to leave his measures dripping until three last drops drip out, as are a householder or wholesaler. Therefore, there is more liquid left in his measures to congeal (Rav; Rashbam).

Alternatively, since the storekeeper sells directly to the consumer, the Rabbis were more concerned for even slight distortions in the measures (Meiri).

This would explain Rabban Shimon ben

Gamliel's implied agreement with this ruling (Meiri). However, even according to Rashbam's explanation of Rabban Shimon ben Gamliel (see above) this is understandable, because even constant usage is not sufficient to prevent the congealment of the thicker layer of residue resulting from his repeated failure to drain out the last three drops from the measure (Rashbam 88a).

וּמְמַחֶה מִשְׁקְלוֹתָיו פַּעַם אַחַת בְּשַׁבָּת, — wipe his weights once a week,

[The scales used in those days were balance scales in which the item being weighed was placed in one pan and known weights in the other until a balance was achieved.] The weights used for weighing moist or greasy products (Rav), such as meat, fish, oil, honey, etc., must be wiped clean once a week because in handling the weights together with them some of their substance sticks to the weights and makes them heavier (Nimmukei Yosef; see mishnah 11). Although this discrepancy would work in favor of the customer, these weights are also used by the seller to purchase from others, and their inaccuracy would then increase the amount of his purchase (Yad Ramah; Meiri).

וּמְקַנֵּחַ מֹאזְנַיִם עַל כָּל מִשְׁקָל וּמִשְׁקָל. — and clean the scales for every weighing.

Every time he uses his scales he must clean out the pans which, due to their concavity, retain more grease and particles than do the weights (Rashbam 88a).

[יא] **אָמַר** רַבָּן שִׁמְעוֹן בֶּן גַּמְלִיאֵל: בַּמֶּה
דְבָרִים אֲמוּרִים? בְּלַח. אֲבָל בְּיָבֵשׁ,
אֵינוֹ צָרִיךְ.

וְחַיָּב לְהַכְרִיעַ לוֹ טֶפַח. הָיָה שׁוֹקֵל לוֹ עַיִן בְּעַיִן,
נוֹתֵן לוֹ גְרוּמָיו: אֶחָד לַעֲשָׂרָה בְּלַח, וְאֶחָד
לַעֲשָׂרִים בְּיָבֵשׁ. מְקוֹם שֶׁנָּהֲגוּ לָמוּד בְּדַקָּה, לֹא

יד אברהם

11.

אָמַר רַבָּן שִׁמְעוֹן בֶּן גַּמְלִיאֵל: בַּמֶּה דְּבָרִים
אֲמוּרִים? — *Rabban Shimon ben Gamliel
said: In regard to what was this stated?*

I.e., in regard to what types of
products did the previous mishnah rule
that a storekeeper must wipe his
weights once a week? Rabban Shimon
ben Gamliel is not disputing the
previous ruling, merely clarifying it
(*Tos. Yom Tov*).

בְּלַח. אֲבָל בְּיָבֵשׁ, אֵינוֹ צָרִיךְ. — *In regard to
moist [commodities]. However, [in the
case] of dry [ones], it is not necessary.*

Only liquids such as wine or oils or
moist or greasy foods leave a sticky
residue on the weights. Dry foods, such
as fruits and spices, do not (*Rashbam
88a*).

Others contend that Rabban Shimon ben
Gamliel does in fact dispute the ruling of the
previous mishnah. Whereas the previous
mishnah maintains that even weights used
for dry products must be cleaned, as a
preventive measure against neglecting to
clean those used for moist products, Rabban
Shimon ben Gamliel requires that they be
cleaned only for moist or greasy items (*Yad
Ramah*)

וְחַיָּב לְהַכְרִיעַ לוֹ טֶפַח. — *He is obligated to
overbalance [the scales] a handbreadth
in [the buyer's] favor.*

The seller must allow the side of the
balance scale which contains the
produce to sink a handbreadth lower

than the side holding the weight
(*Rashbam*), if that is the prevailing
custom (*Tos. Yom Tov* from *Gem*. 88b).
This applies only if the produce in
question weighs at least a *litra* (*Rav*). [A
litra is approximately a pound; see
Aruch.] Otherwise, to demand such an
imbalance would be unfair to the seller
(*Rashbam*). However, even for weights
much greater than a *litra* he is only
obligated to allow one such overweight
for the entire purchase (*Gem*. 89a).

הָיָה שׁוֹקֵל לוֹ עַיִן בְּעַיִן, נוֹתֵן לוֹ גְרוּמָיו: — *[If]
he was weighing for him evenly [lit eye
to eye], he must give him the extra
[weight]:*

I.e., in a place where there is no
custom to overbalance the scale in the
customer's favor (*Rav*), he must add in
something extra to the quantity being
purchased (*Tif. Yis.*). This is based on
the Torah's exhortation to keep a
[measuring] stone which is *whole and
righteous* (*Deut*. 25:15). The *Gemara*
(88b) derives from the extra word
righteous that when a seller measures
out merchandise to a customer, he must
ensure the righteousness of his measure
by adding in a little extra to the amount
stipulated (*Rashbam*).[1] This requirement is fulfilled by overbalancing in
those places where that is the custom
(*Rashbam* 88a). Indeed, where that

---

1. This applies not only to foodstuffs but to all forms of merchandise (*Aruch HaShulchan*
231:14).

11. Rabban Shimon ben Gamliel said: In regard to what was this stated? In regard to moist [commodities]. However, [in the case] of dry [ones], it is not necessary.

He is obligated to overbalance [the scales] a handbreadth in [the buyer's] favor. [If] he was weighing for him evenly, he must give him the extra [weight]: one to ten for moist [commodities] and one to twenty for dry [ones]. [In] a place where it is customary to measure with a small [measure], he may

YAD AVRAHAM

custom exists, he may not balance the scales precisely and add in additional produce instead (*Rambam, Geneivah* 8:14; *Choshen Mishpat* 231:14). [This would seem to be the meaning of the mishnah's statement above that one is *obligated* to overbalance where such is the custom.]

אֶחָד לַעֲשָׂרָה בְּלַח — *one to ten for moist [commodities]*

The *Gemara* (88b) concludes that the text of the mishnah is actually abridged, and in effect should read *one in ten for ten* — i.e., one tenth of a *litra* for a ten *litra* purchase, or one percent of the total. This is derived from the mishnah's use of the phrase 'one *to* ten,' rather than one *in* ten (*Rashbam*). [The seller must add this amount without charge.]

The mishnah chooses this convoluted method of expressing itself, rather than simply saying *one in one hundred*, to indicate that by Biblical law this applies only to a purchase of ten *litra* or more (*Tos.* 88b). In practice, however, this obligation applies regardless of the quantity involved (see *Choshen Mishpat* 231:14).

וְאֶחָד לַעֲשָׂרִים בְּיָבֵשׁ. — *and one to twenty for dry [ones]*.

When selling solids, he need only add one twentieth of a *litra* for each twenty purchased — i.e., a quarter of one percent [one four-hundredth] of the total purchase (*Rav* from *Gem.* 88b). The reason for this distinction is that liquids stick to the utensil from which

they are poured to a greater extent than do drier substances, and the buyer thus does not receive his full measure (*Rashbam*).

The *Gemara* is actually uncertain whether the mishnah means one four-hundredth of the purchase or one two-hundredth. The halachah, however, follows the former view (*Rambam, Geneivah* 8:13; *Choshen Mishpat* 231:14).

In setting the standard for those places where it was already customary to overbalance the scale, the Rabbis did not establish separate standards for moist and dry commodities. Since the custom in those places had been to overbalance the scale the same amount for both, to differentiate between the two would generate confusion and cause the application of the standard for dry commodities to be applied to moist ones as well, at the expense of the buyer. They therefore established the standard appropriate to liquids as a universal rule, at the expense of the seller, since the Torah emphasizes his responsibility to give the buyer more than he pays for (*Yad Ramah*).

מְקוֹם שֶׁנָּהֲגוּ לָמוֹד בְּדַקָּה, — *[In] a place where it is customary to measure with a small [measure]*,

I.e., in a place where it is customary to weigh produce by the *kav* (*Rashbam*).

לֹא יָמֹד בְּגַסָּה; — *he may not measure with a large one*;

He may not weigh it out in units of a *seah*, which is six *kavs* (*Rashbam*), because the buyer loses out. If he weighs by the *kav*, the scale is

יָמַד בְּגַסָּה; בְּגַסָּה, לֹא יָמַד בְּדַקָּה. לִמְחוֹק, לֹא
יִגְדֹּשׁ; לִגְדּוֹשׁ, לֹא יִמְחֹק.

[א] הַמּוֹכֵר פֵּרוֹת לַחֲבֵרוֹ וְלֹא צָמְחוּ, וַאֲפִלּוּ
זֶרַע פִּשְׁתָּן, אֵינוֹ חַיָּב בְּאַחֲרָיוּתָן.
רַבָּן שִׁמְעוֹן בֶּן גַּמְלִיאֵל אוֹמֵר: זֶרְעוֹנֵי גִנָּה שֶׁאֵינָן
נֶאֱכָלִין חַיָּב בְּאַחֲרָיוּתָן.

יד אברהם

overbalanced a handbreadth to his
benefit for each *kav*, whereas when
measuring by the *seah*, he receives only
one increase per *seah* (*Rav*). Additionally, the seller allows a little leeway in
favor of the buyer in each weighing,
making extra weighings beneficial to the
buyer (*Rashbam* 88b according to
Maharsha; cf. Hagahos HaBach).
[Thus, even where the custom is not to
overbalance the scales in the buyer's
favor but to give him a flat amount extra
for the entire sale, the buyer still gains
by having his purchase measured out in
smaller units and the seller is therefore
not permitted to deviate from the local
practice of using small weights.]

בְּגַסָּה, לֹא יָמַד בְּדַקָּה. — *with a large one, he
may not measure with a small one.*

This is the reverse of the previous
case and results in a loss to the seller
(*Rashbam*). He is therefore advised not
to deviate from the custom and measure
with a small measure (*Aruch
HaShulchan* 231:8).[1]

Others explain that it is impossible to
make certain that the measurement of
two smaller amounts will exactly equal
the one measure of a larger quantity.
Rather, at times the former will be more,
and at times the latter will be more.
Therefore, it is prohibited to alter the
prevailing system used in that locale,
since either of the parties may thereby

take a loss (*Yad Ramah*).

לִמְחוֹק, — [*In a place where it is
customary*] *to level,*

I.e., to remove the excess heaped
above the rim of the measuring cup,
leaving a level cup of whatever is being
measured (*Rav*). [This case of the
mishnah deals with products which are
measured by volume rather than
weight.]

לֹא יִגְדֹּשׁ; — *he may not heap;*

The seller may not in such a place
heap his measure, whether or not he
adds to the price (*Rav* from *Gem.* 89a).
This is derived by the *Gemara* from the
verse (*Deut.* 25:15), *You must maintain
an ephah* [a measurement of grain]
which is whole and righteous, in which
the extra word *righteous* is taken to
teach that one may not even measure in
a manner which *could* lead to deceit. In
this case, someone not familiar with the
local custom might be misled into
thinking that the accepted system was
to measure in heaped quantities and
thereby be deceived by a buyer into
measuring his produce in that manner
without receiving compensation for the
added produce. Even if the price is
raised to allow for the heap it is
forbidden, because the observer may
not become aware of this adjustment
(*Rashbam* 89a).

1. [In the following case, *Rashbam* explains the restriction against the seller causing a loss to
himself to be due to the possibility of an observer's mistaken conclusion which could lead to
subsequent corruption (see below). This would seem to apply to this case as well.]

not measure with a large one; with a large one, he may not measure with a small one. [In a place where it is customary] to level, he may not heap; to heap, he may not level.

1. [If] one sells produce to another and it did not grow, even [if these were] seeds of flax, he is not liable. Rabban Shimon ben Gamliel says: [In the case of] garden seeds which are not eaten he is liable.

YAD AVRAHAM

לִגְדּוֹשׁ, לֹא יִמְחֹק. — *to heap, he may not level.*

Similarly, in a place where the custom is to measure out in heaped utensils, the seller may not measure out the purchase in level measures. Here too the practice could lead to corruption by causing some to think that local custom required only level measures, thus leading them to charge the full (heaped) price for a level measure (*Rashbam*). Even if the price is lowered to compensate for the leveling of the measure it is forbidden (*Rav*), because the casual observer might not hear of the price adjustment (*Rashbam*).

Chapter 6

1.

This chapter continues the discussion begun in mishnah 6 of the previous chapter of the laws governing purchases of items whose exact quality or size was not clearly defined.

הַמּוֹכֵר פֵּרוֹת לַחֲבֵרוֹ — *[If] one sells produce to another*

At the time of the sale no indication was given whether the produce was to be used for eating or planting (*Rav*), but the species in question were of a type bought for either purpose — e.g., beans (*Meiri*).

וְלֹא צָמְחוּ, — *and it did not grow,*

[The buyer planted them but they did not grow.]

וַאֲפִלּוּ זֶרַע פִּשְׁתָּן, — *even [if these were] seeds of flax,*

Even if the seeds involved were seeds of flax, which are usually bought for planting (*Rav* from *Gem.* 93a).

אֵינוֹ חַיָּב בְּאַחֲרָיוֹתָן. — *he is not liable.*

The seller does not have to refund the money, because he can claim that they were sold for eating, not planting. This claim is accepted even in the case of flax seeds because the principle of *majority* [i.e., that issues of doubt facing a court may be decided by assuming that the situation at hand is typical of the majority of such cases] is not sufficient to exact money from the one holding it אֵין הוֹלְכִין בְּמָמוֹן אַחַר הָרוֹב] (*Rashbam* 92a, *Rav* from *Gem.* 93a). Therefore, since flax seeds were used by some as an ingredient in making cheese dip (see *Nedarim* 49a), the claim that it was sold for consumption is tenable (*Rashbam*).

רַבָּן שִׁמְעוֹן בֶּן גַּמְלִיאֵל אוֹמֵר: זֵרְעוֹנֵי גִנָּה שֶׁאֵינָן נֶאֱכָלִין — *Rabban Shimon ben Gamliel says: [In the case of] garden seeds which are not eaten*

Such as seeds of cabbage and leek (*Rashbam*).

חַיָּב בְּאַחֲרָיוּתָן. — *he is liable.*

He must refund the buyer the entire

[ב] **הַמּוֹכֵר** פֵּרוֹת לַחֲבֵרוֹ, הֲרֵי זֶה מְקַבֵּל עָלָיו
רֹבַע טְנוֹפֶת לִסְאָה. תְּאֵנִים,
מְקַבֵּל עָלָיו עֶשֶׂר מְתֻלָּעוֹת לְמֵאָה. מַרְתֵּף שֶׁל יַיִן,
מְקַבֵּל עָלָיו עֶשֶׂר קוֹסְסוֹת לְמֵאָה. קַנְקַנִּים בַּשָּׁרוֹן,
מְקַבֵּל עָלָיו עֶשֶׂר פִּיטַסְיָאוֹת לְמֵאָה.

יד אברהם

price of the seeds. Although the buyer did not specify that he was buying the seeds for planting, since they are unfit for anything else, they were clearly bought for this purpose. Since planting is something for which they turned out to be totally unsuited, their purchase was erroneous and inherently invalid (*Nimmukei Yosef*). Thus, even if the seller was unaware of their defect, the sale is void (*Sema* 232:47).

The seller cannot demand that the buyer return the seeds before receiving his money [which would be impossible, since they have already been planted], because it was understood at the time of the sale that he was buying the seeds in order to plant them, and he is therefore not liable for their return (*Nimmukei Yosef*).

However, this applies only if the lack of growth is clearly due to the seeds themselves. If there were other factors which prevented their growth — e.g., a hailstorm — the seller is no longer liable (*Rif*). In the absence of any obvious outside factors to account for the lack of growth, however, the assumption is that the defect was in the seeds (*Rosh*).

Rabban Shimon ben Gamliel's ruling does not dispute anything said earlier in the mishnah. Indeed, the *Gemara* (93b) concludes that the author of the entire mishnah is Rabban Shimon ben Gamliel, and it should be emended to read as follows: ... *even [if they are] seeds of flax, he is not liable. However, [in a case of] garden seeds which are not eaten, he is liable. [These are] the words of Rabban Shimon ben Gamliel. Because Rabban Shimon ben Gamliel says: etc. (Rav).*

2.

If someone sells an item to another and misleads him as to the nature of the object, the purchase is void. If he misleads him only in regard to the quantity, the sale remains valid and the seller must provide the rest of the quantity agreed upon. This mishnah will teach that in many types of sales the subject of the sale commonly contains a certain percentage of refuse or items of inferior quality. In such cases, the buyer is understood to have accepted these as part of the purchase and he is not entitled to any adjustment for it (*Meiri*).

הַמּוֹכֵר פֵּרוֹת לַחֲבֵרוֹ, — *[If] one sells produce to another,*
This refers, in this case, to grain (*Rav; Rashbam*). Rambam (*Mechirah* 18:11), however, takes it to refer to fruit, not grain (*Beis Yosef* 229:1).

הֲרֵי זֶה מְקַבֵּל עָלָיו רֹבַע טְנוֹפֶת לִסְאָה. — *he accepts upon himself a quarter-kav of refuse per seah.*
I.e., the buyer must accept as part of the purchase up to a quarter-*kav* of

refuse in each *seah* of produce (*Rashbam*). A *kav* is one-sixth of a *seah*. Thus, one part in twenty-four is expected to be refuse. This is considered an acceptable part of the purchase because refuse up to this ratio is ordinarily found in a bushel of grain (*Rav*).

If more than this amount is found to be refuse, the seller must sift all of the grain and provide a *seah* of pure grain. The *Gemara* (94a) cites two views for

2. **[I**f] one sells produce to another, he accepts upon himself a quarter-*kav* of refuse per *seah*.
[With] figs, he accepts upon himself ten wormy ones
per hundred. [With] a cellar of wine, he accepts upon
himself ten souring ones per hundred. [With] jars in
Sharon, he accepts upon himself ten inferior ones per
hundred.

YAD AVRAHAM

this. Some explain this to be a penalty —
because the unusually high percentage
of refuse indicates that it was mixed in
deliberately. Others maintain that it is
required by the letter of the law. A
buyer is not really agreeable to any
refuse in his grain but he forgoes up to a
twenty-fourth only to avoid the bother
of sifting it. Therefore, once the seller
forces him to go to this trouble, he does
not waive any amount.

תְּאֵנִים, מְקַבֵּל עָלָיו עֶשֶׂר מַתְלָעוֹת לְמֵאָה. —
[*With*] *figs, he* [the buyer] *accepts upon
himself ten wormy ones per hundred.*

I.e., he must expect up to ten percent
of the figs to be wormy (*Rav*), no matter
what the quantity of figs involved (*Tos.
Yom Tov* from *Rashbam* 83b).

מַרְתֵּף שֶׁל יַיִן, מְקַבֵּל עָלָיו עֶשֶׂר קוֹסְסוֹת לְמֵאָה.
— [*With*] *a cellar of wine, he accepts
upon himself ten souring ones per
hundred.*

The buyer must be prepared to find
up to ten containers out of every
hundred in a deteriorating condition,
soon to be sour (*Rashbam* 83b, *Rambam
Comm.* and *Hil. Mechirah* 17:7).
Though they are still drinkable, they
must be used up quickly. Consequently,
he should not expect to be able to use all
his wine for cooking, in which only
small amounts are used at a time (*Rav*).

The *Gemara* (95b) concludes that the
application of this law depends upon
the precise wording of the purchase
agreement. If the seller said that he was
selling a cellar of wine fit for use in
cooking, all of the wine must be fit for
that purpose and therefore non-
perishable. If he said that he was selling

him 'this cellar,' the sale is valid even if
it has all soured into vinegar (since he
did not mention 'wine'). The ruling of
the mishnah is for a case in which he
said that he was selling him 'this cellar
of wine, which is fit for cooking.' In this
arrangement it is considered acceptable
if up to one-tenth of the containers are
perishable and fit only for immediate
consumption.

If he told him that he is selling him a cellar
of wine, without specifying either a specific
cellar or stating that the wine is good for
cooking, there is a dispute in the *Gemara*
whether the sale is valid if one-tenth of the
containers are in deteriorating condition. The
halachah is that the buyer must accept it (*Rif*;
Rambam loc. cit. 17:7). Accordingly, the
mishnah can also be construed to be
discussing such a case and there is no need to
qualify the simple case of the mishnah in any
way (*Rosh*).

קַנְקַנִּים בַּשָּׁרוֹן, — [*With*] *jars in Sharon,*

[Sharon is a coastal plain in Eretz
Yisrael, between the present day Haifa
and Jaffa.] The mishnah formulates a
rule for Sharon specifically because it
had no set custom regarding the sale of
jars (see below). Wherever there is a set
custom as to what is acceptable in a
purchase, that custom is binding [as
long as the principals do not stipulate
otherwise] (*Nimmukei Yosef*; see
Rambam, Mechirah 18:14, *Kesef Mishneh*). Others explain that Sharon is
singled out because jars were sold there
in abundance (*Meiri*).

מְקַבֵּל עָלָיו עֶשֶׂר פִּיטַסְיָאוֹת לְמֵאָה. — *he
accepts upon himself ten inferior ones
per hundred.*

I.e., ten earthenware jugs which have
not been thoroughly baked and are

[ג] הַמּוֹכֵר יַיִן לַחֲבֵרוֹ וְהֶחֱמִיץ, אֵינוֹ חַיָּב
בְּאַחֲרָיוּתוֹ. וְאִם יָדוּעַ שֶׁיֵּינוֹ
מַחֲמִיץ, הֲרֵי זֶה מֶקַח טָעוּת. וְאִם אָמַר לוֹ, "יַיִן
מְבֻשָּׂם אֲנִי מוֹכֵר לָךְ," חַיָּב לְהַעֲמִיד לוֹ עַד
הָעֲצֶרֶת; וְיָשָׁן, מִשֶּׁל אֶשְׁתָּקַד; וּמְיֻשָּׁן, מִשֶּׁל שָׁלֹשׁ
שָׁנִים:

[ד] הַמּוֹכֵר מָקוֹם לַחֲבֵרוֹ לִבְנוֹת לוֹ בַּיִת, וְכֵן

יד אברהם

therefore unduly porous. Because of this they do a poor job of containing liquids (Rav; Meiri). Others explain this to mean *cracked containers* which have been patched up. They are nevertheless inferior because they do not last as long as uncracked ones (Rashbam 97b, s.v. תנא פיטסיאות).

3.

הַמּוֹכֵר יַיִן לַחֲבֵרוֹ וְהֶחֱמִיץ, אֵינוֹ חַיָּב בְּאַחֲרָיוּתוֹ. — [If] one sells wine to another and it sours, he is not liable.

Even if the wine sours immediately after the purchase (Meiri) the seller is not obligated to refund the buyer for the lost wine, since it was still perfectly good wine at the time of the sale (Rav). [By contrast, the ruling of the previous mishnah concerning the number of jugs of souring wine a buyer accepts (s.v. מרתף) refers to wine which had already begun to sour at the time of the sale (i.e., its taste was already slightly acrid), but was still drinkable (see Rambam, Mechirah 17:7).]

As in the previous mishnah, the mishnah here is discussing a case in which the seller stated that the wine could be used for cooking — i.e., with the expectation that it could last a long time.[1] The reason the sale is valid is because the seller can claim that since his wine showed no signs of deterioration at the time of the sale, the fault may lie with the casks in which the buyer

stored the wine after the sale (since these can often cause wine to turn bad). Therefore, the ruling stated holds true only if the wine soured after being transferred to the buyer's containers. However, if it soured in the seller's containers, the buyer can demand a refund because the fault clearly lies with the seller (Rav from Gem. 98a).

וְאִם יָדוּעַ שֶׁיֵּינוֹ מַחֲמִיץ, — If it is known that his wine sours,

I.e., it occurred every year (Rashbam) for three years (Yad Ramah).

הֲרֵי זֶה מֶקַח טָעוּת. — it is an erroneous purchase.

If, as above, the seller stated that the wine could be used for cooking, the purchase is void. Since this person's wine has a history of souring, its souring is attributed to the wine itself (Rav). However, if the buyer was aware that this person's wine tends to sour, the sale is valid because he obviously accepted the risk (Yad Ramah).

---

1. This is indicated by the mishnah's qualification of this ruling for someone whose wine is known to sour (see below). Had no stipulation been made regarding the expected shelf-life of the wine, even that sale would be valid as long as it was still good wine at the time of the purchase (Gem. 98a).

3. **[I**f] one sells wine to another and it sours, he is not liable. If it is known that his wine sours, it is an erroneous purchase. If he said to him, 'I am selling you spiced wine,' he is responsible for its preservation until Shavuos; 'old wine,' [it must be] from the previous year; 'very old wine,' from three years [previous].

4. **O**ne who sells a place to another to build a house for him [on it], and similarly, one who

YAD AVRAHAM

וְאִם אָמַר לוֹ ,,יַיִן מְבֻשָּׁם אֲנִי מוֹכֵר לָךְ,, — *If he said to him, 'I am selling you spiced wine,'*

Such wine generally lasts until Shavuos, after which time the hot weather may cause it to sour *(Rav).*

Others translate יַיִן מְבֻשָּׁם to mean *superior wine.* Such wine is expected to maintain its superior standing until Shavuos *(Meiri).*

חַיָּב לְהַעֲמִיד לוֹ עַד הָעֲצֶרֶת; — *he is responsible for its preservation* [lit. *to preserve for him] until Shavuos;*

[Since that is the norm for such wine, his mention of its special condition is understood to guarantee that it will last that long.]

Although the mishnah is discussing wine which has been placed in the containers of the buyer (see above), the superior condition of the wine, as stated by the seller, should have protected it from spoilage despite any undetected flaw in the containers. Thus, this holds true only if the containers were checked and were found to be free of any noticeable defects *(Nimmukei Yosef).*

Others contend that the mishnah is not now ruling about wine which actually soured but is simply defining the minimum quality of wine sold under these terms — i.e., it must be good enough to last until Shavuos. If it actually soured before then, however, the buyer can only collect a refund if the wine was still in the seller's containers *(Tos.* 98a).

וְיָשָׁן, מִשֶּׁל אֶשְׁתָּקַד; — *'old wine,'* [*it must be] from the previous year;*

If the seller stated that he was giving him old wine, it must be wine produced the previous year *(Rav;* see *Sema, Choshen Mishpat* 230:18).

וּמְיֻשָּׁן, מִשֶּׁל שָׁלֹשׁ שָׁנִים. — *'very old wine,' from three years [previous].*

If he said that he was selling him very old wine, it must be wine produced two years before, making the present year the third of its existence *(Rashbam).*

In addition, it must last until Succos of that year *(Gem.* 98b), the anniversary of the grapes' harvest, and thus the culmination of its third year. The term *very old wine* implies that it will be good for three full years *(Rashbam).*

4.

The mishnah now reverts to the subject of the fourth and fifth chapters, viz., the definition of what is included in a sale in which all the details have not been specified.

הַמּוֹכֵר מָקוֹם לַחֲבֵרוֹ לִבְנוֹת לוֹ בַיִת, — *One who sells a place to another to build a house for him [on it],*

[I.e., a builder contracted to build a house for someone on the land which he is selling him. The contract, however, did not specify the size of the house to be built.]

In the version to the mishnah cited in the *Gemara,* the phrase *to build a house for him* does not appear (see below, s.v. בַיִת קָטָן).

הַמְקַבֵּל מֵחֲבֵרוֹ לִבְנוֹת לוֹ בֵית חַתְנוּת לִבְנוֹ וּבֵית
אַלְמְנוּת לְבִתּוֹ, בּוֹנֶה אַרְבַּע אַמּוֹת עַל שֵׁשׁ; דִּבְרֵי
רַבִּי עֲקִיבָא. רַבִּי יִשְׁמָעֵאל אוֹמֵר: רֶפֶת בָּקָר הוּא
זֶה. הָרוֹצֶה לַעֲשׂוֹת רֶפֶת בָּקָר בּוֹנֶה אַרְבַּע אַמּוֹת
עַל שֵׁשׁ; בַּיִת קָטָן, שֵׁשׁ עַל שְׁמוֹנֶה; גָּדוֹל, שְׁמוֹנֶה
עַל עֶשֶׂר; טְרַקְלִין, עֶשֶׂר עַל עֶשֶׂר. רוּמוֹ כַּחֲצִי

יד אברהם

וְכֵן, הַמְקַבֵּל מֵחֲבֵרוֹ לִבְנוֹת לוֹ בֵית חַתְנוּת לִבְנוֹ
— and similarly, one who accepts [a
contract] from another to build for him
a wedding house for his son

[I.e., he did not sell him any land but
simply accepted the job of building a
house.]

It was customary when a young man
married for his father to build him a
small annex in which to live adjoining
his own house (Rav; Rashbam).

The mishnah uses the phrase one
who accepts from another in this case
because it is assumed that the land
adjoining the customer's house is
already his and he requires only that the
house be built upon it (Tos. Yom Tov).

וּבֵית אַלְמְנוּת לְבִתּוֹ, — or a widow house
for his daughter,

The daughter's husband died and she
was now moving back to her father's
house. He therefore needed to add on an
annex for her adjacent to his own house
(Rav).

The mishnah talks of a wedding
house for a son and a widow house for a
daughter because it was not customary
for a man to live adjoining his father-in-
law's house. This was to avoid being
suspected of immoral behavior with his
mother-in-law (Rashbam 98a). Therefore, a son lived near his own father
when he married (Rav from Gem. 98b).
Only if a woman was widowed was it
customary for her to move back to her
father's house, and the mishnah

therefore refers to that case to illustrate
a father's building an annex for his
daughter (Rashbam).

בּוֹנֶה אַרְבַּע אַמּוֹת עַל שֵׁשׁ; דִּבְרֵי רַבִּי עֲקִיבָא. —
must build [a house] four cubits by six;
[these are] the words of R' Akiva.

[These are the minimum dimensions
of the house which the contractor must
build.[1]]

Many authorities are of the opinion that
the mishnah's dimensions do not apply to
transactions involving an existing house, in
which case units as small as four cubits by
four are considered an acceptable share for
each party, as indicated by Succah 3a in
regard to partners or heirs dividing their
common property. A structure four by four
can, in fact, serve as a house, albeit a very
minimal one. Thus, where the transaction is
for an existing house of unspecified
dimensions, or where there is a demand by a
partner for the division of a larger house into
individual living quarters, a unit four cubits
by four is recognized as a house, as it is in
regard to several Torah laws (e.g., mezuzah).
However, a person contracting to build a new
house is not likely to go through all the
trouble merely to build such a tiny dwelling.
It is therefore understood that the contract
calls for a larger size structure (Rashba;
Ritva; Beis Yosef, Choshen Mishpat 214:20).
Tosafos (98b) rule that even the division of a
house cannot be based on such small and
unsuitable dimensions.

רַבִּי יִשְׁמָעֵאל אוֹמֵר: רֶפֶת בָּקָר הוּא זֶה. — R'
Yishmael says: This is a cattle-shed.

A structure so small is fit for cattle,
not people! To qualify as a house, it

1. [In studying the dimensions cited in the mishnah, it is important to realize that in former
times most houses were quite small, comprising only the actual living space, while cooking and
storage facilities were outside or in separate structures.]

6
4

accepts [a contract] from another to build for him a wedding house for his son or a widow house for his daughter, must build [a house] four cubits by six; [these are] the words of R' Akiva. R' Yishmael says: This is a cattle-shed. One who wants to make a cattle-shed builds [it] four cubits by six; a small house, six by eight; a large one, eight by ten; a salon, ten by ten.

must be built larger than that (Rav).

הָרוֹצֶה לַעֲשׂוֹת רֶפֶת בָּקָר בּוֹנֶה אַרְבַּע אַמּוֹת עַל שֵׁשׁ; — One who wants to make a cattle-shed builds [it] four cubits by six;

There is a dispute in the Gemara (98b) concerning the authorship of this statement. Some say that it is R' Yishmael, who is explaining his previous statement: A structure four cubits by six cannot be considered a house because we see that even someone building a cattle-shed builds a structure at least four cubits by six and it therefore stands to reason that a house for human habitation must be larger.

R' Akiva, in this view, maintains either that a cattle-shed is smaller than this (Rashbam), or that there is no necessity to assume that a house cannot be the same size as a cattle-shed (Nimmukei Yosef).

The other view in the Gemara is that this statement is R' Akiva's, who is ruling that one who accepts a contract to build a cattle-shed must build one at least four cubits by six. By this ruling, R' Akiva is in effect saying to R' Yishmael that although it is true that a cattle-shed is four cubits by six, a house can also be built with the same dimensions (Rashbam).

בַּיִת קָטָן, שֵׁשׁ עַל שְׁמוֹנֶה; — a small house, six by eight;

One who contracted to build a small house must build one at least six by eight cubits (Rav). This statement is the opinion of R' Yishmael alone, since R' Akiva states explicitly in the beginning of the mishnah that four by six cubits is sufficient for a house of unspecified dimensions (Yad Ramah; Meiri; Ram-

bam, Mechirah 21:5, see Maggid Mishneh).

According to this view, the opinion in the Gemara that R' Akiva is the one who said that a cattle-shed is four by six is difficult to comprehend, since it would have the authorship of the mishnah switching back and forth without any indication of this in the text (Rashba; Ritva). According to this view, therefore, it must be assumed that the Gemara means that the previous phrase of the mishnah was also authored by R' Yishmael but that he is citing the opinion of R' Akiva in this matter, and saying to him that since he agrees that a cattle-shed must be at least four cubits by six, he should also agree that a house must be larger (Beis Yosef, Choshen Mishpat 214).

Others contend that R' Akiva also agrees that a small house must be at least six by eight cubits, and that only a wedding house or widow house may be built four cubits by six (Rashbam; Rav, cited by Beis Yosef). This view can be maintained only according to the version of the mishnah which does not include the words to build a house for him in the opening case of the mishnah (see s.v. וְהַמּוֹכֵר מָקוֹם); thus the mishnah is discussing only the building of a wedding house or a widow house (Meleches Shlomo; cf. Rashba, Ritva).

גָּדוֹל, שְׁמוֹנֶה עַל עֶשֶׂר; — a large one, eight by ten;

If he specified a large house, it must be at least eight cubits by ten (Rav). This is agreed to by both R' Akiva and R' Yishmael (Yad Ramah).

טְרַקְלִין, — a salon,

I.e., a large room or hall used by aristocrats as a drawing room (Rav; Rashbam), rest area (Rabbeinu Gershom), or banquet hall [from the Latin triclinium and Greek triklinion]

אָרְכּוֹ וְכַחֲצִי רָחְבּוֹ. רְאָיָה לַדָּבָר הֵיכָל. רַבָּן שִׁמְעוֹן בֶּן גַּמְלִיאֵל אוֹמֵר: הַכֹּל כְּבִנְיַן הַהֵיכָל.

[ה] **מִי** שֶׁיֶּשׁ לוֹ בוֹר לִפְנִים מִבֵּיתוֹ שֶׁל חֲבֵרוֹ, נִכְנָס בְּשָׁעָה שֶׁדֶּרֶךְ בְּנֵי אָדָם נִכְנָסִין וְיוֹצֵא בְּשָׁעָה שֶׁדֶּרֶךְ בְּנֵי אָדָם יוֹצְאִין. וְאֵינוֹ מַכְנִיס בְּהֶמְתּוֹ וּמַשְׁקֵהוּ מִבּוֹרוֹ; אֶלָּא מְמַלֵּא וּמַשְׁקֶה מִבַּחוּץ. וְזֶה עוֹשֶׂה לוֹ פּוֹתַחַת, וְזֶה עוֹשֶׂה לוֹ פּוֹתַחַת.

יד אברהם

(Aruch). These were most often built as separate structures in the form of pavilions and surrounded by flowers for beauty and fragrance (Gem. 90b; Rashbam; Rabbeinu Gershom).

עֶשֶׂר עַל עֶשֶׂר — ten by ten.

Since it is used as a formal rather than utilitarian area, it must be square [for aesthetic reasons] (Rashbam).

רוּמוֹ כַּחֲצִי אָרְכּוֹ וְכַחֲצִי רָחְבּוֹ. — Its height must equal half its length and width.

[I.e., half the sum of the length and width.] This applies to all of the buildings mentioned in the mishnah. Thus, a small house would be at least seven cubits high; a large house, nine; and a salon, ten (Rav).

רְאָיָה לַדָּבָר הֵיכָל. — Proof to this [is from] the Sanctuary.

I.e., the Sanctuary of the First Temple (Tos. Yom Tov) which was forty cubits long, twenty wide, and thirty high, making its height half the sum of its length and width (Rav).

Although the height of the Second Temple's Sanctuary was more than half the sum of its length and width [it was forty cubits long, twenty wide, and forty high], the example of the First Temple is followed because it is the smaller of the two ratios (Tos. Yom Tov). Gra suggests that since in the Second Temple there was no wall between the Sanctuary and the Holy of

Holies (only a curtain), the two must be counted as one long structure. Taken together their length comes to sixty cubits (Sanctuary = 40, Holy of Holies = 20). Thus, the height of forty is, in fact, one half the sum of the length (60) and the width (20). In fact, it is because this ratio existed in both Temples that the mishnah considers this ratio to be by design rather than merely coincidental (Beur HaGra to mishnah).

רַבָּן שִׁמְעוֹן בֶּן גַּמְלִיאֵל אוֹמֵר: הַכֹּל כְּבִנְיַן הַהֵיכָל. — Rabban Shimon ben Gamliel says: Everything follows the construction of the Sanctuary.

There is a dispute in the Gemara (98b) whether or not Rabban Shimon ben Gamliel is in disagreement with the first statement of the mishnah. Some say that the proof just cited from the dimensions of the Sanctuary is indeed based on the statement of Rabban Shimon ben Gamliel. Thus, this phrase comes to explain the previous case and to say that the formula stated is required because Rabban Shimon ben Gamliel has taught that all structures should ideally be built along the lines of the Sanctuary.

Others explain that Rabban Shimon ben Gamliel is in fact disputing the earlier height requirement. In this view, this phrase is a question: Rabban Shimon ben Gamliel [however] says: Must every structure follow the design of the Sanctuary? Rather, in his view,

6
5

Its height must equal half its length and width. Proof to this [is from] the Sanctuary. Rabban Shimon ben Gamliel says: Everything follows the construction of the Sanctuary.

5. One who owns a pit behind the house of another enters at the time that people ordinarily enter and leaves at the time that people ordinarily leave. He may not bring in his animal to give it to drink from his pit; rather he must fill [a container] and give it to drink outside. Each one may make a lock for himself.

YAD AVRAHAM

the height requirement should follow local custom (Rav). The first Tanna, however, maintains that although length and width cannot follow that of the Sanctuary, because they depend on the space available, height, which is arbitrary, should be built in accordance with those dimensions (Yad Ramah).

5.

The mishnah now begins a discussion of the rules governing a right-of-way which a person has through the property of another.

מִי שֶׁיֵּשׁ לוֹ בּוֹר לִפְנִים מִבֵּיתוֹ שֶׁל חֲבֵרוֹ — One who owns a pit behind the house of another

I.e., a water cistern. They had either divided their property this way, or one had acquired the pit from the other. In either case, the right-of-way was obtained along with it (Rashbam 99a).

נִכְנָס בְּשָׁעָה שֶׁדֶּרֶךְ בְּנֵי אָדָם נִכְנָסִין וְיוֹצֵא בְּשָׁעָה שֶׁדֶּרֶךְ בְּנֵי אָדָם יוֹצְאִין. — enters at the time that people ordinarily enter and leaves at the time that people ordinarily leave.

I.e., he has the right to go through the house to reach his pit only by day, but he has no right to trouble the owner of the house to get up at night to allow him through his home (Rav). Although he acquired a right-of-way through the house, it is assumed that this was the accepted condition to the sale or property division (Rashbam).

However, if he owns an interior room he may pass through at any time. Since it is

customary to make use of a room by day and by night, it must be assumed that night passage was also included in the sale of the right-of-way (Nimmukei Yosef from Ritva).

וְאֵינוֹ מַכְנִיס בְּהֶמְתּוֹ וּמַשְׁקֶה מִבּוֹרוֹ; אֶלָּא מְמַלֵּא וּמַשְׁקֶה מִבַּחוּץ. — He may not bring in his animal to give it to drink from his pit; rather he must fill [a container] and give it to drink outside.

Since it is not necessary to bring the animal to the cistern in order to give it water (Rashbam), the owner of the house is not assumed to have committed himself to allow animals to pass through his home (Meiri). Thus, if he needs water for his animal he must draw the water himself and carry it out to his animal.

It is apparent from this that one who obtains the right-of-way through the property of another in order to reach his own property does not actually own the path through which he is permitted to pass but is only granted rights which allow him to pass through it (Yad Ramah).

וְזֶה עוֹשֶׂה לוֹ פּוֹתַחַת וְזֶה עוֹשֶׂה לוֹ פּוֹתַחַת. —

[137]   THE MISHNAH/BAVA BASRA – Chapter Six: HaMocher Peiros

[ו] **מִי** שֶׁיֵּשׁ לוֹ גִּנָּה לִפְנִים מִגִּנָּתוֹ שֶׁל חֲבֵרוֹ,
נִכְנָס בְּשָׁעָה שֶׁדֶּרֶךְ בְּנֵי אָדָם נִכְנָסִים
וְיוֹצֵא בְּשָׁעָה שֶׁדֶּרֶךְ בְּנֵי אָדָם יוֹצְאִין. וְאֵינוֹ מַכְנִיס
לְתוֹכָהּ תַּגָּרִין; וְלֹא יִכָּנֵס מִתּוֹכָהּ לְתוֹךְ שָׂדֶה
אַחֶרֶת; וְהַחִיצוֹן זוֹרֵעַ אֶת הַדֶּרֶךְ. נָתְנוּ לוֹ דֶּרֶךְ מִן
הַצַּד מִדַּעַת שְׁנֵיהֶם, נִכְנָס בְּשָׁעָה שֶׁהוּא רוֹצֶה
וְיוֹצֵא בְּשָׁעָה שֶׁהוּא רוֹצֶה, וּמַכְנִיס לְתוֹכָהּ תַּגָּרִין.
וְלֹא יִכָּנֵס מִתּוֹכָהּ לְתוֹךְ שָׂדֶה אַחֶרֶת, וְזֶה וָזֶה
אֵינָם רַשָּׁאִים לְזָרְעָהּ.

יד אברהם

Each one may make a lock for himself
[lit. *This one makes ... and this one
makes ...*].

The owner of the cistern may place a
lock on it in order to prevent the owner
of the house from stealing water. The
latter may place an additional lock on
the cistern so that the owner of the

cistern should not be able to draw water
in his absence. This law was instituted
to prevent the woman of the house from
being suspected of infidelity (*Rav* from
Gem. 99b) by people who observe the
owner of the cistern entering constantly
while the woman's husband is not home
(*Nimmukei Yosef*).

6.

מִי שֶׁיֵּשׁ לוֹ גִּנָּה לִפְנִים מִגִּנָּתוֹ שֶׁל חֲבֵרוֹ, — *One
who owns a garden behind the garden
of another*

As in the previous mishnah, the
owner of the inner property has a right-
of-way through the outer property.
This passage runs through the middle of
a garden (*Rav; Rashbam*).

נִכְנָס בְּשָׁעָה שֶׁדֶּרֶךְ בְּנֵי אָדָם נִכְנָסִים וְיוֹצֵא בְּשָׁעָה
שֶׁדֶּרֶךְ בְּנֵי אָדָם יוֹצְאִין. — *enters when
people ordinarily enter and leaves when
people ordinarily leave.*

Since he causes him significant
damage by passing through his garden,
it is self-understood that the owner of
the outer garden did not grant him
unlimited access to the inner garden but
only that which is necessary to work
that garden (*Rashbam*). Thus, he has
the right of access only by day [the
customary time for people to tend their

gardens], not at night when entry is
presumably for some other purpose
(*Rav*).

וְאֵינוֹ מַכְנִיס לְתוֹכָהּ תַּגָּרִין; — *He may not
bring merchants into it;*

I.e., to purchase vegetables from his
garden (*Rashbam*), because this adds
unnecessarily to the traffic through the
garden (*Nimmukei Yosef*). Rather, he
must pick the vegetables himself and
bring them out to the prospective
buyers (*Meiri*).

וְלֹא יִכָּנֵס מִתּוֹכָהּ לְתוֹךְ שָׂדֶה אַחֶרֶת; — *nor
may he enter from it into another field;*

By the same token, he may not use his
right-of-way through the other's garden
as a shortcut to another field which he
owns, because this type of passage was
also never intended in the agreement
(*Rav; Rashbam*). However, once he has

6. One who owns a garden behind the garden of another enters when people ordinarily enter and leaves when people ordinarily leave. He may not bring merchants into it; nor may he enter from it into another field; and the [owner of the] outer [one] may plant the path.

[If] they assigned him a path on the side by mutual consent, he may enter whenever he wishes and leave whenever he wishes, and he may bring merchants into it. However, he may not enter from it into another field, and neither is permitted to plant it.

YAD AVRAHAM

entered his garden to tend it, he may go from there to his other fields (*Ritva*).

וְהַחִיצוֹן זוֹרֵעַ אֶת הַדֶּרֶךְ. — *and the [owner of the] outer [one] may plant the path.*

The owner of the outer garden may plant on the path he granted even though this will make it more difficult for the owner of the inner one to walk through (*Tif. Yis.*). The fact that he granted him right-of-way through the middle of his garden makes it clear that he did not mean to cede his rights to the path entirely [since he would otherwise have given him an access route at the edge of his garden, where it is less intrusive; see below] (*Rav*).

נָתְנוּ לוֹ דֶּרֶךְ מִן הַצַּד מִדַּעַת שְׁנֵיהֶם, — *[If] they assigned him a path on the side by mutual consent,*

I.e., they both agreed that the owner of the inner garden should exercise his right-of-way by passing through at the edge of the other's garden, rather than through the middle of it (*Meiri*).

Others interpret the plural (*they assigned*) to refer to the court; i.e., the assignment of the right-of-way was part of a court settlement to which both parties agreed (*Rabbeinu Gershom; Rashbam 82b, s.v.* וְהָא לָא דְמִיא). As far as the actual ruling is concerned, there is no difference who worked out the arrangement; see *Tur Choshen*

Mishpat 169 (*Tos. Yom Tov*).

נִכְנָס בְּשָׁעָה שֶׁהוּא רוֹצֶה וְיוֹצֵא בְּשָׁעָה שֶׁהוּא רוֹצֶה, וּמַכְנִיס לְתוֹכָהּ תַּגָּרִין. — *he may enter whenever he wishes and leave whenever he wishes, and he may bring merchants into it.*

Since the path is on the side of the garden, passing through causes little or no damage. Thus, we may assume that he was granted full access over this path (*Rashbam 99b*).

וְלֹא יִכָּנֵס מִתּוֹכָהּ לְתוֹךְ שָׂדֶה אַחֶרֶת, — *However, he may not enter from it into another field,*

Although he was granted full access to his garden, the path was not ceded to him entirely. Thus, his right of passage is restricted to using it for access to his garden, not as a general access route to other areas (*Rambam Comm.*).

וְזֶה וָזֶה אֵינָם רַשָּׁאִים לְזָרְעָהּ. — *and neither is permitted to plant it.*

Since it is on the side of the field, the owner of the outer garden is understood to have designated it solely as a pathway for the owner of the inner garden. Consequently, he has no right to plant it (*Rav*). However, he granted only access but not the land itself. Thus, the owner of the access may not plant it either (*Rav; Yad Ramah*).

[ז] **מִי** שֶׁהָיְתָה דֶּרֶךְ הָרַבִּים עוֹבֶרֶת בְּתוֹךְ
שָׂדֵהוּ, נְטָלָהּ וְנָתַן לָהֶם מִן הַצַּד, מַה
שֶּׁנָּתַן נָתַן, וְשֶׁלּוֹ לֹא הִגִּיעוֹ. דֶּרֶךְ הַיָּחִיד אַרְבַּע
אַמּוֹת; דֶּרֶךְ הָרַבִּים שֵׁשׁ עֶשְׂרֵה אַמָּה; דֶּרֶךְ הַמֶּלֶךְ
אֵין לָהּ שִׁעוּר; דֶּרֶךְ הַקֶּבֶר אֵין לָהּ שִׁעוּר. הַמַּעֲמָד
— דַּיָּנֵי צִפּוֹרִי אָמְרוּ: בֵּית אַרְבַּעַת קַבִּין.

יד אברהם

7.

מִי שֶׁהָיְתָה דֶּרֶךְ הָרַבִּים עוֹבֶרֶת בְּתוֹךְ שָׂדֵהוּ, —
[If] someone had a public thoroughfare
passing through his field,

I.e., the public had previously
established a path through that field
(Rav), or the owner had granted it to
them (Rashbam; Meiri).

נְטָלָהּ וְנָתַן לָהֶם מִן הַצַּד, — and he
appropriated it and gave them [another
one] on the side,

[The owner of the field closed off the
path in the middle of his field and
substituted for them a path on the side
of his field.]

מַה שֶּׁנָּתַן נָתַן, וְשֶׁלּוֹ לֹא הִגִּיעוֹ. — what he has
given is given, but his does not become
his [lit. does not reach him].

The path which he established as a
substitute becomes public property, but
the one which he tried to appropriate for
himself does not become his, and they
both belong to the public. Although it
should seemingly make no difference to
the public where in the field they have a
path, removing the route from the
middle of the field to one side of it does
in fact increase the distance to those
coming or going to the other side of the
field. Consequently, he is not permitted
to make this exchange (Gem. 100a).

At the same time, the new path he set
aside for the public becomes theirs
because of the general rule that once a

path has been appropriated by the
public (with the knowledge of the
owner), it cannot be taken from them
(Rav from Gem. 100a). The owner's
silence in the face of their trespass is
taken as evidence of his intention to
grant the right-of-way to the public.
This rule, therefore, applies all the more
so in our case where he granted it to
them explicitly (Rashbam).[1] Although
his granting of the path was based on
the mistaken notion that he could force
an exchange, the Rabbis penalized him
for trying to violate the rights of the
public in this manner and granted them
the path which he mistakenly ceded as
well (Nimmukei Yosef).

דֶּרֶךְ הַיָּחִיד אַרְבַּע אַמּוֹת; — A private path is
four cubits [wide];

One who sells a right-of-way through
his property to another [without
specifying its size] (Rav) must give him
a path four cubits wide, wide enough
for a wagon to pass (Rashbam 99b).
Similarly, if the dimensions of a
previously established path become
questioned, the holder of the path is
allotted a width of four cubits (Yad
Ramah).

This is the opinion of the mishnah.
However, the Gemara (100a) rules in
accordance with the opinion of a baraisa
cited there that two and a half cubits —

1. They must, however, have already taken formal possession of the new path by flattening it
out or making some other improvement in it which would constitute an act of chazakah
acquisition (Gem., Rashbam 100a).

7. [If] someone had a public thoroughfare passing through his field, and he appropriated it and gave them [another one] on the side, what he has given is given, but his does not become his. A private path is four cubits [wide]; a public thoroughfare is sixteen cubits [wide]; the king's thoroughfare has no limit; [and] the path to a grave has no limit. A halting-place — the judges of Tzippori said: An area of four *kavs.*

YAD AVRAHAM

the width necessary for a donkey to pass through with its load — is sufficient. If the path is flanked by walls, in which case a donkey cannot pass through with its load in a space of two and a half cubits, four cubits must be allowed (*Ri Migash*).

דֶּרֶךְ הָרַבִּים — *a public thoroughfare*
If the public is granted the right-of-way through someone's property, or the size of a previously established public thoroughfare comes under question (*Yad Ramah*).

שֵׁשׁ עֶשְׂרֵה אַמָּה; — *is sixteen cubits* [*wide*];
This was the width of the public thoroughfare in the encampment of the Israelites in the desert, as derived by the Gemara (*Shabbos* 99a) from the wagons which carried the Tabernacle (*Rashbam* 99b).

דֶּרֶךְ הַמֶּלֶךְ אֵין לָהּ שִׁעוּר; — *the king's thoroughfare has no limit;*
The Torah grants the king the right to break through people's fences in order to clear a way for himself (*Rav* from *Gem.* 100b). He has the right to trample through their fields and vineyards, and he need not take the trouble to route himself around people's property. There is no limit to the width of this passage; he may use as much area as he [and his entourage] require (*Rambam, Melachim* 5:3).

דֶּרֶךְ הַקֶּבֶר אֵין לָהּ שִׁעוּר. — [*and*] *the path to a grave has no limit.*

The Rabbis ordained that a burial procession need not travel in a roundabout way to carry the body to the grave, even when a direct route entails damaging someone's crops. However, they may not breach fences as may a king (*Rav*).
Alternatively, if someone sells the path to a grave through his field without specifying its size, all of those accompanying the body may pass through with no limit on the area they may traverse (*Rashbam; Meiri*).

הַמַּעֲמָד — — *A halting-place* —
When returning from a burial, it was customary to stop seven times and comfort the mourners, or mourn the deceased, and to impress on everyone present the futility of worldly existence [i.e., that it ultimately ends with death] (*Rashbam* 100b). These seven stops parallel the seven expressions of futility found in the opening verse of the Book of *Koheles* (*Ecclesiastes*).
Others contend that these stops were made on the way to the grave (*Meiri; Rashi* to *Megillah* 123b).

דַּיָּנֵי צִפּוֹרִי אָמְרוּ: בֵּית אַרְבַּעַת קַבִּין. — *the judges of Tzippori said: An area of four kavs.*
If someone sold the right to designate a halting-place on his property (*Meiri*), or such a place had been established there from before (*Yad Ramah*), an area of four *kavs* must be allotted for that purpose. This comes to fifty by thirty-three and one-third cubits (*Rav*).

[ח] **הַמּוֹכֵר** מָקוֹם לַחֲבֵרוֹ לַעֲשׂוֹת לוֹ קֶבֶר,
וְכֵן הַמְקַבֵּל מֵחֲבֵרוֹ לַעֲשׂוֹת לוֹ
קֶבֶר, עוֹשֶׂה תוֹכָהּ שֶׁל מְעָרָה אַרְבַּע אַמּוֹת עַל
שֵׁשׁ, וּפוֹתֵחַ לְתוֹכָהּ שְׁמוֹנָה כּוּכִין: שְׁלֹשָׁה מִכָּאן
וּשְׁלֹשָׁה מִכָּאן וּשְׁנַיִם מִכְּנֶגְדָּן. וְכוּכִין, אָרְכָּן אַרְבַּע
אַמּוֹת, וְרוּמָן שִׁבְעָה, וְרָחְבָּן שִׁשָּׁה. רַבִּי שִׁמְעוֹן

יד אברהם

8.

In Mishnaic times it was customary to bury the dead in catacombs, in the recesses carved into the walls of subterranean chambers. These catacombs would be family burial places, comprising various chambers, each containing a number of recesses to be used as graves. The standard structure of these catacombs was as follows: A central courtyard was formed, and burial chambers were hollowed out at each end of the courtyard. Recesses were then carved into the walls of these chambers to serve as the actual graves (Rashbam 100b), with the opening of the recess being sealed once a body was placed in it (Meiri).

This mishnah establishes the standard dimensions and structure of these catacombs, and anyone who contracts to dig one without specifying the dimensions must adhere to this standard.

הַמּוֹכֵר מָקוֹם לַחֲבֵרוֹ לַעֲשׂוֹת לוֹ קֶבֶר, [If] — *one sells a place to another to make a catacomb for him* [on it],

[I.e., the seller sold a plot of land on which he contracted to construct an underground cemetery for the buyer.]

וְכֵן הַמְקַבֵּל מֵחֲבֵרוֹ לַעֲשׂוֹת לוֹ קֶבֶר, — *and similarly,* [if] *one accepts* [a contract] *from another to dig a catacombs for him,*

[I.e., on property already owned by him.]

עוֹשֶׂה תוֹכָהּ שֶׁל מְעָרָה אַרְבַּע אַמּוֹת עַל שֵׁשׁ, — *he makes the inside of the crypt four cubits by six,*

To fulfill the contract he must excavate an underground chamber four cubits by six, with a height of four cubits (Rashbam 100b from Tosefta). [Actually, more than one chamber is called for, as the mishnah will explain below. The mishnah at this point delineates the structure of the individual crypt.]

The width actually had to be slightly larger than four cubits, so that the casket, which was itself four cubits long, could be turned inside the chamber and placed in a recess (Tos. 101b).

וּפוֹתֵחַ לְתוֹכָהּ שְׁמוֹנָה כּוּכִין: — *and he opens eight recesses into it:*

He must excavate eight recesses in the walls of the chamber which thus open into it (Rashbam).

שְׁלֹשָׁה מִכָּאן וּשְׁלֹשָׁה מִכָּאן, — *three on each side,*

He excavates three recesses in the wall at either side of the chamber entrance; one recess directly to the side of the entrance, one at the far end of the wall, and one in the middle. These side walls were each six cubits long, and since each recess was one cubit wide (see below), this left a space of one and a half cubits between recesses (Rav; Rambam, Mechirah 21:6).

Others contend that the recesses at each end of the wall were removed a half a cubit from the corners at the end of the

8. [If] one sells a place to another to make a catacomb for him [on it], and similarly, [if] one accepts [a contract] from another to dig a catacombs for him, he makes the inside of the crypt four cubits by six, and he opens eight recesses into it: three on each side, and two on the opposite [side]. The recesses [must be] four cubits long, seven [handbreadths] high, and six [handbreadths] wide. R′

YAD AVRAHAM

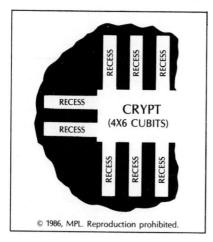

RECESS RECESS RECESS

RECESS

CRYPT
(4X6 CUBITS)

RECESS

RECESS RECESS RECESS

© 1986, MPL. Reproduction prohibited.

wall, leaving a space of one cubit between each recess (*Rashbam; Yad Ramah; Meiri*).

וּשְׁנַיִם מִכְּנֶגְדָן. — *and two on the opposite* [side].

Two more recesses were carved into the wall opposite the entrance to the cave (*Rav*). Since this wall was only four cubits long, and a minimum of one cubit was required between recesses, there was room for only two recesses (*Meiri*). According to *Rav* and *Rambam*, these two were placed at the ends of the wall. Since the wall opposite the entrance was only four cubits long, this left a space of two cubits between them.

According to the second opinion cited above, these were placed half a cubit from the ends of the wall, thus leaving a space of one cubit between them (*Rashbam; Yad Ramah; Meiri*).

וְכוּכִין, אָרְכָּן אַרְבַּע אַמּוֹת, — *The recesses* [*must be*] *four cubits long,*

The [average] corpse is three cubits long and additional space must be allowed for the thickness of the casket. The recess must therefore be four cubits long to accommodate the casket (*Rashbam* 100b).

Others dispute *Rashbam's* assertion that the total height of a person is three cubits, contending that that figure represents the height only up to the shoulder. Thus, the fourth cubit is to allow for the height of the head as well as the thickness of the casket (*Tos.* 100b).[1]

וְרוּמָן שִׁבְעָה, — *seven* [*handbreadths*] *high,*

The height of the recess must be seven handbreadths (one and a sixth cubits) to allow six handbreadths for the height of the casket,[2] plus another handbreadth between the casket and the roof of the chamber (see *Tos. Yom Tov*). This is necessary to prevent the *tumah* of the corpse from extending straight up through the ground and contaminating anyone passing overhead. The space of a handbreadth,

---

1. This dispute is the subject of a great controversy among the *Rishonim* and is fundamental to the question of determining the actual size of the אַמָּה, cubit. See *Shiurim shel Torah* by R′ Yaakov Yisrael Kanievsky, ch. 4.

2. The height of the casket is based on the estimated thickness of a corpse lying on its back.

אוֹמֵר: עוֹשֶׂה תוֹכָהּ שֶׁל מְעָרָה שֵׁשׁ אַמּוֹת עַל
שְׁמוֹנֶה, וּפוֹתֵחַ לְתוֹכָהּ שְׁלֹשָׁה עָשָׂר כּוּךְ: אַרְבָּעָה
מִכָּאן, וְאַרְבָּעָה מִכָּאן, וּשְׁלֹשָׁה מִכְּנֶגְדָּן, וְאֶחָד
מִימִין הַפֶּתַח, וְאֶחָד מִן הַשְּׂמֹאל. וְעוֹשֶׂה חָצֵר עַל
פִּי הַמְּעָרָה, שֵׁשׁ עַל שֵׁשׁ, כִּמְלֹא הַמִּטָּה וְקוֹבְרֶיהָ.
וּפוֹתֵחַ לְתוֹכָהּ שְׁתֵּי מְעָרוֹת: אַחַת מִכָּאן וְאַחַת
מִכָּאן. רַבִּי שִׁמְעוֹן אוֹמֵר: אַרְבַּע, לְאַרְבַּע

יד אברהם

however, acts as a buffer to prevent the contamination from extending upward (Rashbam).

In order to be effective, however, the recesses would have to be left open at one end; otherwise, the *tumah* spreads upward despite the space of a handbreadth (*Tos.* 100b). Others dispute this; see *Tos. Yom Tov.*

וְרָחְבָּן שִׁשָּׁה. — *and six [handbreadths] wide.*

I.e., one cubit. Although the *Gemara* (*Succah* 8a) states that [the average] person is six handbreadths wide [and would thus not fit together with the casket into a space of exactly one cubit], that refers to one who is fully clothed, the bulk of the clothing adding measurably to the total width needed by a person in a *succah*. A lightly dressed corpse, however, takes up slightly less room (*Tos.* 101a).

רַבִּי שִׁמְעוֹן אוֹמֵר: עוֹשֶׂה תוֹכָהּ שֶׁל מְעָרָה שֵׁשׁ אַמּוֹת עַל שְׁמוֹנֶה, — *R' Shimon says: He makes the inside of the crypt six cubits by eight,*

[R' Shimon disputes the size of the burial chamber, giving it larger dimensions and therefore more recesses.]

וּפוֹתֵחַ לְתוֹכָהּ שְׁלֹשָׁה עָשָׂר כּוּךְ: אַרְבָּעָה מִכָּאן, וְאַרְבָּעָה מִכָּאן, וּשְׁלֹשָׁה מִכְּנֶגְדָּן, — *and opens thirteen recesses into it: four on each side, three on the opposite [side],*

Since the length of the chamber is eight cubits in R' Shimon's view, there is room on each side wall for four recesses (each one cubit wide), with spaces of one cubit between them and a half-cubit on each end [4+3+½+½=8]. Along the wall opposite the entrance, three recesses were excavated in the same manner [3+2+½+½=6] (Rashbam).[1]

וְאֶחָד מִימִין הַפֶּתַח, וְאֶחָד מִן הַשְּׂמֹאל. — *one to the right of the entrance and one to the left.*

This refers to the wall opposite the entrance to the chamber. In each corner of that wall, an additional recess was excavated diagonal to the chamber (*Gem.* 101b, as explained by Rashbam).[2] However, if these were to be placed at the same level as the other recesses, their openings would overlap and result in the collapse of the walls between them. The *Gemara* therefore explains that these corner recesses were set lower down than the others so that

1. Even *Rav* and *Rambam,* who did not allow for space in the corners in their interpretations of the previous opinion (s.v. שלשה מכאן), agree to this interpretation of R' Shimon. This is because the mishnah states below that there were two additional chambers on the corners, which clearly indicates that there was space left there (*Tos. Yom Tov*).

2. Placing these two recesses in the two corners adjacent to the chamber entrance would not be acceptable, because the corner recesses, set at a diagonal, would then be jutting into the courtyard. Even lowering them below the floor of the courtyard would be unacceptable since this would result in future funeral processions standing on top of those graves (*Tos. Yom Tov*).

6
8

Shimon says: He makes the inside of the crypt six cubits by eight, and opens thirteen recesses into it: four on each side, three on the opposite [side], one to the right of the entrance and one to the left. He makes a courtyard at the entrance to the crypt, six by six, sufficient space for the bier and those who bury it. He opens two crypts into it: one on each side. R' Shimon says: Four, [one] on each of its four sides.

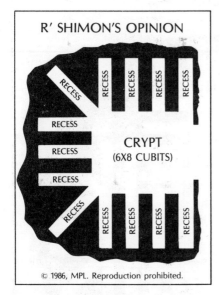

R' SHIMON'S OPINION

RECESS

CRYPT
(6X8 CUBITS)

RECESS

© 1986, MPL. Reproduction prohibited.

the potential overlap passed beneath the upper recesses and did not intrude. Alternatively, these corner recesses were short and were used for the burial of stillbirths (*Gem.* 102b). Because of their small size, they did not do any structural damage to the other recesses (*Tos. Yom Tov*).

וְעוֹשֶׂה חָצֵר עַל פִּי הַמְּעָרָה, — *He makes a courtyard at the entrance to the crypt,*

The mishnah now moves on from its description of the burial chamber to a description of the catacomb as a whole. In addition to the chambers the contractor must provide a central courtyard leading to the crypts (*Rashbam* 101a).

שֵׁשׁ עַל שֵׁשׁ, כְּמְלֹא הַמִּטָּה וְקוֹבְרֶיהָ. — *six by six, sufficient space for the bier and those who bury it.*

I.e., six cubits by six cubits, so that it can accommodate the length of the bier and those who carry it (*Rashbam* 10a).

וּפוֹתֵחַ לְתוֹכָה שְׁתֵּי מְעָרוֹת: — *He opens two crypts into it:*

I.e., a total of two burial chambers, one more in addition to the one already mentioned.

The mishnah first discussed the layout of the crypts because the term *courtyard* is applicable only to a space which opens into a structure of some sort. Consequently, it would have been inappropriate to discuss the courtyard without first mentioning the burial chamber which it was designed to serve (*Rashbam*).

אַחַת מִכָּאן, וְאַחַת מִכָּאן. — *one on each side.*

The width of the cave lay parallel to the courtyard (ibid.).

Rambam (*Mechirah* 21:6) mentions only one chamber and omits any mention of a courtyard or second chamber. Apparently, he considers this part of the mishnah to be a continuation of the opinion of R' Shimon and not universally accepted. However, the quote of R' Shimon again in the next phrase mitigates against this explanation, unless we are to assume that the mishnah records two versions of R' Shimon's view (*Tos. Yom Tov*).

רַבִּי שִׁמְעוֹן אוֹמֵר: אַרְבַּע, לְאַרְבַּע רוּחוֹתֶיהָ. — *R' Shimon says: Four, [one] on each of its four sides.*

I.e., there were four chambers, one on each side of the courtyard. Although

רוּחוֹתֶיהָ. רַבָּן שִׁמְעוֹן בֶּן גַּמְלִיאֵל אוֹמֵר: הַכֹּל לְפִי הַסֶּלַע.

[א] הָאוֹמֵר לַחֲבֵרוֹ ,,בֵּית כּוֹר עָפָר אֲנִי מוֹכֵר לָךְ,'' הָיוּ שָׁם נְקָעִים עֲמֻקִים

יד אברהם

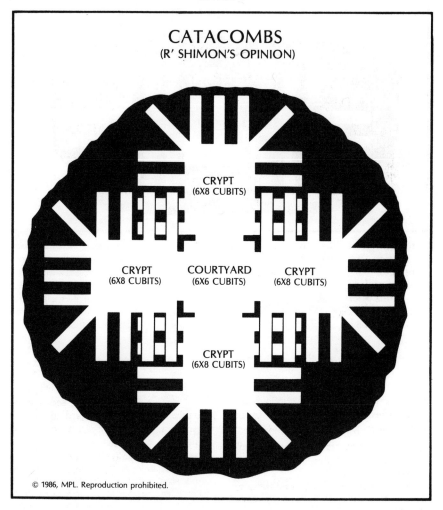

CATACOMBS
(R' SHIMON'S OPINION)

CRYPT
(6X8 CUBITS)

CRYPT
(6X8 CUBITS)

COURTYARD
(6X6 CUBITS)

CRYPT
(6X8 CUBITS)

CRYPT
(6X8 CUBITS)

this would seemingly cause the recesses of the different chambers to overlap at the corners (see diagram), they were dug at different depths to avoid this problem (*Gem.* 101b).

— רַבָּן שִׁמְעוֹן בֶּן גַּמְלִיאֵל אוֹמֵר: הַכֹּל לְפִי הַסֶּלַע. *Rabban Shimon ben Gamliel says: All according to the [nature of the] rock.*

How large a burial chamber is called for by this contract depends on the

Rabban Shimon ben Gamliel says: All according to
the [nature of the] rock.

1. [If] one said to another, 'I am selling you a *beis
kor* of earth,' [and] it contained crevices ten

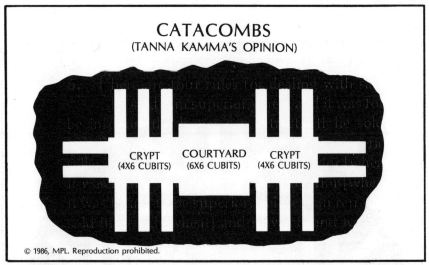

CATACOMBS
(TANNA KAMMA'S OPINION)

CRYPT
(4X6 CUBITS)

COURTYARD
(6X6 CUBITS)

CRYPT
(4X6 CUBITS)

© 1986, MPL. Reproduction prohibited.

consistency of the ground[1] being
excavated. If it is very hard, the
contractor is required to excavate
chambers of only four cubits by six, as
the *Tanna Kamma* ruled above. If it is
not so hard, he must provide chambers
of six by eight, as R' Shimon ruled

(*Rav; Rambam Comm.*). Alternatively,
if the ground is very hard, he need not
leave a cubit of space between each
chamber and he can make more
chambers in each cave. If it is especially
weak, he must leave a larger space and
dig fewer chambers (*Rashbam*).

Chapter 7

1.

This chapter concludes the discussion
of the previous three chapters concerning the laws governing purchases.

הָאוֹמֵר לַחֲבֵרוֹ ,,בֵּית כּוֹר עָפָר אֲנִי מוֹכֵר לָךְ,"
[*If*] *one said to another, 'I am selling you
a beis kor of earth,'*

A *kor* is equal to thirty *seah* and a *beis
kor* is thus an area of land measuring
75,000 square cubits (*Rav*).

Although the term *beis kor* literally
means an area which can hold a *kor* (of

seed) [i.e., in which a *kor* of seed can be
planted], the term in regard to sales is
strictly a measure of land, not yield
(*Rashbam* 102b).

Nevertheless, since he stated that he is
selling a *beis kor* of עָפָר, *earth*, the
implication is that he refers to land which is
fit for planting [though not necessarily in the
quantity of a *kor*]. However, if he said, 'a *beis
kor* of land,' or simply, 'a *beis kor*,' there is
no such implication, and even land which
cannot be planted is included (*Rav*;

1. Although סֶלַע usually means *rock*, in the present context the commentators seem to take it
to mean hard earth (see *Rashbam*, s.v. הכל לפי הסלע and *Rambam Comm.*).

עֲשָׂרָה טְפָחִים, אוֹ סְלָעִים גְּבוֹהִים עֲשָׂרָה טְפָחִים,
אֵינָן נִמְדָּדִין עִמָּהּ; פָּחוֹת מִכָּאן, נִמְדָּדִין עִמָּהּ. וְאִם
אָמַר לוֹ „כְּבֵית כּוֹר עָפָר,'' אֲפִלּוּ הָיוּ שָׁם נְקָעִים
עֲמֻקִים יוֹתֵר מֵעֲשָׂרָה טְפָחִים, אוֹ סְלָעִים גְּבוֹהִין
יוֹתֵר מֵעֲשָׂרָה טְפָחִים, הֲרֵי אֵלּוּ נִמְדָּדִין עִמָּהּ.

[ב] „בֵּית כּוֹר עָפָר אֲנִי מוֹכֵר לָךְ, מִדָּה
בְחֶבֶל,'' פָּחַת כָּל שֶׁהוּא, יְנַכֶּה;

Rashbam).

Tosafos (102b), however, dispute this
distinction and maintain that even if he did
not use the word *earth* explicitly he is
understood to be referring to arable land. The
mishnah cites a case in which he said, 'a *beis
kor* of earth,' only to inform us that even in
such a case if the rocks and crevices are not
ten handbreadths, they are included, as the
mishnah proceeds to explain.

הָיוּ שָׁם נְקָעִים עֲמֻקִים עֲשָׂרָה טְפָחִים, אוֹ סְלָעִים
גְּבוֹהִים עֲשָׂרָה טְפָחִים, — [and] it contained
crevices ten handbreadths deep, or
rocks ten handbreadths high,

I.e., the *beis kor* being sold was
broken up by crevices or had in it rocks
ten handbreadths high and at least four
handbreadths wide. These dimensions
constitute a significant area in their own
right (*Rav*), as may be seen from the
laws of the Sabbath where an area four
handbreadths by four handbreadths
enclosed by a wall ten handbreadths
high constitutes a separate private
domain (*Rashbam* 102b).

אֵינָן נִמְדָּדִין עִמָּהּ; — they are not measured
with it;

They are not included in the *beis kor*
and he must add in level land equal to
the amount of land missing from the
full *beis kor* due to the crevices and

rocks (*Rosh; Rav, Rashbam* as explained by *Tos. Yom Tov*).[1] Even if the
mound or crevice is tillable, it is not
included (*Gem.* 103a). This is because a
person does not want to buy a field
which he must treat as two or three
separate fields (*Rav* from *Gem.*), i.e.,
which he will be forced to plow and
plant separately rather than in one
continuous line (*Rashbam*).

It follows from this that if the entire
field is split across by rocks or a crevice
he must provide a different tract,
because in such a case the land is truly
two completely separate plots of land
(*Rosh; Tur; Rama, Choshen Mishpat*
218:1).

There is a dispute among the authorities as
to the status of the rocks and crevices.
Rambam (*Mechirah* 28:1) rules that even
though they do not count towards the *beis
kor*, they are automatically included in the
sale and become the property of the buyer.
Others contend that they belong to the seller
(*Tur, Choshen Mishpat* 218:1 citing *Rashbam* and *Rosh*). *Ravad* agrees that they
belong to the seller but adds that the buyer
can be forced to buy them since they are
otherwise lost to the seller for all practical
purposes (*Ravad, Mechirah* 28:1, cf.
Rashba).

The mishnah is discussing a case in
which the seller owns a plot of land

1. *Meiri* ascribes to *Rashbam* (and thus by extension to *Rav*, who paraphrases *Rashbam* here)
the view that the seller cannot give him this field at all, but must provide him with an
unbroken *beis kor* of land. However, *Tos. Yom Tov* equates *Rav* (and thus *Rashbam*) with
Rosh and this seems to have been the understanding of *Tur* and *Rama* (218:1) as well (see
notes to *Meiri* here).

7
2

handbreadths deep, or rocks ten handbreadths high, they are not measured with it; [if they were] less than this, they are measured with it. If he said to him, '[I am selling you] like a *beis kor* of earth,' even if it contained crevices deeper than ten handbreadths, or rocks higher than ten handbreadths, they are measured with it.

2. [I]f one said to another,] 'I am selling you a *beis kor* of earth, as measured by a rope,' [if] he gave [even] the slightest amount less he must deduct;

YAD AVRAHAM

larger than a *beis kor* and sold only a portion of it to the buyer. However, if the field in question was the only land he owned, the sale is valid as is, as taught in the next mishnah (*Ritva; Nimmukei Yosef*).

In addition, if he explicitly stated that he was selling him a specific field, the sale is valid, because the buyer accepted that field as is. The mishnah is discussing a case in which he did not specify which *beis kor* of his lands he was selling (ibid.).

פָּחוֹת מִכָּאן, נִמְדָּדִין עִמָּה. — [*if they were*] *less than this, they are measured with it.*

If the rocks or crevices are less than ten handbreadths high or deep, they are counted towards the *beis kor*. Since every field has some small rocks or ruts, these minor breaks are considered an inevitable part of the field (*Rashbam*) and are included in the field even though they are not plantable (*Gem.* 103a). However, if these were so wide that they covered an area of four *kavs* [i.e., fifty cubits by thirty-three and one third cubits, see comm. to 6:7, s.v. דיני], they are so substantial as to be considered separate entities and are no longer included in the purchase (*Tos.*

Yom Tov from *Gem.* 103a).

וְאִם אָמַר לוֹ „כְּבֵית כּוֹר עָפָר,‟ אֲפִלּוּ הָיוּ שָׁם נְקָעִים עֲמֻקִים יוֹתֵר מֵעֲשָׂרָה טְפָחִים, אוֹ סְלָעִים גְבוֹהִין יוֹתֵר מֵעֲשָׂרָה טְפָחִים, הֲרֵי אֵלּוּ נִמְדָּדִין עִמָּהּ. — *If he said to him, '[I am selling you] like a beis kor of earth,' even if it contained crevices deeper than ten handbreadths, or rocks higher than ten handbreadths, they are measured with it.*

By qualifying his description of the parcel of land he proposes to sell with the caveat *like*, he implies that he is selling the *beis kor* as is, whether it be tillable earth or rocks (*Rav, Rashbam*).

However, if the crevice or rock measures more than four *kavs*, it is not included, because the use of the word *earth* indicates that the basic sale must be of tillable land (*Rashbam; Rosh; Ritva*). [Thus, four *kavs* of untillable rock, which is large enough to be considered an area to itself and therefore too large to be viewed as a mere blemish in the overall field, violates that standard.] This, however, is disputed by *Rambam* (*Mechirah* 28:4 as explained by *Tur* 218:5), who considers even more than four *kavs* of rocky land included in the sale made under these terms.

2.

„בֵּית כּוֹר עָפָר אֲנִי מוֹכֵר לָךְ, מִדָּה בְחֶבֶל,‟ — [*If one said to another,] 'I am selling you a beis kor of earth, as measured by a rope'*

[lit. *a measure with a rope*],
I.e., a field with the precise measurements of a *beis kor*, as

הוֹתִיר כָּל שֶׁהוּא, יַחֲזִיר. אִם אָמַר ,,הֵן חָסֵר הֵן
יָתֵר,'' אֲפִלּוּ פָּחַת רֹבַע לִסְאָה אוֹ הוֹתִיר רֹבַע
לִסְאָה, הִגִּיעוֹ. יוֹתֵר מִכָּאן, יַעֲשֶׂה חֶשְׁבּוֹן. מַה הוּא

יד אברהם

measured by a [measuring] rope (Rav).
[Ropes of given lengths were the standard measuring instruments for land — see Eruvin 5:4.]

פָּחַת כָּל שֶׁהוּא, יְנַכֶּה; — [if] he gave [even] the slightest amount less he must deduct;

If the field which he gave was even the least bit less than a full beis kor, the purchase stands, but he must deduct the value of the missing land from the purchase price (Rav).

Although there is a rule that if one overpays for land no price adjustment is necessary, that applies only when the quantity sold was consistent with the agreement but the price was incorrect [in which case he cannot recover his loss because the price of land varies in accordance with many variables (see comm. to 4:4, s.v. רבי אליעזר)]. However, if the quantity is not that which was agreed upon, an adjustment may be demanded (Rashbam 103b).

The Gemara (90a) states when something is sold by measure, any deviation from the agreement voids the purchase. Rashbam (103b) explains that that rule pertains only to movables and not real estate, because the Sages assessed that when one buys real estate he wants the sale to stand even when there is some deviation from the agreed dimensions, as long as it is within the range of what he contracted for. By the same token, the seller's specification of these dimensions is not to be taken as a stipulation requiring these exact numbers but only as a statement that the price will be adjusted according to the actual amount of land given. Thus, it is only a matter of adjusting the price to compensate for the difference.

Tosafos (104a), however, dispute Rashbam's explanation and contend that real estate is also included in the above-mentioned law. They explain that that law applies only when the seller measured the land and then short-changed the buyer. In the instance of our mishnah the field was not

measured prior to the sale and it is therefore understood by both parties that the dimensions quoted in the purchase agreement may not be precise. Consequently, as long as he gives him a parcel of land which people commonly refer to (by rough estimate) as a beis kor, the sale is valid and only the price must be adjusted (Yad Ramah; Nimmukei Yosef). [His stipulation of an exact beis kor is meant only to indicate that he takes responsibility to adjust the price in accordance with the land.]

הוֹתִיר כָּל שֶׁהוּא, יַחֲזִיר. — [if] he gave [even] the slightest amount more he must give back.

If the seller gave the buyer a field containing more land than the agreement called for, the latter must pay him for the extra land or return it, whichever the seller prefers, as the mishnah will explain below (Rav).

There is a question whether this mishnah deals only with a field which the buyer has seen or whether it applies even to a purchase of an unspecified plot of land. Tosafos (104a, s.v. אלא לאו) in the name of Rashba state that only if the buyer saw the field does the shortfall in the dimensions not invalidate the sale since the buyer saw what he was getting and agreed to the sale; his only claim therefore is to an adjustment of the price. If he did not see the field beforehand, but relied on the seller to give him the stipulated amount of land, any shortfall will invalidate the sale because the buyer can claim that he had no desire to buy a smaller piece of land (see below, s.v. אפלו פחת). However, Tosafos there cite another view which considers the sale valid even if the buyer did not see the field (see Maharsha to s.v. פחות).

אִם אָמַר ,,הֵן חָסֵר הֵן יָתֵר,'' — If he said, 'whether less or more,'

If the seller did not guarantee a precise measurement but told the buyer that he was selling him a field of approximately a beis kor (Rav).

אֲפִלּוּ פָּחַת רֹבַע לִסְאָה אוֹ הוֹתִיר רֹבַע לִסְאָה, הִגִּיעוֹ. — even if he gave a quarter-kav

[if] he gave [even] the slightest amount more he must give back. If he said, 'whether less or more,' even if he gave a quarter-*kav* less per *seah* or a quarter-*kav* more per *seah*, it becomes his. [If it was] more than this, he should make a reckoning. What does he give

YAD AVRAHAM

less per seah or a quarter-kav more per seah, it becomes his.

Even if the field was larger or smaller than the size agreed upon by a ratio of a quarter of a *kav* per *seah* [i.e., one twenty-fourth of the total], the sale is valid and no adjustment is necessary. This amounts to a discrepancy of seven-and-a-half *kavs* to a *beis kor*. The mishnah states the ruling per *seah* rather than giving the total for the whole *beis kor* to indicate that this standard applies to the sale of smaller plots of land as well (*Rav*).

The mishnah has dealt with the cases in which the precision of the measurement or its imprecision had been clearly stipulated in the purchase agreement. The *Gemara* (104a) concludes that if the seller did not explicitly stipulate whether the measurement was precise or not, but merely said that he was selling a *beis kor*, it is treated as if he had added *whether less or more* and leeway is allowed. Only if he stipulates that the measurement is precise is he responsible for an exact measurement (*Rav*). The mishnah mentions his saying *whether less or more* only to teach that, even with this stipulation, a discrepancy of more than a quarter-*kav* per *seah* must be adjusted (*Tos.* 104a).

This ruling presents problems. The previous mishnah stated that if the rocks and crevices found in the *beis kor* were less than ten handbreadths high or deep, they are included in the sale. The *Gemara* (103a), however, limited this to rocks and crevices no greater than four *kavs* per *beis kor*, as noted in the comm. to mishnah 1 (s.v. פחות). But if the shortfall of seven and a half *kavs* allowed here holds true even when the seller did not specify 'more or less,' then it should certainly apply where he provided him with a full *beis kor* which contained four *kavs* of rock, since

the rocky terrain is no worse than a complete shortfall in the amount of land agreed upon in the purchase.

Some answer that a general statement of size is treated as an approximation only in a case in which the field in question was sold in its entirety. The previous mishnah, however, referred to a case in which the seller owned other land alongside the field he sold. In such a case he must provide a full *beis kor*, and the question of how much rocky area can be counted becomes relevant (*Ri Migash; Ritva*).

Others distinguish between this mishnah and the previous one in that this mishnah discusses a case in which the buyer is standing in the field at the time of the sale and can see its overall size for himself (see above, s.v. והותיר כל שהוא). Since he saw what he was getting and agreed to the sale, he cannot hold the seller to the precise dimensions stated (unless the deviation exceeds the acceptable limits of approximation). The previous mishnah, however, is discussing a situation in which he had not seen the field, but had relied on the seller for the accuracy of his measurements. The seller is therefore held to the precise terms of his statement, and it is only because up to four *kavs* of rocky or broken ground are considered an acceptable part of a field that the sale is valid. Had these four *kavs* been missing entirely, the sale would be voided (*Tos.* 104a in name of *Rashba*).

יוֹתֵר מִכָּאן, יַעֲשֶׂה חֶשְׁבּוֹן. — [*If it was*] *more than this, he should make a reckoning.*

If the size of the field exceeded the specified size more than a quarter-*kav* per *seah*, the discrepancy is too great to be included in the previously agreed price. Rather, they should calculate how much additional land there is and how much that additional land is worth according to the price per unit of the sale, and this reckoning should be applied to the disposal of the extra land, as the mishnah will explain (*Rav*).

מַחֲזִיר לוֹ? מָעוֹת. וְאִם רָצָה, מַחֲזִיר לוֹ קַרְקַע.
וְלָמָה אָמְרוּ מַחֲזִיר לוֹ מָעוֹת? לְיַפּוֹת כֹּחוּ שֶׁל
מוֹכֵר. שֶׁאִם שִׁיֵּר בַּשָּׂדֶה בֵּית תִּשְׁעָה קַבִּין, וּבַגִּנָּה
בֵּית חֲצִי קַב — וּכְדִבְרֵי רַבִּי עֲקִיבָא בֵּית רֹבַע —
מַחֲזִיר לוֹ אֶת הַקַּרְקַע. וְלֹא אֶת הָרֹבַע בִּלְבַד הוּא
מַחֲזִיר, אֶלָּא אֶת כָּל הַמּוֹתָר.

יד אברהם

Rashbam (followed by Rav) apparently takes the phrase *make a reckoning* to indicate that a new arrangement is being worked out now which was not inherent in the original sale. Accordingly, this phrase applies only to the case in which the field was larger than anticipated and the buyer will be required to purchase the excess as well (see below). If it was smaller, he simply subtracts from the price of the field the value of that which is missing, but he cannot be required to provide more land from another field even if he owns another one adjacent to the one sold (Rashbam).

Others maintain that the phrase may well apply to the latter case as well, and that the mishnah means by it that although at this size the field is significantly smaller than the size agreed upon, he need only reckon the difference and adjust the price, but the sale still holds valid (Nimmukei Yosef). However, if the difference is so great that the parcel of land can no longer be thought of as a *beis kor* even as an approximation, the sale is completely invalidated since it does not even loosely fit the terms of the sale (Tos. Yom Tov).

מַה הוּא מַחֲזִיר לוֹ? מָעוֹת. — *What does he give back? Money.*

[I.e., the buyer must pay for the extra land and keep it, rather than simply return the excess land.] This ruling applies to the first case of the mishnah as well. Thus, whatever amount the buyer received above the exact *beis kor* he was supposed to receive, he must buy from the seller, rather than return it (Rav; Rashbam; Meiri).

וְאִם רָצָה, מַחֲזִיר לוֹ קַרְקַע. — *But if [the seller] prefers, he gives him back the land.*

If the seller wants the extra land back rather than the money for it, the buyer must return it to him (Tif. Yis.).

וְלָמָה אָמְרוּ מַחֲזִיר לוֹ מָעוֹת? — *Why did they say that he gives back money?*

Strictly speaking, the buyer should be allowed to simply return the excess land. The law giving the choice to the seller was a Rabbinic enactment, for the reason the mishnah will now explain (Rav).

לְיַפּוֹת כֹּחוּ שֶׁל מוֹכֵר. — *To improve the position of the seller.*

The Rabbis ordained that the buyer must keep the extra land and pay the seller for it because the excess land is too small a plot to be of any use by itself, and the seller would thus suffer a loss if he had to take it back (Rav). However, if the seller owned another field adjoining this one, the buyer need not purchase the extra land (Gem. 104b).

If the value of the land rose between the time the sale was made and the time they realized that the field was too large, the buyer cannot be forced to pay for it at the higher price. The seller must allow him either to buy it at the price which prevailed at the time of the sale or else take back the extra land (Gem. 104a).

שֶׁאִם שִׁיֵּר בַּשָּׂדֶה בֵּית תִּשְׁעָה קַבִּין, — *So that if there remained an area of nine kavs in the field,*

I.e., since the purpose of the Rabbinic enactment was to protect the seller from being left with a piece of land too small to be worked profitably (Rashbam), the

back? Money. But if [the seller] prefers, he gives him back the land. Why did they say that he gives back money? To improve the position of the seller. So that if there remained an area of nine *kavs* in the field, or half a *kav* in a garden — or a quarter-*kav* according to R' Akiva — he may give him back the land. Moreover, it is not only the quarter-*kav* that he gives back, but all the excess.

YAD AVRAHAM

ruling is different for a parcel of land measuring nine *kavs* beyond a *beis kor*, which is a plot large enough to be considered a field in its own right, as stated above in mishnah 1:6 (*Rav*).

וּבְגִנָּה בֵּית חֲצִי קַב — *or half a kav in a garden* —

The ratio of a quarter-*kav* per *seah* applies to a garden as well as to a field. However, a garden needn't be as large as a field to be viable. Therefore, if the plot being sold was a garden, and the extra land totaled half a *kav*, it is large enough to be defined as a garden of its own, as stated in 1:6 (*Rashbam*).

וּכְדִבְרֵי רַבִּי עֲקִיבָא בֵּית רֹבַע — *or a quarter-kav according to R' Akiva* —

R' Akiva's view in mishnah 1:6 is that a quarter-*kav* is sufficient to be considered a garden (*Rashbam*).

מַחֲזִיר לוֹ אֶת הַקַּרְקַע. — *he may give him back the land.*

[Since the extra land is viable by itself, there is no longer any basis for the Rabbinic enactment protecting the seller. Consequently, the buyer cannot be forced to buy the excess, which he may simply return.]

In summation, if the field was found to be larger or smaller than the *beis kor* agreed upon by seven-and-a-half *kavs* or less, the sale stands without any compensation. If the difference is between seven and a half *kavs* and nine *kavs*, the buyer must purchase the extra *kavs*, the buyer must purchase the extra

land if the seller so desires. Beyond nine *kavs*, he may return the extra land (*Rav*).

וְלֹא אֶת הָרֹבַע בִּלְבַד הוּא מַחֲזִיר, אֶלָּא אֶת כָּל הַמּוֹתָר. — *Moreover, it is not only the quarter-kav that he gives back, but all the excess.*

The *Gemara* explains that this text should be emended to read: *It is not only the excess that he must give back but even the quarter-kav itself* (*Gem.* 104b). Once the land is more than one twenty-fourth larger than the size agreed upon and an adjustment is required, all of the extra land must be returned or paid for, not only that which is beyond the acceptable amount (*Rav*). Similarly, if the land was smaller than the size agreed upon by more than a quarter-*kav* per *seah*, the seller must reimburse the buyer for all of the missing land, not just the fraction which exceeds the acceptable amount (*Rashbam*).

Some authorities contend that this ruling applies only when the discrepancy is more than nine *kavs*, in which case the rule is that the buyer give back the land. Once he gives back land, he must give back all the extra land. However, if the discrepancy exceeded seven and a half *kavs* (i.e., more than a fourth of a *kav* per *seah*), but was less than nine *kavs*, in which case the buyer is required to purchase the excess, he pays only for that which exceeds the seven and a half [or quarter-*kav* per *seah*] (*Ri Migash;* cf. *Rambam, Mechirah* 28:7; *Maggid Mishneh* ad loc.).

[ג] **,,מִדָּה** בְּחֶבֶל אֲנִי מוֹכֵר לָךְ, הֵן חָסֵר הֵן
יָתֵר,'' בָּטֵל ,,הֵן חָסֵר הֵן יָתֵר''
,,מִדָּה בְּחֶבֶל.'' ,,הֵן חָסֵר הֵן יָתֵר, מִדָּה בְּחֶבֶל,''
בָּטֵל ,,מִדָּה בְּחֶבֶל'' ,,הֵן חָסֵר הֵן יָתֵר;'' דִּבְרֵי בֶן
נַנָּס. בְּסִימָנָיו וּבִמְצָרָיו: פָּחוֹת מִשְּׁתוּת, הִגִּיעוֹ; עַד
שְׁתוּת, יְנַכֶּה.

יד אברהם

3.

,,מִדָּה בְּחֶבֶל אֲנִי מוֹכֵר לָךְ, הֵן חָסֵר הֵן יָתֵר,'' —
[If he said,] 'I am selling you ... as
measured by a rope, be it less or more,'

A man selling property to another
defined the sale with two contradictory
statements. First he said that the
dimensions would be as measured by
rope, i.e., precise measurements. He
then added that the field in question was
to be sold as is, whether less or more
than the dimensions stated (Rav).

בָּטֵל ,,הֵן חָסֵר הֵן יָתֵר'' ,,מִדָּה בְּחֶבֶל.'' — [the
condition] 'be it less or more' negates
[the condition of] 'as measured by a
rope.'

Of these contradictory stipulations,
his second statement, which indicates
that the measurements need not be
precise, prevails over the first. Therefore, any inaccuracy which does not
exceed one twenty-fourth of the size of
the field does not require any price
adjustment (Rav; see mishnah 2).

,,הֵן חָסֵר הֵן יָתֵר, מִדָּה בְּחֶבֶל,'' בָּטֵל ,,מִדָּה
בְּחֶבֶל'' ,,הֵן חָסֵר הֵן יָתֵר;'' — [If he said,] '...
be it less or more, as measured by a
rope,' [the condition] 'as measured by a
rope' negates [the condition] 'be it less
or more';

[If he first stipulated that the
dimensions were to be approximate and
then said that they were to be precise,

the final statement is again the
prevailing one and the dimensions must
be accurate to avoid price adjustment.]

דִּבְרֵי בֶן נַנָּס. — [these are] the words of
Ben Nanas.

He maintains that whenever two
contradictory statements are included in
one contract the second one is
considered a retraction of the first, and
it is thus the final statement which
counts (Rashbam 104b). The Gemara
(105a), however, cites the opinion of the
Rabbis who dispute this ruling and
contend that it cannot be known which
is the main condition.[1] Therefore,
whichever statement demands less of
the seller is applied (Rav from Gem.
105a), since the field is in his possession
and we can not exact from him anything
more than he can be proven to owe.[2]
Thus, if the field turned out to be larger
than anticipated, the condition calling
for precise measurements is applied, and
the sale price does not include the extra
land. On the other hand, if it turned out
to be smaller than stated, the condition
'be it less or more' prevails, and the
buyer does not receive any refunds for
the shortfall (Rashbam 104b).

If the plot was smaller than stated and the
buyer has not yet paid for it, his position
would seem to be the stronger because he is
in possession of the money and it is the seller

---

1. Although it would seem logical to assume that the final statement is the seller's final word,
the fact that he switched without clarifying allows for the possibility that he regretted the latter
statement immediately and therefore did not bother to elaborate (Ritva).

2. [The field is considered to be in the possession of the seller even if the buyer has already
performed an act of acquisition, because possession of land, as a determinant of ownership, is
not defined as the one presently holding the land; rather, in cases of doubt it is assigned to the
last definite owner (see preface to 3:1).]

3. [If he said,] 'I am selling you ... as measured by a rope, be it less or more,' [the condition] 'be it less or more' negates [the condition of] 'as measured by a rope.' [If he said,] '... be it less or more, as measured by a rope,' [the condition] 'as measured by a rope' negates [the condition] 'be it less or more'; [these are] the words of Ben Nanas.

[If he described it] by its marks and boundaries: [if the difference is] less than a sixth, he must accept it; [but anything] down to a sixth, he deducts.

YAD AVRAHAM

who wishes to exact something from him, namely full price for less than a complete *beis kor*. Thus, in this case, the statement which favors the buyer should be applied. This indeed is the position taken by *Ravad (Hil. Mechirah* 28:11). However, *Maggid Mishneh* there rules that even if the buyer has not yet paid, the terms of the contract are applied in favor of the seller. Since the sale has taken effect and its validity is not in question, the buyer is obligated by the terms of the contract to pay the full purchase price. The only issue is how much land he deserves, but this, as explained above, must be decided in favor of the seller since he is in possession of the land. This appears to be the position of *Rashbam* as well *(Tos. Yom Tov).*

בְּסִימָנָיו וּבִמְצָרָיו: — [*If he described it] by its marks and boundaries:*

If the seller described to the buyer the *beis kor* he was selling by giving its identifying marks and boundaries *(Rav; Rambam Comm.).*

פָּחוֹת מִשְּׁתוּת, הִגִּיעוֹ; — [*if the difference is] less than a sixth, he must accept it* [lit. *it comes to him*];

As the *Gemara* (106a) explains this,[1] it means that if the shortfall in the land is less than a sixth, or even a sixth, of the amount called for, the buyer must accept the property as is, without any reduction in the price *(Rav).*

By saying a *beis kor* without stipulating that it is to be a precise measurement, he has already indicated that an inaccuracy up to one twenty-fourth of the total does not affect the sale (see comm. to mishnah 2, s.v. אפלו פחת). Since he specified its boundaries as well, he is understood to be saying that this is the field being sold, no matter what its size. Nevertheless, since he did say a *beis kor*, it is clear that he intended the dimensions to be binding to some degree *(Rashbam* 106a). We therefore assume that the degree intended is that which we find pertinent to other sales situations. This is one sixth, which is the degree of inaccuracy which, in the sale of movables, calls for an adjustment *(Yad Ramah).* [This is the law of אוֹנָאָה, *fraudulent overcharge.* If the overcharge amounts to a sixth of the price, the sale stands but the seller must refund the overcharge; if it comes to less than a sixth, no adjustment is required *(Bava Metzia* 4:3; *Choshen Mishpat* 227).]

עַד שְׁתוּת, יְנַכֶּה. — [*but anything] down to a sixth, he deducts.*

I.e., if the field was found to be smaller than a *beis kor*, and the shortfall was any large fraction of the total down to a sixth, the price must be adjusted accordingly, with the buyer receiving a refund. Similarly, if the field exceeded a *beis kor* by a similar amount, the buyer

---

1. There is actually a dispute in the *Gemara* concerning a case in which the discrepancy was exactly one sixth of the total. The halachah follows the opinion of Rav Huna that the sale is valid as is *(Rif; Rosh; Rambam, Mechirah* 28:12), and the mishnah has been explained accordingly *(Rav).*

[ד] **הָאוֹמֵר** לַחֲבֵרוֹ ,,חֲצִי שָׂדֶה אֲנִי מוֹכֵר
לָךְ,'' מְשַׁמְּנִין בֵּינֵיהֶן, וְנוֹטֵל חֲצִי
שָׂדֵהוּ. ,,חֶצְיָה בַּדָּרוֹם אֲנִי מוֹכֵר לָךְ,'' מְשַׁמְּנִין
בֵּינֵיהֶן, וְנוֹטֵל חֶצְיָה בַּדָּרוֹם, וְהוּא מְקַבֵּל עָלָיו
מְקוֹם הַגָּדֵר, חָרִיץ, וּבֶן חָרִיץ. וְכַמָּה הוּא חָרִיץ?
שִׁשָּׁה טְפָחִים. וּבֶן חָרִיץ? שְׁלֹשָׁה.

יד אברהם

must return the extra land *(Rashbam)* if it is nine *kavs* or more. If it is smaller, the seller may choose between repossessing the extra land or reimbursement, as explained in the previous mishnah *(Rambam, Mechirah 28:12)*.

4.

הָאוֹמֵר לַחֲבֵרוֹ ,,חֲצִי שָׂדֶה אֲנִי מוֹכֵר לָךְ,'' — [If] one says to another, 'I am selling you half the field,'

[Without specifying which half.]

מְשַׁמְּנִין בֵּינֵיהֶן, וְנוֹטֵל חֲצִי שָׂדֵהוּ. — they divide [the field] between them qualitatively, and he takes half his field.

Rather than dividing the field into two parts of equal sizes, they divide it into two parts of equal value. If one part of the field is superior to the rest, a smaller portion of that land is equal in value to a larger parcel of the inferior land. Thus, when the division is made, it is made [if the seller wishes] along the lines of value [משמנין from שֶׁמֶן, *fat*], not acreage *(Rav)*, because the seller may claim that this was what he intended when he proposed to divide the field *(Rashbam 107b)*.[1] The seller, who generally has the upper hand when the terms of the sale are in doubt, as explained in the previous mishnah, takes the smaller tract of superior land and the buyer receives the larger portion of inferior land. This arrangement is beneficial to the seller because people generally prefer having a smaller plot of superior land to a larger plot of inferior quality *(Rav)*.

Others translate מְשַׁמְּנִין to mean *evaluate*.[2] They evaluate the entire field, and the buyer receives land worth half the total value from the poorer section of the field *(Rambam Comm.; Meiri)*.

Even R' Akiva who maintains (4:2) that one who sells property does so generously, providing the buyer with all that his purchase requires, would agree here that the seller takes the superior parcel. His rule applies only to determining what ancillary items are included in the sale, not the identity of the basic object sold *(Yad Ramah)*.

,,חֶצְיָה בַּדָּרוֹם אֲנִי מוֹכֵר לָךְ,'' מְשַׁמְּנִין בֵּינֵיהֶן, וְנוֹטֵל חֶצְיָה בַּדָּרוֹם. — [If he said,] 'I am selling you its southern half,' they divide [the field] between them qualitatively, and he takes [equal to] its southern half.

They evaluate the worth of the southern half of the field, and the seller may then give him land of that value from the poorest part of the field even though it is not in the southern sector. The seller can maintain that what he meant was that he was selling a percentage of his field equal in value to the southern half of the field *(Rav, Rashbam)*. [Thus, here too the field is divided according to its quality, with the

1. However, if the language used was such that it clearly referred to a division by size, not value, this claim is not tenable and they divide it into two parts of equal size *(Aruch HaShulchan 218:20)*.

2. The Kafich edition of *Rambam's Commentary* in fact has the reading מְשַׁמִין, a more expected form for the verb meaning *to evaluate*.

4. [**I**f] one says to another, 'I am selling you half the field,' they divide [the field] between them qualitatively, and he takes half his field. [If he said,] 'I am selling you its southern half,' they divide [the field] between them qualitatively, and he takes [equal to] its southern half. He accepts upon himself the place for the fence, a [wide] ditch, and a narrow ditch. How wide is a [wide] ditch? Six handbreadths. And the narrow ditch? Three [handbreadths].

YAD AVRAHAM

seller taking the better piece. The only difference between this case and the first is that whereas in the first case the buyer received a share equal to half the value of the whole field, here he receives a piece equal to the value of its southern half.]

Others maintain that he gives him the southern portion of the field, whether it is of superior or inferior quality. However, he does not give him half the actual field but rather the portion at the southern end of the field which is worth half the value of the entire field (*Nimmukei Yosef; Meiri; Rambam, Mechirah* 21:22).

וְהוּא מְקַבֵּל עָלָיו מְקוֹם הַגָּדֵר, חָרִיץ, וּבֶן חָרִיץ. — *He accepts upon himself the place for the fence, a [wide] ditch, and a narrow ditch.*

The buyer accepts upon himself to provide the space for a fence, a ditch, and a small ditch to protect his field (*Rav*), and he cannot demand of the seller that he provide the space for these necessities (*Yad Ramah*). *Rashbam*, however, explains this to mean that the seller must provide the space for these items, because one who sells a field is assumed to include all that is necessary for the field unless he specifies otherwise.

Some maintain that one who buys a field from another automatically assumes the responsibility to take whatever steps are necessary to prevent his being the cause of

any damage to the neighboring fields (*Maggid Mishneh, Hil. Shecheinim* 2:17; see comm. to 1:2, s.v. מקום שנהגו לגדור). Therefore, the seller can rightfully demand of the buyer that he provide the place for a fence and ditches so that no animals come from the field of the latter into that of the former (*Rashash*).[1]

These ditches are placed behind the fence so that small animals, such as martens (*Rambam Comm.*), should not be able to jump onto the fence and enter his field. If he were to dig only a wide ditch, the animal might be able to jump down into it, and because of its width, jump from inside the ditch to the other side of it. By adding a narrow ditch between the wide ditch and the wall, the animal is prevented from getting up on the second side of the wide ditch by depriving it of a decent foothold on that side (*Tif. Yis.*). Nor can the animal climb into the narrow ditch and use that as a springboard to get over to the fence, because the ditch is too narrow to allow that (*Rambam Comm.*). A narrow ditch alone would also not be sufficient because the animal would jump straight across it (*Rav from Gem.* 108a). Both together, however, are too wide for it to jump across (*Rambam Comm.*).

וְכַמָּה הוּא חָרִיץ? שִׁשָּׁה טְפָחִים. — *How wide is a [wide] ditch? Six handbreadths.*

I.e., six handbreadths wide and extending along the entire length of the

---

1. As explained previously (comm. to 1:3, s.v. אין מחייבין אותו), although one is not compelled to build a partition four cubits high between fields to ensure privacy (see mishnah 1:2), a ten-handbreadth wall can be demanded to keep the animals which belong to each of them from entering the other's field (*Tos. Yom Tov* to 1:3, from gloss to *Rashi* 4b).

[א] **יֵשׁ** נוֹחֲלִין וּמַנְחִילִין; וְיֵשׁ נוֹחֲלִין וְלֹא
מַנְחִילִין, מַנְחִילִין וְלֹא נוֹחֲלִין, לֹא
נוֹחֲלִין וְלֹא מַנְחִילִין.
וְאֵלּוּ נוֹחֲלִין וּמַנְחִילִין: הָאָב אֶת הַבָּנִים, וְהַבָּנִים
אֶת הָאָב, וְהָאַחִין מִן הָאָב — נוֹחֲלִין וּמַנְחִילִין.
הָאִישׁ אֶת אִמּוֹ, וְהָאִישׁ אֶת אִשְׁתּוֹ, וּבְנֵי אֲחָיוֹת

יד אברהם

border between the two fields *(Rashbam 107b).*

שְׁלֹשָה? חֲרִיץ וּבֵן — *And the narrow*

ditch? Three [handbreadths].

Additionally, a space of one handbreadth is left between the two ditches *(Rav from Gem. ibid.).*

Chapter 8

1.

This chapter deals with the laws of inheritance. It defines who is entitled to inherit under Torah law and how inheritance is to be apportioned.

The Torah assigns priority in inheritance to the relative who is closest to the deceased *(Num. 27:11).* The more closely one is related, the better is his position for inheritance. It would thus seem that two relatives should either both qualify as heirs to each other or neither should. The mishnah, however, informs us that this is not the case and there are those whose relationship regarding inheritance is not reciprocal *(Yad Ramah).*

יֵשׁ נוֹחֲלִין וּמַנְחִילִין; — *There are those who inherit and bequeath;*

There are those who stand to inherit from certain of their relatives should those relatives die, as well as to bequeath to those relatives should they predecease those relatives *(Rav).*

The *Tanna* uses this double expression, *inherit and bequeath,* rather than simply stating, 'There are those who inherit one another,' in order to be consistent with the phraseology of the remainder of the mishnah where inheriting and bequeathing are not reciprocal *(Rashbam).*

וְיֵשׁ נוֹחֲלִין וְלֹא מַנְחִילִין, — *and there are those who inherit but do not bequeath,*

I.e., they inherit specific relatives, but those relatives would not inherit them if they were to predecease those relatives *(Rashbam).*

מַנְחִילִין וְלֹא נוֹחֲלִין, — *who bequeath but do not inherit,*

These are the counterparts of those included in the preceding category

(Rashbam 108a).

לֹא נוֹחֲלִין וְלֹא מַנְחִילִין. — *[and] who neither inherit nor bequeath.*

There are those who despite their kinship are not considered relatives as regards inheritance.

וְאֵלּוּ נוֹחֲלִין וּמַנְחִילִין: — *These inherit and bequeath:*

Sometimes the mishnah begins a listing with the first category mentioned, and sometimes with the last one cited. In this case, the former structure is used *(Tos. Yom Tov).*

הָאָב אֶת הַבָּנִים, — *A father [his] sons,*

A father inherits his sons when they have no offspring of their own (see mishnah 2), and they in turn are his heirs *(Rashbam).*

That a father inherits his sons is derived from the verse *(Numbers 27:8): If a man dies without a son, you shall transfer his inheritance to his daughter.*

8
1

1. **T**here are those who inherit and bequeath; and there are those who inherit but do not bequeath, who bequeath but do not inherit, [and] who neither inherit nor bequeath.

These inherit and bequeath: A father [his] sons, sons their father, and brothers from the [same] father — inherit and bequeath. A man his mother, a man his wife, and [his] sisters' sons — inherit but do not

The verse uses the word *transfer* rather than simply saying *give* in order to allude to another party who is eligible to inherit if there is no son but is nonetheless passed over in favor of the daughter *(Nimmukei Yosef)*. This refers to the father, who is passed over in favor of the daughter, but is next in line when there are no children. He takes precedence even over the deceased's brothers *(Rav from Gem.* 109a).[1]

That a father bequeaths to his sons is clearly contained in the verse cited above, which states that only if there are no sons does a daughter inherit *(Rav from Gem.* 110a).

וְהַבָּנִים אֶת הָאָב, — *sons their father,*

[Sons inherit their father and they bequeath to him.]

Although this is included in the previous statement, the mishnah repeats it so that we should derive from the redundancy that it is the sons who inherit, not the daughters [i.e., when there are sons] *(Tos.* 108a).

וְהָאַחִין מִן הָאָב — נוֹחֲלִין וּמַנְחִילִין. — *and brothers from the [same] father — inherit and bequeath.*

Two brothers from the same father, even if they do not have the same mother, inherit each other when the deceased brother leaves no offspring and their father is no longer alive *(Rashbam).* This is stated explicitly (ibid. v. 10): *If he has no daughter, then you shall give his legacy to his brothers.*

This completes the list of those who inherit and bequeath. The mishnah now proceeds to list those who inherit but do not bequeath.

הָאִישׁ אֶת אִמּוֹ, — *A man his mother,*

A man inherits his mother, as derived from the verse *(Num.* 36:8): *And every daughter who inherits a legacy from the tribes of the children of Israel.* The word *tribes* (plural) indicates that it is possible for her to inherit from the portion of two separate tribes. This can occur only if she inherits both her father *and* her mother, who can be from different tribes. Although this verse deals with daughters, not sons, the inheritance that a daughter receives from her mother is equated with that which she receives from her father (both are contained in the single word *tribes).* From this the *Gemara* derives that just as sons take precedence over daughters in a father's legacy, so too they have priority in the mother's *(Rav from Gem.* 111a).

However, a man does not bequeath to his mother, since the verse (ibid. v. 11) specifies that inheritance belongs to relatives from one's מִשְׁפָּחָה, *family.* From the verse *(Num.* 1:2), *according to their families, the house of their fathers,* we infer that the word מִשְׁפָּחָה in Scripture refers solely to family from the father's side *(Rashbam; Gem.* 109b).

וְהָאִישׁ אֶת אִשְׁתּוֹ, — *a man his wife,*

A man inherits his wife even if she leaves sons *(Rashbam* 111b). There is a

1. The Torah does not mention the inheritance of the father explicitly because it is unnatural that a father should survive his children *(Meiri).*

נוֹחֲלִין וְלֹא מַנְחִילִין. הָאִשָּׁה אֶת בָּנֶיהָ,
וְהָאִשָּׁה אֶת בַּעֲלָהּ, וַאֲחֵי הָאֵם — מַנְחִילִין וְלֹא
נוֹחֲלִין. וְהָאַחִים מִן הָאֵם לֹא נוֹחֲלִין וְלֹא מַנְחִילִין.

[ב] סֵדֶר נְחָלוֹת כָּךְ הוּא: ,,אִישׁ כִּי יָמוּת וּבֵן
אֵין לוֹ, וְהַעֲבַרְתֶּם אֶת נַחֲלָתוֹ לְבִתּוֹ"
— בֵּן קוֹדֵם לְבַת, וְכָל יוֹצְאֵי יְרֵכוֹ שֶׁל בֵּן קוֹדְמִין

יד אברהם

difference of opinion in the *Gemara* (111b-113a) whether a husband's inheritance of his wife's legacy is of Biblical or Rabbinic origin. The halachah is also in dispute (see *Rambam, Nachalos* 1:8 and *Raavad* and *Maggid Mishnah* there).

וּבְנֵי אֲחָיוֹת — *and [his] sisters' sons* [lit. *the sisters' sons*] —

A man inherits his mother's brother if the latter has no closer heirs. [The plural *sisters* refers to the sisters of the deceased uncle (*Rashbam*).] Since a sister is eligible to inherit her brother [if he dies without children or brothers], her son receives the legacy through her if she is already deceased (*Rashbam* 108a; see mishnah 2). The converse, however, does not apply — the man does not bequeath to his mother's brother. Since the mother herself does not inherit her son (see above), she obviously cannot be the link to pass her son's legacy along to her brother.

Actually, this phrase, which literally translates as *the sisters' sons*, is interpreted by some to mean that a man inherits his mother's sister. It would refer to sisters from the same father who inherit each other and thus pass this eligibility to inherit to their respective sons. However, the difficulty with this alternate interpretation is that the following grouping in the mishnah, which lists those who bequeath but do not inherit, is derived merely by reversing the roles of the subjects in this phrase, those who inherit but do not bequeath. Were we to interpret *sisters'*

sons to mean that a man inherits his aunt, this passage would then contain nothing to correspond to *the mother's brothers* in the following phrase (*Rashbam* 108a).

נוֹחֲלִין וְלֹא מַנְחִילִין — *inherit but do not bequeath.*

[All of these individuals inherit those mentioned but do not bequeath to them, as explained.]

הָאִשָּׁה אֶת בָּנֶיהָ, וְהָאִשָּׁה אֶת בַּעֲלָהּ — *A woman her sons, and a woman her husband,*

[A woman bequeaths to her son or husband, but cannot inherit them.] This entire passage is superfluous, since it is merely the inverse of the previous category. The *Gemara* (114b) explains that it is nevertheless listed to equate a woman's bequeathing to her son with her bequeathing to her husband. Just as a husband does not inherit his wife if he predeceases her, so too a son does not inherit his mother if he predeceases her. This means that just as a husband is not considered an heir of his wife after his own death in order to be able to pass the legacy on to *his* heirs (see mishnah 2), so too a son does not inherit his mother after his death to pass her legacy on to his father's family [e.g., his brother from a different mother]. Rather, the woman's legacy in such cases is passed on to her paternal relatives (*Yad Ramah*; cf. *Rashbam* to *Gem.* 114b; *Tos.* there; *Tos. Yom Tov*).

bequeath. A woman her sons, and a woman her husband, and the mother's brothers — bequeath but do not inherit. Brothers by the [same] mother neither inherit nor bequeath.

2. The order of inheritance is as follows: *'If a man should die, and he has no son, you shall transfer his legacy to his daughter' (Numbers 27:8) —* A son takes precedence over a daughter, and all the descendants of a son take precedence over a

YAD AVRAHAM

וַאֲחֵי הָאֵם — מַנְחִילִין וְלֹא נוֹחֲלִין. — *and the mother's brothers — bequeath but do not inherit.*

Although this case, too, is superfluous, being the inverse of *his sisters' sons* mentioned above, it is mentioned along with the others of its category in order to complete the corresponding list *(Rashbam to 114b, s.v.* אף האשה את בנה*).*

וְהָאַחִים מִן הָאֵם לֹא נוֹחֲלִין וְלֹא מַנְחִילִין. — *Brothers by the [same] mother neither*

inherit nor bequeath.

[Brothers who are related only through their mother but who are of different fathers neither inherit nor bequeath each other.] This is because the Torah mandates that inheritance go strictly through the father's side *(Gem.* 109b; see above). It goes without saying that if they are related from the father's side as well, that their additional relationship from the mother's side does not disqualify them as heirs *(Rashbam).*

2.

When someone who is next in line to inherit dies, his position in the line of inheritance is not lost, but is passed along to his descendants. Thus, the descendant of a close heir, though several generations removed from the person leaving the estate, will inherit rather than a more distant heir of the same generation, as the mishnah will explain.

סֵדֶר נְחָלוֹת כָּךְ הוּא: — *The order of inheritance is as follows:*

[I.e., this is the order of precedence concerning inheritance. Whoever takes precedence over another receives the entire legacy while the other receives nothing.]

„אִישׁ כִּי יָמוּת, וּבֵן אֵין לוֹ, וְהַעֲבַרְתֶּם אֶת נַחֲלָתוֹ לְבִתּוֹ" — בֵּן קוֹדֵם לְבַת, וְכָל יוֹצְאֵי יְרֵכוֹ שֶׁל בֵּן קוֹדְמִין לְבַת. — *'If a man should die, and he has no son, you shall transfer his legacy to his daughter' (Num. 27:8) — A son takes precedence over a daughter,*

and all the descendants of a son take precedence over a daughter.

E.g., Yaakov has a son Reuven, and a daughter Dinah. Not only does Reuven take precedence over Dinah, his sister, to inherit Yaakov, their father, but even if Reuven is no longer alive, his offspring take his place to inherit Yaakov rather than Dinah *(Rashbam).* The Torah prescribes the transfer of inheritance to a daughter only if the deceased *has no son* whatsosever, which is not the case if his deceased son has been survived by issue (see *Gem.* 115a

לְבַת. בַּת קוֹדֶמֶת לְאַחִין, יוֹצְאֵי יְרֵכָהּ שֶׁל בַּת
קוֹדְמִין לְאַחִין. אַחִין קוֹדְמִין לַאֲחֵי הָאָב, יוֹצְאֵי
יְרֵכָן שֶׁל אַחִין קוֹדְמִין לַאֲחֵי הָאָב. זֶה הַכְּלָל: כָּל
הַקּוֹדֵם בְּנַחֲלָה, יוֹצְאֵי יְרֵכוֹ קוֹדְמִין; וְהָאָב קוֹדֵם
לְכָל יוֹצְאֵי יְרֵכוֹ.

יד אברהם

and *Rashbam* ad loc.).

בַּת קוֹדֶמֶת לְאַחִין, — *A daughter takes precedence over brothers,*

[The Torah (v. 9) states: *And if he has no daughter, then you shall give his legacy to his brothers.* This clearly indicates that if he does have a daughter, she takes precedence over her uncles, the deceased's brothers.]

יוֹצְאֵי יְרֵכָהּ שֶׁל בַּת קוֹדְמִין לְאַחִין. — *[and] the descendants of a daughter take precedence over brothers.*

[If the daughter died before the father but left offspring, they inherit their grandfather rather than his brothers.] Here, too, the Torah writes, *And if he has no daughter,* which means no daughter whatsoever, i.e., no surviving issue from his daughter (*Gem.* 115a).

אַחִין קוֹדְמִין לַאֲחֵי הָאָב, — *Brothers take precedence over the father's brothers,*

[The deceased's brothers take precedence over the deceased's paternal uncles.[1] This is stated in the verse (ibid. v. 10), *And if he has no brothers, then you shall give his legacy to his father's brothers.*]

Not only do brothers of the deceased take precedence over their uncles, but so do the sisters of the deceased and her offspring (*Tos. Yom Tov; Rashbam*). However, where the deceased is survived by a brother and sister, only the brother inherits (*Gem.* 113b; see *Rashbam* ad loc.).

יוֹצְאֵי יְרֵכָן שֶׁל אַחִין קוֹדְמִין לַאֲחֵי הָאָב. — *[and] the descendants of brothers take precedence over the father's brothers.*

[This is derived from the same verse, *And if he has 'no' brothers,* which means no vestige of his brothers.]

זֶה הַכְּלָל: כָּל הַקּוֹדֵם בְּנַחֲלָה, יוֹצְאֵי יְרֵכוֹ קוֹדְמִין; — *This is the rule: Whoever takes precedence in the inheritance, his descendants take precedence;*

The reason is that we view the deceased's estate as if it had become the property of the one who had priority to inherit (even though he is no longer alive), and his heirs thus inherit it from him (*Yad Ramah*).

An exception to this rule is a husband, who does not inherit his wife after her death in order to pass her possessions on to his descendants [from another wife] (ibid. from *Gem.* 114b). Another exception is that a son does not inherit his mother after his death to pass her estate on to his brothers by his father but by a different mother (*Gem.* ibid; see commentary to mishnah 1, s.v. האשה).

וְהָאָב קוֹדֵם לְכָל יוֹצְאֵי יְרֵכוֹ. — *but the father takes precedence over all his descendants.*

A man whose son or daughter dies takes precedence over his other offspring — i.e., the deceased's brothers and sisters — in the inheritance. However, he does not precede the offspring of the deceased himself (*Rashbam*). [Thus, the phrase *all his descendants* denotes those who are his descendants only but not the deceased's.]

As noted previously (comm. to mishnah 1, s.v. האב), the use of the word *transfer* rather than *give,* in the verse mandating the inheritance of the

1. The mother's brothers are not in line to inherit because inheritance passes only through the paternal side, as taught in mishnah 1.

**8
2**

daughter. A daughter takes precedence over brothers, [and] the descendants of a daughter take precedence over brothers. Brothers take precedence over the father's brothers, [and] the descendants of brothers take precedence over the father's brothers. This is the rule: Whoever takes precedence in the inheritance, his descendants take precedence; but the father takes precedence over all his descendants.

YAD AVRAHAM

daughter, indicates that there is another heir, besides those mentioned in the passage, who is passed over in favor of the deceased's daughter, namely, the deceased's father. By the same token, we derive from this that he is passed over only in favor of the daughter, but not in favor of any other heir *(Gem.* 109a).

Similarly, a grandfather takes precedence over his own offspring in the inheritance of his grandson. Thus, if a man's grandson dies, leaving no children, living father, or brothers, the grandfather inherits rather than any of the grandfather's sons, who are the deceased's uncles. However, the brothers of the deceased have priority over him since they are the direct heirs of the deceased's father, who, if he were alive, would have preceded the grandfather to inherit the deceased *(Gem.* 116b).

The order of inheritance is thus as follows: (1) If a man dies, his sons inherit him. If one of those sons has predeceased him, that son's offspring take his share of the inheritance. (2) If the man dies and no son or descendant (male or female) of his son survives him, then his daughters inherit him. [Daughters, too, transfer their share of the inheritance to their descendants if the daughters predecease their father.] (3) If the deceased leaves no offspring whatsoever, his father inherits him. (4) If the father is no longer living, then the

father's sons, who are the deceased's brothers from the same father, inherit. (5) If the deceased's brothers are no longer alive, then their sons or the descendants of their sons — or, if they have no sons, their daughters or the descendants of their daughters — inherit. [If the brothers have died, one leaving sons and another leaving only daughters, the daughters of the latter inherit together with the sons of the former, since they are inheriting by virtue of their father who was a son (see mishnah 3).] (6) If the deceased is not survived by brothers or their offspring, his sisters inherit him; or, if they are dead, their offspring. (7) If the deceased is not survived by any brother or sister or their offspring, then the inheritance reverts to his father's father. (8) If the father's father is dead, then the father's brothers inherit; or, if they too are dead, their offspring inherit. (9) If these heirs do not exist, then the father's sister inherits, either for herself, or, if she is not living, for her offspring. If there are no relatives at this level, then the legacy reverts to the father's grandfather and his progeny. This process continues, going back as many generations as is necessary and then tracing their descendants forward until an heir is found *(Rav).*

3.

The mishnah cites an historic example of the law stated in the previous mishnah, that the daughter of the deceased's son inherits in place of her father *(Rashbam* 116b).

11
stttt

[ג] **בְּנוֹת** צְלָפְחָד נָטְלוּ שְׁלֹשָׁה חֲלָקִים בַּנַּחֲלָה: חֵלֶק אֲבִיהֶן, שֶׁהָיָה עִם יוֹצְאֵי מִצְרַיִם; וְחֶלְקוֹ עִם אֶחָיו בְּנִכְסֵי חֵפֶר; וְשֶׁהָיָה בְּכוֹר, נוֹטֵל שְׁנֵי חֲלָקִים.

יד אברהם

There is a dispute in the *Gemara* (117a) concerning the apportionment of the Land of Israel to the children of Israel. Some are of the opinion that within each tribe, the land was divided among the people who left Egypt although they had already died before the conquest of the Land of Israel. Each share was then divided among the heirs of its recipient. Support for this view is adduced from the verse (*Numbers* 26:55), *According to the names of the tribes of their fathers they shall inherit.*

Others contend that the land was divided according to those who entered the Land of Israel with Joshua, as stated in the verse (ibid. v. 53), *To these you shall apportion the land.* The other passage cited above which states that the land was apportioned according to those who left Egypt is meant to teach us that after the land was divided by the number of those entering, those shares were then reapportioned according to those who left Egypt.

For example: If Reuven and Shimon were brothers who left Egypt, and Reuven had ten sons while Shimon had only one, and these sons entered the land with Joshua. According to the first opinion, Reuven and Shimon would each posthumously receive one portion in the land. Shimon's only son would inherit Shimon's entire portion of land by himself while Reuven's ten sons would divide Reuven's portion ten ways. However, according to the second opinion, the eleven sons would be given eleven shares in the land. These shares would then revert to their fathers, Reuven and Shimon, with each of them receiving five and one half. Consequently, Reuven's ten sons would divide Reuven's five and a half portions while Shimon's one son would receive Shimon's five and a half portions (*Rashbam*).

בְּנוֹת צְלָפְחָד — *The daughters of Tzelophechad*

The Torah (*Numbers* 27:1-7) relates that the daughters of Tzelophechad came to Moshe claiming their father's share in Eretz Yisrael, since he had died in the desert without leaving any sons to inherit him. Moshe was instructed by God to grant them their father's share in the land as their claim was indeed valid.

נָטְלוּ שְׁלֹשָׁה חֲלָקִים בַּנַּחֲלָה: — *took three shares of the inheritance:*

The daughters of Tzelophechad received three shares of the inheritance in the Holy Land to divide among themselves (*Rav*).

חֵלֶק אֲבִיהֶן, שֶׁהָיָה עִם יוֹצְאֵי מִצְרַיִם; — *the share of their father, who was among those who left Egypt;*

This *Tanna* is of the opinion that the Land of Israel was divided among those who left Egypt (see preface). Therefore, since Tzelophechad was in that group, he was entitled to a portion in the land, and his daughters inherited it (*Rav* from *Gem.* 117a).

וְחֶלְקוֹ עִם אֶחָיו בְּנִכְסֵי חֵפֶר; — *and his share among his brothers in the estate of Chepher;*

Chepher, the father of Tzelophechad, was also among those who left Egypt. Therefore, Chepher's sons were entitled to divide his share of the land in addition to receiving shares of their own. Consequently, Tzelophechad's daughters also received his share of Chepher's portion in the land after it was divided among Tzelophechad's

3. The daughters of Tzelophechad took three shares of the inheritance: the share of their father, who was among those who left Egypt; and his share among his brothers in the estate of Chepher; and that which, being a first-born, he takes two portions.

YAD AVRAHAM

brothers (Rashbam).

וְשֶׁהָיָה בְכוֹר, — and that which, being a first-born,

Tzelophechad was Chepher's first-born.

Although Scripture (I Chronicles 7:15) writes, *The name of the second was Tzelophechad,* it does not mean that he was not the first-born, but refers rather to the fact that he was the second generation from Gilead, the father of Chepher (Rashbam).

נוטֵל שְׁנֵי חֲלָקִים. — he takes two portions.

[The Torah states (Deut. 21:17), *But the first-born ... he shall recognize to give him a double share in all that will be found to him.* I.e., if the first-born child is a son, and there are other sons as well, the first-born gets double the share of any of the others. E.g., if there were three sons altogether, the estate would be divided into four shares, the first-born would get two shares (or half the estate) and the other two brothers would each get one share (a quarter of the estate).

Thus, Tzelophechad inherited a double share of Chepher's legacy. These two shares, plus Tzelophechad's personal share, gave his daughters three shares to divide among themselves.]

The fact that all of these allotments belonged to Tzelophechad is derived from the verse (loc. cit. v. 7), 'You shall give to them a portion of the inheritance among the brothers of their father, and you shall transfer the inheritance of their father to them.' You shall give to them refers to the portion of their father; among the brothers of their father refers to the inheritance of their grandfather; and you shall transfer the inheritance of their father to them refers to the double portion granted to him by right of being the first-born (Gem. 118b).[1]

Although the law is that a first-born receives a double portion only of that which was already in the father's possession at the time he died, but not of that which became part of his estate after his death, Eretz Yisrael was considered as if it had already been acquired by those who left Egypt (Rav from Gem. 119a; see Tos. Yom Tov), since any gift which has been announced through prophecy is considered as already received (Meiri).

Even if we assume that Tzelophechad died before Chepher, his daughters were still eligible to receive his double share in Chepher's portion of the land (Rashbam). That which a first-born does not inherit a double share from possessions not yet acquired applies only to those possessions still unacquired by his father at the time of the *latter's* death. However, those double portions which do not reach the first-born in 'his lifetime (i.e., he predeceased his father) are transferred to his heirs along with his basic share of inheritance (Nimmukei Yosef).

---

1. Actually, the daughters of Tzelophechad had received a fourth share in the land as well, since Tzelophechad had a brother who died childless. This brother's portion in the land was, therefore, inherited by his brothers, Tzelophechad's share being passed along to his daughters (see Joshua 17:5; Rashi and Radak thereon; Gem. 119a). The mishnah does not mention this fourth portion because nothing would be added to our understanding of the laws of inheritance. From that which they inherited from their grandfather, Chepher, we see that a son's daughter inherits his portion of his father's legacy even where there are brothers. Once this is known, it follows naturally that the daughter also inherits his share in the possessions of his brother, and it is not necessary for the mishnah to point this out (Rashbam).

[ד] אֶחָד הַבֵּן וְאֶחָד הַבַּת בְּנַחֲלָה, אֶלָּא שֶׁהַבֵּן נוֹטֵל פִּי שְׁנַיִם בְּנִכְסֵי הָאָב וְאֵינוֹ נוֹטֵל פִּי שְׁנַיִם בְּנִכְסֵי הָאֵם; וְהַבָּנוֹת נִזּוֹנוֹת מִנִּכְסֵי הָאָב וְאֵינָן נִזּוֹנוֹת מִנִּכְסֵי הָאֵם.

[ה] הָאוֹמֵר ,,אִישׁ פְּלוֹנִי, בְּנִי בְּכוֹר, לֹא יִטֹּל פִּי שְׁנַיִם''; ,,אִישׁ פְּלוֹנִי, בְּנִי, לֹא יִירַשׁ עִם אֶחָיו'' — לֹא אָמַר כְּלוּם, שֶׁהִתְנָה עַל מַה שֶּׁכָּתוּב בַּתּוֹרָה.

יד אברהם

4.

אֶחָד הַבֵּן וְאֶחָד הַבַּת בְּנַחֲלָה, — *Both the son and daughter* [have the same laws] *concerning inheritance,*

I.e., the laws of inheritance are uniform for both the son and the daughter (when there is no son) regardless of which relative they are inheriting. Thus, they inherit the possessions of their mother subject to the same conditions that apply to inheriting the possessions of their father (*Rav* from *Gem.* 122b).

The mishnah cannot be understood literally, that the laws of a son and daughter concerning inheritance are identical, because the Torah states explicitly (*Numbers* 27:8; see mishnah 2) that a daughter inherits only if there is no son (*Gem.* ibid.).

אֶלָּא שֶׁהַבֵּן נוֹטֵל פִּי שְׁנַיִם בְּנִכְסֵי הָאָב — *except that the son takes a double share of the father's estate*

A son who is a first-born takes a double share in his father's legacy, as stated in the verse (*Deut.* 21:17), *to give him a double share* (ibid.).

וְאֵינוֹ נוֹטֵל פִּי שְׁנַיִם בְּנִכְסֵי הָאֵם; — *but does not take a double share of the mother's estate;*

A first-born son does not receive a double portion of his mother's legacy. This is indicated by the verse (loc. cit.), *to him is the law of the first-born* (*Gem.* 111b); the pronoun *him* can be construed to refer to the father — i.e., only to the possessions of the father does the law of the first-born apply but not to the possessions of the mother (*Rashbam*).

וְהַבָּנוֹת נִזּוֹנוֹת מִנִּכְסֵי הָאָב — *and the daughters are supported from the father's estate*

After a man dies his daughters' sustenance is paid for by his estate until they reach adulthood or marry. If the estate is not large enough to support the daughters and still leave a remainder for the sons to inherit, their support takes priority (see below, 9:1; *Rav* ibid.). The reason for this priority is that every Jewish husband binds himself to the obligations of the *kesubah* which stipulates that his daughters from this wife will be supported from his estate. Thus, the amount required for this support was already under obligation before the father's death and is therefore not considered part of his inheritable estate (*Tif. Yis.* ibid.).

וְאֵינָן נִזּוֹנוֹת מִנִּכְסֵי הָאֵם. — *but they are not supported from the mother's estate.*

The daughters are not entitled to support from their mother's estate; rather, the sons inherit the entire estate. This is because this support is a stipulation of the *kesubah*, and thus

4. **B**oth the son and daughter [have the same laws] concerning inheritance, except that the son takes a double share of the father's estate but does not take a double share of the mother's estate; and the daughters are supported from the father's estate but they are not supported from the mother's estate.

5. **O**ne who says, 'That man, my first-born son, shall not take a double share'; [or] 'That man, my son, shall not inherit with his brothers' — has not said anything, because he has stipulated [contrary] to what is written in the Torah.

applies only to the properties of the father, who is obligated by the *kesubah* (*Rashbam* from *Kesubos* 4:11).

However, the daughters do receive a dowry from their mother's legacy as they would from that of their father. Since the Rabbinic ordinance requiring this was not enacted as part of the *kesubah*, it applies to the mother's estate as well as the father's (*Yad Ramah*).

5.

The mishnah now deals with one who wishes to alter the division of his estate from the standard prescribed by the Torah.

הָאוֹמֵר ,,אִישׁ פְּלוֹנִי, בְּנִי בְּכוֹר, לֹא יִטֹּל פִּי שְׁנַיִם'' — *One who says, 'That man, my first-born son, shall not take a double share';*

[This demand runs contrary to the Torah's laws of inheritance, which dictate that a double portion be allotted to the first-born son (see mishnah 3,4).]

,,אִישׁ פְּלוֹנִי, בְּנִי, לֹא יִירַשׁ עִם אֶחָיו'' — [or] *'That man, my son, shall not inherit with his brothers' —*

This is a separate case, in which he excluded one of his sons from the inheritance entirely (*Rashbam*).

לֹא אָמַר כְּלוּם, שֶׁהִתְנָה עַל מַה שֶׁכָּתוּב בַּתּוֹרָה. — *has not said anything — because he has stipulated [contrary] to what is written in the Torah.*

[These stipulations are invalid since one does not have the power to alter the procedures of inheritance prescribed by

the Torah. Similarly, his stipulation to disinherit an heir is void since the Torah mandates that the heir should inherit. Though one may ordinarily attach conditions to legal procedures which he effects, this applies only to the stipulation of additional conditions. One is not, however, empowered to stipulate that a consequence mandated by the Torah should be void.] The only way that one can disinherit a son or deprive the first-born of a double share is to distribute his estate as gifts prior to his death so that nothing is left subject to the laws of inheritance (*Rav;* see below).

Even R' Yehudah, who maintains that stipulations to alter procedures prescribed by the Torah are valid in monetary matters (*Kiddushin* 19b) [and the halachah is in accordance with his opinion], agrees that this is true only if the party affected by the stipulations consents to them (*Gem.* 126b). In our case, however, the son who was excluded from the inheritance never consented to that provision (*Rashbam*).

Others, referring to other Rabbinic sources, explain that since the Torah (*Num.*

הַמְחַלֵּק נְכָסָיו לְבָנָיו עַל פִּיו, רִבָּה לְאֶחָד וּמִעֵט
לְאֶחָד, וְהִשְׁוָה לָהֶן אֶת הַבְּכוֹר — דְּבָרָיו קַיָּמִין,
וְאִם אָמַר מִשׁוּם יְרֻשָּׁה, לֹא אָמַר כְּלוּם. כָּתַב —
בֵּין בַּתְּחִלָּה, בֵּין בָּאֶמְצַע, בֵּין בַּסּוֹף — מִשׁוּם
מַתָּנָה, דְּבָרָיו קַיָּמִין.
הָאוֹמֵר ,,אִישׁ פְּלוֹנִי יִירָשֵׁנִי,'' בְּמָקוֹם שֶׁיֵּשׁ בַּת;

יד אברהם

27:11) refers to the order of inheritance as a חֻקַּת מִשְׁפָּט, *a fixed statute of law*, it is inviolate [unlike other monetary matters] *(Meiri; Rambam, Nachalos* 6:1).

Further in this mishnah, we find the opinion of R' Yochanan ben Beroka who states that the Torah empowers a person to designate all or part of his legacy for a specific heir, and the halachah is in accordance with this view. Although this phrase of the mishnah, which invalidates the father's disinheriting of a son, would appear to be at odds with R' Yochanan ben Beroka's view, the commentators point out that this is not the case. R' Yochanan ben Beroka's ruling only permits a person to assign his estate to those of his heirs whom he chooses. Although in so doing he may assign even all of his legacy to one heir and thereby leave nothing for the other heirs to inherit, he cannot *directly* exclude one of his rightful heirs from inheriting[1] *(Nimmukei Yosef)*. Since he has not specifically designated his legacy to his other heirs, it naturally reverts to all who are eligible to inherit *(Ri Migash* to 130a).

הַמְחַלֵּק נְכָסָיו לְבָנָיו עַל פִּיו, — *One who apportions his estate to his sons orally,*

[The mishnah is now referring to a sickbed testament in which the father specifies the term *gift* in his apportionment rather than merely expressing his desire as to how the *inheritance* should be distributed (see below).]

The mishnah specifies orally because one who dictates action in monetary matters on his sickbed is granted the authority by Rabbinic enactment to implement his desires by word of mouth

alone, without the ordinarily required formal transactions and legal documents [see 9:6] *(Rav)*.

The Rabbis ordained that someone who is lying in bed enfeebled by sickness may issue oral instructions that his possessions be given to another, and his words have the legal validity of a formal act of transfer. This was enacted in order to prevent any deterioration in his condition resulting from his fear that his dispositions would not be carried out *(Gem.* 147b; *Rambam, Zechiyah* 8:2). [The actual transfer of ownership does not take effect until his death (see mishnah, 9:6). Thus it is in effect a sickbed will.]

רִבָּה לְאֶחָד וּמִעֵט לְאֶחָד, — *increasing [the share of] one and decreasing [the share of] one,*

I.e., he gave one a larger share and thereby diminished the share of another *(Nimmukei Yosef)*. Alternatively, the second half of this phrase means that he explicitly decreased the share of one of his heirs *(Tos. Yom Tov)*.

וְהִשְׁוָה לָהֶן אֶת הַבְּכוֹר — *or making the first-born equal to them* —

[He gave the first-born only a single share instead of the double portion to which he is entitled.] In all of these cases, he granted these shares as gifts prior to his demise, rather than indicating that the estate be inherited in this manner *(Rav)*.

1. Some authorities maintain that this invalidation applies only in a case in which he entirely disinherited one of his heirs; however, if he excludes an heir from only part of his inheritance, it is valid *(R' Hai Gaon,* cited by *Meiri)*. Others dispute this distinction and contend that it is invalid in all cases *(Yad Ramah)*.

8
5
One who apportions his estate to his sons orally, increasing [the share of] one and decreasing [the share of] one, or making the first-born equal to them — his words are upheld. But if he said [that it was to be] by inheritance, he has not said anything. [If] he wrote — whether in the beginning, the middle, or the end — [that it was to be] a gift, his words are upheld.

One who says, 'That man shall inherit me,' in a case in which there is a daughter; [or] 'My daughter

YAD AVRAHAM

דְּבָרָיו קַיָּמִין. — *his words are upheld.*
This is not considered a stipulation contrary to the laws of the Torah, because a man may give his possessions as a gift to anyone he wishes (*Rav*). Having done so, he dies leaving no possessions to be subject to the Torah's laws of inheritance (*Rashbam*).

וְאִם אָמַר מִשּׁוּם יְרֻשָּׁה, לֹא אָמַר כְּלוּם. — *But if he said [that it was to be] by inheritance, he has not said anything.*
If he dictates that one of his sons should *inherit* a larger share of the estate and one of them a smaller portion, or that his first-born son should inherit a single share alone, his instructions are void, because he is stipulating against the laws of the Torah (*Rav*).

As previously mentioned, the view of R' Yochanan ben Beroka (and the halachah) is that a person is empowered to dictate the various amounts that his heirs should receive. This statement of the mishnah follows the opinion of the Rabbis, who maintain that one cannot adjust the allotment of his inheritance. The mishnah tells us here that according to this view he cannot even alter the amount to be received by any of his heirs, and he is certainly unable to exclude one of the heirs entirely (*Rashbam*).

Others contend that this statement is consistent with the opinion of R' Yochanan ben Beroka as well. The mishnah is discussing a case in which he altered both the portion of the first-born and that of another son. Since his directive concerning the share of the first-born is null, even according to R' Yochanan ben Beroka (see comm. below), the rest of his instructions are also invalidated

(*Ri Migash; Meiri;* see below, s.v. וְעַל מִי).

כָּתַב — בֵּין בַּתְּחִלָּה, בֵּין בָּאֶמְצַע, בֵּין בַּסּוֹף — מִשּׁוּם מַתָּנָה, — *[If] he wrote — whether in the beginning, the middle, or the end — [that it was to be] a gift,*
I.e., if he said or wrote in a document (*Rambam Comm;* see *Choshen Mishpat* 281:7): 'The field should be given to so-and-so and he will inherit it' (*given* appears in the beginning); or, 'So-and-so shall inherit the field; it should be given to him and he will inherit it' (*given* appears in the middle); or 'So-and-so should inherit it and it will be given to him' (*given* appears at the end) (*Rav*).

דְּבָרָיו קַיָּמִין. — *his words are upheld.*
Since the entire directive deals with one transaction, and he describes it as a gift at some point, the bequest is understood to be a gift (*Yad Ramah*).

If he dictated a gift to one of the heirs and inheritance to another, they are considered to be included in one transaction — and the reference to a gift for one validates the transaction with regard to the other as well. This applies only if they were both included in one continuous statement with no time lapse between them (ibid. from *Gem.* 129a; *Rambam, Nachalos* 6:6).

הָאוֹמֵר ,,אִישׁ פְּלוֹנִי יִירָשֵׁנִי,'' בְּמָקוֹם שֶׁיֵּשׁ בַּת; — *One who says, 'That man shall inherit me,' in a case in which there is a daughter;*
[I.e., someone who is not his son. He is thus trying to designate as his heir

„בְּתִּי תִירָשֵׁנִי," בְּמָקוֹם שֶׁיֵּשׁ בֵּן — לֹא אָמַר
כְּלוּם, שֶׁהִתְנָה עַל מַה שֶׁכָּתוּב בַּתּוֹרָה. רַבִּי יוֹחָנָן
בֶּן בְּרוֹקָה אוֹמֵר: אִם אָמַר עַל מִי שֶׁהוּא רָאוּי
לִירָשָׁה, דְּבָרָיו קַיָּמִין; וְעַל מִי שֶׁאֵין רָאוּי לִירָשָׁה,
אֵין דְּבָרָיו קַיָּמִין. הַכּוֹתֵב אֶת נְכָסָיו לַאֲחֵרִים
וְהִנִּיחַ אֶת בָּנָיו, מַה שֶׁעָשָׂה עָשׂוּי, אֲבָל אֵין רוּחַ
חֲכָמִים נוֹחָה הֵימֶנּוּ. רַבָּן שִׁמְעוֹן בֶּן גַּמְלִיאֵל

יד אברהם

someone not entitled to inherit.] The
following rule of the mishnah would
certainly apply to a case in which there
is a son (Tif. Yis.), as is clear from the
mishnah's next statement.

„בְּתִּי תִירָשֵׁנִי," בְּמָקוֹם שֶׁיֵּשׁ בֵּן — [or] 'My
daughter shall inherit me,' in a case in
which there is a son —

[Whereas a daughter ordinarily
inherits nothing whatsoever when the
deceased has also left over a son. Here,
too, he is trying to alter the normal order
of inheritance.]

לֹא אָמַר כְּלוּם, שֶׁהִתְנָה עַל מַה שֶׁכָּתוּב בַּתּוֹרָה.
— he has not said anything, because he
has stipulated [contrary] to what is
written in the Torah.

The mishnah specifies a case in which
the heir designated by the father is
ineligible to inherit anything at all by
law, which implies that only in such an
instance is his directive void. However,
if the father instructed that one of the
eligible heirs should receive the entire
legacy, it would be valid (Gem. 130a).
This statement, then, is actually the
opinion of R' Yochanan ben Beroka
which follows (ibid.).

רַבִּי יוֹחָנָן בֶּן בְּרוֹקָה אוֹמֵר: אִם אָמַר עַל מִי
שֶׁהוּא רָאוּי לִירָשָׁה, דְּבָרָיו קַיָּמִין; — R'
Yochanan ben Beroka says: If he said
[this] about one who is eligible for the
inheritance, his words are upheld;

I.e., he willed his estate to one of the
several people in line to inherit, e.g., if
he gave the entire inheritance to one of

his sons, or to one of his daughters
when there were no sons.

The validity of this selective
inheritance is derived from the verse
(Deut. 21:16), And it shall be on the day
that he bequeaths to his sons, which
implies that the father has the authority
to dictate the amounts of his sons'
inheritance (Rav from Gem. ibid.).

וְעַל מִי שֶׁאֵין רָאוּי לִירָשָׁה, אֵין דְּבָרָיו קַיָּמִין.
and [if] about one who is not eligible for
the inheritance, his words are not
upheld.

E.g., if he dictated that his daughter
inherit in place of his sons, his
instructions are void, because she is not
eligible to inherit anything whatsoever
when there are sons (Rav).

Although the structure of the
mishnah would lead one to believe that
R' Yochanan ben Beroka disputes the
mishnah's preceding statement, this is
not the case, as explained above. Rather,
the mishnah is emended by the Gemara
(130a) to read as follows: One who says,
'That man shall inherit me,' in a case in
which there is a daughter, etc., has not
said anything. However, in the case of a
son among sons or a daughter among
daughters, if he said that one should
inherit all of his property, his words are
upheld; as R' Yochanan ben Beroka
says, etc.

An alternate explanation proposed by the
Gemara is that R' Yochanan ben Beroka
disputes the mishnah's preceding statement,
and in fact holds that a person can designate
his entire legacy not only to one among

shall inherit me,' in a case in which there is a son — he has not said anything, because he has stipulated [contrary] to what is written in the Torah. R' Yochanan ben Beroka says: If he said [this] about one who is eligible for the inheritance, his words are upheld; and [if] about one who is not eligible for the inheritance, his words are not upheld.

One who signs over his property to another and sets aside his sons, what he did is done, but the Sages are not pleased with him. Rabban Shimon ben

YAD AVRAHAM

equally eligible heirs, but even to an heir who is second in the line of succession to the inheritance (e.g., to a daughter when there are sons). In contrast, the first *Tanna* holds that no alteration whatsoever in the distribution of inheritance is valid, not even to a son among sons. Accordingly, the statement of the first *Tanna* — *One who says, 'That man shall inherit me,' in a case in which there is a daughter ... has not said anything* — was not intended to imply that in the case of equally eligible heirs such a stipulation is valid. Rather, the statement was chosen in response to R' Yochanan ben Beroka, who, in this view, considers such a bequest valid even to someone further down the line of heirs (*Gem.; Rashbam*).

Even R' Yochanan ben Beroka concedes that one cannot deprive his first-born of his double share, as stated explicitly in the verse (*Deut.* 21:16), *He cannot give precedence to the son of the beloved [wife] in the face of the son of the despised [wife] who is the first-born* (*Rav* from *Gem.* 130b).[1]

The halachah follows the opinion of R' Yochanan ben Beroka (*Rav* from *Gem.* 130a; *Choshen Mishpat* 281:1).

The question is raised in the *Gemara* (131a) whether R' Yochanan ben Beroka's opinion applies only to one

who is on his deathbed, as indicated by the verse *on the day that he bequeaths to his sons,* or to anyone who dictates the terms of his inheritance. Since the *Gemara* does not resolve this question, one cannot, in practice, deprive a son of his rightful inheritance by transferring it to another son unless he is on his deathbed (*Choshen Mishpat* 281:5).

הַכּוֹתֵב אֶת נְכָסָיו לַאֲחֵרִים וְהִנִּיחַ אֶת בָּנָיו, — *One who signs over his property to another and sets aside his sons,*

[This refers to one who transfers his estate by giving it away as a gift before his death to one who is not qualified to inherit.]

מַה שֶּׁעָשָׂה עָשׂוּי, — *what he did is done,*

The gift is valid. This has already been stated above. It is repeated here only as a preface to the following statement (*Rashbam*).

אֲבָל אֵין רוּחַ חֲכָמִים נוֹחָה הֵימֶנּוּ. — *but the Sages are not pleased with him.*

Even if his sons do not conduct themselves properly, he is still encouraged to allow them to inherit him, because some of their eventual descen-

1. Although Yaakov took the right of the first-born from Reuven, his eldest, and gave it to Yosef (see *Genesis* 49:3,4; *Rashi* ad loc.), that was before the Torah was given at Sinai, and the laws of inheritance, as dictated by the Torah, were not yet in effect (*Yad Ramah*).

Some authorities maintain that if the will altering the terms of the inheritance in regard to several of the sons included a provision depriving the first-born of his double share, the entire will is void (*Yad Ramah*; see above, s.v. ואם אמר משום ירושה). Others contend that the remainder of the will is still valid (*Nimmukei Yosef*).

אוֹמֵר: אִם לֹא הָיוּ בָנָיו נוֹהֲגִין כַּשׁוּרָה, זָכוּר לְטוֹב.

[ו] הָאוֹמֵר ,,זֶה בְּנִי,'' נֶאֱמָן. ,,זֶה אָחִי,'' אֵינוֹ
נֶאֱמָן, וְנוֹטֵל עִמּוֹ בְּחֶלְקוֹ. מֵת,
יַחְזְרוּ נְכָסִים לִמְקוֹמָן. נָפְלוּ לוֹ נְכָסִים מִמָּקוֹם

יד אברהם

dants may behave righteously and they will benefit from the legacy (*Rav* from *Gem.* 133b).

The literal translation of this idiom is: but the spirit of Sages does not rest easy because of him (*Rashbam* as explained by *Sema* 282:2).

רַבָּן שִׁמְעוֹן בֶּן גַּמְלִיאֵל אוֹמֵר: אִם לֹא הָיוּ בָנָיו נוֹהֲגִין כַּשׁוּרָה, זָכוּר לְטוֹב. — *Rabban Shimon ben Gamliel says: If his sons did not conduct themselves properly, he is remembered for good.*

[I.e., his transfer of the inheritance to another is approved.]

The halachah follows the opinion of the first *Tanna*, that even when the sons behave improperly transfer of the inheritance to someone else is discouraged (*Rav* from *Gem.* 133b; *Choshen Mishpat* 282).

6.

The mishnah discusses the credibility of one who declares another to be his son or brother. The obvious pertinence of this issue is to determine the latter's status in regard to inheritance. However, it also affects the question of *yibum* — the law that if a man dies childless his brother must either marry his widow or release her through the ceremony of *chalitzah* (see *Deut.* 25:5).

הָאוֹמֵר ,,זֶה בְּנִי,'' נֶאֱמָן. — *One who says, 'This is my son,' is believed.*

He is believed that this person is his son [although there are no witnesses to that effect], and the son therefore inherits him (*Rav*). There is no reason for the father to lie about this merely to make this man his heir, because if he wanted, he could grant him his possessions as a gift (*Rashbam* 134b, s.v. פשיטא).[1] This ruling is obvious, and the main point of the mishnah is that he is also believed to free his wife from falling to *yibum* in case he has no other children but is known to have brothers (*Rav* from *Gem.* 134b). This is because he could divorce her (just before his death) if he desired and thereby avoid the issue of *yibum* entirely (*Gem.*).

Although divorcing her is not the perfect alternative to *yibum*, since she would thereby become forbidden to marry a *Kohen* (*Lev.* 21:7), a disqualification that would not result from *yibum*, it is unlikely that this is of concern to him (*Nimmukei Yosef*).

,,זֶה אָחִי,'' — [*If he said*,] *'This is my brother,'*

Reuven related to his brother, Shimon, that a third person, Levi, is also their brother, and must therefore share in their father's inheritance. Shimon, however, claims to have no knowledge in this matter [nor are there any independent witnesses to confirm the story] (*Tif. Yis.*).

אֵינוֹ נֶאֱמָן — *he is not believed,*

1. Some authorities maintain that he is therefore believed only in regard to possessions which he presently owns, since he could give them to his son as a gift, but if he receives other possessions afterwards, the alleged son does not inherit them (*Rashbam* 134b). Others contend that once he is believed to declare him his son, the latter is accepted as such completely, and he inherits from that which the father acquires later as well (*Rosh; Rama; Choshen Mishpat* 279:1).

Gamliel says: If his sons did not conduct themselves properly, he is remembered for good.

6. One who says, 'This is my son,' is believed. [If he said,] 'This is my brother,' he is not believed, but he must share his portion with him. [If] he died, the possessions return to their place. [If] possessions fell to him from another source, his

YAD AVRAHAM

Reuven is not believed to allow Levi to inherit, since Shimon does not recognize Levi as their brother *(Rav)*. Similarly, if Reuven had no other brothers, and his wife was therefore assumed to be exempt from *yibum*, he is not believed to cause her to fall to him in *yibum (Rashbam*, loc. cit.).

However, if Levi was previously presumed to be a brother, and several of the brothers protested that he was not, they are not believed to disqualify him from sharing in their inheritance *(Meiri)*.

וְנוֹטֵל עִמּוֹ בְּחֶלְקוֹ. — *but he must share his portion with him.*

[Reuven, who proclaimed Levi to be a brother, must share his portion of the inheritance with him, because a person's admission of anything to his detriment is believed in regard to himself even if it lacks the quality of evidence needed to establish the matter in court. Since Reuven claims that Levi is his brother, he is, in effect, admitting that he, Reuven, does not deserve half the estate but only a third, with the difference going to Levi.] Thus, if the father, Yaakov, died leaving three fields to be divided equally among his sons, his two known sons, Reuven and Shimon, each receive one and a half fields. However, according to Reuven's claim that Levi is also a brother, each brother is entitled to only one field, and Levi's rightful share of one field was wrongly divided between Reuven and Shimon. Therefore, Reuven must give the extra half-field which he received to Levi. Thus, Shimon, who does not recognize

Levi as their brother, receives one and a half fields; Reuven receives one field, and Levi would be granted the extra half-field which had been apportioned to Reuven *(Rav)*.

מֵת, — *[If] he died,*

If Levi, the one whose status was in doubt, subsequently died *(Rav)* and did not leave any children *(Tif. Yis.)*.

יַחְזְרוּ נְכָסִים לִמְקוֹמָן. — *the possessions return to their place.*

That portion of the father's legacy which Levi received from Reuven return to Reuven's possession, and the other brother, Shimon, who does not recognize the deceased, Levi, to be his brother, has no share in those possessions which Levi received from Reuven's portion of their father's legacy. If Levi was in fact a brother, then he was entitled, as his share of the father's estate, to the extra half-field which Shimon had refused to give him. Since Shimon already has this in his possession, he already has one-half of what Levi should have actually received from their father. Thus Shimon retains that half, while the other half reverts to Reuven. If Levi was, in fact, *not* a brother, then Shimon, obviously, does not inherit him, while Reuven gets back that which he had given to Levi *(Rashbam)*.

נָפְלוּ לוֹ נְכָסִים מִמָּקוֹם אַחֵר, — *[If] possessions fell to him from another source,*

I.e., if Levi had other property besides

בבא
בתרא
ח/ו

אַחֵר, יִירְשׁוּ אֶחָיו עִמּוֹ.
מִי שֶׁמֵּת, וְנִמְצֵאת דְּיַתִּיקִי קְשׁוּרָה עַל יְרֵכוֹ,
הֲרֵי זוֹ אֵינָהּ כְּלוּם. זִכָּה בָהּ לְאַחֵר, בֵּין מִן הַיּוֹרְשִׁין
בֵּין שֶׁאֵינוֹ מִן הַיּוֹרְשִׁין, דְּבָרָיו קַיָּמִין.

יד אברהם

the half-share he received from Reuven, either property that he had inherited from another source[1] or had otherwise acquired himself (Rav).

יִירְשׁוּ אֶחָיו עִמּוֹ — *his brothers inherit with him.*

Reuven's brothers would inherit together with him, since he admitted to them that Levi was their brother (Rav). However, this holds true only if they never claimed to be certain that Levi was not their brother. Otherwise, their claim of non-relation would be considered an admission that they have no rights to his inheritance (Rav from Gem. 135a).

Actually, since it has not been established clearly that Levi was a brother, Levi is objectively considered to have died without any discoverable heirs.[2] Therefore, if a third party was first to take possession of Levi's property, the brothers would not be able to exact it from him in court, since the burden of proof is on the one who seeks to change the existing status (see preface to ch. 3). The mishnah must be discussing a case in which Reuven was first to take possession upon Levi's death, and the other brothers claim the right to share with him in the inheritance based on Reuven's identification (Rashash).

מִי שֶׁמֵּת, וְנִמְצֵאת דְּיַתִּיקִי — *[If] one died, and a will was found*

As explained in mishnah 5 (s.v. המחלק נכסיו), the Rabbis ordained that a sickbed disposition of property is effective even in the absence of a formal transaction or document. The mishnah here refers to a case in which these sickbed instructions were not issued verbally but rather written down in legal document form (Rav).

An alternate approach is that this mishnah does not refer to a legal document but rather to a note written simply as a reminder of the sick man's wishes concerning the transfer of his possessions after his death (Ravad cited by Rashba; Meiri).

The word דְּיַתִּיקִי can be construed as an abbreviation of the phrase דָּא תְּהֵא לְמֵיקָם וּלְמֶהֱוֵי, *this shall be upheld* (ibid. from Gem. 135b). [It was the common practice of the Sages to apply Aramaic meanings to words of whose Greek origin they were fully aware (see Tos. Anshei Shem to Sheviis 10:3).]

Some interpret this phrase to denote: this [will] be upheld [after my death] (Rashbam). Others explain that this phrase actually appears in the will (Ran) and refers not to the provision of the will but is rather a prayer for the ailing donor: May this [man] endure and live, but if I die ... (Nimmukei Yosef from Tosefta).

קְשׁוּרָה עַל יְרֵכוֹ — *tied to his thigh,*

The document was found tied to the deceased's thigh, so that it is clear that it was written with the consent of the deceased and not by someone else without the deceased's knowledge

1. Rav stipulates that this inheritance came to him when he was still alive. The reason for this is that the mishnah cannot be dealing with Levi's inheritance from his father's family, since the brothers would inherit that in their own right. Since the mishnah must mean that Levi inherited from his wife or mother, it must be that Levi was still alive when they died since a dead man does not inherit his wife or mother to pass the inheritance along to his brothers (see comm. to mishnah 1, s.v. האשה את בניה). However, the mishnah apparently could have meant that Levi inherited from his children, in which case he could inherit them even after his death to pass the inheritance along to his brothers (see Tos. Yom Tov; Rashash; see, however, Mahariach).

2. [Since the question of Levi's brotherhood remains open, it is obvious that none of his other close relationships can be established, else there would be no doubt.]

משניות / בבא בתרא — פרק ח: יש נוחלין   [174]

brothers inherit with him.

[If] one died, and a will was found tied to his thigh, it is void. [If] he granted title to someone else with it, whether from the heirs or not, his words are upheld.

YAD AVRAHAM

(Rav).

הֲרֵי זוֹ אֵינָהּ כְּלוּם. — *it is void.*

Nevertheless, this will is of no legal consequence, since the fact that the deceased had the document written indicates that he intended the transfer of ownership to take effect only with the handing over of the document. This, however, can no longer be done since transfer of a document is not valid after the death of the owner *(Rav).*

According to the alternate view that the mishnah is discussing a document written merely as a reminder, the reason it is not valid is because the deceased never issued his instructions verbally. Therefore, it is possible that he wrote the document for the sake of recording his intended instructions which he subsequently reconsidered and never issued. Alternatively, he might have wanted these instructions to become effective only upon the receipt of this document, which now has no legal validity, since it is received after the donor's death *(Meiri).*

Rambam (Hil. Zechiyah 9:24) states that even if there were witnesses signed on the document, and they had performed an act of acquisition on behalf of the recipient, the gift is not valid, since the gift is not designed to take effect until after the donor's demise, and he might have changed his mind *(Maggid Mishnah*, ad loc.).

זָכָה בָהּ לְאַחֵר, בֵּין מִן הַיּוֹרְשִׁין בֵּין שֶׁאֵינוֹ מִן הַיּוֹרְשִׁין, דְּבָרָיו קַיָּמִין. — *[If] he granted title to someone else with it, whether from the heirs or not, his words are upheld.*

The ailing donor had previously written a document giving all his property to one person. He then changed his mind and decided to give those possessions to someone else. He did so by giving the document to this second person and saying to him, 'Acquire what is written in this [document].' Although the document is made out to someone else, the gift to the second person is valid, even if the new recipient is not eligible to inherit the deceased. His oral gift of the property to the new recipient is no different from any other oral instructions issued by an ailing person and its effect is not diminished by the document [whose presence is not required for a sickbed gift] *(Rashbam;* see *Tur Choshen Mishpat* 250; *Tos. Yom Tov).*

An alternate interpretation of this phrase is that the ailing donor handed the document to a third party in order that the latter acquire it on behalf of the recipient mentioned in the document. Ordinarily, a document can be acquired on behalf of someone else only by a person who is not considered an extension of the donor. In this case, however, even if that third party is the donor's heir and we were to consider him an extension of the donor, the transfer is valid *(Ravad,* cited by *Tur, Choshen Mishpat* 250; see *Aruch HaShulchan* 250:40), because it is actually the words of the deceased which effect the transfer and not the document *(Ritva).*

7.

As explained in the commentary to mishnah 5 (s.v. הכותב נכסיו), one who is in his sickbed was granted the authority to give away his possessions orally without any formal act of transfer, and the gift takes effect after death *(Gem.* 147a). However, the gift of a healthy man cannot take effect in this manner, even with a formal act of

[ז] **הַכּוֹתֵב** נְכָסָיו לְבָנָיו צָרִיךְ שֶׁיִּכְתֹּב: מֵהַיּוֹם
וּלְאַחַר מִיתָה; דִּבְרֵי רַבִּי יְהוּדָה.
רַבִּי יוֹסֵי אוֹמֵר: אֵינוֹ צָרִיךְ.

הַכּוֹתֵב נְכָסָיו לִבְנוֹ לְאַחַר מוֹתוֹ, הָאָב אֵינוֹ יָכוֹל
לִמְכֹּר, מִפְּנֵי שֶׁהֵן כְּתוּבִין לַבֵּן; וְהַבֵּן אֵינוֹ יָכוֹל
לִמְכֹּר, מִפְּנֵי שֶׁהֵן בִּרְשׁוּת הָאָב. מָכַר הָאָב,
מְכוּרִין עַד שֶׁיָּמוּת. מָכַר הַבֵּן, אֵין לַלּוֹקֵחַ בָּהֶן
כְּלוּם עַד שֶׁיָּמוּת הָאָב. הָאָב תּוֹלֵשׁ וּמַאֲכִיל לְכָל

יד אברהם

transfer; if he directs that the transfer take place after his death the entire transaction is void, since at the designated time of acquisition the belongings are no longer his but his heirs. This mishnah discusses the manner in which a healthy person can give over his possessions so that the transfer is binding from now but does not fully take effect until after his death (Meiri).

הַכּוֹתֵב נְכָסָיו לְבָנָיו — *One who signs over his property to his sons*

A healthy man [who had been previously married] desired to remarry, but he wanted to ensure that, upon his death, his sons from his previous marriage would not lose their rights to his possessions because of the *kesubah* of his new wife. However, he did not want to give them his properties outright, because he would thereby lose the rights to them while he was still alive. He therefore drew up a document dictating the transfer of his properties to them after his death (Rashbam).

צָרִיךְ שֶׁיִּכְתֹּב: מֵהַיּוֹם וּלְאַחַר מִיתָה; דִּבְרֵי רַבִּי יְהוּדָה. — *must write: from today and after death; [these are] the words of R' Yehudah.*

[In order to prevent the document from being invalid by virtue of the transfer taking effect only after his death, he must specify that it is to take effect *from today and after death* — i.e., the transfer begins today but does not culminate until after his death.] This is understood to mean that ownership of the actual land itself is transferred immediately, but the donor retains the rights to its produce until his death (Rav from Gem. 136a).

This ruling applies only if the recipient was given the document before the demise of the donor. Otherwise, it is void, because the document does not take effect until after it is handed over, and it has no legal force after the donor's death (Yad Ramah).

רַבִּי יוֹסֵי אוֹמֵר: אֵינוֹ צָרִיךְ. — *R' Yose says: He need not.*

R' Yose maintains that the donor need not specify that the transfer begin immediately, since the date written on the document is sufficient evidence of his intent to that effect; otherwise, since it is not to take effect until after his death, there is no reason for him to date the document at all (Rav from Gem. 136a).

The halachah follows the opinion of R' Yose (Rav; Rambam, Zechiyah 12:15; Choshen Mishpat 258:1).

הַכּוֹתֵב נְכָסָיו לִבְנוֹ לְאַחַר מוֹתוֹ, — *[If] one signs over his possessions to his son to [take effect] after his death,*

A father wrote a document which awarded his son the land itself immediately and the produce after the father's death, as explained above (Rav).

הָאָב אֵינוֹ יָכוֹל לִמְכֹּר, מִפְּנֵי שֶׁהֵן כְּתוּבִין לַבֵּן; — *the father cannot sell [them], because they are signed over to the son;*

The father cannot sell both the field

7. One who signs over his property to his sons must write: from today and after death; [these are] the words of R' Yehudah. R' Yose says: He need not.

[If] one signs over his possessions to his son to [take effect] after his death, the father cannot sell [them], because they are signed over to the son; and the son cannot sell [them], because they are in the possession of the father. [If] the father [went and] sold [them], they are sold until his death. [If] the son [went and] sold [them], the buyer has no share in them until the father dies. The father may detach

YAD AVRAHAM

[and its produce] without the participation of the son, since the land itself belongs to the latter (Rav).

וְהַבֵּן אֵינוֹ יָכוֹל לִמְכּוֹר, מִפְּנֵי שֶׁהֵן בִּרְשׁוּת הָאָב. — and the son cannot sell [them], because they are in the possession of the father.

The son cannot sell without the father's participation, since the latter still has the rights to the produce (Rav).

מָכַר הָאָב, מְכוּרִין עַד שֶׁיָּמוּת. — [If] the father [went and] sold [them], they are sold until his death.

If the father sold the field, the produce which the field bears until the father's death belongs to the buyer, since the father owns the rights to the produce (Rav).

Some commentators explain that this holds true only if the buyer, upon discovering that the seller was not the absolute owner of the field, wishes to uphold the purchase. However, if he wishes to nullify the sale, he may do so on the grounds that he thought that he was acquiring the field entirely when in reality he was receiving only its produce for the duration of the seller's lifetime. Obviously, if the buyer knew the true condition of the sale, he cannot back out (Nimmukei Yosef).

Others contend that since the buyer received the object he wanted but was mistaken only regarding the degree of ownership he was receiving, the sale is valid.

The fact that he did not receive his entire purchase entitles him to receive reimbursement of his extra payment, but not to nullify the sale entirely (Meiri).

מָכַר הַבֵּן, אֵין לַלּוֹקֵחַ בָּהֶן כְּלוּם עַד שֶׁיָּמוּת הָאָב. — [If] the son [went and] sold [them], the buyer has no share in them until the father dies.

If the son sold the field while the father was still living, the buyer does not acquire the rights to the produce until the father's death (Rav). Once the father dies, however, the buyer acquires the produce, since the father's rights terminated with his death.

This is true even if the son predeceased his father and thus never actually took over the land. Since the land itself belonged to the son his sale of it was valid (Gem. 136b), and the father's right of use terminates with his death.

This is actually the subject of an important dispute. R' Yochanan maintains that if someone has the rights to all of the produce of a field it is considered that the field itself is in his possession (קִנְיַן פֵּרוֹת כְּקִנְיַן הַגּוּף). Thus, in our case, the son's sale of the field while the father is alive has no validity at all since it is still in the father's possession and the buyer, therefore, has no right to it later. Resh Lakish, however, contends that the rights to the produce are not

מִי שֶׁיִּרְצֶה, וּמַה שֶׁהִנִּיחַ תָּלוּשׁ הֲרֵי הוּא שֶׁל
יוֹרְשִׁין.

הִנִּיחַ בָּנִים גְּדוֹלִים וּקְטַנִּים, אֵין הַגְּדוֹלִים
מִתְפַּרְנְסִים עַל הַקְּטַנִּים, וְלֹא הַקְּטַנִּים נִזּוֹנִין עַל
הַגְּדוֹלִים; אֶלָּא חוֹלְקִין בְּשָׁוֶה.

נָשְׂאוּ הַגְּדוֹלִים, יִשְׂאוּ הַקְּטַנִּים. וְאִם אָמְרוּ
קְטַנִּים ,,הֲרֵי אָנוּ נוֹשְׂאִים כְּדֶרֶךְ שֶׁנְּשָׂאתֶם אַתֶּם,"

יד אברהם

considered tantamount to ownership of the field (קִנְיַן פֵּרוֹת לָאו כְּקִנְיַן הַגּוּף). Thus, the son's ownership of it was in effect even when the father was alive and his sale of it was consequently valid (Gem. 136b). The halachah follows the view of Resh Lakish (Choshen Mishpat 157:5).

הָאָב תּוֹלֵשׁ וּמַאֲכִיל לְכָל מִי שֶׁיִּרְצֶה, — The father may detach [produce] and give to eat to whomever he wishes,

The father may detach produce from the field which he signed over to his son and give it to whomever he wishes (Rav), since he retains a life interest in the property.

וּמַה שֶׁהִנִּיחַ תָּלוּשׁ הֲרֵי הוּא שֶׁל יוֹרְשִׁין. — and what [produce] he leaves over detached [from the field] belongs to the heirs.

When the father dies, any produce already detached from the field belongs to all his heirs, and not exclusively to the son to whom he gave the field. Since it was detached during the father's lifetime, it already became his property and thus part of his estate. However, the produce which is still attached to the ground, even that which is ready to be harvested, belongs entirely to the son who owns the field itself (Rav; Rashbam).[1]

This ruling that the attached produce belongs entirely to the owner of the field

itself applies only to a field which one gave to his son, because a person seeks his son's benefit and it may therefore be assumed that his intention was to include in the gift whatever was still attached to it at the time of his death. However, if a man gives a field to someone other than his son, even that produce which is still attached to the ground at the time of the father's death belongs to the heirs (Rav from Gem. 137a), because attached produce ordinarily belongs to the one under whose ownership it grew, and not to the one who acquired the rights to the land after the produce was already grown (Tos. Yom Tov).

הִנִּיחַ בָּנִים גְּדוֹלִים וּקְטַנִּים, — [If] he leaves older and younger sons,

[The mishnah now returns to the topic of ordinary inheritance. A man died without leaving a will and was survived by older and younger sons. Pending the division of the estate, the children are supported from the common estate. Older children have different needs than younger ones. The mishnah will define how much each may take to meet his special needs.]

אֵין הַגְּדוֹלִים מִתְפַּרְנְסִים עַל הַקְּטַנִּים, — the older ones are not supported at the expense of the younger ones,

1. Others, however, contend that any produce which is ready to be harvested is considered as if already detached and belongs to all the heirs (Rosh; see Tos. Yom Tov). Although Rav follows the view of Rashbam here that produce ready to be harvested is not considered as if it were already detached, in mishnah 5:7 he seems to have followed the opposite view; see comm. there, s.v. ותלש כל שהוא.

8
7
[produce] and give to eat to whomever he wishes, and what [produce] he leaves over detached [from the field] belongs to the heirs.

[If] he leaves older and younger sons, the older ones are not supported at the expense of the younger ones, nor are the younger ones fed at the expense of the older ones; rather they divide equally.

[If] the older ones married, the younger ones may marry. If the younger ones said, 'We will marry just as you married,' we do not listen to them. Rather,

YAD AVRAHAM

There is a tendency for the older sons to spend more on clothing than the younger children. Nevertheless, they may not take extra money from the estate to cover their greater expenses (Rav).

If the eldest son requires more expensive clothing in order to engage in business to support the family, he is permitted to draw from the estate for it (Gem.; Rosh), unless the other brothers explicitly deny him this right (Tos., Bava Kama 11b, s.v. בגדול; Choshen Mishpat 286:2).[1]

וְלֹא הַקְטַנִּים נְזוֹנִין עַל הַגְּדוֹלִים; — nor are the younger ones fed at the expense of the older ones;

Although the younger children tend to incur greater expenses for food since they are less organized in their eating habits, they may not cover this extra expense from the common estate (Rav).

אֶלָא חוֹלְקִין בְּשָׁוֶה. — rather they divide equally.

Each draws an equal amount of support money, and each must pay for his needs out of his allowance (Rav).

According to some authorities, this applies only if the younger sons refused the older ones the right to pay for their extra expenses from the estate. Otherwise, as long as the

inheritance has not been divided, all of the heirs may take from it in accordance with their needs, for they are considered like partners, who generally do not demand a strict accounting of their respective expenditures (Rashba; Choshen Mishpat 286:1). Others contend that they are never allowed to take more than their share, and if they did, they must recompense the other brothers (Meiri; R' Yeshaya, cited by Tur 286).

נָשְׂאוּ הַגְּדוֹלִים, יִשְׂאוּ הַקְּטַנִּים. — [If] the older ones married, the younger ones may marry.

If the older sons covered their wedding expenses with money from the undivided estate, the younger ones may do the same (Rav from Gem. 139a). If they are not yet ready to marry, they may subtract from the estate prior to its division the money that they will eventually need for their wedding expenses (Meiri).

וְאִם אָמְרוּ קְטַנִּים ,,הֲרֵי אָנוּ נוֹשְׂאִים כְּדֶרֶךְ שֶׁנְּשָׂאתֶם אַתֶּם,'' אֵין שׁוֹמְעִין לָהֶם. — If the younger ones said, 'We will marry just as you married,' we do not listen to them.

If the older sons married in the lifetime of their father, the younger sons do not have the right to cover their wedding expenses from the common estate (Rav from Gem. 139a).

1. Rashbam contends that he does not have a permit to spend the money of the inheritance on such clothing. The Gemara means only that if he did so, the others cannot demand reimbursement. Rashba's view (as cited by Ritva; cf. Pischei Teshuvah to Choshen Mishpat ad loc.), on the other hand, is that even if the brothers protested, the eldest is still permitted to pay for these clothes from the inheritance.

אֵין שׁוֹמְעִין לָהֶם. אֶלָּא, מַה שֶּׁנָּתַן לָהֶם אֲבִיהֶם, נָתַן.

[ח] **הִנִּיחַ** בָּנוֹת גְּדוֹלוֹת וּקְטַנּוֹת, אֵין הַגְּדוֹלוֹת מִתְפַּרְנְסוֹת עַל הַקְּטַנּוֹת, וְלֹא הַקְּטַנּוֹת נִזּוֹנוֹת עַל הַגְּדוֹלוֹת; אֶלָּא חוֹלְקוֹת בְּשָׁוֶה.

נָשְׂאוּ גְדוֹלוֹת, יִשְׂאוּ קְטַנּוֹת. וְאִם אָמְרוּ קְטַנּוֹת "הֲרֵי אָנוּ נוֹשְׂאוֹת כְּדֶרֶךְ שֶׁנְּשָׂאתֶם אַתֶּם," אֵין שׁוֹמְעִין לָהֶן.

זֶה חֹמֶר בַּבָּנוֹת מִבַּבָּנִים: שֶׁהַבָּנוֹת נִזּוֹנוֹת עַל הַבָּנִים וְאֵין נִזּוֹנוֹת עַל הַבָּנוֹת.

יד אברהם

אֶלָּא, מַה שֶּׁנָּתַן לָהֶם אֲבִיהֶם, נָתַן. — *Rather, whatever their father gave them, he gave.*

Whatever their father gave them while he was still alive is theirs [but no more] (Rav). Even if the father had promised to pay for their marriages, they cannot take that amount from the inheritance (Ritva).

8.

הִנִּיחַ בָּנוֹת גְּדוֹלוֹת וּקְטַנּוֹת, — *[If] he leaves older and younger daughters,*

A man died and left no sons, and his daughters are thus his heirs (Rav).

אֵין הַגְּדוֹלוֹת מִתְפַּרְנְסוֹת עַל הַקְּטַנּוֹת, וְלֹא הַקְּטַנּוֹת נִזּוֹנוֹת עַל הַגְּדוֹלוֹת; אֶלָּא חוֹלְקוֹת בְּשָׁוֶה. — *the older ones are not supported at the expense of the younger ones, nor are the younger ones fed at the expense of the older ones; rather they divide equally.*

As explained in the previous mishnah concerning sons, their unequal respective expenses are not subtracted from the common estate but rather from their individual portions (Rashbam).

נָשְׂאוּ גְדוֹלוֹת, יִשְׂאוּ קְטַנּוֹת. — *[If] the older ones married, the younger ones may marry.*

If the older ones covered their wedding expenses from the common inheritance, the younger daughters may do likewise (Gem. 139a).

Others explain that this mishnah teaches us that even if the elder daughter brought the entire legacy into her marriage, the younger one can collect her share from the husband of the elder (Gem. 139a), even if nothing of the original inheritance is still extant, and her claim is for reimbursement rather than the return of the actual articles of inheritance (Ritva).

וְאִם אָמְרוּ קְטַנּוֹת "הֲרֵי אָנוּ נוֹשְׂאוֹת כְּדֶרֶךְ שֶׁנְּשָׂאתֶם אַתֶּם," אֵין שׁוֹמְעִין לָהֶן. — *If the younger ones said, 'We will marry just as you married,' we do not listen to them.*

[As explained in the previous mishnah regarding sons, if the older daughters married in their father's lifetime at his expense, the younger daughters cannot claim this amount from the common estate even if the

whatever their father gave them, he gave.

8. [If] he leaves older and younger daughters, the older ones are not supported at the expense of the younger ones, nor are the younger ones fed at the expense of the older ones; rather they divide equally.

[If] the older ones married, the younger ones may marry. If the younger ones said, 'We will marry just as you married,' we do not listen to them.

This is the stringency of daughters over sons: That the daughters are fed at the expense of the sons but they are not fed at the expense of the daughters.

YAD AVRAHAM

father had promised the same to his younger daughters.]

זֶה חֹמֶר בְּבָנוֹת מִבְּבָנִים: שֶׁהַבָּנוֹת נִזוֹנוֹת עַל הַבָּנִים וְאֵין נִזוֹנוֹת עַל הַבָּנוֹת. — *This is the stringency of daughters over sons: That the daughters are fed at the expense of the sons but they are not fed at the expense of the daughters.*

When a man dies and leaves both sons and daughters, the daughters who are still minors are fed from the father's estate (see 9:1) even if they require greater expenditures than the sons *(Rif)*. This is by virtue of their mother's *kesubah*, one of whose conditions was that any daughters born of the marriage are to be supported until they marry (see *Kesubos* 4:11). However, if he left only daughters, they inherit equally, and

those who are minors are not entitled to spend more than their share of the legacy on their food. The special *kesubah* provision for the support of the daughters applies only when there are sons, because the daughters do not inherit anything. When there are no sons the daughters are the heirs of the estate and they are therefore not covered by this special provision *(Rav; Rashbam* 139a). [Similarly, sons who are minors do not share this privilege, and they may not cover their expenses from the inheritance beyond their fair share.]

Alternatively, if the estate is insufficient to cover the needs of the daughters and leave over inheritance for the sons to divide, the daughters must nevertheless be fed (see 9:1). However, if there are only daughters, they all inherit equally *(Nimmukei Yosef)*.

Chapter 9

1.

The ninth chapter continues the discussion concerning the laws of inheritance. This mishnah deals with the allocation of the deceased's properties between his sons and daughters. Although, by Torah law, a daughter does not inherit anything whatsoever when there are sons (8:2), the Rabbis ordained that a man must stipulate a provision in his *kesubah* (marriage contract) that his daughters receive support from his estate until they marry or attain twelve and a half years of age *(Kesubos* 4:11). This mishnah is also found in *Kesubos* 13:3.

[א] **מִי** שֵׁמֵת וְהִנִּיחַ בָּנִים וּבָנוֹת — בִּזְמַן
שֶׁהַנְּכָסִים מְרֻבִּים, הַבָּנִים יִירְשׁוּ וְהַבָּנוֹת
יִזּוֹנוּ; נְכָסִין מֻעָטִין, הַבָּנוֹת יִזּוֹנוּ וְהַבָּנִים יִשְׁאֲלוּ עַל
הַפְּתָחִים. אַדְמוֹן אוֹמֵר: בִּשְׁבִיל שֶׁאֲנִי זָכָר
הִפְסַדְתִּי? אָמַר רַבָּן גַּמְלִיאֵל: רוֹאֶה אֲנִי אֶת דִּבְרֵי
אַדְמוֹן.

[ב] **הִנִּיחַ** בָּנִים, וּבָנוֹת, וְטֻמְטוּם — בִּזְמַן
שֶׁהַנְּכָסִים מְרֻבִּים, הַזְּכָרִים דּוֹחִין
אוֹתוֹ אֵצֶל נְקֵבוֹת. נְכָסִין מֻעָטִין, הַנְּקֵבוֹת דּוֹחוֹת

יד אברהם

מִי שֵׁמֵת וְהִנִּיחַ בָּנִים וּבָנוֹת — **One who
died and left sons and daughters —**

A man died without leaving instructions as to how to distribute his possessions among his children (Nimmukei Yosef).

בִּזְמַן שֶׁהַנְּכָסִים מְרֻבִּים, — **when there is
much property,**

I.e., there is sufficient property to allow both for the sons and the daughters to be supported until the daughters become twelve and a half years old (Rav from Gem. 139b).

הַבָּנִים יִירְשׁוּ וְהַבָּנוֹת יִזּוֹנוּ; — **the sons inherit
it and the daughters are supported;**

The estate becomes the property of the sons (Rosh), and they must provide the daughters with food and clothing (Ritva) until the daughters marry or come of age (Rashbam). However, if the courts see that the sons are careless with their finances, the courts may take from them sufficient property to support the daughters (Rosh).

נְכָסִין מֻעָטִין, — **[when] there is little
property,**

I.e., less than the amount described above (Rav).

הַבָּנוֹת יִזּוֹנוּ — **the daughters are supported**

The possessions are placed in the hands of the courts or a trustee appointed by them, and the daughters receive their support from those possessions (Yad Ramah; Nimmukei Yosef).

וְהַבָּנִים יִשְׁאֲלוּ עַל הַפְּתָחִים. — **and the sons
must go begging** [lit. ask at the doors].

The sons receive only whatever properties remain after the daughters' support has been secured. If it is not sufficient for their needs, they must go begging (Tif. Yis.).

This applies only to real property. However, if the father left over movable property, although the Rabbis ordained that the daughters must receive support from these as well, they did not grant them precedence over the sons in such properties. Therefore, if there is insufficient property to provide for both the sons and the daughters, they both receive support equally (Rif; Rosh; Even Haezer 112:12).

אַדְמוֹן אוֹמֵר: בִּשְׁבִיל שֶׁאֲנִי זָכָר הִפְסַדְתִּי? — **Admon says: Because I am a male, I
lose?**

Why should the son, who is the true heir (as evidenced by the distribution of properties when they are sufficiently large), be superseded in a small estate by the daughter, who receives support from the estate only by Rabbinic enactment? Is it not enough if the Rabbinic enactment is construed to equate the daughter to the sons, without

9
1-2

1. One who died and left sons and daughters — when there is much property, the sons inherit it and the daughters are supported; [when] there is little property, the daughters are supported and the sons must go begging. Admon says: Because I am a male, I lose? Said Rabban Gamliel: I approve of Admon's view.

2. [If] he left sons, daughters, and a *tumtum* — when there is much property, the males can relegate him to the females. [If there is] little

YAD AVRAHAM

granting the daughters greater rights *(Gem. 141b; Ritva)?* Therefore, in Admon's view when there is little property the sons and daughters are supported equally *(Rashbam).*

אָמַר רַבָּן גַּמְלִיאֵל: רוֹאֶה אֲנִי אֶת דִּבְרֵי אַדְמוֹן. — *Said Rabban Gamliel: I approve of Admon's view* [lit. *see the words of Admon*].

Although Admon's position is supported by Rabban Gamliel, the halachah, nevertheless, does not follow Admon's opinion *(Rav; Rif; Rambam, Ishus 19:17; Even Haezer 112:11).*

The reason that the daughters take precedence is that their father obligated himself to this support in the *kesubah,* when he married their mother, long

before his death and the inheritance of the sons. Thus, the portion of the estate necessary to provide this support is, in this case, not subject to the sons' right to inherit *(Tif. Yis.).*

Others, however, contend that due to Rabban Gamliel's support of his position, the view of Admon is the accepted one *(Rashbam).* An alternate approach to this entire mishnah is that Admon himself is not disputing the ruling of the first *Tanna,* but only expressing his amazement at the fact that the enactment was ordained in such a manner *(Rabbeinu Tam, cited by Rosh).*

If the deceased left a wife, her support takes precedence over that of even the daughters. Therefore, if there are insufficient funds to support them both, the widow is supported and the daughters must go begging *(Rav from Gem. 141a).*

2.

This mishnah discusses the status of a *tumtum* — one whose genitals are not visible. The Sages maintain that though such a person's gender cannot be determined, he is, in fact, either male or female. Rabban Shimon ben Gamliel contends that such a person is not included in either classification, but rather constitutes a separate category *(Rashbam;* see *Temurah* 5:2; *Bechoros* 41b; see below, s.v. ילדה טמטום).

הִנִּיחַ בָּנִים, וּבָנוֹת, וְטֻמְטוּם — בִּזְמַן שֶׁהַנְּכָסִים מְרֻבִּים, הַזְּכָרִים דּוֹחִין אוֹתוֹ אֵצֶל נְקֵבוֹת. — [*If*] *he left sons, daughters, and a tumtum — when there is much property, the males can relegate him to the females.*

I.e., the *tumtum* does not inherit together with the sons because he cannot prove that he is indeed a male

and thus entitled to share in the apportionment. Therefore, the brothers have the right to treat him as a female; see below *(Rav).*

נְכָסִים מְעַטִּין, הַנְּקֵבוֹת דּוֹחוֹת אוֹתוֹ אֵצֶל זְכָרִים. — [*If there is*] *little property, the females can relegate him to the males.*

אוֹתוֹ אֵצֶל זְכָרִים.

הָאוֹמֵר ,,אִם תֵּלֵד אִשְׁתִּי זָכָר, יִטֹּל מָנֶה" —
יָלְדָה זָכָר, נוֹטֵל מָנֶה. ,,נְקֵבָה מָאתַיִם" — יָלְדָה
נְקֵבָה, נוֹטֶלֶת מָאתַיִם. ,,אִם זָכָר מָנֶה; אִם נְקֵבָה
מָאתַיִם" — וְיָלְדָה זָכָר וּנְקֵבָה, זָכָר נוֹטֵל מָנֶה,
וְהַנְּקֵבָה נוֹטֶלֶת מָאתַיִם. יָלְדָה טֻמְטוּם, אֵינוֹ נוֹטֵל.
אִם אָמַר ,,כָּל מַה שֶּׁתֵּלֵד אִשְׁתִּי, יִטֹּל," הֲרֵי זֶה

יד אברהם

When the estate is small and thus distributed to the daughters rather than to the sons (see preceding mishnah), the *tumtum* does not receive support along with the daughters because he cannot prove that he is indeed female and thus entitled to share with them (*Rav*).

However, since he is necessarily either male or female (according to the Sages — see preface), he shares together with those who receive the lesser amount (*Gem.* 140b). Thus, if there is much property, he must at least receive support like a daughter. If there is little property, he shares in the inheritance which is left after awarding the daughters their support (*Tos. Yom Tov*).

There is another opinion in the *Gemara* (140b), that this portion of the mishnah follows the view that a *tumtum* is a distinct category (see preface). Accordingly, he receives neither the inheritance of a son nor the support of a daughter.

There is a dispute in the *Gemara* (141a) whether the acquisition which one makes on behalf of an unborn fetus has any validity. The *Gemara's* conclusion (142b) is that it is not valid unless the fetus is his own child since 'a person's mind is close to his child' (ibid.; see below).

הָאוֹמֵר ,,אִם תֵּלֵד אִשְׁתִּי זָכָר, יִטֹּל מָנֶה" —
יָלְדָה זָכָר, נוֹטֵל מָנֶה. — *One who says, 'If my wife bears a male [child], let him take one hundred [zuzin]' — if she bore a male, he takes one hundred [zuzin].*

A man declared on his sickbed that should the child whom his wife is carrying be a male, he should receive a gift of one hundred *zuzin* (*Rav*). Although a fetus is not capable of acquiring anything, and thus the bestowal of a gift upon him should have no validity, the Rabbis ordained that a sickbed gift given to him by his father does take effect (see comm. to 8;5, 9:6). Otherwise, the father's inability to have his gift to his unborn child validated might cause his health to deteriorate, given the father's strong feelings for his son (*Nimmukei Yosef* citing *Ritva* to 142b).

Others contend that even if the father is healthy he can bestow a gift upon his fetus son (*Rashbam; Meiri; Rambam, Mechirah* 22:10; see *Maggid Mishneh* ibid.). [They understand the statement of the *Gemara*, that a person's mind is close to his son, to be a reason for the validity of the gift by law. Apparently, they consider the inability of a fetus to acquire anything not to be an inherent legal deficiency but rather due to the donor's inability to relate fully to the fetus' existence. This causes him to lack the level of resolution necessary to effect an acquisition. Accordingly, the special feeling which a father has for his own child is sufficient to compensate for that lack.]

Others offer another reason why the mishnah must be discussing one who makes a sickbed gift: otherwise, the statement of the father would be an אַסְמַכְתָּא, a commitment made on an uncertain assumption [see comm.

property, the females can relegate him to the males.

One who says, 'If my wife bears a male [child], let him take one hundred [*zuzin*]' — if she bore a male, he takes one hundred [*zuzin*]. '[If] a female, [let her take] two hundred [*zuzin*]' — if she bore a female, she takes two hundred [*zuzin*]. [If he said,] 'If a male, one hundred; if a female, two hundred,' and she bore a male and a female, the male takes one hundred and the female takes two hundred. [If] she bore a *tumtum*, he does not take [anything]. If he said, 'Whatever my wife bears, let him take,' he takes. If

YAD AVRAHAM

to 10:5], which is not valid (*Ri Migash; Yad Ramah; Rambam, Zechiyah* 8:5; see *Maggid Mishneh* ibid.). Others disagree, and contend that such commitments are invalid only when made against one's will on the assumption that the necessity for them will not materialize (see 10:5). In this case, however, the father wants to give his son the gift; therefore, it is valid (*Ritva; Nimmukei Yosef;* cf. *Meiri*).

נְקֵבָה מָאתַיִם״ — יָלְדָה נְקֵבָה, נוֹטֶלֶת מָאתַיִם. — '[If] a female, [let her take] two hundred [zuzin],' — if she bore a female, she takes two hundred [zuzin].

[This is in essence a repetition of the previous case, but in regard to a female.] The mishnah cites a larger amount for a daughter than for a son — indicating that it would be expected for the father to grant her more — because a man is likely to be more concerned for the financial future of his daughter whose options are more limited (*Gem.* 141a).

אִם זָכָר מָנֶה; אִם נְקֵבָה מָאתַיִם״ — וְיָלְדָה זָכָר וּנְקֵבָה, זָכָר נוֹטֵל מָנֶה, וְהַנְּקֵבָה נוֹטֶלֶת מָאתַיִם. — [If he said,] 'If a male, one hundred; if a female, two hundred,' — and she bore a male and a female, the male takes one hundred and the female takes two hundred.

If twins were born (*Rav*), he must keep both sides of his pledge, and give the son one hundred zuz and the daughter two hundred. Although he

pledged only to give to one or the other, since his children are dear to him, and it is clear that he desired to give the stated gifts to his son or daughter, it is assumed that such intent is present even in the event of twins (*Teshuvos HaRosh* §81; cited by *Tos. Yom Tov*).

Others contend that since he pledged to give only one child, he would not be obligated to give anything in the event of twins. The mishnah should be understood to mean *if she bore a male or a female,* not both together (*Rashbam* 140b).

יָלְדָה טֻמְטוֹם, אֵינוֹ נוֹטֵל. — [If] she bore a tumtum, he does not take [anything].

This is the opinion of Rabban Shimon ben Gamliel, who maintains that a *tumtum* is neither a son nor daughter (*Gem.* 140b), but forms a separate category (*Rashbam*). [Therefore, he was not included in the pledge.]

There is an opinion in *Bechoros* (41b) that even Rabban Shimon ben Gamliel agrees that a *tumtum* is either a male or a female. However, the mishnah assumes that one who stipulates a male or female refers to a person of definite gender and therefore does not include a *tumtum* in his intention (*Tos.* 141a, s.v. אלא לאביו).

אִם אָמַר ,,כָּל מַה שֶׁתֵּלֵד אִשְׁתִּי, יִטֹּל,״ הֲרֵי זֶה יִטֹּל. — If he said, 'Whatever my wife bears, let him take,' he takes.

Under these circumstances, a *tumtum* also receives the gift, and we cannot

יִטֹּל. וְאִם אֵין שָׁם יוֹרֵשׁ אֶלָּא הוּא, יוֹרֵשׁ אֶת הַכֹּל.

[ג] הִנִּיחַ בָּנִים גְּדוֹלִים וּקְטַנִּים — הִשְׁבִּיחוּ
גְדוֹלִים אֶת הַנְּכָסִים, הִשְׁבִּיחוּ
לָאֶמְצַע. אִם אָמְרוּ ,,רְאוּ מַה שֶּׁהִנִּיחַ לָנוּ אַבָּא;

יד אברהם

assume that he did not include such a
child in his intentions (Tif. Yis.).

— וְאִם אֵין שָׁם יוֹרֵשׁ אֶלָּא הוּא, יוֹרֵשׁ אֶת הַכֹּל.
*If there is no other heir but him, he
inherits everything.*

Although Rabban Shimon ben
Gamliel holds that a *tumtum* is not
included in either the category of son or
daughter, he nevertheless inherits in the
absence of other children. This is
derived from the verse giving the

inheritance to the deceased's brothers if
he leaves no children — וְאִם אֵין לוֹ בַּת,
and if he has no daughter (Num. 27:9),
which implies that he has no offspring
whatsoever. From this we derive that a
child who is neither a son nor a
daughter is also eligible to inherit
(Rashbam; see comm. to 8:2, s.v. אִישׁ כִּי
יָמוּת). Alternatively, the *tumtum* is
included in the general category stated
in the verse (ibid. v. 11), *who is close to
him from his family (Rashbam).*

3.

The mishnah now discusses the case of heirs who make improvements in an estate prior to its division. The question under consideration is how much of that
improvement belongs solely to the brothers who make the improvements and how
much to the general estate.

This issue must be considered in the context of the general rules governing the
distribution of improvements made by one person in the property of another. In
this regard, there is a distinction between one who makes improvements in a
property with the consent of the owner and one who does so unbidden. A person
who enters another person's field and, without the consent of the owner, makes
improvements in it, is not entitled to any part of the profit generated by those
improvements. He is entitled only to reimbursement for his expenses and even this
only to the extent that they are covered by the profits. [I.e., if the expenses exceed
the profits earned, he receives only the value of the profits as reimbursement.]
However, one who makes the improvements *with* the consent of the owner [with no
price being set in advance], or in circumstances in which such consent could be
assumed, receives a share of the profit commensurate with the standard percentages
paid to sharecroppers in that locale. If the profits generated came to less than the
expenses, he must be fully reimbursed for his expenses (and labor) (Bava Metzia
101a; Choshen Mishpat 375).

The law is somewhat different in the case of a partner who improves a jointly
owned property in the absence of the other partners. Since a partner has the right to
act for the benefit of the partnership in the absence of the other partners, he is
considered the equivalent of one who improves a property with the consent of the
owner and (if the profit exceeds the expenses) he is therefore paid for his
improvements like a sharecropper [in addition to receiving his share as a partner]
(Choshen Mishpat 178; see Aruch HaShulchan ibid.).

there is no other heir but him, he inherits everything.

3. **[**If**]** he left sons who were of age as well as minors — [if] those of age improved the properties, they improved [them] for the common estate. If they said, 'See what our father left us; we

YAD AVRAHAM

The mishnah now considers this question in regard to brothers who have inherited their father's estate but have not yet divided it.

הִנִּיחַ בָּנִים גְּדוֹלִים וּקְטַנִּים — — [If] he left sons who were of age as well as minors —

The deceased left some sons who were of age and some who were still minors. Actually, the ruling which follows would apply equally if all the sons were of age but only some of them were involved in making the improvements. The mishnah specifies that some were still minors because in such a case it is common for the older sons to take sole responsibility for the estate (Tos. 143b; cf. Rosh; Nimmukei Yosef).

Others contend that the laws stated in this mishnah apply only to a situation in which some of the sons were minors (Ravad cited by Rashba, Bava Metzia 40a; see below, s.v. השביח לאמצע and fn. there).

הִשְׁבִּיחוּ גְּדוֹלִים אֶת הַנְּכָסִים, — [if] those of age improved the properties,

I.e., they made improvements in the estate before it was divided. These improvements were made by workers hired by the older brothers to work the estate (Rav).

הִשְׁבִּיחוּ לָאֶמְצָע. — they improved [them] for the common estate [lit. for the middle].

If the improvements were financed from the monies of the estate (Rav from Gem. 143b), they belong to the estate, and the son who arranged for them to be done is not recompensed for his administrative efforts (Rosh; see Pilpula Charifta §6). He does not receive any

special consideration for his initiative in hiring the workers because it is assumed that brothers who share an estate willingly and freely contribute this relatively minor effort for the common benefit (Nimmukei Yosef, see Tos. 143b; cf. Maharsha).[1]

However, if the elder brothers paid for the improvements from their own money — or they did the actual labor themselves (Nimmukei Yosef) — the improvements belong solely to them (Rav from Gem. loc. cit.; see below, s.v. אם אמרו). Even so, if the effort involved entailed only that which even a child could do, the benefits belong to the estate as a whole (Gem. 144a).

Some explain that this applies only if there are younger brothers who are old enough to be able to perform the work in question, since the older brothers should have trained them to do it rather than labor themselves or hire others to do the work. If the children are too young to work, the older brothers receive the benefits for themselves (Meiri; Tur and Shulchan Aruch, Choshen Mishpat 287:1).

This is disputed, however, by Ritva and Nimmukei Yosef who contend that regardless of the age of the children, if the work involved was so simple that it could have been done by a child, the profits belong to all the brothers equally. The assumption is that when such trivial work is performed by the older brothers, they do so on behalf of everyone gratis.

אִם אָמְרוּ ,,רְאוּ מַה שֶׁהִנִּיחַ לָנוּ אַבָּא; הֲרֵי אָנוּ עוֹשִׂים וְאוֹכְלִין". — If they said, 'See what our father left us; we shall labor and eat

---

1. Some contend that this assumption is valid only when the brothers who do not contribute to the improvements are minors. Thus, our mishnah is quite specific when it states that he left sons of age and minors (Ravad cited by Rashba, Bava Metzia 40a).

הֲרֵי אָנוּ עוֹשִׂים וְאוֹכְלִין," הִשְׁבִּיחוּ לְעַצְמָן. וְכֵן הָאִשָּׁה שֶׁהִשְׁבִּיחָה אֶת הַנְּכָסִים הִשְׁבִּיחָה לָאֶמְצַע. אִם אָמְרָה ,,רְאוּ מַה שֶׁהִנִּיחַ לִי בַעֲלִי; הֲרֵי אֲנִי עוֹשָׂה וְאוֹכֶלֶת," הִשְׁבִּיחָה לְעַצְמָהּ.

יד אברהם

[for ourselves],'

If the older brothers declared this to the younger ones (Rashbam) before a Jewish court (Yerushalmi, cited by Tos.).

הִשְׁבִּיחוּ לְעַצְמָן — *they have improved [them] for themselves.*

They receive the entire appreciation produced by their improvements. Included in their public notification of their intention to develop the property solely for their personal gain and not for the common good was an offer to divide the estate immediately (Rashbam). Therefore, even though the court (which is charged with safeguarding the interests of underaged orphans) was slow in dividing the estate, the profits earned by the older brothers' improvements belong entirely to them and not to the estate. Accordingly, the mishnah refers only to profits generated and coming out of what would have amounted to their share of the estate [had it been partitioned] (Rashbam as explained by Tos. 143b).

Tos. (ibid.), however, reject this view on various grounds and conclude that even if the whole estate was developed, using all the resources of the estate, the entire profit belongs to the older brothers. [In Tos.' view, no offer of partition accompanied their declaration.] Although the law is that one of several partners who improves the common property receives only a percentage of the profit for his efforts, rather than the entire amount of appreciation (see preface), that is because the other partners could have generated this appreciation as well. In this case, however, since the minors are incapable of improving the estate, they

are willing to allow their older brothers to do so even if they keep the entire profit (Tos.). Indeed, partners enter a joint venture in order to earn a profit and they therefore insist on their rightful share of the appreciation. Brothers who inherit their father's estate, on the other hand, did not embark on a profit-making venture and thus do not feel that they have been deprived of anything if a brother can profit individually by his efforts from the estate (Rosh).

Since this arrangement presumes the consent of the minors, who are incapable of giving legal consent, this declaration can be effective only if it is made before the court. Since it is the responsibility of the courts to protect the interests of orphaned minors, if the older brothers declared before the court their intention to develop the estate for their own profit and the court allowed them to improve the entire estate rather than demand that they first divide the property, it can be assumed that the court considered it to be in the best interests of the minors to do so (Rosh).

Thus, if all of the brothers were of age the declaration of those who wish to improve the property need not be made before the court; it is sufficient if it is made before witnesses. Having done so, the developers receive the benefits themselves because the lack of initiative or protest on the part of the remaining brothers is taken as acquiesence to the plan (Rosh; Rama, Choshen Mishpat 287:1).

Others explain the mishnah's statement that *they have improved for themselves* to mean that they receive the entire appreciation from their eventual share of the estate plus a percentage of the profits from the remainder equivalent to one who makes improvements in someone else's field (Ramban; Ritva; Yad

shall labor and eat [for ourselves],' they have improved [them] for themselves.

Similarly, a wife who improved the properties improved them for the common estate. If she said, 'See what my husband left me; I shall labor and eat [for myself],' she has improved [them] for herself.

YAD AVRAHAM

Ramah; Meiri). According to this interpretation, the mishnah does not mean to say that the improvement is entirely theirs, but only that they effected the improvements for their own benefit alone, and they therefore receive a larger share of the profits than if they had expended their efforts on behalf of the common estate (Yad Ramah). Accordingly, even if the younger brothers are minors, the older brothers need not declare their intentions before a court and it is sufficient for them to do so merely in the presence of wittnesses (Nimmukei Yosef, Rashbam).

Rambam (Hil. Nachalos 9:2) writes that even in this latter part of the mishnah, which deals with improvements made after the developer's declaration of intent, the statement of the mishnah that they receive the entire benefit applies only if they financed the improvements from their own money. However, if it was paid for from the estate, the profits belong to the common estate (see Maggid Mishneh, Kesef Mishnah ad loc.). In the case where they did not make any declaration, Rambam maintains that the profits are divided equally even if it was financed entirely by the older brothers' (Choshen Mishpat 287:12; Sma §1).

וְכֵן הָאִשָּׁה שֶׁהִשְׁבִּיחָה אֶת הַנְּכָסִים — Similarly, a wife who improved the properties

This refers to a wife who is one of several heirs to her husband's estate (Rav from Gem. 144a). For example, a man married his brother's daughter and subsequently died without leaving any children. [His brother had previously died, leaving only daughters.] In such a case, his nieces, including his wife, are all equal heirs to his estate (Rav).

In case the wife of the deceased is not his heir, she may either collect her kesubah or else be supported from the estate (until she remarries). In either case, she would not be in line to profit from improvements she effects in the estate (Rashbam 1441).

הִשְׁבִּיחָה לָאֶמְצַע — improved them for the common estate.

This law is the same as the one stated above in regard to the sons. It is restated in regard to a wife because we might otherwise think that since it is not customary for her to involve herself in improving the estate, the fact that she does so is tantamount to a declaration that she is doing so entirely for the sake of her own profit (Gem. 144a).

אִם אָמְרָה ,,רְאוּ מַה שֶׁהִנִּיחַ לִי בַּעְלִי; הֲרֵי אֲנִי עוֹשָׂה וְאוֹכֶלֶת,'' הִשְׁבִּיחָה לְעַצְמָהּ. — If she said, 'See what my husband left me; I shall labor and eat [for myself],' she has improved [them] for herself.

This, too, must be restated in order to preclude the assumption that the enhancement of her reputation which would result from her efforts on behalf of the orphans is of such value to her that she can be assumed to have retracted her position claiming the profits entirely for herself (Rav from Gem. 144a).

However, if she receives support from the estate, she does not receive the profits, because the earnings of a widow being supported from her husband's estate belong to the heirs [Kesubos 11:1] (Rashbam). Others contend that she would still receive the same compensation received by one who on his own initiative improves the property of another (Rosh; see Tur, Even Haezer 95).

4.

Brothers who have not yet divided their father's estate are considered partners in that estate. Thus, any benefit or liability resulting from the partnership is

[ד] **הָאַחִין** הַשֻּׁתָּפִין, שֶׁנָּפַל אֶחָד מֵהֶן
לְאֻמָּנוּת, נָפַל לָאֶמְצַע. חָלָה
וְנִתְרַפֵּא, נִתְרַפֵּא מִשֶּׁל עַצְמוֹ.
הָאַחִין שֶׁעָשׂוּ מִקְצָתָן שׁוֹשְׁבִינוּת בְּחַיֵּי הָאָב,
חָזְרָה שׁוֹשְׁבִינוּת, חָזְרָה לָאֶמְצַע, שֶׁהַשּׁוֹשְׁבִינוּת

יד אברהם

distributed equally, whereas any benefit or liability produced or incurred by an individual is assumed only by that individual. As partners, the brothers can also support their basic needs from the common estate.

הָאַחִין הַשֻּׁתָּפִין, — [If] brothers were partners,

This refers to brothers who have not yet divided their inheritance and are thus considered partners in the estate (Nimmukei Yosef). Additionally, the brothers are all drawing their basic support from the undivided estate, not from their own resources (Meiri). Brothers who are not partners, or partners who are not brothers, are not included in this law (Ritva; Nimmukei Yosef).

Other versions of the mishnah read brothers or partners, indicating that it applies to other partners as well (Rosh; see Tos. Yom Tov).

שֶׁנָּפַל אֶחָד מֵהֶן לְאֻמָּנוּת, — [and] one of them happened into a profession,

One of them was appointed by the government as a tax collector (Rav from Gem. 144b). It was customary to rotate the position each month or two to a member of a different family (Rav, Rashbam).

נָפַל לָאֶמְצַע. — it belongs to the common estate.

The profits from this position are shared by all the brothers, since the position was granted to him as a representative of the family rather than on the force of his own credentials.

However, if he secured the position by virtue of his merit — i.e., his employer clearly stated that this was the case (Tos. Yom Tov) — the profits belong entirely to him (Rav from Gem. 144b).

This applies only to a government appointment. If he secured a different position, even if his brothers trained him for it, his earnings belong entirely to him (Meiri). However, if each of the brothers has a profession [and they are living together from the estate], they share their combined earnings equally (Ritva, cited by Nimmukei Yosef).

חָלָה וְנִתְרַפֵּא, נִתְרַפֵּא מִשֶּׁל עַצְמוֹ. — [If] he fell ill and was healed, he is healed from his own [money].

If he became ill through his own negligence — e.g., from overexposure to heat or cold — he is responsible for his medical expenses. However, if he was not to blame, his bills are covered by the estate (Rav from Gem. 144b). This applies only to a program of treatment which has a fixed medical fee. However, if the treatment of his illness entails open-ended medical expenses, then these expenses fall under the category of basic support and are paid from the estate even if the illness was the result of his own negligence[1] (Tos. 144b; Choshen Mishpat 177:2, from Tosefta).

Others (based on a variant reading of

---

1. Although the mishnah (8:7) stated previously that the younger brothers cannot pay their extra food expenses from the estate, nor the older brothers their greater expenses for clothing, that is because the imbalance between them in these areas is constant. Medical expenses, however, are occasional (Tos. 144b) and could fall upon anyone [and it is therefore equitable to ordain that if they are incurred by any of the brothers, the estate should cover them] (Meiri).

Nimmukei Yosef explains that the previous mishnah, which disallows the drawing of unequal expenditures from the common estate, applies only to discrepancies between minors

4. [If] brothers were partners, [and] one of them happened into a profession, it belongs to the common estate. [If] he fell ill and was healed, he is healed from his own [money].

Brothers, some of whom gave groomsmen's gifts during their father's lifetime, [when] the groomsmen's gifts are returned, they return to the common estate, for groomsmen's gifts are collectible

Tosefta) take the opposite approach — viz., that illnesses incurred through negligence are never covered by the estate. Even illnesses which strike unavoidably are paid for by the estate only if the medical fees are open ended. If the fee is fixed, even if he contracted the illness through no fault of his own, he must pay these expenses on his own (*Meiri; Rama*, ibid.; see commentators there).

Rambam states that all of this applies only as long as they have not divided the estate. Once they divide, each is completely responsible for his own expenses even though one of them became sick before the division (*Nimmukei Yosef*).

◈§ שׁוּשְׁבִינוּת / Groomsmen's gifts

It was customary in the days of the Talmud for the friends of a groom to bring gifts of food to the wedding and *Sheva Berachos* (the feasts of celebration during the first seven days of marriage) and to celebrate those feasts together with the groom. The groom was expected to reciprocate at the weddings of those who had done this for him. Such gifts are referred to as שׁוּשְׁבִינוּת, and those who present them are called שׁוּשְׁבִינִים, groomsmen (*Rav; Meiri*).

הָאַחִין שֶׁעָשׂוּ מִקְצָתָן שׁוּשְׁבִינוּת בְּחַיֵּי הָאָב —

Brothers, some of whom gave [lit. *made*] *groomsmen's gifts during their father's lifetime,*

If the father sent one of his sons with gifts to a groom, without specifying that he was sending them on behalf of this particular son (*Rav from Gem.* 144b).

חָזְרָה שׁוּשְׁבִינוּת, חָזְרָה לָאֶמְצָע, — [when] *the groomsmen's gifts are returned, they return to the common estate,*

Since the gifts were given on behalf of the entire family, when the groom reciprocates at the wedding of that son, the gifts belong to all of the brothers equally, not only to the one who conveyed him the original gifts. However, if the father had specified that he was sending the gifts on behalf of this specific son, he alone is considered the groomsman [even though the father financed the gifts] and the reciprocal gifts brought to his wedding are his alone (*Rav from Gem.* 144b).

If the groom had specifically requested that the father send that particular son to the wedding, the gifts are automatically assumed to have been made on his behalf (*Ritva*).

There is another opinion in the *Gemara* that when the father sends one of his sons with the groomsmen's gifts it is assumed to be given on that son's behalf. The mishnah is discussing a case in which that son

and adults. However, where all the brothers are of age (as in the case of our mishnah) each draws his family's individual needs from the common estate, even though these needs vary depending on family size and other factors. These disparities are assumed to be acceptable to all the brothers since they are more than compensated by the financial standing accorded them by the collective resources of their partnership.

Rashba (cited by *Maggid Mishneh, Nachalos* 9:12) maintains that unequal income needs are generally drawn from the common estate regardless of the brothers' ages. The mishnah (8:7) which disallows this refers only to instances in which some of the brothers specifically protested such an arrangement.

נִגְבֵּית בְּבֵית דִּין. אֲבָל הַשּׁוֹלֵחַ לַחֲבֵרוֹ כַּדֵּי יַיִן וְכַדֵּי שֶׁמֶן, אֵין נִגְבִּין בְּבֵית דִּין, מִפְּנֵי שֶׁהֵן גְּמִילוּת חֲסָדִים.

[ה] הַשּׁוֹלֵחַ סִבְלוֹנוֹת לְבֵית חָמִיו, שָׁלַח שָׁם מֵאָה מָנֶה, וְאָכַל שָׁם סְעוּדַת חָתָן אֲפִלּוּ בְּדִינָר, אֵינָן נִגְבִּין. לֹא אָכַל שָׁם סְעוּדַת

יד אברהם

subsequently married, and the original groom participated in his celebration. However, before he had the opportunity to repay the gifts, the new groom died. Since he left no children, his possessions are inherited by the *yavam*, the brother who marries the deceased's widow in *yibum* (see preface to 8:6). Nevertheless, the *yavam* does not inherit the groomsmen's gifts given now by the original groom, because they were not yet in the possession of the deceased before he died, and a *yavam* has no greater rights than the other brothers in items which did not come into the deceased's possession until after his death.

שֶׁהַשּׁוֹשְׁבִינוֹת נִגְבֵּית בְּבֵית דִּין. — *for groomsmen's gifts are collectible in court.*

The original giving of these gifts is considered to have been a loan, to be repaid on the event of the marriage of the groomsman (*Rav*). [Therefore, their repayment is not an optional gift which can be designated for the new groom alone, but rather constitutes repayment of a legal debt which must be made to the original lender, in this case the entire family.]

This obligation to repay the gifts and celebrate applied only if the circumstances of the groomsman's subsequent marriage were similar to those of the original groom [for the groomsman can insist that he obligated himself only to that particular degree of celebration (*Rashbam*)]. Thus, if the original groom had married a woman who had never been previously married, he is obligated to reciprocate only if the groomsman does the same. If he marries a widow, he cannot demand a return gift from the previous

groom unless he too had married a widow. If the original marriage was a public celebration, the obligation to reciprocate pertains only to such a celebration. The same holds true if the original celebration was a private one (*Rav* from *Gem.* 145b).

This custom of reciprocal groomsmen's gifts no longer prevails (*Even Haezer* 60).

אֲבָל הַשּׁוֹלֵחַ לַחֲבֵרוֹ כַּדֵּי יַיִן וְכַדֵּי שֶׁמֶן, אֵין נִגְבִּין בְּבֵית דִּין, מִפְּנֵי שֶׁהֵן גְּמִילוּת חֲסָדִים. — *However, if one sent to another jars of wine or oil, they are not collectible in court, because they [were given] as an act of kindness.*

If the gifts were not sent at the time of the wedding, or if they were sent at that time but the sender did not participate in the celebration, they are not included in the category of groomsmen's gifts and do not obligate reciprocation (*Rav; Rashbam*).

Others interpret this statement of the mishnah in an entirely different manner. Only gifts of money are included in the category of groomsmen's gifts, but not those of other items, such as wine or oil (*Rambam, Zechiyah* 7:9). Others include articles of clothing in the same category as money (*Yad Ramah*).

A third interpretation is as follows: Only those things which are ordinarily sent as gifts to the wealthy — e.g., fancy meats, delicacies, or other types of expensive gifts — obligate reciprocation. Articles which are usually sent to the poor — e.g., such staples as wine or oil — are given as charitable gifts, and do not require repayment (*Meiri*).

in court. However, if one sent to another jars of wine or oil, they are not collectible in court, because they [were given] as an act of kindness.

5. **[I**f] one sent wedding gifts to the house of his father-in-law, [even if] he sent a hundred *maneh* there, and he ate there a groom's meal worth [as little] as a *dinar*, they cannot be reclaimed. [If] he

YAD AVRAHAM

5.

In Mishnaic times, *erusin*, the first (betrothal) stage of marriage (performed today by the giving of the marriage ring at the *chupah*), was customarily performed up to a year prior to *nisuin*, the final stage after which the couple lives together (see General Introduction to ArtScroll *Kiddushin*). It was customary for the groom to send gifts of jewelry and food to his bride the day following the *erusin*, when she was still living in her father's house. At times, the groom would go to his father-in-law's house and join them in celebrating the marriage. If the marriage was subsequently dissolved prior to *nisuin*, the groom has a claim that he be repaid for the gifts he sent. The mishnah discusses when such a claim is valid and when it is not.

הַשּׁוֹלֵחַ סְבְלוֹנוֹת לְבֵית חָמָיו, — [If] one sent wedding gifts to the house of his father-in-law,

This refers only to one who sent these gifts after *erusin*, because only then is there a possibility that he waives his right to be recompensed if the marriage is not consummated (*Ritva*).

שָׁלַח שָׁם מֵאָה מָנֶה, — [even if] he sent a hundred maneh there,

Even if he sent the large sum of one hundred *maneh* (a *maneh* is one hundred *zuzin*), and he did not specify his intention in sending this gift (*Rashbam*).

וְאָבַל שָׁם סְעוּדַת חָתָן אֲפִלּוּ בְּדִינָר, — and he ate there a groom's meal worth [as little] as a dinar,

The groom ate a celebration feast with a minimum value of a *dinar* at his father-in-law's house. However, if he ate less than a *dinar's* worth, it is negligible, and the law is the same as if he did not eat at all — i.e., he can reclaim his gifts [if the marriage is dissolved before *nisuin*] (*Rav* from *Gem.* 146a).

אֵינָן נִגְבִּין. — they cannot be reclaimed.

If the groom or bride died, or he divorced her on his initiative, he cannot reclaim the gifts that he sent her, because he is assumed to have waived his right to do so in the affectionate spirit of the celebration feast (*Rav*). However, if she refused to complete the marriage [and he was therefore forced to divorce her], she must repay him for his gifts. Nevertheless, the gifts of food which were already eaten are repaid at only two-thirds of their regular value (*Gem.* 146b), since the bride ate them under the assumption that they were hers and she would not have eaten them so freely if she would have had to purchase them at full value (*Rashbam*).

This ruling applies only to those gifts which are given on the assumption that they will be used up while she is still in her father's house. However, those gifts which are by their nature expected to last into the completed marriage must be returned even if the husband initiated the divorce or one of them died, and even if he had joined them in the festivities (*Rashbam* from *Gem.* 146a).

Money is included in the category of items

חָתָן, הֲרֵי אֵלּוּ נִגְבִּין. שָׁלַח סִבְלוֹנוֹת מְרֻבִּין שֶׁיַּחְזְרוּ עִמָּהּ לְבֵית בַּעֲלָהּ, הֲרֵי אֵלּוּ נִגְבִּין. סִבְלוֹנוֹת מְעַטִּין שֶׁתִּשְׁתַּמֵּשׁ בָּהֶן בְּבֵית אָבִיהָ, אֵינָן נִגְבִּין.

[ו] **שכיב** מְרַע שֶׁכָּתַב כָּל נְכָסָיו לַאֲחֵרִים, וְשִׁיֵּר קַרְקַע כָּל שֶׁהוּא, מַתְּנָתוֹ

יד אברהם

which are meant to be used up in her father's house, since it is spent to buy other things. Clothing, too, is included in this category, unless he gave her several changes of clothing, which she would be unlikely to wear out while still in her father's house (Nimmukei Yosef).

לֹא אָכַל שָׁם סְעוּדַת חָתָן, הֲרֵי אֵלּוּ נִגְבִּין. — [If] he did not eat a groom's meal there, they can be reclaimed.

[If the husband never ate the groom's meal at his father-in-law's house, there is lacking the affectionate spirit of the meal which causes the husband to waive his rights to reclaim the gifts should the marriage be dissolved.]

If he drank a dinar's worth, it is the same as if he ate (Gem. 146a).

שָׁלַח סִבְלוֹנוֹת מְרֻבִּין, שֶׁיַּחְזְרוּ עִמָּהּ לְבֵית בַּעֲלָהּ, הֲרֵי אֵלּוּ נִגְבִּין. — [If] he sent many wedding gifts, [on the understanding] that they return with her to her husband's house, they can be reclaimed.

If the groom sent gifts and specified that he was sending them to her on the understanding that they will be brought into their home after nisuin, these gifts can be reclaimed if the marriage is dissolved [regardless of the cause] (Rav), even if he ate a dinar's worth at the celebration (Rashbam).

This applies even if he sent her only a few gifts. The mishnah states that he sent her many because customarily when he sends her an abundance of gifts he intends for her to retain them until after the nisuin and he so specifies; whereas those gifts which are designed to be used up before the marriage is

completed are generally fewer in number (Rav; Rashbam).

סִבְלוֹנוֹת מְעַטִּין, שֶׁתִּשְׁתַּמֵּשׁ בָּהֶן בְּבֵית אָבִיהָ, אֵינָן נִגְבִּין. — [If he sent] few wedding gifts, [on the understanding] that she use them in her father's house, they cannot be reclaimed.

If he specified that the gifts were meant for her use in her father's house, which ordinarily occurs only if he sends a few gifts, he cannot demand their return if the marriage is dissolved (Rav) even if he did not eat at the feast (Rashbam).

Thus, the first part of the mishnah, which makes return of the bridal gifts dependent upon whether or not the husband celebrated the groom's feast, applies when the husband did not specify anything when he sent the gifts. This latter part of the mishnah applies when the husband did specify his intent. We then follow his specifications regardless of whether or not he celebrated the groom's feast (Rashbam 146a). However, others contend that this latter portion of the mishnah comes to explain the first half [and thus also deals with a case in which he did not specify his intent]. If he sent her an abundance of gifts — i.e., gifts which may be expected to last beyond the time of nisuin — the gifts can be reclaimed even if he did partake of the celebration feast. The initial statement of the mishnah that he cannot demand compensation if he participated in the meal applies only to a case in which he sent her few gifts — i.e., gifts which were likely to be used up while she was still in her father's house (Yad Ramah; Ritva; Meiri).

Some authorities maintain that the Gemara's final decision is not in accordance with the mishnah. Rather, whether or not he

9
6

did not eat a groom's meal there, they can be reclaimed. [If] he sent many wedding gifts, [on the understanding] that they return with her to her husband's house, they can be reclaimed. [If he sent] few wedding gifts [on the understanding] that she use them in her father's house, they cannot be reclaimed.

6. [I]f] one who was lying ill wrote [away] all his property to others, but retained some

YAD AVRAHAM

participated in the feast, and whether or not the gifts were expected to last until the *nisuin*, they can all be reclaimed. The only exceptions to this are food items which were already consumed. However, if she refuses to consummate the marriage, even such items must be repaid, but only at two-thirds their regular value *(Rambam, Zechiyah* 5:21).

6.

Ordinarily, any transfer of ownership requires a formal act of acquisition *(kinyan)* to take effect (see preface to 5:7). However, the Rabbis ordained that one who is lying ill and in fear of dying may issue even oral instructions that his belongings be given to another, and his words have the validity of an act of acquisition. The transfer of ownership under these conditions takes effect upon his death [in contrast to a regular transaction which must take effect during the owner's lifetime or not at all]. This was enacted in order to prevent any deterioration of the ill person's condition resulting from his apprehension that his wishes will not be carried out *(Gem.* 147b; *Rashbam).*

When it is clear that his intent to give away his possessions is due only to his apprehension that he may die, the gift is null if he recovers from his illness, even if a formal act of acquisition was made *(Gem.* 146b; *Rashbam).* However, our assessment of his intent depends upon the circumstances of his instructions. If he stated clearly that he was giving away his possessions because he expected to die, or if his medical condition was grave and he was in clear danger of dying, his gift is nullified if he should recover. However, if he was not so ill (nor did he express a belief that his death was imminent), it cannot be automatically assumed that he issued his instructions only because he expected to die. Therefore, his gift is nullified in the event of his recovery only if there are indications from the manner of the gift that his directive was meant to take effect only if he dies *(Nimmukei Yosef* to *Gem.* 151b, 152a). In this regard, the mishnah will distinguish between a directive disposing of the sick person's entire estate, and one disposing of only part of his possessions.

שְׁכִיב מְרַע שֶׁכָּתַב כָּל נְכָסָיו לַאֲחֵרִים, — *[If]* one who was lying ill wrote [away] all his property to others,

I.e., he stated in writing that all his possessions be given to others but did not specify that he was doing so because he expected to die from his current

illness *(Yad Ramah;* see preface).

וְשִׁיֵּר קַרְקַע כָּל שֶׁהוּא, — *but retained* [lit. *left over] some property,*

The donor excluded some property from his gift, which he retained for himself. Although the mishnah men-

[195]   THE MISHNAH/BAVA BASRA — Chapter Nine: *Mi SheMeis*

בבא
בתרא
ט/ו

קַיֶּמֶת. לֹא שִׁיֵּר קַרְקַע כָּל שֶׁהוּא, אֵין מַתְּנָתוֹ
קַיֶּמֶת.
לֹא כָתַב בָּהּ שְׁכִיב מְרַע, הוּא אוֹמֵר שְׁכִיב

יד אברהם

tions only real property, the same ruling
applies if he retained movable property
(Rav from Gem. 150b).

מַתְּנָתוֹ קַיֶּמֶת. — *his gift is upheld.*

If he recovers from his illness, the gift
is still valid. The fact that he retained
some of his possessions and did not
distribute all of them (as might be
expected of a dying man) raises the
possibility that he thought he would
survive and still need property for
himself.[1] If this is true, then the part of
his estate which he gave as a gift he
meant to be valid even if he recovered. It
is therefore upheld even if he recovers
(Gem. 149b; Rashbam).

Although this assumption cannot be a
certainty (since he may have been retaining
some of his belongings for the sake of his
rightful heirs), since he gave this gift without
in any way indicating that he was doing so
because he feared he was dying [and since his
medical condition was not at that moment
critical (Nimmukei Yosef)], we cannot nullify
it unless we are certain that it was meant to be
effective only in the event of his death (Yad
Ramah). Only when he gives away all his
property is it clear that he is doing so because
of his expectation of death (Nimmukei
Yosef).

Furthermore, his (possible) consideration of his future needs removes
this gift from the category of a sickbed
gift and restores it to the category of an
ordinary gift. Thus, despite his illness,
his partial gift is not valid unless it was
accompanied by a formal act of
acquisition, and mere oral instructions
are insufficient. If no act of acquisition
was performed in regard to this partial
gift, the gift is null and void even if the
donor indeed dies of his illness. Thus,
the mishnah must be discussing a
written declaration accompanied by a

regular act of acquisition (Rav from
Gem. 151b).

However, if he made it clear at the
time that his partial gift *was* made in the
belief that he was about to die, it is
considered a sickbed gift and it requires
no act of acquisition to take effect. By
the same token, should he recover the
gift is *not* upheld (ibid.).

לֹא שִׁיֵּר קַרְקַע כָּל שֶׁהוּא, — [*If*] *he did not
retain any property,*

I.e., he stated explicitly that he was
giving everything he owns to the
recipient, or it was definitely known
that he owned no possessions other than
those which he signed over (Nimmukei
Yosef).

However, if he signed over all his known
possessions, but it is not firmly established
that he had no other belongings, it is possible
that he has additional property elsewhere
which he retained for himself. Accordingly,
the gift is thus valid even if he recovers
(Gem. 148b). Nimmukei Yosef explains that
this applies when he specified that he was
giving certain possessions to specific people,
rather than stating explicitly that he was
ceding all of his belongings. Since a dying
man will usually state explicitly that he is
giving away all his belongings, his failure to
do so gives rise to the reasonable suspicion
that he has yet other possessions which are
not being transferred.

Alternatively, since this mishnah deals
with a sickbed gift which was deeded by the
donor to the recipient through an act of
acquisition valid for a healthy person (as
explained above), this deed can be nullified
upon the donor's recovery only if it can be
proven that the donor made this gift because
he expected to die (which would be the case if
he, in fact, deeded all his property). Thus it
must be proven that the donor left over no
other property before the gift can be nullified
(Rosh).

1. Some authorities contend that this law applies only if he left for himself sufficient
belongings to support himself after he recovers (Rosh, see Gem. 149b), while others rule that it
applies to any retention (Rif; see Choshen Mishpat 250:4).

9
6

property, his gift is upheld. [If] he did not retain any
property, his gift is not upheld.
[If] he did not record in it [that he was] lying ill,

YAD AVRAHAM

אֵין מַתְּנָתוֹ קַיֶּמֶת. — *his gift is not upheld.*

If the donor recovers, the gift is void because it is apparent from the fact that he retained nothing for himself that he gave it only because he thought he was dying *(Rav).*

However, the gift would be valid if he dies even if no regular act of acquisition had been performed [since it was a deathbed will] *(Rav).*

The *Gemara* (152a) records a dispute between Rav and Shmuel in regard to a sickbed gift accompanied by a regular act of acquisition. It is Rav's opinion that since his oral instructions would have sufficed, we construe the redundant regular act of acquisition as intended to give the recipient the additional benefits of an ordinary act of transfer. Therefore this gift would be valid even if the donor recovers. Shmuel, however, maintains that the regular act of transfer in effect nullifies the sickbed gift completely, since it is construed as an attempt by the donor to effect the terms of his oral will solely by way of a regular act of acquisition. Now a will's terms take effect only after the donor's death — but a regular act of acquisition cannot transfer property posthumously. This is because one of the axioms of any transfer is that the property involved belong to the one effecting its transfer. Once a person has died, his property is no longer his, having already been acquired by the rightful heirs through inheritance. [It is one of the unique features of a sickbed will that it can transfer property posthumously.] Consequently, since the donor intended the gift to be transferred via his regular act of acquisition only after his death, the entire gift is null and void. The halachah follows the view of Shmuel *(Choshen Mishpat* 250:17).

This entire dispute, however, seems to be contradicted by our mishnah which, as explained above (s.v. מתנתו קימת), is discussing a situation in which the sickbed will was accompanied by a regular act of acquisition. Specifically, Shmuel's view (the view accepted as halachah) is problematic since the mishnah has just stated that if he

wrote away all his property and recovered the gift is not upheld — implying that had he died, the sickbed will would have been a valid gift even though it was accompanied by a regular act of acquisition.

One possible answer is suggested by the *Gemara's* statement that if the regular act of acquisition was clearly described as being to reinforce the sickbed gift (and not to supplant it), even Shmuel agrees that the rules of a sickbed gift pertain. Thus, some authorities explain that the mishnah is discussing a case where this was clearly stipulated. Although a regular act of acquisition would seem to indicate that he does not mean to cede the property by means of the Rabbinic enactment, the mishnah is discussing one who stated that the act of acquisition was meant to accentuate the transfer rather than to be its sole basis *(Nimmukei Yosef).*

Tosafos explain that Shmuel's ruling applies only to one who wrote in the will document itself that a regular act of acquisition had also been made. The mishnah, however, is dealing with a situation in which this was not recorded in the document. Therefore, the laws governing the directive of one who is lying ill still apply *(Tos.* 152a).

Ritva explains that the mishnah is discussing a case in which he gave him a deed for the property but performed no other act of acquisition. [The giving of the deed alone cannot serve as evidence that he means to effect the transfer in the regular manner, because it may have been given solely for the sake of guaranteeing its execution.] Nevertheless, it is a legitimate form of acquisition if only real property is involved and the gift is therefore valid if he dies *(Ritva).*

לֹא כָתַב בָּהּ שְׁכִיב מְרַע, — *[If] he did not record in it [that he was] lying ill,*

He wrote a will giving all his property to others without retaining anything for himself *(Tif. Yis.),* but he did not write into it the wording commonly used for a sickbed will — *when he was sick and lying in his bed;* nor did he write the wording commonly used for a regular

[197]   THE MISHNAH/BAVA BASRA — Chapter Nine: *Mi SheMeis*

מְרַע הָיָה, וְהֵן אוֹמְרִים בָּרִיא הָיָה, צָרִיךְ לְהָבִיא
רְאָיָה שֶׁהָיָה שְׁכִיב מְרַע; דִּבְרֵי רַבִּי מֵאִיר.
וַחֲכָמִים אוֹמְרִים: הַמּוֹצִיא מֵחֲבֵרוֹ עָלָיו הָרְאָיָה.

[ז] **הַמְחַלֵּק** נְכָסָיו עַל פִּיו — רַבִּי אֱלִיעֶזֶר
אוֹמֵר: אֶחָד בָּרִיא וְאֶחָד מְסֻכָּן,
נְכָסִים שֶׁיֵּשׁ לָהֶן אַחֲרָיוּת נִקְנִין בְּכֶסֶף, וּבִשְׁטָר

יד אברהם

gift document — *when he was going on his feet in the streets* [i.e., healthy] *(Rav)*.

הוּא אוֹמֵר שֶׁכִּיב מְרַע הָיָה, — [*and*] *he says that he was lying ill,*
The donor later wishes to retract his gift by claiming that it was a sickbed gift which is nullified by his recovery *(Rav)*.

וְהֵן אוֹמְרִים בָּרִיא הָיָה, — *whereas they say that he was healthy,*
The recipients claim that he was not lying ill at the time he wrote away his property and that the gift was therefore the regular gift of a healthy person which cannot be canceled *(Rav)*.

צָרִיךְ לְהָבִיא רְאָיָה שֶׁהָיָה שְׁכִיב מְרַע; דִּבְרֵי רַבִּי מֵאִיר. — *he must bring proof that he was lying ill;* [*these are*] *the words of R' Meir.*
Since he is presently healthy, we have no cause to assume that he was otherwise at the time the document was drawn unless it can be proven *(Rav from Gem. 154a).*

וַחֲכָמִים אוֹמְרִים: הַמּוֹצִיא מֵחֲבֵרוֹ עָלָיו הָרְאָיָה. — *But the Sages say: The one who exacts from another must bring the proof.*

The Sages maintain that the above principle of retroactive status does not suffice to remove the property in question from the one who presently has them in his possession. Rather, the burden of proof rests on the recipients — who are attempting to exact the property from the donor — to disprove the donor's claim *(Rav from Gem. 154a).*

There is another opinion in the *Gemara* (ibid.) that, barring proof to the contrary, the Sages would ordinarily accept the fact that he is now healthy as sufficient basis to assume that this was his status when the document was written. Nevertheless, the donor's claim that he was bedridden is believed because it is buttressed by the fact that had he wished to lie he could have claimed that the document was a forgery. Thus, the only evidence proving that the gift ever took place is based on the donor's admission that the document was properly written — but he himself denies its validity on other grounds. Consequently, this cannot be used to undermine his position. Accordingly, if the recipients can prove that the document is legitimate [so that its validity is established independently of the donor's admission], their claim would be accepted. R' Meir, however, contends that once one has conceded the authenticity of a document, he is no longer believed to contest its ramifications on the basis of that which he could have declared it a forgery.

7.

The previous mishnah was based on the principle that one who is lying ill was granted the authority to distribute his possessions orally, with his instructions having the legal validity of a regular act of acquisition. The mishnah now relates that this principle is actually the subject of a dispute among the *Tannaim*.

[and] he says that he was lying ill, whereas they say that he was healthy, he must bring proof that he was lying ill; [these are] the words of R' Meir. But the Sages say: The one who exacts from another must bring the proof.

7. **[**I**f]** someone distributes his property orally — R' Eliezer says: Whether he is healthy or dangerously ill, properties which can become subject to a lien are acquired through money, a document, or

YAD AVRAHAM

הַמְחַלֵּק נְבָסָיו עַל פִּיו — — [If] someone distributes his property orally —

This must refer to one who willed belongings orally to someone who is not entitled to them according to the laws of inheritance. Otherwise, R' Eliezer, who invalidates an oral gift (see below), himself states elsewhere (130a) that one is entitled to orally alter distribution of his estate among the eligible heirs (Yad Ramah, Meiri from 130a-b; see 8:5).

Others explain the mishnah to be discussing even one who distributes his possessions among his sons as a gift (Rashi to Gittin 14b). [Apparently, Rashi maintains that the person's instructions must specify whether he means inheritance or a gift; if he specified a gift, the fact that his instructions would have been valid for inheritance is of no consequence.]

רַבִּי אֱלִיעֶזֶר אוֹמֵר: — R' Eliezer says:

However, other versions to the mishnah read R' Elazar (Tos.; Rif; Rosh; see Tos. Yom Tov).

אֶחָד בָּרִיא וְאֶחָד מְסֻכָּן, — Whether he is healthy or dangerously ill,

I.e., the legal requirements for this distribution of his property are identical whether he is healthy or dangerously ill. R' Eliezer does not accept the principle that the words of one who is lying ill are equivalent to an act of acquisition (Rav). [Therefore, in all cases, a proper act of acquisition must be performed, as described below.]

Since the mishnah specifies one who is dangerously ill, rather than one who

is simply lying ill, it is clear that R' Eliezer's opinion applies even if he stated explicitly that he was distributing his possessions because he expected to die. As explained in the preface to mishnah 6, the law concerning one who is dangerously ill and makes a gift without stipulation is identical with that of one who is not known to be so gravely ill but who states explicitly that his gift is based on his expectation of dying (Yad Ramah). In addition, the case described below makes it clear that the mishnah deals with a gift given in the clear expectation of dying, as will be explained there (Rashbam).

Just as R' Eliezer equates one who is ill to one who is healthy concerning the validity of an oral gift, he also equates them in regard to a case in which an act of acquisition was performed and the original owner subsequently recovered. Thus just as the gift is valid in the case of a healthy donor, so too it is valid in the case of a sick donor who subsequently recovered, and he cannot undo it claiming that he meant to give it only on the assumption that he was dying (Rashbam).

נְבָסִים שֶׁיֵּשׁ לָהֶן אַחֲרָיוּת — properties which can become subject to a lien

I.e., real properties, which can be mortgaged to a creditor, because their permanence guarantees their availability for collection. The word אַחֲרָיוּת means recourse — i.e., that the lender can seize them as payment for his loan from buyers who bought them from the debtor after the loan was made (Rav to

וּבַחֲזָקָה. וְשֶׁאֵין לָהֶן אַחֲרָיוּת אֵין נִקְנִין אֶלָּא
בִּמְשִׁיכָה. אָמְרוּ לוֹ: מַעֲשֶׂה בְּאִמָּן שֶׁל בְּנֵי רוֹכֵל
שֶׁהָיְתָה חוֹלָה וְאָמְרָה ,,תְּנוּ כְבִינָתִי לְבִתִּי; וְהִיא
בִּשְׁנַיִם עָשָׂר מָנֶה,'' וָמֵתָה, וְקִיְּמוּ אֶת דְּבָרֶיהָ.
אָמַר לָהֶן: בְּנֵי רוֹכֵל, תְּקַבְּרֵם אִמָּן. וַחֲכָמִים
אוֹמְרִים: בְּשַׁבָּת דְּבָרָיו קַיָּמִין, מִפְּנֵי שֶׁאֵין יָכוֹל
לִכְתּוֹב, אֲבָל לֹא בְחֹל. רַבִּי יְהוֹשֻׁעַ אוֹמֵר: בְּשַׁבָּת
אָמְרוּ, קַל וָחֹמֶר בְּחֹל.

יד אברהם

Kiddushin 1:5).

Although movable property can also be
seized for a debt, it is not subject to a lien.
Thus, once it has been sold, it has been put
beyond the reach of any of the seller's
creditors. Real estate, on the other hand, can
become subject to a lien, which in the Torah
law means that if the debtor owned land at
the time he incurred the debt but
subsequently sold it, that land can be
attached by the creditor for payment if the
debtor has no remaining assets of his own.
The buyer's only recourse is to attempt to
obtain a refund from the seller; see below,
10:8.

נִקְנִין בְּכֶסֶף, — *are acquired through
money,*

The transfer of the property is
effected when the buyer gives the value
of the land, or even a part of its value
[with a minimum of a *perutah*], to the
seller, for the purpose of acquisition
(Meiri, ibid.; see *Yad Avraham* comm.
to *Kiddushin* 1:5).

וּבִשְׁטָר, — *a document,*

The owner writes a document stating
that his field is being acquired by the
recipient. Handing the document over
to him effects the transfer of the
property (Rav loc. cit.).

וּבַחֲזָקָה. — *or an act of possession.*

[The transfer can also be effected by
the recipient's performance of an act
which indicates his possession of the
land in the presence of the seller.] For
example, he digs up part of the land, or
partially fences it in, or locks it up or

breaches the existing enclosure (Rav loc.
cit.).

וְשֶׁאֵין לָהֶן אַחֲרָיוּת — *Those which cannot
become subject to a lien*
[I.e., movable property.]

אֵין נִקְנִין אֶלָּא בִּמְשִׁיכָה. — *are acquired only
through meshichah.*

Meshichah means to pull an article
and make it move. This is a formal act of
acquisition suitable for movables [see
above, preface to 5:7]. The mishnah
specifies *meshichah* because that is the
method most commonly used for
movables. However, the other ways of
taking possession by hand, such as
lifting or having the object handed over
to the recipient by the owner, are also
valid (see above, preface to 5:7).

אָמְרוּ לוֹ: — *They said to him:*
[The Sages said to R' Eliezer.]

מַעֲשֶׂה בְּאִמָּן שֶׁל בְּנֵי רוֹכֵל שֶׁהָיְתָה חוֹלָה — *It
occurred with the mother of the sons of
Rochel that she was ill*

She stated explicitly that she was
issuing her instructions on the assumption that she was dying (Gem. 151b).

וְאָמְרָה ,,תְּנוּ כְבִינָתִי לְבִתִּי; וְהִיא בִּשְׁנַיִם עָשָׂר
מָנֶה,'' — *and she said, 'Give my veil to
my daughter; it is worth twelve maneh,'*

This is the translation of *Rav*. Others
render כבינה, *a brooch* used to clasp a
cloak around the neck (Rashbam to
151b). A third interpretation is that it is
a type of crown (Tos.).

an act of possession. Those which cannot become subject to a lien are acquired only through *meshichah*. They said to him: It occurred with the mother of the sons of Rochel that she was ill and she said, 'Give my veil to my daughter; it is worth twelve *maneh*,' and she died, and they upheld her words. He said to them: [As to] the sons of Rochel, their mother should bury them. The Sages say: On the Sabbath his words are upheld, because he cannot write, but not on weekdays. R' Yehoshua says: They said [it] on the Sabbath, and certainly on weekdays.

YAD AVRAHAM

וָמֵתָה, וְקִימוּ אֶת דְּבָרֶיהָ. — *and she died, and they upheld her words.*

[The Sages of her time upheld her instructions and gave the article to the daughter — although a daughter does not inherit where there are sons (above, 8:2). Thus it is evident that the oral instructions of one who is ill were considered, by the Sages of the earlier generation, as binding.]

אָמַר לָהֶן: בְּנֵי רוֹכֵל, תְּקַבְּרֵם אִמָּן. — *He said to them: [As to] the sons of Rochel, their mother should bury them.*

R' Eliezer retorted that no proof can be brought from their case because they were sinners whom the Rabbis fined by allowing their mother to transfer their inheritance to her daughter (Rav).

Actually, R' Eliezer and the Sages are in dispute as to whether the sons of Rochel were sinners. These men maintained thorns in a vineyard, which R' Eliezer considers a transgression of the laws of *kilayim* of the vineyard, the prohibition on growing other species together with grapes. The Sages, however, contend that thorns are not included in this prohibition and there was thus no reason for the Sages of their time to fine them; their proof from that case is therefore valid in their opinion (Gem. 156b; see Kilayim 5:8).

The halachah is in accordance with the opinion of the Sages (Rav).

וַחֲכָמִים אוֹמְרִים: — *The Sages say:*

These 'Sages' are none other than R' Eliezer, who maintains that, with the exception of the Sabbath, the oral instructions of one who is ill have no validity (Yad Ramah).

Other versions in fact read R' Eliezer says. These versions had the reading of R' Elazar for the first opinion recorded in the mishnah (Tos. Yom Tov).

בְּשַׁבָּת דְּבָרָיו קַיָּמִין, מִפְּנֵי שֶׁאֵין יָכוֹל לִכְתּוֹב, — *On the Sabbath his words are upheld, because he cannot write,*

[If one who is lying ill issued oral instructions on the Sabbath to distribute his possessions, his words are upheld, because he has no other recourse. Since it is the Sabbath, one is not permitted to perform an act of acquisition or to write a document, and his condition may deteriorate if he does not see that his wishes will be carried out (Rashbam).

אֲבָל לֹא בְחֹל. — *but not on weekdays.*

If he issued his instructions during the week, they are not binding (Rav) because if it is indeed of sufficient importance to him to see that his wishes will be carried out, he has the option of performing an act of acquisition or having a deed written and given over (Rashbam).

רַבִּי יְהוֹשֻׁעַ אוֹמֵר: בְּשַׁבָּת אָמְרוּ, קַל וַחֹמֶר בְּחֹל. — *R' Yehoshua says: They said [it] on the Sabbath, and certainly on weekdays.*

כַּיּוֹצֵא בוֹ, זָכִין לְקָטָן, וְאֵין זָכִין לְגָדוֹל. רַבִּי
יְהוֹשֻׁעַ אוֹמֵר: לְקָטָן אָמְרוּ, קַל וָחֹמֶר לְגָדוֹל.

[ח] **נָפַל** הַבַּיִת עָלָיו וְעַל אָבִיו, אוֹ עָלָיו וְעַל
מוֹרִישָׁיו, וְהָיְתָה עָלָיו כְּתֻבַּת אִשָּׁה
וּבַעַל חוֹב — יוֹרְשֵׁי הָאָב אוֹמְרִים, הַבֵּן מֵת
רִאשׁוֹן וְאַחַר כָּךְ מֵת הָאָב; בַּעֲלֵי הַחוֹב אוֹמְרִים,
הָאָב מֵת רִאשׁוֹן וְאַחַר כָּךְ מֵת הַבֵּן — בֵּית שַׁמַּאי

יד אברהם

If his verbal instructions are valid on the Sabbath, when the regular methods of acquisition are not permitted and the property is thus not fit to be transferred, they are certainly binding during the week, when all acquisitions can be performed and the property is thus fit to be transferred (Rashbam).

The halachah is in accordance with this view. Thus, the verbal instructions of one who is lying ill are valid whether on the Sabbath or during the week, as if they were recorded in a deed and handed over (Rav).

כַּיּוֹצֵא בוֹ, — Similarly,

The following dispute is based on the same principles as the previous one. In both instances, the first *Tanna* contends that only a situation in which the normal manner of acquisition is impossible calls for the acceptance of an irregular alternative, whereas R' Yehoshua counters that the greater a person's capacity to acquire possession the more diverse forms of acquisition must be seen to be effective for him

(Yad Ramah).

זָכִין לְקָטָן, — one can acquire on behalf of a minor,

Since a minor does not have the legal ability to make acquisitions on his own behalf, the Rabbis enacted that an adult can acquire an object on his behalf (Rashbam).

וְאֵין זָכִין לְגָדוֹל. — but one cannot acquire on behalf of an adult.

One cannot acquire on behalf of another adult since the other adult is capable of making acquisition for himself (ibid.).

רַבִּי יְהוֹשֻׁעַ אוֹמֵר: לְקָטָן אָמְרוּ, קַל וָחֹמֶר לְגָדוֹל. — R' Yehoshua says: They said [it] for a minor, and certainly for an adult.

If acquisition made on behalf of a minor, who is incapable of acquiring for himself, is valid, it is certainly valid when done on behalf of an adult, who is capable of making acquisitions, and who can even appoint an agent to do so in his place (ibid.).

8.

The remainder of this chapter deals with the rules governing the disposition of an inheritance when several family members die at approximately the same time but the precise order of death, and thus the precedence of inheritance, between them is not clear.

Similarly, one can acquire on behalf of a minor, but one cannot acquire on behalf of an adult. R' Yehoshua says: They said [it] for a minor, and certainly for an adult.

8. [If] a house collapsed upon a man and his father, or upon him and one from whom he inherits, and there was a wife's *kesubah* or a creditor's [claim outstanding] against him — the father's heirs claim [that] the son died first and then the father; [while] the creditors claim [that] the father died first and then the son — Beis Shammai say: They

YAD AVRAHAM

נָפַל הַבַּיִת עָלָיו וְעַל אָבִיו, — [If] *a house collapsed upon a man* [lit. *him*] *and his father,*

A house collapsed, killing a man and his father, and it is not known which of them died first (*Rashbam*). The same law applies if they died in any other manner and the order of their deaths could not be ascertained (*Meiri*).

אוֹ עָלָיו וְעַל מוֹרִשָׁיו, — *or upon him and one from whom he inherits,*

E.g., a house fell on Reuven and his brother, or his father's brother, and they died along with him leaving no closer relatives than Reuven himself (*Rashbam*).

וְהָיְתָה עָלָיו כְּתֻבַּת אִשָׁה וּבַעַל חוֹב — *and there was a wife's kesubah or a creditor's [claim outstanding] against him —*

Reuven was survived by his wife, who, as a widow, is now owed the money of their marriage contract, or he owed money to another creditor, and he left no money or possessions from which they could collect other than his possible inheritance (*Rashbam*).

יוֹרְשֵׁי הָאָב אוֹמְרִים, הַבֵּן מֵת רִאשׁוֹן וְאַחַר כָּךְ

מֵת הָאָב; — *the father's heirs claim [that] the son died first and then the father;*

The father's heirs — i.e., Reuven's brothers (*Rashbam*) — claim that Reuven died first and thus never inherited his father.[1] Therefore, Reuven's creditors have no claim on the father's inheritance, since no part of it ever belonged to Reuven, their debtor (*Rav*).

The mishnah discusses the case of a house which collapsed on a man and his father. The same ruling would apply in the case of a man and any other relative from whom he stands to inherit (*Rashbam*).

The same would apply if the father's closest relatives were his grandsons, Reuven's sons. Although their relationship to their grandfather is obviously through Reuven, if Reuven is not living when his father dies they inherit directly from the grandfather, and the possessions never enter Reuven's estate to be liable to collection by his creditors (*Rashbam* 157a from *Gem.* 159b).

בַּעֲלֵי הַחוֹב אוֹמְרִים, הָאָב מֵת רִאשׁוֹן וְאַחַר כָּךְ — מֵת הַבֵּן — *[while] the creditors claim [that] the father died first and then the son —*

---

1. Obviously, they cannot assert this with certainty. The intent is that their claim to the property is based on this possibility.

אוֹמְרִים: יַחֲלֹקוּ. וּבֵית הִלֵּל אוֹמְרִים: נְכָסִים
בְּחֶזְקָתָן.

[ט] נָפַל הַבַּיִת עָלָיו וְעַל אִשְׁתּוֹ — יוֹרְשֵׁי
הַבַּעַל אוֹמְרִים הָאִשָּׁה מֵתָה רִאשׁוֹנָה
וְאַחַר כָּךְ מֵת הַבַּעַל, יוֹרְשֵׁי הָאִשָּׁה אוֹמְרִים הַבַּעַל
מֵת רִאשׁוֹן וְאַחַר כָּךְ מֵתָה הָאִשָּׁה — בֵּית שַׁמַּאי

יד אברהם

This possibility is to the benefit of the widow and creditors, since if the father died even a moment before the son, a share of the estate was inherited by the son immediately before he died, thus rendering it collectible for their debt (Rav).

The mishnah is discussing a case in which Reuven had explicitly obligated himself to pay his debt from any properties which would enter his possession after the debt was incurred. Otherwise, properties which did not belong to him at the time of the loan would not be collectible from his heirs after his death (Nimmukei Yosef from Gem. 157a).

בֵּית שַׁמַּאי אוֹמְרִים: יַחֲלֹקוּ. — Beis Shammai say: They divide [the estate].

Since it cannot be determined who really died first, the general rule for resolving unprovable monetary claims must be applied — i.e., the money remains in the possession of whoever had it up to that point. This would seem to favor the heirs over the creditors, since the money indisputably comes to them as part of the estate and the only question is whether the creditors can then press a claim against it. However, Beis Shammai are of the opinion that the

creditor's possession of a document to the loan is considered tantamount to holding the money of the loan itself. Thus, if the money came to the son before he died, the creditors would have gained immediate 'possession' of it, legally speaking. Since it is *not* known who died first, the creditors are considered to be as much in possession of the money as the heirs, and they divide accordingly (Rav from Yevamos 38b).

וּבֵית הִלֵּל אוֹמְרִים: נְכָסִים בְּחֶזְקָתָן. — But Beis Hillel say: The property retains its status.

[Beis Hillel dispute the contention that possesion of a loan document is tantamount to possession of the money.] Thus, the properties are considered to be in the possession of the heirs, while the creditors are considered to be in the position of trying to exact the properties from that possession. The creditors must therefore bring proof to their claim that the father died before the son in order to collect (Rav).

It is clear from this mishnah that a creditor can collect only from that which the debtor acquired while still alive. Otherwise, even if the son died first, the creditors would be able to collect from that which he would have inherited had he lived (Yad Ramah).

9.

The mishnah deals with three types of assets which a married woman has: the kesubah; נִכְסֵי צֹאן בַּרְזֶל, fixed-value property [lit. iron-sheep property]; and נִכְסֵי מְלוֹג, usufruct property.

Kesubah in this context refers to the debt undertaken by the husband — and

divide [the estate]. But Beis Hillel say: The property retains its status.

9. [If] a house collapsed upon a man and his wife — the husband's heirs claim [that] the wife died first and then the husband, [while] the wife's heirs claim [that] the husband died first and then the

YAD AVRAHAM

recorded in the marriage contract — to pay his wife two hundred *zuzin*, plus whatever additions are included in the contract, in the event of his death or their divorce.

Fixed-value properties are those properties that the wife brings into the marriage, for which the husband accepts responsibility to return to her in case he divorces her or dies, at the value at which they were assessed at the time of their wedding. Any capital gains belong to him, but she is protected against depreciation or loss of the properties. Thus, their value to her remains fixed throughout the marriage.

Melog, usufruct properties, are properties that the wife brings into a marriage which the husband may use and profit from but for whose value he does not accept responsibility. Thus, in case they are divorced or he dies, the properties are returned to her as they stand at that time; if they increased in value, the gain is hers; if they depreciated or were lost, she suffers the loss.

נָפַל הַבַּיִת עָלָיו וְעַל אִשְׁתּוֹ — — [*If*] *a house collapsed upon a man* [lit. *him*] *and his wife* —

[Both the husband and wife died in the collapse of the house, but it is not known which of them died first. This creates uncertainty as to the disposition of the wife's property, since a husband inherits his wife. Thus, if the wife died first, her property passed to the husband and on his death to his heirs. If the husband died first, her property passes to her family upon her death.]

The mishnah speaks of a case in which they had no children from their marriage (*Rashbam*). [If they had children, these children would be the heirs to both the husband and the wife and would thus have a definite claim to the estate. Their claim would, therefore, take precedence over that of any other of their father's relatives, such as sons from previous marriages, whose claim to the estate is not certain (cf. comm. to mishnah 10, s.v. נפל הבית).]

יוֹרְשֵׁי הַבַּעַל אוֹמְרִים — *the husband's heirs claim*

E.g., his father, his brother, or his children by another wife (*Rashbam*).

הָאִשָּׁה מֵתָה רִאשׁוֹנָה וְאַחַר כָּךְ מֵת הַבַּעַל, — [*that*] *the wife died first and then the husband,*

Thus, the wife's heirs do not inherit anything, because the husband first inherited his wife and then passed the legacy on to his heirs (*Rav*).

יוֹרְשֵׁי הָאִשָּׁה אוֹמְרִים הַבַּעַל מֵת רִאשׁוֹן — וְאַחַר כָּךְ מֵתָה הָאִשָּׁה — [*while*] *the wife's heirs claim* [*that*] *the husband died first and then the wife* —

Therefore, the husband never inherited his wife's possessions. In addition, since his wife outlived him, the *kesubah* became due upon his death and is thus to be collected from his estate and passed on to the wife's heirs (*Yad Ramah*).

Ordinarily, a woman must first swear that she has not received her *kesubah* in advance before she can collect it from the husband's heirs (*Gittin* 4:3). Accordingly, her heirs would not be able to collect her *kesubah*, since a person cannot give over to his heirs the right to swear and collect (*Shevuos* 48a). The mishnah must therefore be discussing a situation in which she would not have been obligated to swear — e.g., the husband added a clause to the *kesubah* exempting her from the obligation to swear in order to collect

אוֹמְרִים: יַחֲלקוּ. וּבֵית הִלֵּל אוֹמְרִים: נְכָסִים
בְּחֶזְקָתָן; כְּתֻבָּה בְּחֶזְקַת יוֹרְשֵׁי הַבַּעַל; נְכָסִים
הַנִּכְנָסִים וְהַיּוֹצְאִין עִמָּהּ בְּחֶזְקַת יוֹרְשֵׁי הָאָב.

[יז] **נָפַל** הַבַּיִת עָלָיו וְעַל אִמּוֹ, אֵלּוּ וָאֵלּוּ מוֹדִים

יד אברהם

(*Yad Ramah; Nimmukei Yosef; Meiri*).

Others contend that since the basis for her heirs being able to collect is that the possessions are considered to have been in her possession (see below), she would be able to pass on to her heirs the right to swear and collect (*Tos.*). In such a case they would only have to swear that to the best of their knowledge the *kesubah* was never collected (see *Shevuos* ibid.).

בֵּית שַׁמַּאי אוֹמְרִים: יַחֲלֹקוּ. — *Beis Shammai say: They divide* [*the estate*].

Since it cannot be determined who died first and who the rightful heirs are, the wife's estate is divided between the two sets of heirs. This includes both her fixed-value and *melog* properties as well as the value of her *kesubah*. Although her *kesubah* would seem to be only a debt to be collected by the wife and thus in the possession of the husband's heirs, Beis Shammai consider possession of a loan document tantamount to money which was already collected, as explained in the previous mishnah. The wife is thus considered to have been equally in possession of the amount stated in the *kesubah* with her husband, and their heirs therefore divide it (*Ramah*; see *Yevamos* 38b).

However, according to one opinion in *Yevamos* (ibid.), even Beis Shammai agree that the *kesubah* is considered to be in the possession of the husband (*Rashbam; Tos. Yom Tov*), because a *kesubah* is not meant to be collected in his lifetime [and is therefore, at the time of his death, not considered as tantamount to having been collected] (*Rashi to Yevamos* ad loc.). Thus, according to this view, the *kesubah* is not divided, but goes entirely to the husband's heirs.

This is said in regard to the mishnah (ibid. 4:3) concerning a woman whose husband

died without children, leaving her a *yevamah;* she subsequently inherited possessions and died, before the *yavam* performed *yibum* or *chalitzah* (see preface to 8:6). The mishnah there discusses the question of who is to inherit her *kesubah* and properties. There, too, Beis Shammai say that her heirs and the husband's heirs — i.e., his brothers, who were eligible to perform *yibum* — divide the possessions. Concerning that statement, the *Gemara* says that it refers to her possessions but not to the *kesubah.*

Others contend that only in regard to the case in *Yevamos* does the *Gemara* make such a distinction, because after her husband dies, she has no rights to the *kesubah* until one of the brothers frees her from *yibum* through the process of *chalitzah.* In our case, however, her rights to the *kesubah* exist immediately after her husband's death (*Tos.*).

וּבֵית הִלֵּל אוֹמְרִים: נְכָסִים בְּחֶזְקָתָן; — *But Beis Hillel say: The property retains its status;*

[Beis Hillel are of the opinion that since the line of inheritance is questionable, the property should be left in the possession of whoever controlled it up to that point.]

The general term — *property* — refers here specifically to the fixed-value properties. Beis Hillel does not clarify who previously had control of this property and a case can be made either way. On the one hand, they are primarily the wife's properties, but on the other hand the husband is the one who loses or gains with their appreciation or depreciation (*Rav, Rashbam* 158a). Therefore, they are considered to be in the possession of both of them equally and their respective heirs divide these properties (*Rav from Gem.* 158b).

9   wife — Beis Shammai say: They divide [the estate].
10   But Beis Hillel say: The property retains its status;
the *kesubah* is in the possession of the husband's
heirs; the possessions which enter and go out with
her are in the possession of the father's heirs.

10. **[**I**f]** a house collapsed upon a man and his

כְּתֻבָּה בְּחֶזְקַת יוֹרְשֵׁי הַבַּעַל; — *the kesubah is
in the possession of the husband's heirs;*
   The debt stated in the *kesubah* is in
the possession of the husband's heirs,
since it was not yet collected *(Rav)*. [As
explained in the previous mishnah, Beis
Hillel do not consider possession of a
loan document tantamount to possession of the money.]
   Some commentators maintain that the
mishnah should read *and the kesubah* etc.,
since it is a separate case *(Rav; Rashbam)*.
However, even according to the version
which reads *the kesubah*, it can still be
understood to be a second case *(Ritva;* cf.
Meiri).

נְכָסִים הַנִּכְנָסִים וְהַיּוֹצְאִין עִמָּהּ — *the
possessions which enter and go out with
her*
   This refers to the *melog* properties,
which enter into the marriage with her

and leave with her as well, in whatever
condition they may be, whether
improved or deteriorated *(Rav)*.

בְּחֶזְקַת יוֹרְשֵׁי הָאָב. — *are in the possession
of the father's heirs.*
   I.e., the heirs of the wife's father, who
are in effect the heirs of the wife *(Rav)*.
Her heirs may be referred to in this
manner because she received these
possessions by inheritance from her
father *(Rashbam)*. [Those properties
remained her properties during their
marriage, since she was affected by any
fluctuation in their value].
   The mishnah refers to them as the father's
heirs, to be consistent with the wording of
the mishnah in *Yevamos* (4:3) and *Kesubos*
(8:6) which are similar to this one *(Tos. Yom
Tov)*. Other versions read *the wife's heirs
(Rif)*.

10.

נָפַל הַבַּיִת עָלָיו וְעַל אִמּוֹ, — *[If] a house
collapsed upon a man* [lit. *him*] *and his
mother,*
   The collapse killed him and his
widowed mother[1] but it is unknown
who died first. The sons's relatives —
e.g., his brothers from his father's side,
who are not of this mother *(Rashbam)* —
claim that the mother died first.
Accordingly, the son inherited her
possessions before his death, and these

possessions now fall to them. The
relatives of the mother, however — e.g.,
her brothers, who are not heirs of her
son [since a mother does not inherit her
son] (ibid.) — claim that the son died
first; thus, the mother's legacy never
entered his possession, and they now
inherit these possessions *(Rav)*.[2]
   The mishnah is discussing a situation in
which the woman had no other son *(Rav)*. If
she had, that son would inherit the entire

1. If her husband were still alive, he would inherit his wife, even if she predeceased her son;
thus, the son's heirs would have no claim whatsoever.
2. The possessions do not pass through the dead son's estate to *his* heirs, even though he was
his mother's closest relative, because a man does not inherit his mother after his death to pass
the inheritance on to his relatives *(Gem.* 159b; see comm. to 8:1, s.v. האשה את בניה).

שֶׁיַּחֲלֹקוּ. אָמַר רַבִּי עֲקִיבָא: מוֹדֶה אֲנִי בָּזֶה
שֶׁהַנְּכָסִים בְּחֶזְקָתָן. אָמַר לוֹ בֶּן עַזַּאי: עַל הַחֲלוּקִין
אָנוּ מִצְטַעֲרִין, אֶלָּא שֶׁבָּאתָ לַחֲלֹק עָלֵינוּ אֶת
הַשָּׁוִין?

[א] **גֵּט** פָּשׁוּט עֵדָיו מִתּוֹכוֹ; וּמְקֻשָּׁר עֵדָיו
מֵאֲחוֹרָיו.

יד אברהם

estate, since he is a definite heir of his mother, while any other claimant is at best only a possible heir. This is because the remaining son inherits at least a portion of his mother's estate regardless of who died first: If the son died first in the collapse and then the mother, the remaining son is the sole heir of his mother's estate. However, even if the mother died first, the remaining son at least shared her inheritance with his brother who died in the collapse. Since it is unclear who died first, the remaining son would inherit everything based on a principle in Torah law that one whose status is in question must defer to one whose status is certain (*Rashbam;* see *Yevamos* 38a).

Others contend that this rule would apply only if the mother's second son had the same father as the son who died in the collapse. In such a case, he has a definite claim on the entire inheritance, since he is an heir of both that son [if he had no children] and his mother, while any paternal brothers [i.e., brothers only through the father but by different mothers] can only inherit the dead son's portion of his mother's legacy if she died before him. Even then they must share that portion with her surviving son who is also a brother. Their questionable position is thus inferior to that of the full brother of the deceased [i.e., one who shares the same father and mother]. However, if the mother's second son does not have the same father as the dead son and thus is an heir only of the mother, but not of the dead son himself, his definite claim to half of his mother's possessions would not grant him precedence concerning the half which may have been inherited by the dead son (*Tos.*).

אֵלוּ וָאֵלוּ מוֹדִים שֶׁיַּחֲלֹקוּ. — *all* [lit. *these and these*] *agree that they divide.*

Since the claims on both sides are based on equal possibilities of inheritance, both Beis Shammai and Beis Hillel

agree that the respective heirs divide the mother's possessions equally (*Rav*). This is not similar to the case (mishnah 8) in which the house collapsed killing a man and his father, since, in that situation, one claim is based on inheritance while the other side claims only the right to collect a debt from the estate (*Rashbam*). Neither is it similar to the case of the previous mishnah in which a man and his wife died in a simple accident. There the husband was considered to be in possession of some of the properties in question and the wife in possession of others. Thus Beis Hillel assign the properties to whomever had control of them previously. In this instance, however, everything was in the possession of the woman, and all claims are based on the possibility of inheritance from her [i.e., the claim of her relatives that they inherit directly from her and the claim of the son's relatives that they inherit from her through the dead son] (*Rav*).

Although, in the previous mishnah, the husband's relatives also claim that the wife died first and the husband inherited her properties, thereby passing it along to them, the inheritance of a wife by her husband is a Rabbinic statute according to the prevailing opinion and cannot grant his heirs parity with those of the woman (*Tos. Yom Tov;* see comm. to 8:1, s.v. והאיש את אשתו).

Others explain that a son is expected to inherit his mother rather than vice versa; therefore the Rabbis enacted that in the event that they both die, his position — and thus that of his heirs — is considered equal to that of his mother in regard to her belongings. Concerning a man and his wife, however, there is no reason to assume that he will survive her rather than she him; therefore,

mother, all agree that they divide. Said R' Akiva: I agree in this [case] that the possessions retain their status. Said Ben Azzai to him: On the disputed issues we are pained, and you come to dispute the unanimous?

1. **A**n open document [has] its witnesses on the inside; and a bound [document has] its

his position in regard to her possessions is inferior to hers (*Tos.* 158a, s.v. בית הלל).

אָמַר רַבִּי עֲקִיבָא: מוֹדֶה אֲנִי בָזֶה — *Said R' Akiva: I agree in this [case]*

R' Akiva says that in this mishnah's case as well, it is only Beis Shammai who say that the respective heirs divide the disputed property. Beis Hillel, however, argue and rule that the properties retain their status.

R' Akiva uses the expression 'I agree' only to parallel that same expression used by the mishnah's first *Tanna* [i.e., *all agree*] (*Rashbam*).

שֶׁהַנְּכָסִים בְּחֶזְקָתָן. — *that the possessions retain their status.*

I.e., they fall to the heirs of the mother and thereby remain within the tribe to which they had hitherto belonged (*Rav* from *Gem.* 158b). Even her *kesubah* is included in this, since

once she collected it from her husband it was incorporated into the assets of the tribe of her father before the house collapsed on her (*Rashbam*).

אָמַר לוֹ בֶּן עַזַּאי: עַל הַחֲלוּקִין אָנוּ מִצְטַעֲרִין, אֶלָּא שֶׁבָּאתָ לַחֲלוֹק עָלֵינוּ אֶת הַשָּׁוִין — *Said Ben Azzai to him: On the disputed issues we are pained, and you come to dispute the unanimous?*

We are sufficiently pained by those issues which Beis Shammai and Beis Hillel disputed explicitly; and you come to add that they dispute yet another issue in which the first *Tanna* maintains that they are in accord (*Rav*).

Nevertheless, the halachah is in accordance with the opinion of R' Akiva. Thus, the mother's estate passes completely to the mother's heirs rather than to the son's (*Rambam, Nachalos* 5:6; *Choshen Mishpat* 280:10).

Chapter Ten

1.

Having discussed legal documents in the previous chapter (mishnah 6), the mishnah concludes this tractate with a general discussion of the rules governing legal documents (*Tos.* 160a, s.v. גט פשוט).

גֵּט פָּשׁוּט — *An open document*

I.e., an ordinary legal document, in contrast to one which is folded and sewn, as will be discussed below (*Rav*).

The term *get* [although usually used in reference to divorce documents in particular] applies to all legal documents (*Rav*).

עֵדָיו מִתּוֹכוֹ; — [has] *its witnesses on the inside;*

After all of the pertinent information has been written, the witnesses sign their names under the text (*Meiri*).

וּמְקֻשָּׁר — *and a bound [document]*

A bound document is a normal legal document prepared in a different manner. The scribe writes one or two lines, and leaves the next line blank. The written lines are then folded over on the blank one and sewn down over it (*Rav,*

מֵאֲחוֹרָיו. פָּשׁוּט שֶׁכָּתְבוּ עֵדָיו מֵאֲחוֹרָיו, וּמְקֻשָּׁר
שֶׁכָּתְבוּ עֵדָיו מִתּוֹכוֹ, שְׁנֵיהֶם פְּסוּלִים. רַבִּי חֲנִינָא
בֶּן גַּמְלִיאֵל אוֹמֵר: מְקֻשָּׁר שֶׁכָּתְבוּ עֵדָיו מִתּוֹכוֹ
כָּשֵׁר, מִפְּנֵי שֶׁיָּכוֹל לַעֲשׂוֹתוֹ פָשׁוּט. רַבָּן שִׁמְעוֹן בֶּן

יד אברהם

Rashbam).

Others contend that even on a bound document, no lines were left blank. The document was written in the same manner as a regular one, with one line following the other, but was then folded and signed in the manner described *(Tos.; Ran; Rosh,* cited by *Shita Mekubetzes).*

All documents consist of two parts: the טוֹפֶס, *standard text* for that type of document (e.g., in the case of a divorce, the fact that a marriage is being dissolved and that the woman is henceforth free to remarry), and the תּוֹרֶף, the part containing the information specific to this particular document (e.g., the names, date, place etc.). Only the תּוֹרֶף was bound in the above manner *(Rashbam).*

This method of writing documents was instituted by the Rabbis for *gittin* (divorce documents) to be used where the husband was a *Kohen.* This was to remedy a situation in which a short-tempered *Kohen* might, in a fit of anger, divorce his wife and subsequently regret it. Since a *Kohen* is prohibited to marry a divorcee (Lev. 21:7), once he divorced her he could never undo his rash deed. Therefore, to make the divorce process of a *Kohen* more cumbersome so that he would have time to regain his composure and retract his decision, the Rabbis instituted this type of *get,* which takes longer to prepare, for *Kohanim.* Having enacted this process for *gittin,* they extended the ordinance to apply to other documents as well, should the parties choose to use it *(Rav from Gem.* 160b).

עֵדָיו מֵאֲחוֹרָיו — *[has] its witnesses on the*

outside.

[The outside of each fold requires the signature of a witness,[1] with a different witness on each fold.]

Theoretically, since the witnesses did not sign on the bottom as in a regular document, there was nothing to clearly mark the end of the agreed upon wording. This would enable an un-scrupulous person to add his own conditions to the document. Conse-quently, all such documents were required to conclude with the words שָׁרִיר וְקַיָּם, *firm and established,* to indicate the end of the agreed upon wording. Any subsequent statements were invalid *(Gem.* 160b).

There is another opinion in the *Gemara* (ibid.), that the witnesses signed on the back of the document across its length, with their names beginning opposite the point where the text of the document ended, thus effectively marking the last legitimate line in the document.

פָּשׁוּט שֶׁכָּתְבוּ עֵדָיו מֵאֲחוֹרָיו, וּמְקֻשָּׁר שֶׁכָּתְבוּ עֵדָיו מִתּוֹכוֹ, שְׁנֵיהֶם פְּסוּלִים. — *An open one whose witnesses wrote on the outside, and a bound one whose witnesses wrote on the inside, are both invalid.*

If the proper procedure for these documents was reversed, with the simple open document being signed on the outside and the bound one on the inside, the documents are invalid because they were not drawn up in accordance with Rabbinic law *(Rav; Rashbam).* [As legal instruments, all documents have to be framed according to the prescribed form.]

Others explain the invalidity of such documents to be based on that which

1. The witnesses do not sign as soon as the individual folds are sewn, for then they would be attesting to an unfinished document. First, the entire document must be written and read by all witnesses, and then folded, sewn and signed in the prescribed manner.

witnesses on the outside. An open one whose witnesses wrote on the outside, and a bound one whose witnesses wrote on the inside, are both invalid. R' Chanina ben Gamliel says: A bound one whose witnesses wrote on the inside is valid, because he can make it an open one. Rabban Shimon ben Gamliel

YAD AVRAHAM

the *Gemara* (164b) says that bound documents were dated differently than open ones. Open documents were dated by the year of the reign of the present monarch; in bound documents an extra year was added — e.g., in the first year of his reign it was dated the second — and, thus, the actual date of the *get* was one year prior to the date stated. This was done to add to the differences between a bound document and an open one, and thereby increase the difficulty encountered in drawing up one of the former (*Rashbam* ad loc.).

Thus, if the witnesses signed one in the manner reserved for the other, it could be presented as the wrong type of document, and its date would be misleading; therefore, the Rabbis voided it (*Tos.; Ramah; Meiri;* see below).

There is another view, that the mishnah is discussing a case in which the document was signed in two places — once correctly and once in the manner of the other type of document. Since we assume that the one for whom the document is being drawn up surely specified one particular type of document in his instructions to the witnesses, one of the sets of signatures was obviously made on the witnesses' own initiative, and any document drawn up contrary to the instructions of the owner is invalid (*Nimmukei Yosef;* cf. *Ritva*).

רַבִּי חֲנִינָא בֶּן גַּמְלִיאֵל אוֹמֵר: מְקֻשָּׁר שֶׁכָּתְבוּ עֵדָיו מִתּוֹכוֹ כָּשֵׁר, מִפְּנֵי שֶׁיָּכוֹל לַעֲשׂוֹתוֹ פָשׁוּט. — *R' Chanina ben Gamliel says: A bound one whose witnesses wrote on the inside is valid, because he can make it an open one.*

If he were to tear out the stitches and open the document, it would be an open document with proper testimony;

therefore, in R' Chanina ben Gamliel's view, it is valid even if it was not opened (*Rav*).

Although there are blank lines on the document (see above), that does not affect its validity (*Rashi* ·to *Kiddushin* 49a, s.v. שיכבול לעשותו פשוט). *Tos.* there point out that each blank line would have a witness signing on it [so that it is clear that these lines were left blank in the original].

However, in the reverse case, that of an open document which is signed on the outside, it is invalid because it cannot be converted into a bound document. Since a bound document must be dated one year ahead (see above) of its actual date, if an open document were made into a bound one its valid date would be assumed to be one year earlier than stated. Thus, its effectiveness would be assumed to begin earlier than is actually the case, thereby rendering it a pre-dated document, which is invalid [*Sheviis* 10:5] (*Meiri*). In the case of a bound document converted to an open one, the date of its effectiveness would be post-dated, which is valid (*Tos., Gittin* 17a, s.v. ריש לקיש).

A document, in addition to serving as proof of the debt, is also the vehicle for securing a lien on any real estate owned by the debtor at the time of the loan. Once a lien takes effect, it remains in effect even if the property is sold. As a result, if the debtor should default on his debt and own no assets, the creditor may exercise his lien and attach the sold property as payment for the debt. The buyer's only recourse is to sue the seller for a refund (see below, 10:8). By pre-dating the document, the creditor is wrongly given the power to exercise a lien on real estate sold before the debt was incurred, which, in truth, never became subject to the lien.

גַּמְלִיאֵל אוֹמֵר: הַכֹּל כְּמִנְהַג הַמְּדִינָה.

[ב] גֵּט פָּשׁוּט עֵדָיו בִּשְׁנַיִם, וּמְקֻשָּׁר, בִּשְׁלֹשָׁה. פָּשׁוּט שֶׁכָּתוּב בּוֹ עֵד אֶחָד, וּמְקֻשָּׁר שֶׁכָּתוּב בּוֹ שְׁנֵי עֵדִים, שְׁנֵיהֶם פְּסוּלִין.

יד אברהם

The first *Tanna*, however, contends that even a bound document which is changed to an open one is void because of the incorrect date, for the following reason: Normally, when a borrower repays a debt the lender is obligated to return the loan document to him so he can destroy it. This is to protect the borrower from being dunned a second time for the money. If the lender claims to have lost the document, however, there is no alternative but for the lender to give the borrower a receipt for his payment. Generally, this suffices to protect the borrower. However, if the debt was recorded in a bound document and the lender should falsely claim that the document was lost and give the borrower a receipt for his payment dated with the date that he actually received the money, he could then change his bound document to an open one, thus rendering its date effective one year later than the true date of the loan. With this newly opened document he could sue for payment a second time, claiming that a second loan took place after the payment of the first one (the one recorded in the receipt with an earlier date). Therefore, such a document is void (*Tos.* from *Gem.* 164b).[1]

R' Chanina ben Gamliel, however, contends that one cannot offer a receipt in lieu of the loan document; and if the lender cannot produce the loan document, the borrower is not obligated to pay. Therefore, the above situation could never materialize (*Gem.* ibid.).

Rambam (*Hil. Geirushin* 1:25) maintains that even though post-dated documents are generally valid, a post-dated divorce document is invalid. Accordingly, he must explain R'

Chanina ben Gamliel to be discussing only other legal documents, but not divorce documents (*Kesef Mishneh* ad loc.).

Even R' Chanina validates such a document only if the one who had it drawn up did not specify whether he desired an open document or a bound one. However, if he told the scribe to write a bound document and the latter did so, but had the witnesses sign on the inside, the document would be invalid, because he cannot make it open, since if he converts it to an open document he is violating the terms of his assignment (*Yad Ramah*).

רַבָּן שִׁמְעוֹן בֶּן גַּמְלִיאֵל אוֹמֵר: הַכֹּל כְּמִנְהַג הַמְּדִינָה. — *Rabban Shimon ben Gamliel says: All in accord with the custom of the land.*

As the *Gemara* explains this, Rabban Shimon ben Gamliel's point refers to a locale where the prevailing custom was to use either type of document, but in this instance the scribe was instructed to write one particular kind. Rabban Shimon ben Gamliel maintains, as a general rule, that wherever there are two ways of doing something, both being exactly equal, and one gives instructions that it be done in one of those ways (but does not explicitly exclude the other way), we assume that he does not really care which way it is done, since people in his area do it both ways. Thus, even if it was done the other way it is also valid. Therefore, in our case, we may assume that he does not really care whether an open or bound document is utilized, and

---

1. According to *Rav* and *Rashbam*, who explain the reasoning of the first *Tanna* to be simply because the document is not in accordance with the Rabbinic enactment, the above is mentioned in the *Gemara* only to question the reasoning of R' Chanina ben Gamliel.

says: All in accord with the custom of the land.

2. **A**n open document requires two witnesses, and a bound one, three. An open one in which one witness is signed, and a bound one in which two witnesses are signed, are both invalid.

the document is valid even if it was drawn up in the opposite manner from the one he ordered. The Sages, however, contend that his instructions are binding, and any change by the scribe invalidates the document (Rav from

Gem. 165a). The halachah is in accordance with the opinion of the Sages (Rav).

In these times, the custom is not to use bound documents (Nimmukei Yosef; Rama, Choshen Mishpat 42:1).

2.

גֵּט פָּשׁוּט עֵדָיו בִּשְׁנַיִם, — An open document requires two witnesses,

I.e., only two witnesses are required to be signed on it (Rashbam).[1]

וּמְקֻשָּׁר, בִּשְׁלֹשָׁה. — and a bound one, three.

At least three witnesses must be signed on a bound document, one on each of the three folds which such a document is minimally required to have (Rashbam). If there are more than three folds more witnesses must be added, one for each fold (Gittin 81b).

However, only two of the witnesses have to be valid witnesses; all the other witnesses signed on a bound document can even be people who are generally invalidated from serving as witnesses (Gittin 81b), since the extra witnesses are not really required to validate the document (see Rashi ad loc.; Yad Avraham comm. to Gittin 8:9, s.v. כנסה בגט קרח and 8:10, s.v. הכל משלימין עליו).

פָּשׁוּט שֶׁכָּתוּב בּוֹ עֵד אֶחָד, וּמְקֻשָּׁר שֶׁכָּתוּב בּוֹ שְׁנֵי עֵדִים, שְׁנֵיהֶם פְּסוּלִין. — An open one in which one witness is signed [lit. written], and a bound one in which two witnesses are signed [lit. written], are both invalid.

I.e., just as a regular document which is signed by only one witness is void by Torah law, so too is a bound document which is signed by two witnesses (Rav from Gem. 165b).[2]

Although a bound document obviously requires three witnesses only by virtue of Rabbinic law, if it has only two witnesses it is treated as if it were Biblically invalid. If it is used for a divorce, the divorce is void; if it is used for a loan, there is no lien on the borrower's property [as is normally the case for a loan recorded in a document] (Rashbam). In addition, in the case of a divorce document, any child born of a subsequent marriage is illegitimate [in the absence of another valid divorce] (Tos. ad loc.).

1. This is the prescribed form of drawing up a legal document. However, even a document without the signature of any witness is valid if it was handed over to the party concerned in the presence of two witnesses (Yad Ramah; see Gittin 9:4 and Yad Avraham Comm. there).

2. This interpretation is offered by the Gemara because the statement of the mishnah that a document with only one witness is not valid is so obvious as to be superfluous.

כָּתַב בּוֹ ,,זוּזִין מְאָה, דְּאִנּוּן סִלְעִין עֶשְׂרִין,'' אֵין
לוֹ אֶלָּא עֶשְׂרִין. ,,זוּזִין מְאָה, דְּאִנּוּן תְּלָתִין סִלְעִין,''
אֵין לוֹ אֶלָּא מָנֶה. ,,כְּסַף זוּזִין דְּאִנּוּן ...'' וְנִמְחַק,
אֵין פָּחוֹת מִשְׁתַּיִם. ,,כְּסַף סִלְעִין דְּאִנּוּן ...''
וְנִמְחַק, אֵין פָּחוֹת מִשְׁנָיִם. ,,דַּרְכּוֹנוֹת דְּאִנּוּן ...''
וְנִמְחַק, אֵין פָּחוֹת מִשְׁתַּיִם. כָּתוּב בּוֹ מִלְמַעְלָה
מָנֶה, וּמִלְמַטָּה מָאתַיִם, מִלְמַעְלָה מָאתַיִם
וּמִלְמַטָּה מָנֶה — הַכֹּל הוֹלֵךְ אַחַר הַתַּחְתּוֹן. אִם

יד אברהם

,,זוּזִין מְאָה,'' בּוֹ כָּתַב — [If] he wrote in it,
'one hundred zuzin,

If the document stated that one
person lent another one hundred zuzin
(the plural of zuz) (Tif. Yis.).

עֶשְׂרִין סִלְעִין דְּאִנּוּן — which are twenty
selas,'

[This was the wording of the
document.] There are four zuzin to a
sela; thus one hundred zuzin are
actually the equivalent of twenty-five
selas (Rav). Since the document states
two contradictory sums, we are faced
with the question of deciding how much
the actual loan was and which sum was
recorded in error.

עֶשְׂרִין אֶלָּא לוֹ אֵין — he receives only
twenty [selas].

It is possible to interpret this
document in such a manner that both
statements are true by assuming that he
lent him one hundred inferior zuz coins,
which are worth only twenty selas
(Rav). Since that is the smallest amount
which he surely owes, we use the rule
that the burden of proof rests with the
one seeking to exact money (see above,
preface to 3:1), and that is all he pays.
If, however, the borrower had already
paid the greater amount and now wants
to recover the difference, the burden of
proof rests with the borrower and the
lender is not obligated to return the
money (Rashbam).

,,זוּזִין מְאָה, דְּאִנּוּן תְּלָתִין סִלְעִין,'' אֵין לוֹ אֶלָּא
מָנֶה. — [If he wrote,] 'one hundred zuzin

which are thirty selas,' he receives only
a maneh.

One hundred zuzin come to twenty-
five standard selas, but, employing the
same rationale as above, we interpret the
document to mean one hundred zuzin
which are the equivalent of thirty
inferior selas, or twenty-five regular
selas (Rav). [A maneh is one hundred
zuzin.]

,,כְּסַף זוּזִין דְּאִנּוּן ...'' וְנִמְחַק, — [If it stated,]
'silver zuzin which are ...' and [the rest]
was erased,

I.e., the number of zuzin was erased
(Rav).

מִשְׁתַּיִם פָּחוֹת אֵין. — it is not less than two
[zuzin].

[Although the amount has been
erased, he can collect two zuzin with
this document, since the use of the
plural form — zuzin — is evidence that
at least that amount is involved.] He
cannot collect more than two based on
this document, since he has no evidence
to support such a claim (Nimmukei
Yosef).

This mishnah thus teaches that if an
erasure is found in a document, we assume
the missing information to be within the
context of the previous words, and do not
entertain the possibility that some other
information — which could invalidate the
entire document — was written and erased
(Yad Ramah).

,,כְּסַף סִלְעִין דְּאִנּוּן ...'' וְנִמְחַק, אֵין פָּחוֹת
מִשְׁנָיִם. — 'Silver selas which are ...' and
[the rest] was erased, it is not less than

10
2

[If] he wrote in it, 'one hundred *zuzin*, which are twenty *selas*,' he receives only twenty [*selas*]. [If he wrote,] 'one hundred *zuzin* which are thirty *selas*,' he receives only a *maneh*. [If it stated,] 'silver *zuzin* which are ...' and [the rest] was erased, it is not less than two [*zuzin*].' Silver *selas* which are ...' and [the rest] was erased, it is not less than two [*selas*]. 'Darkons which are ...' and [the rest] was erased, it is not less than two [*darkons*]. [If] above was written, one hundred [*zuzin*], and below, two hundred [*zuzin*], [or] above two hundred and below one hundred — everything follows the bottom [state-

YAD AVRAHAM

two [*selas*].

Although a *sela* is a larger coin than a *zuz*, and the document could conceivably have stated *silver selas which are seven zuzin*, referring to inferior *selas* (see above), we do not concern ourselves with this possibility, but rather take for granted that it refers to regular *selas* (*Tif. Yis.*). We only consider such a possibility in a case such as the previous one, in which the wording of the document contradicts itself unless we assume such an explanation (*Ritva, Rashba* cited by *Meleches Shlomo*).

דַּרְכּוֹנוֹת,, — *'Darkons*

A *darkon* equaled two *selas* (*Rambam Comm.* to *Shekalim* 2:1; see *Yad Avraham* comm. ibid.).

דְּאָנוּן ... "וְנִמְחַק, אֵין פָּחוֹת מִשְׁתַּיִם. — *which are ...' and* [*the rest*] *was erased, it is not less than two* [*darkons*].

Darkons were gold coins, which were not readily available to be given in payment. Therefore, one might assume that the document had mentioned them only to specify that inferior *darkons* were involved (*Tif. Yis.*).

כָּתוּב בּוֹ מִלְמַעְלָה מָנֶה, — [*If*] *above was written, one hundred* [*zuzin*],

[I.e., the main text of the document stated that a *maneh* — one hundred *zuzin* — was owed.]

וּמִלְמַטָּה מָאתַיִם, — *and below, two hundred* [*zuzin*],

[All the primary information in a document is written twice. First it is stated in detail, and towards the end of the document (usually when describing the property lien) it is given again in summation.]

When the document repeated the amount of the loan (*Rav*), in describing the extent of the property lien effected by the transaction (*Meiri*), the amount of the loan was given as two hundred *zuzin*.

מִלְמַעְלָה מָאתַיִם וּמִלְמַטָּה מָנֶה — הַכֹּל הוֹלֵךְ אַחַר הַתַּחְתּוֹן. — [*or*] *above two hundred and below one hundred — everything follows the bottom* [*statement*].

The sum mentioned at the end is the one accepted by the court, and the assumption is made that it represents a retraction of the original figure. (*Nimmukei Yosef*).

We interpret the second statement to be clarifying the first (as in the previous case of the mishnah) only when the two are stated together in one clause, so that it is clear that the second is meant to clarify the first. In this case, though, they are two entirely separate statements, recorded in two different parts of the document. Thus, the more likely explanation here is that there was a change of heart (*Yad Ramah; Meiri*).

כֵּן, לָמָּה כּוֹתְבִין אֶת הָעֶלְיוֹן? שֶׁאִם תִּמָּחֵק אוֹת
אַחַת מִן הַתַּחְתּוֹן, יִלָּמֵד מִן הָעֶלְיוֹן.

[ג] **כּוֹתְבִין** גֵּט לְאִישׁ אַף עַל פִּי שֶׁאֵין אִשְׁתּוֹ
עִמּוֹ, וְהַשּׁוֹבֵר לְאִשָּׁה, אַף עַל פִּי
שֶׁאֵין בַּעֲלָהּ עִמָּהּ; וּבִלְבַד שֶׁיְּהֵא מַכִּירָן; וְהַבַּעַל

יד אברהם

Additionally, there is no reasonable way to reconcile the contradiction between one hundred and two hundred. Therefore, we are forced to assume that there was a change (Nimmukei Yosef).

However, if the second amount was written on the last line of the document it is ignored (Rav) because of the rule that one cannot derive any conclusions from the bottom line of a document. This is because whatever is recorded in the last line is inherently suspect, since the witnesses may have inadvertently left a space between the end of the text and their signature, which was later filled in by the holder of the document (Tos. Yom Tov). However, this applies only when that which is written on the bottom line favors the creditor, who had been holding the document, since we must then consider the possibility of tampering. If it favors the debtor, it is accepted as valid (Ritva; Nimmukei Yosef). If the document had the words שָׁרִיר וְקַיָם, firm and established, to indicate its ending, then it is all valid, even the last line (see above).

אִם כֵּן, לָמָּה כּוֹתְבִין אֶת הָעֶלְיוֹן? — If so, why is the top written?

Since everything is repeated at the end of the document, when the specifics of the property lien are stated (Rashbam), and we rely entirely on that which is stated in that bottom statement (Nimmukei Yosef), what purpose does the first statement of the document serve?

שֶׁאִם תִּמָּחֵק אוֹת אַחַת מִן הַתַּחְתּוֹן, יִלָּמֵד מִן הָעֶלְיוֹן. — So that if one letter from the bottom should be erased, it will be derived from the top.

For example, if a man named Chanani borrowed money, and the bottom line of the document identified Chanan as the debtor, he would not be able to avoid payment by claiming he was not the borrower, because we would rely on what was written on the top line — Chanani — to assume that the letter yud was erased from his name at the bottom (Nimmukei Yosef from Gem. 166b).

However, only one letter can be filled in through this process, not more (Gem. ibid.).

3.

Generally, for documents to be legally valid they must be written with the knowledge and consent of the one to whose detriment they are. For example, a loan document can only be written with the authorization of the borrower. [The lender, of course, may refuse to lend him money without receiving such a document. Nevertheless, the document may only be issued with the borrower's consent.] One exception to this is the get, bill of divorce, for the reason to be explained below. This mishnah discusses different types of documents with regard to who must authorize their writing.

כּוֹתְבִין גֵּט לְאִישׁ אַף עַל פִּי שֶׁאֵין אִשְׁתּוֹ עִמּוֹ, — We may write a get for a man even though his wife is not with him,

The scribe may draw up a divorce document for the husband, and

witnesses may validate it by signing it, without the wife being present. This renders the get a valid instrument of divorce which may then be used by the husband to divorce his wife at anytime.

ment]. If so, why is the top written? So that if one letter from the bottom should be erased, it will be derived from the top.

3. We may write a *get* for a man even though his wife is not with him, and a receipt for a woman, even though her husband is not with her; provided that we recognize them; and the husband

YAD AVRAHAM

The wife's consent is not required for the formulation of this document since (according to strict Torah law) a husband has the right to divorce his wife even against her will[1] (*Rav*).

When a woman is married, her husband receives any benefits derived from her possessions (*Kesubos* 4:4). If he sells any of these benefits — such as the produce of her fields — the sale is valid for as long as the marriage lasts. Once the marriage dissolves, the *melog* (usufruct) property (see above, 9:8) reverts to her and any earnings taken from that property subsequent to the divorce by the husband or the person to whom he leased the property must be repaid to her. Accordingly, a *get* written in her absence and not actually used to divorce her until sometime later might allow her to collect that produce unlawfully, since the date on the *get* will be earlier than her actual divorce.

However, the rule is that when a woman utilizes her *get* to collect, she is required to bring proof of the actual date of her divorce. Thus, there is no danger that the *get* will be used improperly to collect produce sold during the marriage (*Nimmukei Yosef; Meiri;* see *Bava Metziah* 19a).

Furthermore, it is unlikely that a husband will have a *get* written for him and then delay the divorce, thus causing the *get* to be outdated. It is the nature of a person to put off for as long as possible becoming involved in a crisis. Thus, a man would not have a *get* drawn up unless he intended to use it immediately (*Tos.;* see *Gittin* 18a).

and a receipt for a woman, even though her husband is not with her;

A woman can order the writing of a receipt for her *kesubah* in the absence of her husband, since it can be used only to his benefit, and it is permissible to effect one's benefit [in his absence] without his being aware of it (*Rav*).

Here too, however, there is room for concern that she may sell the rights to her *kesubah* after the receipt is written and dated, but before she actually collects. For example, if the receipt for the *kesubah* payment was written (but not yet collected) on the first of Nissan, and she then sold the rights to her *kesubah* on the fifteenth of that month, when the buyer later comes to collect the *kesubah,* the husband would be able to produce this receipt dated the first of the month to prove that he already paid before the rights were sold, thus voiding the sale. The buyer would then have to go through the bother of taking the wife (the seller) to court to recover his loss.

The reason we are not concerned about this possible abuse is because even after selling the rights to the *kesubah,* she would still be able to waive the debt, thereby causing the buyer to lose the debt he bought.[2] He would then have to take her to court to retrieve the money he paid. Since she could cause the buyer the loss either way, there is no point in preventing the possibility of her doing so in this manner (*Bava Metzia* 20a; *Tos. Yom Tov, Bava Metzia* 1:7).

וְהַשּׁוֹבָר לְאִשָּׁה, אַף עַל פִּי שֶׁאֵין בַּעֲלָהּ עִמָּהּ; — ‏

וּבִלְבַד שֶׁיְּהֵא מַכִּירָן; — *provided that we*

---

1. This is the Biblical law as well as the applicable law throughout Biblical Mishnaic and Talmudic times. However, in the eleventh century, *Rabbeinu Gershon Meor HaGolah* instituted a ban on a man divorcing his wife against her will (*Rama, Even HaEzer* 119:5).

2. This is true anytime a lender sells his loan to another. He nevertheless retains the right to forgive the debt at any time. He would, however, have to refund the money to the buyer.

נוֹתֵן שָׂכָר.

כּוֹתְבִין שְׁטָר לַלֹּוֶה אַף עַל פִּי שֶׁאֵין מַלְוֶה עִמּוֹ,
וְאֵין כּוֹתְבִין לַמַּלְוֶה עַד שֶׁיְּהֵא לֹוֶה עִמּוֹ; וְהַלֹּוֶה
נוֹתֵן שָׂכָר.

יד אברהם

recognize them;

Though a *get* may be written without the wife's presence, and a *kesubah* receipt without the husband's, the scribe and the witnesses must at least recognize the identity of the absent party before they are permitted to draw up the divorce or receipt document for them. This is necessary to prevent a man from entering into a conspiracy with the wife of another man who happened to have the same name as he does to help her obtain a fraudulent divorce. This he could do by ordering a *get* written with her name in it [since only he must appear before the scribe and his name coincides with that of this other woman's husband], and then giving her the *get*. She would then be able to use this fraudulent *get* as proof of her divorce, though *her* husband never in fact divorced her. Similarly, in the case of the receipt, if only the wife is known to the scribe and not the husband, she might have a receipt written with some other man's name in it, give it to him, and thereby unlawfully free him from paying the *kesubah* to his wife (*Rav* from *Gem*. 167b).

וְהַבַּעַל נוֹתֵן שָׂכָר. — *and the husband pays the fee.*

He pays the fee for the *get*, because the Torah specifies (*Deut*. 24:1), *and he shall write ... and he shall give* [the *get*]..., indicating that the husband is responsible for the writing of the *get* (*Gem*. 168a). He also pays for the receipt, because he is the one who benefits from it (*Rashbam*). However, in a place where the custom is to write a *kesubah* and, when the husband pays, for the wife to simply return the *kesubah* as proof of payment rather than give a receipt, were she to lose the

kesubah and therefore be required to issue a receipt, she must bear its cost (*Nimmukei Yosef*).

It later became customary for the wife to pay for the *get*, so that she should not be kept waiting for her divorce due to the husband's reluctance to bear the cost (*Gem*. loc. cit.). This was not considered a violation of the Scriptural dictate that he have it written, since it was still drawn up at his behest (*Nimmukei Yosef*, ad loc.). Others contend that in order to comply with the Scriptural dictate, the document must actually be his. Therefore, when the woman pays the scribe, she must stipulate that in consideration of the money the scribe transfer the materials from which the *get* will be written to the husband's ownership, so that it should be his *get* (*Rashba*, cited by *Meleches Shlomo*, s.v. והלוקח נותן את השכר).

— כּוֹתְבִין שְׁטָר לַלֹּוֶה אַף עַל פִּי שֶׁאֵין מַלְוֶה עִמּוֹ,
We may write a document for a borrower even though the lender is not with him,

A man can order the writing and signing of a document obligating him to repay a loan even in the absence of the lender named in the document, and even though the witnesses signing did not see the loan take place. Since the borrower is the only one who stands to lose from this document, only his consent is needed to draw it up (*Yad Ramah*).

However, this applies only if the borrower performed an act of acquisition subjecting his possessions to a lien for that debt from the moment the bond is signed. Otherwise, the lien would not take effect until the loan is actually made, but an unscrupulous lender could use this document to collect unlawfully from possessions which the borrower sold after the document was drawn up but before the debt was incurred (ibid., *Nimmukei Yosef*, *Meiri* from *Bava Metzia* 13a). [As explained below

pays the fee.

We may write a document for a borrower even though the lender is not with him, but we do not write for a lender unless the borrower is with him; and the borrower pays the fee.

YAD AVRAHAM

(preface to mishnah 8), once a lien takes effect on a borrower's property, it remains in effect even after the property is sold.]

If the designated lender protests the writing of the document because he is concerned that people will hear about it and think he is wealthy, he may prevent it from being written (Rama, Choshen Mishpat 39:12).

We are not, however, concerned that the loan may never be made but that the lender will nevertheless use the document to collect the money illegally, because that is a risk that the debtor knowingly accepted when he had the document drawn up.

Others contend that the nature of such a document is, that it obligates the debtor to pay regardless of whether a loan is made. Thus, the creditor would be collecting legitimately (Ritva; Rashi to Bava Metzia loc. cit.).

In this case, too, the witnesses may not sign unless they recognize the borrower and know the purported lender. Otherwise, someone could have a document drawn up obligating another person to pay a debt (Rambam, Hil. Malveh 24:3).

Maggid Mishnah questions why they need recognize the lender, when the document is solely to the detriment of the borrower, and he is the one commissioning it (see Derisha to Choshen Mishpat 49:2).

וְאֵין כּוֹתְבִין לְמַלְוֶה עַד שֶׁיְהֵא לֹוֶה עִמּוֹ; — but we do not write for a lender unless the borrower is with him;

[The lender's word that a loan took place cannot serve as the basis for issuing a loan document.] Although this ruling is obvious, the mishnah includes it to maintain a parallel with the previous case of a divorce (Rashba).

Others explain that the mishnah means to include by this even a situation in which the debtor performed an act of acquisition before witnesses, obligating himself to pay this debt from that time on, even though no loan yet took place. The creditor subsequently requested that the witnesses draw up a document to that effect. Since the debtor is the one who is detrimentally affected by this document, he is the only one who can authorize its writing (Ramban; Ritva).

Alternatively, the mishnah may refer to a situation in which the creditor requested that the document be drawn up in advance of the loan and held in readiness by the witnesses until the loan actually takes place (thus avoiding any danger that it will be used unlawfully). Nevertheless, they may not comply with his wishes, since the document is false when written (Yad Ramah; Maggid Mishneh loc. cit. 23:5).

וְהַלֹוֶה נוֹתֵן שָׂכָר. — and the borrower pays the fee.

This would appear to be obvious, since the loan is made for the benefit of the borrower. However, the mishnah includes by this even a case in which the money is being lent for the sake of a business venture from which the lender will receive a share of the profits (Rav from Gem. 168a). Nevertheless, since the borrower is considered the primary beneficiary of the transaction, he pays the fee (Tos. Yom Tov).

If the lender lost the document and required another, he must pay the fee (Nimmukei Yosef to Gem. ibid.).

It is apparent from this mishnah that the one who must bear the expense of having the appropriate document drawn up is not the one who benefits from the document itself, but rather the one who benefits from the transaction for which the document is drawn up. Otherwise, the lender would be required to pay for the bond, since it is written for his sake (Yad Ramah).

כּוֹתְבִין שְׁטָר לְמוֹכֵר אַף עַל פִּי שֶׁאֵין לוֹקֵחַ
עִמּוֹ, וְאֵין כּוֹתְבִין לְלוֹקֵחַ עַד שֶׁיְּהֵא מוֹכֵר עִמּוֹ;
וְהַלּוֹקֵחַ נוֹתֵן שָׂכָר.

[ה] **אֵין** כּוֹתְבִין שְׁטָרֵי אֵרוּסִין וְנִשׂוּאִין אֶלָּא
מִדַּעַת שְׁנֵיהֶם; וְהֶחָתָן נוֹתֵן שָׂכָר. אֵין

יד אברהם

כּוֹתְבִין שְׁטָר לְמוֹכֵר אַף עַל פִּי שֶׁאֵין לוֹקֵחַ עִמּוֹ,
— *We may write a document for a seller
even though the buyer is not with him,*

[I.e., we may write up a bill of sale
attesting to the transfer of a property
from one person to another at the behest
of the seller, even if the buyer named in
the document is not present.] This refers
to a situation in which an act of
acquisition was made on behalf of the
buyer, validating the transfer of the
property from the date the document is
written. Otherwise, the person named in
the document as the buyer could use it
unlawfully to seize the property of
someone who bought the field after this
document was written but before any
transfer actually took place (*Yad
Ramah*). [For example: Reuven wants to
buy a property from Shimon but, not
having ready cash, he draws up a
contract on the first of Nissan, and asks
Shimon to wait until he can pay him.
However, on the fifteenth of Nissan
Shimon sells the property to Levi.
Subsequently, when Reuven has the
money, he could use the document to
prove that he had bought the property
first and take the property away from
Levi.]

However, it is only permitted to write
up a bill of sale for the seller without the
prior consent of the buyer if this does
not pose any threat to the buyer's
interests. Thus, the bill of sale must
record that the buyer was not a party to
its writing and therefore is not to be held
responsible for what it says. Otherwise,
it could be used to coerce the buyer to
consummate a transaction he never

intended to enter. Even if it records that
the buyer has already paid (and
therefore does not threaten him with
having to give the seller money he
doesn't owe), the document must still
note the absence of the buyer because
the transaction may necessitate his
paying taxes. Furthermore, he may not
wish to be known as the owner of this
property for some other reason (ibid.).

Others contend that our sole concern is
that the buyer should not have to pay the
seller for property he never wanted.
Therefore, it is sufficient if the document
records that the property was already paid
for (*Nimmukei Yosef*).

Ritva, however, is of the opinion that all
these precautions are unnecessary. Since it is
permitted to write such a document for a
seller without the buyer being present, the
courts would never recognize a bill of sale in
the hands of the seller as evidence of the
buyer's consent to the sale.

וְאֵין כּוֹתְבִין לְלוֹקֵחַ עַד שֶׁיְּהֵא מוֹכֵר עִמּוֹ; — *but
we do not write for a buyer unless the
seller is with him;*

[We cannot draw up a bill of sale at
the behest of a buyer without the seller's
participation because he may not in fact
have bought the property.] This ruling
of the mishnah is seemingly obvious.
Ramban explains that the mishnah
means to teach regarding a case in which
the seller transacted through two people
to transfer his field to the buyer, though
the buyer was not present. The buyer
then approaches these two people, in
the absence of the seller, to write up a
document attesting to this transfer.
Though they are witnesses to the
transfer, they may not write up the

10
4

We may write a document for a seller even though the buyer is not with him, but we do not write for a buyer unless the seller is with him; and the buyer pays the fee.

4. We do not write documents of betrothal and marriage except with the knowledge of both [parties]; and the groom pays the fee. We do not

YAD AVRAHAM

document without the express authorization of the seller (*Tos. Yom Tov* from *Tur, Choshen Mishpat* 238).

According to *Rashba*, however, in such a case they would be empowered to draw up such a document even without the seller's express consent. Thus, the mishnah's ruling cannot refer to such a case. In this view, the mishnah's ruling, though obvious, is stated to maintain the symmetry with the earlier cases. Alternatively, it refers to a case in which the buyer agrees to let the witnesses hold the document until the sale is completed (from *Tos. Yom Tov*).

וְהַלוֹקֵחַ נוֹתֵן שָׂכָר. — *and the buyer pays the fee.*

[Since this transaction primarily benefits the buyer, he bears the cost of writing up the bill of sale.] Even if the seller was anxious to sell this field because of its inferior quality — or its great distance from where he lived (*Rashbam*) — the buyer pays the fee (*Gem.* loc. cit.), because an exchange of property is always considered to be a greater benefit to the buyer (*Nimmukei Yosef*).

4.

The previous mishnah listed those documents which may be written at the behest of just one of the parties to the transaction. The present mishnah will list those whose execution requires the authorization of both parties.

אֵין כּוֹתְבִין שְׁטָרֵי אֵרוּסִין — *We do not write documents of betrothal*

This refers to documents which spell out the obligations accepted by each of the two parties to the marital agreement (*Rashbam* from *Moed Katan* 18b).

Alternatively, this refers to the document with which *kiddushin* (betrothal) is effected (see *Tos. R' Akiva*). [A document is one of three mechanisms by which a betrothal may be effected; see *Kiddushin* 1:1.]

וְנִשּׂוּאִין — *and marriage*

I.e., a *kesubah* [a marital contract] (*Rashbam*), including a description of the dowry (*Meiri*).

אֶלָּא מִדַּעַת שְׁנֵיהֶם; — *except with the knowledge of both [parties];*

I.e., with their consent, since they

both stand to lose if the details are not recorded correctly (*Meiri*).

וְהֶחָתָן נוֹתֵן שָׂכָר. — *and the groom pays the fee.*

The groom must bear the expense of writing the document because he benefits by receiving the dowry. Additionally, the structure of the marriage transaction is that the groom acquires the bride as his wife, rather than vice versa (*Nimmukei Yosef*; see General Introduction to ArtScroll *Kiddushin*). Even if the groom is a Torah scholar, and the bride's father is anxious for the marriage to take place, the groom must pay the fee because he is considered the primary beneficiary (*Gem.* 168a).

If two separate documents were written, one describing the obligations of the groom

כּוֹתְבִין שִׁטְרֵי אֲרִיסוּת וְקַבְּלָנוּת אֶלָּא מִדַּעַת שְׁנֵיהֶם; וְהַמְקַבֵּל נוֹתֵן שָׂכָר. אֵין כּוֹתְבִין שִׁטְרֵי בֵרוּרִין וְכָל מַעֲשֵׂה בֵית דִּין אֶלָּא מִדַּעַת שְׁנֵיהֶם; וּשְׁנֵיהֶם נוֹתְנִים שָׂכָר. רַבָּן שִׁמְעוֹן בֶּן גַּמְלִיאֵל אוֹמֵר: שְׁנֵיהֶם כּוֹתְבִין שְׁנַיִם, לָזֶה לְעַצְמוֹ וְלָזֶה לְעַצְמוֹ.

יד אברהם

towards the bride and one defining those of the bride towards the groom, each one pays for the document from which they benefit (Nimmukei Yosef).

אֵין כּוֹתְבִין שִׁטְרֵי אֲרִיסוּת — We do not write a sharecropping contract
I.e., an arrangement in which a tenant farmer leases land in return for a percentage of the crop (Rav).

וְקַבְּלָנוּת — or a rental contract
In which the tenant pays a fixed amount of produce regardless of how much is actually grown (ibid.).

אֶלָּא מִדַּעַת שְׁנֵיהֶם; — except with the knowledge of both [parties];
The consent of both parties is required since this document obligates each of the parties to the other (Yad Ramah).

וְהַמְקַבֵּל נוֹתֵן שָׂכָר. — and the tenant [lit. recipient] pays the fee.
The tenant is deemed the main beneficiary of this arrangement, because he now has a means to make a living. This holds true even in a situation in which the field must lie fallow for a year or two, so that the tenant does not receive any immediate benefit (Gem. 168a).

אֵין כּוֹתְבִין שִׁטְרֵי בֵרוּרִין — We do not write documents of designation
In which each of the parties records

the judge he has selected, as well as the third judge selected by the other two. Also included are the pleadings of each of the litigants, to prevent them from changing their claims once the trial begins (Rav).[1]

Two litigants who agree to take their case to trial may select a court in the following manner: One litigant selects one judge, the other a second, and both judges then pick a third (Sanhedrin 3:1).

וְכָל מַעֲשֵׂה בֵית דִּין — or any court judgments
This refers to a document issued by the court after it has decided a case, in which the court grants the creditor the right to collect his debt forcibly from the properties of the debtor when the latter is not forthcoming with payment. It also includes a document which specifies the actual transfer of a specific property to the creditor by virtue of such a collection (Bava Metzia 16b; Rashi ad loc.).

אֶלָּא מִדַּעַת שְׁנֵיהֶם; — except with the knowledge of both [parties];
In this case, their actual consent is obviously not required, only their awareness that the document is being drawn up. Otherwise, anyone who made an argument in court which could be beneficial to his disputant would be able to prevent it from being recorded! (Yad Ramah).

1. The Gemara seems to indicate that there are two separate interpretations to this case: one, that this refers to documents in which the selection of the judges is recorded, and the other, that this refers to the document in which their claims are recorded by the court scribes (Tos. Yom Tov). However, Rav apparently understands the Gemara to mean that one view considers that only the claims were recorded, whereas the other view maintains that the selection of judges was also recorded.

10
4

write a sharecropping contract or a rental contract except with the knowledge of both [parties]; and the tenant pays the fee. We do not write documents of designation or any court judgments except with the knowledge of both [parties]; and they both share in the fee. Rabban Shimon ben Gamliel says: The two of them write two [documents], one for each [party].

YAD AVRAHAM

וּשְׁנֵיהֶם נוֹתְנִים שָׂכָר. — *and they both share in the fee.*

This refers to the case of documents of designation (*Rashbam*). [In the case of judicial decisions, the one asking for the document would obviously be the one to pay for it.]

רַבָּן שִׁמְעוֹן בֶּן גַּמְלִיאֵל אוֹמֵר: שְׁנֵיהֶם כּוֹתְבִין שְׁנַיִם, לָזֶה לְעַצְמוֹ וְלָזֶה לְעַצְמוֹ. — *Rabban Shimon ben Gamliel says: The two of them write two [documents], one for each [party].*

The two witnesses signing the document write up two documents, a separate one for each of the litigants (*Rashbam*). Each document records only the pleadings of the litigant to whom it is issued (*Rav*).

Rabban Shimon ben Gamliel refers only to the case of the documents outlining each party's claims. Even he agrees, however, that only one copy is made of the document recording the court's decision, which is then given to the party that requires it (*Yad Ramah*). Others contend that even court decisions are written twice and copies given to both parties (*Meiri*).

The dispute between Rabban Shimon ben Gamliel and the *Tanna Kamma* is as follows: The first *Tanna* contends that although each of them is entitled to a copy of his claims, if one of them wishes to spare himself the expense of having a separate document drawn up for each, he can insist that all the information be recorded in one document as long as he agrees to leave it in the possession of the other party. His own right to see it whenever he wishes is, of course, guaranteed (*Ramban*).

Rabban Shimon ben Gamliel, however, maintains the opposing party may decline, claiming that sharing the record of his pleading with his litigant is comparable to "having a lion crouching nearby" (*Gem.* 168a). I.e., he is afraid that if his opponent has a record of his claims and supporting arguments in front of him, he will review them constantly and seek new supporting claims of his own and there will be endless quarreling between them (*Rashbam*).[1]

Others explain the concern to be that he will constantly demand that he go with him to the courts with the documents, thereby causing him much bother (*Yad Ramah*; cf. *Meiri*).

The halachah is not in accordance with the opinion of Rabban Shimon ben Gamliel (*Rav*; cf. *Tos. Yom Tov*; *Tos. R' Akiva Choshen Mishpat* 13:3).

1. From this it is clear why *Rav* understood the *document of designation* to refer of necessity to a designation of claims as well as judicial choices. Since Rabban Shimon ben Gamliel maintains that two separate documents are required, so that each should not have constant access to the other's arguments and find ways to defeat him, it is clear that the mishnah cannot be referring to a document in which only the choice of judges has been recorded. Hence *Rav's* interpretation that both opinions in the *Gemara* must agree that the arguments are surely recorded and the question is only whether the choice of judges is also recorded (*Tos. Yom Tov*). [However, according to the second explanation of Rabban Shimon ben Gamliel, this line of reasoning does not hold true, and it is thus possible to explain the *document of designation* to refer solely to the designation of judges.]

[ה] מִי שֶׁפָּרַע מִקְצָת חוֹבוֹ וְהִשְׁלִישׁ אֶת שְׁטָרוֹ,
וְאָמַר לוֹ „אִם לֹא נָתַתִּי לְךָ מִכָּאן וְעַד
יוֹם פְּלוֹנִי, תֵּן לוֹ שְׁטָרוֹ" — הִגִּיעַ זְמַן וְלֹא נָתַן,
רַבִּי יוֹסֵי אוֹמֵר: יִתֵּן. רַבִּי יְהוּדָה אוֹמֵר: לֹא יִתֵּן.

[ו] מִי שֶׁנִּמְחַק שְׁטַר חוֹבוֹ, מְעִידִין עָלָיו עֵדִים,

יד אברהם

5.

The mishnah now discusses the law of אַסְמַכְתָּא, *asmachta,* which is a conditional commitment made by one person to pay another person money only because he does not believe that circumstances will require him to live up to the terms of that agreement. In the case of this mishnah, this occurs when a person volunteers to pay something to another if he doesn't live up to an agreed upon obligation. Since he does this only because he assumes he will surely live up to his obligation and not because he actually intends to carry out the commitment, there are those who maintain that the commitment is not binding. This is the subject of a dispute among the *Tannaim* (Rav).

מִי שֶׁפָּרַע מִקְצָת חוֹבוֹ וְהִשְׁלִישׁ אֶת שְׁטָרוֹ, — *One who paid part of his debt and gave his [loan] document to a third party,*

The creditor and debtor were not willing to bother writing up a receipt for the amount paid (Rav; see mishnah 6), so they agreed to give the loan document to a third party to hold until the rest of the loan is paid.

וְאָמַר לוֹ — *and said to him,*

In order to assure the quick repayment of the remainder of the debt (Nimmukei Yosef).

„אִם לֹא נָתַתִּי לְךָ מִכָּאן וְעַד יוֹם פְּלוֹנִי, תֵּן לוֹ שְׁטָרוֹ" — *'If I do not pay you between now and such-and-such a day, give him his [loan] document' —*

The debtor tells the third party that if he does not pay the rest by the appointed day, the third party should return the bond to the lender, and thereby render the debtor liable to repay the entire loan, even the part which he has already paid. Although no act of acquisition was performed to obligate him to pay the amount already paid, this statement is considered tantamount to declaring that he retroactively renders the money already paid to be a gift, and

the entire debt is thus still intact (Ritva; Meiri; Tos. R' Akiva).

[if] — הִגִּיעַ זְמַן וְלֹא נָתַן, רַבִּי יוֹסֵי אוֹמֵר: יִתֵּן. *the time came and he did not pay, R' Yose says: He should give [the document].*

R' Yose maintains that although this is an *asmachta* (since the debtor clearly had no intention of allowing this to happen), it is a binding commitment. Thus, when the debtor misses the deadline, the third party must fulfill the commission and give the document to the creditor, thus enabling him to collect the entire debt (Rav from Gem. 168a).

רַבִּי יְהוּדָה אוֹמֵר: לֹא יִתֵּן. — *R' Yehudah says: He should not give [it].*

Since the debtor was never asked to make this generous commitment, we assume that he never really intended to pay this amount and made the commitment only because he was sure that he would be able to repay the remainder by the assigned date. Though circumstances in fact prevented him from doing so, he is not held responsible because we do not consider it a real agreement. Thus, the debtor is not required to pay a second time the part he

5. **O**ne who paid part of his debt and gave his [loan] document to a third party, and said to him, 'If I do not pay you between now and such-and-such a day, give him his [loan] document' — [if] the time came and he did not pay, R' Yose says: He should give [the document]. R' Yehudah says: He should not give [it].

6. **[**If] someone's loan document was erased, wit-

YAD AVRAHAM

already paid. Consequently, the trusted third party should not hand over the document to the creditor *(Rashbam)*. Even the creditor never fully relied upon the debtor's assurance *(Nimmukei Yosef)*.

The halachah follows the opinion of R' Yehudah, that such a commitment is not binding *(Rav from Gem.* loc. cit.; *Choshen Mishpat* 55:1, 207:12). However, if they cemented the commitment with an act of acquisition in the

presence of a prestigious court,[1] and he gave the document to that court on behalf of the one who stands to benefit from the commitment, the stipulation is binding *(Rav)*.

Some authorities maintain that in a case in which the beneficiary himself was given the document to hold until the designated day, and it was stipulated that the payment would take effect retroactively from that day, the commitment is binding even without the involvement of the courts *(Rabbeinu Tam,* cited by *Tos.;* see *Tos. Yom Tov)*.

6.

מִי שֶׁנִּמְחַק שְׁטַר חוֹבוֹ, — *[If] someone's loan document was erased,*

The mishnah speaks of a case where there are witnesses who saw that the document faded by itself or was ruined by water dripping on it[2] *(Rav, Rashbam)*, but they do not know the terms that were written within *(Yad Ramah)*.

Others explain the case under discussion to be one in which the ink on the bond was partially erased but still legible, and the bearer is concerned that it will soon be completely obliterated and no longer readable *(Rosh; Yad Ramah,* first opinion; *Meiri; Rambam, Hil. Malveh* 23:12).

מְעִידִין עָלָיו עֵדִים, — *witnesses attest to it,*

I.e., witnesses who know what was written in it, and the date on which it was written, testify to its former contents *(Rav)*.

According to the view that the document was not yet fully erased, the mishnah means that he should get two witnesses to read the document. They can then attest to its contents and to the fact that it was in the process of fading *(Meiri; Rambam,* loc. cit.).

This would be relied upon to issue a new document only if the original document is destroyed; otherwise, he may get other witnesses to also look and see that it is fading, go to another court, and get another

1. According to some, this refers to a court which is expert on the laws of such stipulations. *Rambam (Comm.,* ed. Kafich), however, rules that only a court ordained in Eretz Yisrael is qualified for this role *(Rav)*.

2. However, if the lender erased it himself, or was negligent and left it in a place where it was susceptible to erasure, the document is not replaced, since it is evident from his failure to protect it that this note has already been repaid *(Choshen Mishpat* 41:2). Even if the witnesses are unsure as to how it came to be erased, no replacement is issued *(Sma* 42:18).

וּבָא לִפְנֵי בֵית דִּין וְעוֹשִׂין לוֹ קִיּוּם: אִישׁ פְּלוֹנִי בֶן
פְּלוֹנִי נִמְחַק שְׁטָרוֹ בְּיוֹם פְּלוֹנִי, וּפְלוֹנִי וּפְלוֹנִי
עֵדָיו.

מִי שֶׁפָּרַע מִקְצָת חוֹבוֹ, רַבִּי יְהוּדָה אוֹמֵר:
יַחֲלִיף. רַבִּי יוֹסֵי אוֹמֵר: יִכְתֹּב שׁוֹבָר. אָמַר רַבִּי
יְהוּדָה: נִמְצָא זֶה צָרִיךְ לִהְיוֹת שׁוֹמֵר שׁוֹבָרוֹ מִן
הָעַכְבָּרִים. אָמַר לוֹ רַבִּי יוֹסֵי: כָּךְ יָפֶה לוֹ, וְלֹא

יד אברהם

new document. He can do this a number of times and keep collecting his debt over and over (*Tur* and *Shulchan Aruch, Choshen Mishpat* 41:1).

וּבָא לִפְנֵי בֵית דִּין — *and he comes before the court*

[He must bring these witnesses to court to testify to the validity of the original document.] He need not bring the document itself (*Ritva; Nimmukei Yosef; Rambam,* loc. cit.).

וְעוֹשִׂין לוֹ קִיּוּם: — *and they draw up a validation:*

The witnesses draw up a validation before the courts (*Rav; Rashbam; Nimmukei Yosef*).

Others maintain that only the court has the authority to write a validation; thus the mishnah is here referring to the court before whom the witnesses testify (*Tos.; Yad Ramah; Rambam,* loc. cit.; see *Choshen Mishpat* 41:1).

אִישׁ פְּלוֹנִי בֶן פְּלוֹנִי נִמְחַק שְׁטָרוֹ בְּיוֹם פְּלוֹנִי, — *The document of so-and-so, the son of so-and-so, was erased, of* [lit. on] *such-and-such a date,*

I.e., the date of the original document was such-and-such. The amount of the debt must also be included (*Tif. Yis.*).

וּפְלוֹנִי וּפְלוֹנִי עֵדָיו. — *and so-and-so and so-and-so were his witnesses.*

They record the witnesses who had been signed on the original document as well as those who testified to its contents at the replacement proceeding (*Rosh; Nimmukei Yosef; cf. Tos.*).[1]

If the court itself investigated the validity of the original document and verified it, they do not need to record the identity of the original witnesses, but only that they were found to be valid. The bond can then be collected without further testimony (*Nimmukei Yosef;* cf. *Gem.* 168b).

This process is necessary even if the witnesses who signed the original document were to testify at the time of collection, because a loan which is not documented cannot be collected from assigned properties (*Tos.;* see *Rashash,* ad loc.).

מִי שֶׁפָּרַע מִקְצָת חוֹבוֹ, — *[If] one paid part of his debt,*

I.e., the borrower paid only part of a debt which had been recorded in a document, and he is concerned that the creditor should not use the document to collect the entire debt again (*Rashbam*), and they could not agree on a third party to whom to entrust the document (*Nimmukei Yosef; Meiri*).

Even if the creditor is not willing to accept

1. Seemingly, the testimony upon which the replacement document is based should be invalid, since there is a general rule against accepting second-hand testimony. This testimony is in essence second-hand because these witnesses never saw the actual loan take place. However, in this case there is an important difference. The law does allow witnesses to testify that they were in court and heard two others testify to a loan and the court accept their testimony. That is not considered second-hand testimony because they are talking about an event, the acceptance of testimony, which they saw. A legal document is considered *the equivalent to testimony accepted in court* (*Gittin* 3a); therefore these witnesses in our mishnah are also considered as testifying to an event (*Ramban; Ritva; Choshen Mishpat* 23:4).

nesses attest to it, and he comes before the court and they draw up a validation: **The document of so-and-so, the son of so-and-so, was erased, of such-and-such a date, and so-and-so and so-and-so were his witnesses.**

[If] one paid part of his debt, R' Yehudah says: He should exchange [the document]. R' Yose says: He should write a receipt. Said R' Yehudah: This results in his needing to safeguard his receipt from the mice. R' Yose said to him: It is fitting for him, so that this

YAD AVRAHAM

partial payment, and he tells the debtor that he must either pay the entire debt or leave the document in the hands of the lender, the borrower has the right to insist that he take the partial payment and follow the procedures described below *(Yad Ramah;* see below, s.v. ולא יורע).

רַבִּי יְהוּדָה אוֹמֵר: יַחֲלִיף. — *R' Yehudah says: He should exchange* [the document].

He should destroy the original document and draw up another, with only the remainder of the debt recorded in it *(Rav).*

The date recorded on this new document would be the date on which the original one was written, in effect making this a pre-dated document. The reason for pre-dating it is because the loan was made on an earlier date, and any properties sold by the debtor since that time are thus mortgaged to the lender. Consequently any new document to this loan would need to be dated from the time of the original loan in order not to impair the lender's lien. Although it is generally forbidden to sign a pre-dated document, R' Yehudah permits it here [since this is not really a new document but only the rewriting of a pre-existing one] *(Gem.* ibid.).

רַבִּי יוֹסֵי אוֹמֵר: יִכְתֹּב שׁוֹבֵר. — *R' Yose says: He should write a receipt.*

[The lender has the right to retain the original bond, and the borrower should draw up a receipt for the amount he paid and be responsible for its

safekeeping.]

Theoretically, they could simply record between the lines of the original document, that such-and-such an amount had been paid, thus sparing the borrower the expense of drawing up a receipt and the responsibility of its safekeeping. Since a document with erasures on it is void, there would be no fear of the bearer changing the notation. However, according to R' Yehudah, this is not prescribed, so as not to flaw the document of the creditor [since a document with notations would raise suspicions as to its legitimacy]. According to R' Yose, a receipt was required in order to motivate the borrower to pay up his debt quickly, as explained below *(Yad Ramah).*

אָמַר רַבִּי יְהוּדָה: נִמְצָא זֶה צָרִיךְ לִהְיוֹת שׁוֹמֵר שׁוֹבְרוֹ מִן הָעַכְבָּרִים. — *Said R' Yehudah: This results in his needing to safeguard his receipt from the mice.*

R' Yehudah rejects R' Yose's solution because it places upon the borrower the burden of guarding his receipt from being destroyed, since, if it is lost, the creditor will be able to collect the entire original debt with the original document. The creditor, on the other hand, loses nothing by having a new bond drawn up with only the remaining debt recorded on it *(Rav).*

אָמַר לוֹ רַבִּי יוֹסֵי: כָּךְ יָפֶה לוֹ, — *R' Yose said to him: It is fitting for him,*

It is fitting for the lender that this arrangement be implemented. R' Yose is of the opinion that a replacement document could not be pre-dated and the present date would have to be

יוֹרַע כֹּחוֹ שֶׁל זֶה.

[ז] שְׁנֵי אַחִין, אֶחָד עָנִי וְאֶחָד עָשִׁיר, וְהִנִּיחַ לָהֶן אֲבִיהֶן מֶרְחָץ וּבֵית הַבַּד — עֲשָׂאָן לְשָׂכָר, הַשָּׂכָר לָאֶמְצַע; עֲשָׂאָן לְעַצְמָן, הֲרֵי הֶעָשִׁיר אוֹמֵר לֶעָנִי „קַח לְךָ עֲבָדִים וְיִרְחֲצוּ בַּמֶּרְחָץ; קַח לְךָ זֵיתִים, וּבֹא וַעֲשֵׂם בְּבֵית הַבַּד.‟

יד אברהם

recorded. This would cause the lender a loss since he could now exercise his lien only from a much later date (Rav).

Others interpret: It is fitting for the borrower that he be encumbered with the safekeeping of a receipt so that he will expedite payment of his debt (Nimmukei Yosef).

וְלֹא יוֹרַע כֹּחוֹ שֶׁל זֶה. — *so that this one's position not be impaired.*

The position of the lender should not be impaired by requiring a new document to be written which would have to be dated from the time it is drawn up, thereby limiting his options for collection by preventing him from seizing properties which were sold after

the original debt was incurred but before the new document was written (Rav; Rambam Comm.). [1]

Another interpretation is as follows: It is beneficial for the borrower that he be required to hold a receipt, because, otherwise, the lender would not accept partial payment, since it obligates him to rewrite the document and date it from the present time (Rashba). [2]

The halachah is that the creditor has the option of drawing up a new document or giving a receipt. If a new document is drawn, the date depends on who draws it up. If it is prepared by the court, they use the original date; but if it is prepared by the witnesses themselves, the present date is used (Choshen Mishpat 54:1, Beis Yosef and Rama).

7.

The previous mishnah recorded an instance in which the law confers an unwarranted advantage to one party over another — viz., the opinion of R' Yose that one who pays part of his debt must accept a receipt which, if lost, would enable the lender to [unlawfully] collect the entire debt again. In connection with this, the mishnah now cites another situation in which one can obtain an undeserved financial advantage over another (Tos. Yom Tov from Rif).

שְׁנֵי אַחִין, אֶחָד עָנִי וְאֶחָד עָשִׁיר, וְהִנִּיחַ לָהֶן אֲבִיהֶן מֶרְחָץ וּבֵית הַבַּד — — [If there were] *two brothers, one poor and one wealthy, and their father left them a bathhouse or an olive press —*

[Their father died and left them an inheritance consisting of a bathhouse or an olive press.] This refers to a case in which the bathhouse or press was not divisible. Otherwise, either brother

1. The *Gemara* (171a) explains that, although R' Yehudah himself is of the opinion that the document is dated from the time of the original loan, R' Yose in his counter-argument misunderstood his position, and thought that he required the new document to be dated from the time it is written.

2. [Apparently, *Rashba* disagrees with the opinion of *Rama*, stated above (s.v. מי שפרע), that the borrower can force the lender to accept partial payment. However, it is possible that *Rashba* says this only according to R' Yose's understanding of R' Yehudah (see fn.1), that the

one's position not be impaired.

7. [If there were] two brothers, one poor and one wealthy, and their father left them a bathhouse or an olive press — [if] he had made them for renting, the rent is divided; [if] he made them for themselves, the wealthy one can say to the poor one, 'Acquire servants, and let them bathe in the bathhouse; acquire olives, and come process them in the olive press.'

YAD AVRAHAM

could coerce the other to divide it, since the laws concerning partnerships provide that either partner can dissolve the partnership at any time, provided the item is divisible without impairing its function (*Yad Ramah*; see 1:6).

עֲשָׂאָן לְשָׂכָר, הַשָּׂכָר לָאֶמְצַע; — [if] *he had made them for renting, the rent is divided;*

[If the father had built them to use as a commercial enterprise rather than for his personal needs, the rich brother cannot force the poor brother to convert it to private use, for which he has little use (see below). Rather, the properties should continue to be rented, with each brother receiving half the profits.]

עֲשָׂאָן לְעַצְמָן, — [if] *he had made them for themselves,*

If the father had made these for his own private use, either brother has the right to insist that it be maintained in that manner. This works to the disadvantage of the poor brother who, lacking a household staff or olive holdings, has little or no personal use for them (*Rav; Yad Ramah; Rambam, Shecheinim* 1:2).

Others contend that the intent of the father is not binding upon the sons. Rather, the mishnah is distinguishing between a large bathhouse or olive press, which is suitable

for rental to the public, and a small one, which is not (*Maggid Mishneh, Shecheinim* 1:2; cf. *Kesef Mishneh* ad loc.).

הֲרֵי הֶעָשִׁיר אוֹמֵר לֶעָנִי ,,קַח לְךָ עֲבָדִים, — *the wealthy one can say to the poor one, 'Acquire servants,*

So that they will heat up the bathhouse for you (*Rav*). [This is said facetiously, since, being poor, he obviously cannot acquire servants.]

וְיִרְחֲצוּ בַמֶּרְחָץ; — *and let them bathe in the bathhouse;*

I.e., let the members of your household bathe there (*Tif. Yis.*).

Normally, they would share the bathhouse by using it on alternate days. However, the days the bathhouse would come to the poor brother are useless to him, since he can neither afford to use it personally nor rent it out (as explained above, s.v. עשאן לעצמן). Consequently, we apply the rule that 'where one gains and the other suffers no loss thereby, we force him to acquiesce [to its use]' (*Bava Kamma* 21b). Thus, we force the poor brother to allow the rich one to use it all week (*Nimmukei Yosef*).

קַח לְךָ זֵיתִים, וּבֹא וַעֲשֵׂם בְּבֵית הַבַּד.". — *acquire olives, and come process them in the olive press.'*

[This, too, is said facetiously.]

Although it has been previously established (*Gem.* 13a; see comm. to 1:6, s.v. ואם לאו) that where a property is not divisible

lender incurs a loss with the rewriting of the document by virtue of that which he is now unable to use his lien from the earlier date since only the new date is recorded. However, since in truth we record the earlier date, even *Rashba* may agree that the creditor has no legitimate reason to refuse partial payment.]

שְׁנַיִם שֶׁהָיוּ בְּעִיר אַחַת, שֵׁם אֶחָד יוֹסֵף בֶּן
שִׁמְעוֹן וְשֵׁם אַחֵר יוֹסֵף בֶּן שִׁמְעוֹן, אֵין יְכוֹלִין
לְהוֹצִיא שְׁטָר חוֹב זֶה עַל זֶה; וְלֹא אַחֵר יָכוֹל
לְהוֹצִיא עֲלֵיהֶן שְׁטָר חוֹב. נִמְצָא לְאֶחָד בֵּין
שְׁטָרוֹתָיו ,,שְׁטָרוֹ שֶׁל יוֹסֵף בֶּן שִׁמְעוֹן פָּרוּעַ,"
שְׁטָרוֹת שְׁנֵיהֶן פְּרוּעִין. כֵּיצַד יַעֲשׂוּ? יְשַׁלֵּשׁוּ. וְאִם
הָיוּ מְשֻׁלָּשִׁים, יִכְתְּבוּ סִימָן. וְאִם הָיוּ מְסַמָּנִין,

יד אברהם

either partner can demand that the partnership be dissolved by offering his partner the choice of either buying him out or selling out to him, in this case the poor brother cannot present this ultimatum, since he lacks the resources to buy if his rich brother chooses to sell (*Rav*).

Nevertheless, the wealthy brother can impose this choice upon the poor one, thus forcing him to sell his share (*Nimmukei Yosef*).

However, if the poor brother presented the other with this ultimatum, saying he would borrow money in order to buy the latter's share, it is valid (*Rambam loc. cit.*).

שְׁנַיִם שֶׁהָיוּ בְּעִיר אַחַת, שֵׁם אֶחָד יוֹסֵף בֶּן שִׁמְעוֹן וְשֵׁם אַחֵר יוֹסֵף בֶּן שִׁמְעוֹן — *Two people in the same town both named Yosef ben Shimon* [lit. *one's name is Yosef ben Shimon and the other's name is Yosef ben Shimon*],

This follows in the same mishnah, because this is also a case in which someone may end up with unearned financial gain at another's expense, since anyone with a bond against either of these two individuals will not be able to collect, as will be explained (*Rosh*).

אֵין יְכוֹלִין לְהוֹצִיא שְׁטָר חוֹב זֶה עַל זֶה; — *cannot produce a document of indebtedness against each other;*

Neither can press a claim against the other on the basis of a document which states that Yosef ben Shimon owes money to Yosef ben Shimon. This is

because the one being sued can claim that the document actually recorded a debt which the other once owed him, which he returned to him when the debt was paid (*Rav*).

וְלֹא אַחֵר יָכוֹל לְהוֹצִיא עֲלֵיהֶן שְׁטָר חוֹב. — *nor can another produce a document of indebtedness against them.*

Without more specific identification, a third party can also not successfully press a claim against either one of them, because each of them can claim that the debtor mentioned in the document is the other individual by that name.[1]

The implication of this statement is that in the reverse situation, in which one of them produced a document against a third party, it would be valid. We do not suspect that the loan may have actually been made by the other man with the same name, because the fact that this one has possession of the document is considered ample proof that he is the creditor cited within. Even though in other cases we are concerned that a document may have been lost by the creditor and found by another, it would be most improbable to assume that one Yosef ben Shimon lost the bond and it just happened to be found by the other.

However, there is another opinion cited in a *baraisa* which disputes this point and contends that we must consider the possibility that one of them gave the document to his namesake to hold. The *Tanna* of the *baraisa* maintains that the debt recorded in a document cannot be transferred

---

1. However, if according to the date on the document one of the two individuals was a minor at the time the loan was made, it can be assumed that the borrower cited in the document was the other (*Ritva; Nimmukei Yosef*).

10
7

Two people in the same town both named Yosef ben Shimon, cannot produce a documents of indebtedness against each other; nor can another produce a document of indebtedness against them. [If] one found among his documents [a receipt stating], 'The note of Yosef ben Shimon is paid,' both their notes are [treated as] paid. What should they do? They should [record] the third [generation]. If they were [identical] for three [generations], they should write a description. If they were alike, they

YAD AVRAHAM

with the transfer of the document. Consequently, the bearer of the bond does not necessarily have the right to collect the debt recorded within, and the defendant can therefore refuse to pay the bearer on the grounds stated above. The *Tanna* of the mishnah, however, is of the opinion that the debt can be transferred in this manner; accordingly, possession of the document can be used as proof that the bearer either was the original creditor or else acquired the right to collect the debt with the transfer of the document *(Gem.* 172b-173a; *Rashbam,* ad loc.).

נִמְצָא לְאֶחָד בֵּין שְׁטָרוֹתָיו ,,שְׁטָרוֹ שֶׁל יוֹסֵף בֶּן שִׁמְעוֹן פָּרוּעַ,'' שְׁטָרוֹת שְׁנֵיהֶן פְּרוּעִין. — *[If] one found among his documents [a receipt stating], 'The note of Yosef ben Shimon is paid,' both their notes are [treated as] paid.*

I.e., if one who had borrowed money from each of the Yosef ben Shimons found a receipt which stated that his debt to Yosef ben Shimon had been paid, neither of the two can collect from him, since he can deny each debt by claiming that the receipt refers to that person *(Tos. Yom Tov* from *Gem.* 173a).

However, they can circumvent this ploy by one of them giving power of attorney to the other to act as his agent to collect his debt for him. Armed with this document, he can collect the outstanding debt, since he now has the authority to collect whichever one was not yet paid *(Rashbam;* ad loc.).

Alternatively, someone lent money to

two men named Yosef ben Shimon, and recorded each debt in a document which clearly identified the borrower (see below). The lender then found among his papers a document which stated that Yosef ben Shimon's debt had been paid, without specifying which of the two. He can no longer collect from either of them, since each can claim that he is the one to whom that document refers *(Gem.* 173a).

כֵּיצָד יַעֲשׂוּ? — *What should they do?*

How can these two people draw up documents and administer their debts without being required to identify themselves each time through outside sources *(Meiri)?*

יְשַׁלֵּשׁוּ. — *They should [record] the third [generation].*

They should identify themselves by going back to the third generation, and record the names of their grandfathers as well as their fathers [thus clarifying which of the two is intended] *(Rav).*

וְאִם הָיוּ מְשֻׁלָּשִׁים, — *If they were [identical] for three [generations],*

I.e., the names of their grandfathers were also identical *(Rav).*

יִכְתְּבוּ סִימָן. — *they should write a description.*

They should record some identifying description to clarify which of the two is intended — e.g., the one with the limp *(Rav).*

יִכְתְּבוּ ,,כֹּהֵן.''

הָאוֹמֵר לִבְנוֹ ,,שְׁטָר בֵּין שְׁטָרוֹתַי פָּרוּעַ, וְאֵינִי
יוֹדֵעַ אֵיזֶהוּ,'' שְׁטָרוֹת כֻּלָּן פְּרוּעִין. נִמְצָא לְאֶחָד
שָׁם שְׁנַיִם, הַגָּדוֹל פָּרוּעַ וְהַקָּטָן אֵינוֹ פָּרוּעַ.
הַמַּלְוֶה אֶת חֲבֵרוֹ עַל יְדֵי עָרֵב לֹא יִפָּרַע מִן
הֶעָרֵב. וְאִם אָמַר ,,עַל מְנָת שֶׁאֶפָּרַע מִמִּי
שֶׁאֶרְצֶה,'' יִפָּרַע מִן הֶעָרֵב. רַבָּן שִׁמְעוֹן בֶּן גַּמְלִיאֵל

יד אברהם

,,כֹּהֵן.'' יִכְתְּבוּ מְסֻמָּנִין, הָיוּ וְאִם — *If they
were alike* [lit. *they are identified*], *they
should write 'Kohen.'*

I.e., if one is a *Kohen* and the other is
not (ibid.). If they are both *Kohanim* [or
neither is *(Tos.)*.], they should go back
as many generations as necessary to
record an ancestor whose name is
different than the name of the ancestor
of the other one (*Gem.* loc. cit.).

In a case in which one is identified as a
Kohen, the witnesses to the document must
know that he is in fact a *Kohen*, since that
knowledge is vital to the collection of the
debt (*Tos. Yom Tov*).

לִבְנוֹ הָאוֹמֵר — *If someone said to his son,*
I.e., immediately prior to his death
(*Rashbam*).

,,אֵיזֶהוּ. יוֹדֵעַ וְאֵינִי פָּרוּעַ, שְׁטָרוֹתַי בֵּין שְׁטָר —
*'One of my notes is paid, but I do not
know which,'*

He had several loan documents in his
possession, each naming a different
person as the debtor, and he recalled
that one of them had been paid (*Yad
Ramah*). He had not returned the note,
because the borrower had trusted him
not to collect a second time. He was now
concerned that after his demise his son
would collect all the notes, including,
unwittingly, the one already paid
(*Rashbam*).

פְּרוּעִין. כֻּלָּן שְׁטָרוֹת — *all the notes are paid.*

All the notes in his possession must
be considered as paid, and the son
cannot collect any of them, except those
which the debtor admits to still owing
(*Rashbam*). One may not exact money

from another when there is any doubt as
to his right to do so (*Yad Ramah*).

The same ruling would apply if the father
knew which debt was paid but died before
being able to identify it. In either case,
however, if a receipt was found in the
possession of one of the debtors stating that
his debt had been paid, it can be assumed that
this is the one to which the father referred,
and the other debts may all be collected
(*Ritva*).

שְׁנַיִם, שָׁם לְאֶחָד נִמְצָא — [*If*] *two* [*notes*]
from one person were found there,

If the father possessed two documents recording two separate loans to
the same debtor (*Rav*).

פָּרוּעַ. אֵינוֹ וְהַקָּטָן פָּרוּעַ הַגָּדוֹל — *the larger
one is* [*treated as*] *paid and the smaller
one is not* [*considered*] *paid.*

Since the father stipulated that *one* of
the debts was paid, we can be certain
that one of the debts of this debtor is
still outstanding. Where we have a
larger and smaller debt, the larger must
be assumed to have been paid, because
there is no way to disprove the
possibility that this is the case. Since one
of the two is certainly not paid, the
smaller is considered outstanding and
must be paid (*Rav*).

However, if the father had stated that a
number of notes in his possession had been
paid, even ten notes from the same debtor are
void, because there is no way to determine
the number he meant (*Yad Ramah*).

◆§ עָרֵב §◆ / A guarantor

If someone accepts upon himself to
guarantee the loan of another at the time
the loan is made, his commitment is

10

7

should write 'Kohen.'

If someone said to his son, 'One of my notes is paid, but I do not know which,' all the notes are paid. [If] two [notes] from one person were found there, the larger one is [treated as] paid and the smaller one is not [considered] paid.

One who lends to another through a guarantor may not collect from the guarantor. If he said, 'On condition that I can collect from whomever I wish,' he may collect from the guarantor. Rabban Shimon

YAD AVRAHAM

binding even if he performs no act of acquisition to obligate himself for this debt (Rambam, Hil. Malveh 25:2). Although he received no money for his obligation, and although a commitment is usually considered binding only if a transaction takes place, the fact that the lender considered the guarantor a man of integrity and had faith in his commitment is considered sufficient satisfaction for the guarantor to be bound by the obligation he assumed (ibid. from Gem. 173b; see Kiddushin 7a). This is derived from Scriptural reference (Proverbs 20:16; 6:1-3).

The lender can only go to the guarantor after trying unsuccessfully to recover his money from the borrower. If at the time he guaranteed the loan, however, he told the lender, 'Give him the money and I will give it to you,' he becomes an עָרֵב קַבְּלָן, kablan guarantor — a guarantor who has accepted the debt unconditionally, and the lender can collect from him even without first trying to collect from the borrower (Rambam, loc. cit. §4; Gem. 174a).

הַמַּלְוֶה אֶת חֲבֵרוֹ עַל יְדֵי עָרֵב — One who lends to another through a guarantor

I.e., the latter agreed to guarantee the loan at the time it was made [and the lender agreed to the loan only because of the guarantee] (Tif. Yis.).

לֹא יִפָּרַע מִן הֶעָרֵב. — may not collect from the guarantor.

He may not collect from the

guarantor unless he first takes the borrower to court to recover the debt from him. If it is then established in court that the latter is unable to repay the loan he may collect from the guarantor (Rav from Gem. 173b). Even if the borrower is not known to own any property from which the lender could collect, it must first be established through the courts that this is indeed the case before the lender may proceed to collect from the guarantor (Tos. 173b, s.v. חסורי מחסרא; Rosh, ibid.; Yad Ramah; Nimmukei Yosef). Similarly, if the borrower is not presently available, [i.e. — he is ill or away], the lender must await his return and try to collect from him before turning to the guarantor (Tos., loc. cit.; Rosh, ibid.). However, others contend, that in that case he may go straight to the guarantor (Rashbam).

If all the borrower has is property of inferior quality with which to repay the debt, the creditor must still accept that rather than collect better property from the guarantor [in spite of the fact that a lender has the right to collect his debt from fields of medium quality (see Gittin 5:1)] (Meiri).

However, if the borrower refuses to heed a court summons and cannot be forced into coming to court, the lender may then claim directly from the guarantor (Tos. loc. cit.; Rosh ibid.; Rambam, Hil. Malveh 25:3). Others disagree, and contend that even in such a case due process must still be exercised against the borrower before turning to the guarantor (Meiri).

וְאִם אָמַר „עַל מְנָת שֶׁאֶפָּרַע מִמִּי שֶׁאֶרְצֶה,"

אוֹמֵר: אִם יֵשׁ נְכָסִים לַלּוֶה, בֵּין כָּךְ וּבֵין כָּךְ לֹא
יִפָּרַע מִן הֶעָרֵב. וְכֵן הָיָה רַבָּן שִׁמְעוֹן בֶּן גַּמְלִיאֵל
אוֹמֵר: הֶעָרֵב לְאִשָּׁה בִּכְתֻבָּתָהּ, וְהָיָה בַּעֲלָהּ
מְגָרְשָׁהּ, יַדִּירֶנָּה הֲנָאָה, שֶׁמָּא יַעֲשׂוּ קְנוּנְיָא עַל
נְכָסִים שֶׁל זֶה, וְיַחֲזִיר אֶת אִשְׁתּוֹ.

יד אברהם

יִפָּרַע מִן הֶעָרֵב. — *If he said, 'On condition that I can collect from whomever I wish,' he may collect from the guarantor.*

If the lender stipulated at the time of the loan that he have the right to collect from either the borrower or the guarantor, he may do so, if the borrower has no known real property, or if he cannot be brought to court just now. Otherwise, he must collect from the borrower (*Tos.* 173b; *Rosh*, ibid.).

However, according to many commentators, if he specified that he should be able to collect from the guarantor even if the borrower has the wherewithal to pay, the stipulation is valid (*Nimmukei Yosef*). Others disagree (*Rashba*, cited ad loc.).

רַבָּן שִׁמְעוֹן בֶּן גַּמְלִיאֵל אוֹמֵר: אִם יֵשׁ נְכָסִים לַלּוֶה, בֵּין כָּךְ וּבֵין כָּךְ לֹא יִפָּרַע מִן הֶעָרֵב. — *Rabban Shimon ben Gamliel says: In either case [lit. whether like this or like this], if the borrower has property, he may not collect from the guarantor.*

Based on the manner in which the *Gemara* interpreted the words of the first *Tanna* (see above), there seems to be no dispute between him and Rabban Shimon ben Gamliel. The *Gemara* therefore concludes that the mishnah is to be emended as follows: *When is the above stated* [that the lender can collect from the guarantor]? *When the borrower has no possessions. However, if the borrower has possessions, he* [the lender] *may not collect from the guarantor. However, in the case of a kablan* (see above), *even if the borrower has possessions, he may collect from the*

kablan. *Rabban Shimon ben Gamliel says: Whether* [the guarantor is] *a regular guarantor or a kablan guarantor, he* [the lender] *may not collect from the guarantor if the borrower has possessions* (*Rav* from *Gem.* 173b).[1]

The halachah, however, follows the *Tanna Kamma* (*Rambam, Hil. Malveh* 25:4; *Choshen Mishpat* 129:15).

וְכֵן הָיָה רַבָּן שִׁמְעוֹן בֶּן גַּמְלִיאֵל אוֹמֵר: — *Similarly, Rabban Shimon ben Gamliel said:*

I.e., just as in the previous case Rabban Shimon ben Gamliel is lenient towards the guarantor and protects him from loss, so too his following ruling is one which protects the guarantor (*Nimmukei Yosef*).

הֶעָרֵב לְאִשָּׁה בִּכְתֻבָּתָהּ, — [*If one was*] *the guarantor of a woman's kesubah,*

[I.e., he guaranteed the husband's *kesubah* obligations to the wife.] Ordinarily, one who guarantees a *kesubah* is not liable to the woman if the husband cannot pay, since he committed himself to be a guarantor only for the sake of bringing the man and woman together but without any intention of accepting liability. He did not cause her any loss with this deception (*Gem.* 174b), since a woman desires to get married even if she is not assured of being able to collect her *kesubah* (*Rashbam* 174b). The only exception to this is a father who guarantees the *kesubah* of his son (*Gem.* ibid.), who fully commits himself to his son's obligation because of his love for

---

1. According to this explanation of the *Gemara*, the intent of the words *in either case* mentioned in the mishnah is whether he is a simple guarantor or a kablan (*Tif. Yis.*) [rather than whether or not the lender stipulated that he be able to collect from the guarantor].

ben Gamliel says: In either case, if the borrower has property, he may not collect from the guarantor. Similarly, Rabban Shimon ben Gamliel said: [If one was] the guarantor of a woman's *kesubah*, and her husband was divorcing her, he must vow not to derive any [further] benefit from her, to prevent them from plotting against this one's property and [then] remarrying.

YAD AVRAHAM

his son (*Rabbeinu Gershom* ad loc.). This is the case to which the mishnah refers (*Tos.* ad loc., s.v. בר מערב).

וְהָיָה בַעֲלָה מְגָרְשָׁה, — *and her husband was divorcing her,*

Thus, the *kesubah* payment came due, but the husband was unable to pay the *kesubah*, causing the woman to turn to the guarantor (*Tif. Yis.*).

יַדִּירֶנָּה הֲנָאָה, — *he must vow not to derive any [further] benefit from her,*

The husband must make a *neder* (vow) under the jurisdiction of the public — a type of vow which cannot be canceled — that he will never benefit from her. Thereby, he prohibits himself from ever remarrying her (*Rav*).

שֶׁמָּא יַעֲשׂוּ קְנוּנְיָא עַל נְכָסִים שֶׁל זֶה, וְיַחֲזִיר אֶת אִשְׁתּוֹ. — *to prevent them from plotting against this one's property and [then] remarrying [lit. and he will remarry his wife].*

We are concerned that the couple may have conspired to cheat the guarantor by divorcing, collecting the *kesubah* from him, and then remarrying and enjoying the benefits of his money (*Rav*). Although the guarantor can claim compensation from the husband, we are concerned that the husband will spend all the money before the case comes to court, making it very difficult for the guarantor to collect (*Nimmukei Yosef*).

The halachah follows Rabban Shimon ben Gamliel in this last matter (*Rambam Ishus* 17:9; *Even Haezer* 102:7).

8.

Along with a personal obligation to repay a debt from any possessions he owns, a borrower is also subject to a lien on his real properties, which enables the creditor to collect the debt from any real estate the borrower owns at the time of the loan. This lien prevails even if the property is subsequently transferred to the ownership of another. Consequently, if the borrower is unable to meet his obligations, the creditor can collect from these properties even though they are no longer owned by the borrower.[1] However, as stated in this mishnah, this applies only if the debt is recorded in a legal document, not if it is transacted and witnessed orally.

There is a dispute in the *Gemara* (175b) concerning the origin of this distinction. Ulla maintains that by Biblical law every loan carries an automatic lien on the borrower's property which persists even after property is sold. However, the Rabbis enacted that a loan transacted orally cannot be collected from sold properties, to protect those who purchase real estate from the danger of having their land appropriated by the seller's creditors. They did not extend this to include a

1. In such a case, the buyer's only recourse is to try to recover his money from the borrower who sold him the property.

[ח] הַמַּלְוֶה אֶת חֲבֵרוֹ בִּשְׁטָר גּוֹבֶה מִנְּכָסִים

מְשֻׁעְבָּדִים; עַל יְדֵי עֵדִים, גּוֹבֶה
מִנְּכָסִים בְּנֵי חֹרִין. הוֹצִיא עָלָיו כְּתָב יָדוֹ שֶׁהוּא
חַיָּב לוֹ, גּוֹבֶה מִנְּכָסִים בְּנֵי חֹרִין.
עָרֵב הַיּוֹצֵא לְאַחַר חִתּוּם שְׁטָרוֹת, גּוֹבֶה
מִנְּכָסִים בְּנֵי חֹרִין. מַעֲשֶׂה בָא לִפְנֵי רַבִּי יִשְׁמָעֵאל,

יד אברהם

documented loan, because such a loan is generally public knowledge and it is therefore up to the buyer to protect himself with a thorough search to discover any liens on the property before buying it. Oral loans, however, are not widely publicized and the Rabbis therefore acted to protect the buyer.

Rabbah, on the other hand, contends that Biblical law does not mandate any automatic property lien when a loan is transacted. Rather, it was the Rabbis who ordained that a documented loan carry such a lien in order to assure the availability of loans for those who need them. They did not include orally transacted loans, because the buyer of the properties would have no way of knowing about the lien and would suffer a loss.

The prevailing view is that of Ulla (Rambam, Malveh 11:4).

הַמַּלְוֶה אֶת חֲבֵרוֹ בִּשְׁטָר גּוֹבֶה מִנְּכָסִים מְשֻׁעְבָּדִים; — *One who lends another money with a document collects from mortgaged properties;*

If the borrower has no money or property with which to repay the loan, the lender may attach any property subject to his lien (Nimmukei Yosef). This includes not only those properties which were sold by the borrower subsequent to the loan [whose loss to the buyer is not total since he is eligible for a refund], but even those which were given as a gift [whose collection is a complete loss to the present owner] (Yad Ramah).

Even if the document does not state that a lien was taken, it is assumed to be an oversight of the scribe who wrote the document, and the lien is nevertheless in effect (Rav from Bava Metzia 14a). We may safely assume that a person would not be so careless with his money as to lend it without a lien which would guarantee repayment, especially if the lien is his for the asking (Rashi to Bava Metzia ad loc.).

עַל יְדֵי עֵדִים, גּוֹבֶה מִנְּכָסִים בְּנֵי חֹרִין. — *with witnesses, he collects [only] from*

available [lit. *free*] *properties.*

[I.e., he can collect only from properties which are still in the borrower's possession.] Without the combination of witnesses and a document, there is not likely to be sufficient publicity concerning the loan to allow potential purchasers of the borrower's property to be aware of the existence of a lien and we must therefore protect them (Rashbam; see preface).

הוֹצִיא עָלָיו כְּתָב יָדוֹ שֶׁהוּא חַיָּב לוֹ, — *[If] he produced his handwritten [note] that he is indebted to him,*

[The lender produced a document signed by the borrower which stated that the latter owed the former a sum of money,] but there were no witnesses signed upon the document (Rav).

Some commentators hold that the same would apply to a document written by the borrower in his own handwriting but not signed at all (Meiri). Others contend that if it is not signed it is of no value (Ran to Gittin 86a).

גּוֹבֶה מִנְּכָסִים בְּנֵי חֹרִין. — *he collects [only] from available properties.*

Without the involvement of witnesses the loan does not receive

10
8

8. One who lends another money with a document collects from mortgaged properties; with witnesses, he collects [only] from available properties. [If] he produced his handwriten [note] that he is indebted to him, he collects [only] from available properties.

[If] a guarantor appears below the document's signatures, he collects [only] from available properties. A case came before R' Yishmael, and he

YAD AVRAHAM

sufficient publicity to protect the buyers (Rav).

However, if witnesses were signed on the document, although it is written in the first person — i.e., I, so-and-so, borrowed etc. — it has the validity of a regular loan document and the lender can collect from mortgaged properties (Beis Yosef, Choshen Mishpat 69; Meleches Shlomo).

Another major distinction between a loan recorded in a document and one attested to orally is that in the case of an undocumented loan the borrower is believed to say he paid, but not in the case of a documented one. This is because we assume no person would repay a loan and leave the document in the hands of the lender. Therefore, if the creditor still has the note, it is clear that the borrower did not yet repay the debt (Shevuos 41a,b) [unless, of course, he can produce a receipt]. In the case of a document signed by the borrower rather than by witnesses, some authorities maintain that the borrower is believed to say that he repaid (Rif; Rambam, Malveh 11:3; Ramban, Milchamos; Ran), because people tend to be less careful with such a document, and it is conceivable that he paid the loan without making certain to retrieve it (Nimmukei Yosef). Others reject this distinction and rule that, in this respect, it is similar to a document signed by witnesses, and the borrower's claim to have repaid is not believed in the face of the note held by the lender (Rashbam to 176a, s.v. ג"הג; Yad Ramah §49; Baal Hamaor).

עֶרֶב הַיּוֹצֵא לְאַחַר חִתּוּם שְׁטָרוֹת, — [If] a guarantor appears below the document's signatures,

I.e., after the witnesses signed the document, a guarantor added in his own hand a postscript stating, 'I, so-and-so,

am a guarantor' (Rav).

גּוֹבֶה מִנְּכָסִים בְּנֵי חֹרִין. — he collects [only] from available properties.

I.e., if the lender collects from the guarantor it can only be from his available properties, not from properties already sold. Since there are no witnesses attesting to his guarantee, his obligation is tantamount to a loan transacted orally (Rav).

The mishnah is discussing a situation in which there are witnesses who recognize this to be the guarantor's signature. However, if witnesses signed on the guarantee, it would be analogous to having witnesses signed to an obligation, and the lender would have a lien on the guarantor's properties (ibid.).

It emerges from this that a guarantor can become obligated even after the loan has been transacted. However, this is only if an act of acquisition is performed to legalize his commitment (Rav, based on Gem. 176a). [Thus, the mishnah is discussing a case in which such an act of acquisition was performed] (Yad Ramah; Rashbam to 176b, s.v. שלא; בשעת מתן מעות; Rambam loc. cit.).

Others rule that only a guarantor who obligates himself orally after the loan has been transacted requires an act of acquisition; one who signs on the document to the loan does not, since his signature gives it legal status (Ramban; Rashba; Ritva).

A 'guarantor of the courts' does not require an act of acquisition to obligate himself (Gem. 176b). Some explain this to refer to a situation in which the court was ready to force a borrower to pay when a guarantor stepped forward and accepted

וְאָמַר: גּוֹבֶה מִנְּכָסִים בְּנֵי חוֹרִין. אָמַר לוֹ בֶּן נַנָּס:
אֵינוֹ גוֹבֶה לֹא מִנְּכָסִים מְשֻׁעְבָּדִים וְלֹא מִנְּכָסִים
בְּנֵי חוֹרִין. אָמַר לוֹ: לָמָה? אָמַר לוֹ: הֲרֵי הַחוֹנֵק אֶת
אֶחָד בַּשּׁוּק, וּמְצָאוֹ חֲבֵרוֹ וְאָמַר לוֹ „הַנַּח לוֹ,"
פָּטוּר, שֶׁלֹּא עַל אֱמוּנָתוֹ הִלְוָהוּ. אֶלָּא אֵיזֶהוּ עָרֵב
שֶׁהוּא חַיָּב? „הַלְוֵהוּ, וַאֲנִי נוֹתֵן לָךְ," חַיָּב, שֶׁכֵּן עַל
אֱמוּנָתוֹ הִלְוָהוּ. אָמַר רַבִּי יִשְׁמָעֵאל: הָרוֹצֶה
שֶׁיַּחְכִּים יַעֲסֹק בְּדִינֵי מָמוֹנוֹת, שֶׁאֵין לָךְ מִקְצוֹעַ
בַּתּוֹרָה גָּדוֹל מֵהֶן, שֶׁהֵן כְּמַעְיָן הַנּוֹבֵעַ. וְהָרוֹצֶה
שֶׁיַּעֲסֹק בְּדִינֵי מָמוֹנוֹת יְשַׁמֵּשׁ אֶת שִׁמְעוֹן בֶּן נַנָּס.

יד אברהם

responsibility to pay (Rambam, Malveh 25:2). Others understand it to refer to any guarantor who assumes his obligation before a court of law (Tur, Choshen Mishpat 129).[1]

מַעֲשֶׂה בָּא לִפְנֵי רַבִּי יִשְׁמָעֵאל, וְאָמַר: גּוֹבֶה מִנְּכָסִים בְּנֵי חוֹרִין. אָמַר לוֹ בֶּן נַנָּס: אֵינוֹ גוֹבֶה — לֹא מִנְּכָסִים מְשֻׁעְבָּדִים וְלֹא מִנְּכָסִים בְּנֵי חוֹרִין. A case came before R' Yishmael, and he said: He collects [only] from available properties. Ben Nannos said to him: He collects neither from mortgaged properties nor from available properties.

Ben Nannos contends that any guarantor who obligates himself after the money has already been lent is not bound to his guarantee whatsoever (Rav), since he received nothing in return, not even the satisfaction of the leader relying on him to make the loan. A person cannot legally obligate himself for a debt unless a transaction takes place in which he receives something in

return for accepting the obligation (Yad Ramah).

אָמַר לוֹ: לָמָה? — He said to him: Why?
[R' Yishmael asked Ben Nannos for his reason.]

אָמַר לוֹ: הֲרֵי הַחוֹנֵק אֶת אֶחָד בַּשּׁוּק, — He said to him: [If] someone was choking someone in the street,

Some commentators understand this literally (Rambam, Malveh 26:1). Others interpret it figuratively to refer to someone who was pressuring his debtor to repay him (R' Hai Gaon cited by Nimmukei Yosef).

וּמְצָאוֹ חֲבֵרוֹ וְאָמַר לוֹ „הַנַּח לוֹ," — and another encountered him and said, 'Let him alone,'

[I.e., he promised to pay over a sum of money if the person choking the other (or pressuring him to pay his debt) would leave him be.]

1. Although a guarantor who assumes his obligation after the loan is made does not have the satisfaction that the lender relied upon him to part with his money, and is therefore unable to obligate himself without an act of acquisition (see comm. to mishnah 7, s.v. ערב), the fact that in the court's eyes he is trusted as a guarantor is enough satisfaction to make his obligation binding even without an act of acquisition (Tos. Yom Tov).

said: He collects [only] from available properties. Ben Nannos said to him: He collects neither from mortgaged properties nor from available properties. He said to him: Why? He said to him: [If] someone was choking someone in the street, and another encountered him and said, 'Let him alone,' he is exempt, because he did not lend him due to his trust in him. Rather, which is a guarantor who is liable? [If he said,] 'Lend him, and I will give you,' he is liable, because he lent him due to his trust in him. Said R' Yishmael: One who wishes to become wise should involve himself in [the study of] monetary laws, as there is no branch of Torah greater than them, because they are like a welling fountain. And one who wishes to involve himself in monetary laws should serve Shimon ben Nannos.

YAD AVRAHAM

פָּטוּר, שֶׁלֹא עַל אֲמוּנָתוֹ הִלְוָהוּ. — *he is exempt, because he did not lend him due to his trust in him.*

[So, too, in this case, there is no basis for his obligation.]

R' Yishmael, however, disagrees in this case as well, and maintains that he would be obligated to fulfill his commitment (*Gem.* 176a).

אֶלָּא אֵיזֶהוּ עָרֵב שֶׁהוּא חַיָּב? ,,הַלְוֵהוּ, וַאֲנִי נוֹתֵן לָךְ,'' חַיָּב, שֶׁכֵּן עַל אֲמוּנָתוֹ הִלְוָהוּ. — *Rather, which is a guarantor who is liable? [If he said,] 'Lend him, and I will give you,' he is liable, because he lent him due to his trust in him.*

[That satisfaction is sufficient to be considered receiving something in return.]

אָמַר רַבִּי יִשְׁמָעֵאל: הָרוֹצֶה שֶׁיַּחְכִּים יַעֲסֹק בְּדִינֵי

מָמוֹנוֹת, שֶׁאֵין לְךָ מִקְצוֹעַ בַּתּוֹרָה גָּדוֹל מֵהֶן, שֶׁהֵן כְּמַעְיָן הַנּוֹבֵעַ. — *Said R' Yishmael: One who wishes to become wise should involve himself in [the study of] monetary laws, as there is no branch of Torah greater than them, because they are like a welling fountain.*

Monetary law, more than any other branch of Torah law, requires the involvement of human logic making decisions and drawing analogies between one case and another (*Tif. Yis.*).

וְהָרוֹצֶה שֶׁיַּעֲסֹק בְּדִינֵי מָמוֹנוֹת יְשַׁמֵּשׁ אֶת שִׁמְעוֹן בֶּן נַנָּס. — *And one who wishes to involve himself in monetary laws should serve Shimon ben Nannos.*

Nevertheless, the halachah follows the opinion of R' Yishmael concerning the discussion in this mishnah (*Rav* from *Gem.* 176a).

סליק מסכת בבא בתרא